THE GERMAN MELTING-POT

Also by Wolfgang Zank

WIRTSCHAFT UND ARBEIT IN OSTDEUTSCHLAND

3/97

LR/

UNIVERSITY OF
WOLVERHAMPT?

WP 2137180 6

The German Melting-Pot

Multiculturality in Historical Perspective

Wolfgang Zank
Assistant Professor
Aalborg University
Denmark

First published in Great Britain 1998 by
MACMILLAN PRESS LTD
Houndmills, Basingstoke, Hampshire RG21 6XS and London
Companies and representatives throughout the world

A catalogue record for this book is available from the British Library.

ISBN 0–333–71041–X

 First published in the United States of America 1998 by
ST. MARTIN'S PRESS, INC.,
Scholarly and Reference Division,
175 Fifth Avenue, New York, N.Y. 10010

ISBN 0–312–21303–4

Library of Congress Cataloging-in-Publication Data
Zank, Wolfgang.
The German melting-pot : multiculturality in historical
perspective / Wolfgang Zank.
p. cm.
Includes bibliographical references and index.
ISBN 0–312–21303–4 (cloth)
1. Pluralism (Social sciences)—Germany—History.   2. Minorities–
–Germany—History.   I. Title.
HM276.Z36 1998
306'.0943—dc21   97–42336
                                                                   CIP

© Wolfgang Zank 1998

This book is printed on paper suitable for recycling and made from fully managed and sustained forest sources.

10   9   8   7   6   5   4   3   2   1
07   06   05   04   03   02   01   00   99   98

Printed and bound in Great Britain by
Antony Rowe Ltd, Chippenham, Wiltshire

To Ulla

Contents

- 'Inner unification' and the 'wall in the minds'
- The xenophobic wave and the new immigration
  policy
- Contradictory integration

List of Figures

1 Introduction

GERMANY – A MULTICULTURAL NATION-STATE

Fifty years after the end of the Second World War, Germany seems to have reached the stage of boredom, at least seen from the perspective of the international media. Some years ago this was still quite different: unification was a dramatic event in itself, and it immediately provoked fears of a Greater Germany which would dominate Europe (if not start a new war); racist attacks on foreigners seemed to confirm the worst expectations. But then the level of xenophobic violence declined again, the right-wing party *Die Republikaner* ended with a poor 1.9 per cent at the national elections in 1994, and Helmut Kohl continued as chancellor. At present (1996) there seems to be nothing at hand which could bring internal German affairs back onto the front pages of the international media.

The relative calmness is in certain aspects surprising, given the point that Germany is divided by deep cultural contrasts, some of which in other places mark the front lines of civil wars. The word 'culture' is used here in a broad sense, as an ensemble of values, norms, symbols and 'images' which structure people's perception of the world. The cultural differences in Germany are most visible in the foreign immigrant population (roughly 7.5 million people),[1] particularly in the Turks. But also the three million *Aussiedler*, ethnic Germans from Eastern Europe, have been bringing different values to Germany; they often came from remote rural areas which remained largely untouched by the cultural mainstreams which have shaped (West) German society since 1945. Asylum applicants have been coming from countries as distant as Ghana and Sri Lanka. Not so important in quantitative terms but of a certain symbolical value is the immigration of Jews from the former Soviet Union (relatives included, about 45 000 up to 1996).[2]

The impact of immigration upon German society can perhaps best be illustrated by the following calculation: if the German refugees and expellees who after 1945 came from the former German territories are counted as immigrants as well, then by 1989 one-third of all inhabitants of West Germany were either immigrants, or

1

descendants of immigrants.³ And in 1992 in relation to her population, Germany was the largest immigration country in the world.⁴

But also among the 'innate' Germans deep cultural gaps are
noticeable. One of these gaps divides East and West Germans. Forty
years under different social systems have left marks on the men-
tality of both populations. Much older of origin but still traceable
is the confessional gap which separates Protestants from Catholics.
This cultural divide has lost much of its previous sharpness because religion in general has lost importance. But still, about three-
quarters of the German population believe in God or in a Higher
Being. For 52 per cent of the West Germans religion is 'rather
important', or even 'very important'.⁵ On the other hand, about a
quarter of the population does not believe either in God or in a
Higher Being, and the proportion is rising.⁶ That means that life
and death, the world beyond the reach of experience and science,
the 'last realities' (Max Weber) look completely different for different
groups of Germans.

Repeatedly history has been the source of emotional debates,
not to say agonizing polemics. One example was the sharp controversy in 1995 about the role of the German army in the Second
World War (a misused heroic fighting force, or the largest criminal
organization in German history?).⁷ When looking back, Germans
often see completely different things.

All Western societies, not the least West Germany, have been
transformed by a 'Silent Revolution' (Ronald Inglehart)⁸ which led
to a decline of 'materialist' and a growing importance of 'post-
materialist' values. Sociologists have grouped German society into
several different social milieux (see below); even in small areas an
enormous variety of lifestyles, attitudes and values can be discerned.⁹

Simply as a matter of fact, Germany is a multicultural society.¹⁰
But strangely enough, this cultural diversity hampers cooperation
and the division of labour only to a limited extent. There are tensions, disrespect, violence, but seen in proportion, the overwhelming day-to-day normality is an undramatic living together, or at
least side by side. The answer to this mystery partly lies in the fact
that Germany *in some aspects* is quite *homogeneous*, more homogeneous than the other large EU member states Great Britain, France,
Spain and Italy. The parliamentary democracy and the basic characteristics of the social order have practically no enemies and political extremism is quantitatively weak. Hidden extremist propensities
and resentments among the population are difficult to measure but

comparative research has produced no evidence that they are more widespread in Germany than in the other EU countries.[11] Germany is also homogeneous in the sense that there is no separatism, not even regionalism. Many Germans feel a deep sense of regional identity, and the German regions vary very much from each other as to customs, mentalities, food and drinking habits, architecture or dialect. But regional identity easily goes together with a national identity, here understood as a sentiment of belonging to one nation. There is no political movement which could be compared to Sinn Fein or to Scottish Nationalists, to Corsican separatists, to ETA or to the Lega Nord. No German political party was founded in order to represent the interests of one region only, let alone to make it independent. Not even the Bavarian CSU (*Christlich Soziale Union*) can be grouped under this heading; the CSU is mainly the Bavarian branch of the CDU/CSU. Not even in East Germany where in 1991 86 per cent of the population felt they were treated as second-rank citizens[12] was there a base for a regional party. No political party demands the reversion of unification, not even the post-communist PDS (*Partei des Demokratischen Sozialismus*), which is strong in East Germany and weak in the West, but defines itself as a German party.

Also, in linguistic terms, Germany is rather homogeneous today. There are, apart from immigrants, a few people who speak a non-German idiom as their first language (Frisians, Danes, slavonic Sorbs). But these linguistic minorities amount to only about 0.1 per cent of the population. The German language is divided into dialects, but the knowledge of German standard speech is so widespread, its status so uncontested that few problems arise. No one demands that Low German or Bavarian should be made the official language to be taught in school or to be used in court. In this respect Germany fundamentally differs from the other large West European countries; in Germany there is nothing which could be compared to Gaelic or Welsh, to Breton or Provençal, to Catalan, Galician or Basque, or to Sardic. The solid position of German standard speech is a result of Germany's relatively strong educational system, but it reflects also the rather unproblematic relation between the regions and the central power; if there were regionalism or separatism, the activists of these movements certainly would claim that, say, Bavarian or Rhenanian constitute proper languages in their own right.

To sum up, Germany today displays a rich variety of cultural currents, but is nevertheless quite homogeneous in certain fields. The cultural diversity seldom impedes cooperation and coexistence, and it is not in contradiction to a sentiment of belonging to one nation. Therefore, Germany can be labelled a multicultural nation-state. Nation is here understood as: a group of people who are citizens of one state and who are connected by a feeling of belonging to one group.

German society is confronted with the problem of integrating a wide range of different cultural groups. In a historical perspective this problem is not new. By about 1895, Germany was divided by deep cultural cleavages into four large *social-moral milieux* (see below) which were closely affiliated to competing political parties: a conservative-agrarian Protestant milieu in northern and northeast Germany, a bourgeois-liberal, predominantly urban Protestant milieu, a Catholic milieu and a socialist workers' movement.

Besides these four macro milieux there were several other groups with separate cultural identities. Many people spoke a non-German language, the Jews were a very successful religious minority, while many artists and writers met in bohemian groups and mentally lived in their own world. And Germany was already in 1895 an immigration country.

If we go another two hundred years back in time, to 1695, the picture is no less multicultural. At that time Germany, as a nation-state, did not exist. There was, however, a loose confederation called the 'Holy Roman Empire of the German Nation'. The formal head of this confederation was an emperor, but the political power rested mainly with the princes of the numerous territories. This 'Holy Roman Empire' comprised huge territories which today are part of Czechia, Belgium, France, Italy, former Yugoslavia and Poland, and the linguistic pattern varied accordingly. But the German-speaking parts did not constitute a linguistic unity because the population at large used mutually incomprehensible dialects. German intellectuals were active in creating a standard speech, but the educated and ruling classes mostly used French or Latin. And given the massive impact which religion had upon daily life and the perception of the world, the confessional gaps deeply separated mental worlds.

Multiculturality is not a peculiarity of German history, 'for any nation of even middling size had to construct its unity on the base of evident disparity' (Eric J. Hobsbawm).[13] The specific content of the multicultural cocktail has been different at different historical times, and so have been the mechanisms which allowed (with uneven success) for the integration of the different groups. But the basic problem, namely that societies must integrate culturally different groups, has been almost constant in modern history.

THE PITFALLS OF BIOLOGICAL ANALOGIES AND 'NATIONAL IDENTITIES'

The emphasis which is placed here upon multiculturality might surprise readers who are familiar with the concept of national identity. Certainly, the members of one nation share the feeling of belonging to one group, one nation. The development of this sentiment in Germany is one of the subjects of the present book. This group sentiment has been a factor of paramount political importance. The nation-state and its laws constitute the framework of society. Government and taxation are accepted as legitimate as long as it is the *national* government which empties the pockets, and not a foreign one. Everything which seems to threaten the nation-state provokes fierce reactions. This is one of the reasons why the process of European integration has often run into difficulties.

The common feeling of belonging to one nation is affirmed daily by symbols. The flag, the national football team, the language, the navy, the queen or president, the currency, the anthem – there is a long list of items with which the citizens can identify, and which symbolically express their commonness. And if some hostile individuals mistreat one of these symbols, for instance by burning the flag, many citizens who have never met before can simultaneously feel severely hurt. Particularly in times of war this group feeling becomes of paramount importance since most people automatically tend to rally round their own government, and against the people living in the neighbouring country. This is the reason why shaky dictatorships have a tendency to look for outer conflicts.

The feeling of belonging to one national group and the symbols by which this group-feeling is expressed can conveniently be summarized under the term national identity.

The borders of the nation-state also constitute a barrier for human solidarity. High taxation and social contributions are accepted as long as they are used to remedy misery *within* the national borders. But in all European countries it is politically very difficult to raise even modest sums of taxpayers' money for development aid to Third World countries where misery is much harsher.

The nation-state also constitutes a hindrance to communication since the media to a great extent focus on internal affairs. This partly reflects the group feeling: what happens to 'others' is not so important. But it is also less important in an objective sense: if one's own government raises taxes or introduces speed limits, it has direct consequences for one's own situation, whereas similar decisions in the neighbouring country are at best of indirect importance. Furthermore, political campaigning must be directed towards fellow-nationals – they can vote at the next elections; the citizens of the neighbouring country cannot.

In most cases the national boundaries are also language barriers, and the language differences reinforce the inward bias of communication. Many people do not have sufficient command of foreign languages to read foreign newspapers or follow foreign TV. In many cases language, in an almost 'natural' way, seems to separate those who belong to one's own group from those who do not – one kind of people one can easily talk to, others one cannot, at least not without further training. Language therefore often becomes a powerful symbol of national group-feeling.

The inward bias of communication means that the people in the neighbouring countries often appear somewhat nebulous, which creates good conditions for the development of national stereotypes. National stereotypes are still very widespread and are therefore important cultural factors. This inward bias also means that many writers, actors and singers have an audience which ends at the national borders and the images they create are practically unknown in neighbouring countries. To mention one example, there is hardly a Dane who doesn't know the singer Kim Larsen, but outside Denmark hardly anyone has heard of him. The existence of authors, singers and images which can be found more or less in only one country eases communication and hidden allusions among the compatriots, a fact which in turn reinforces the 'we-feeling'. Moreover, political systems are different from country to country, and this often implies different political styles. A Danish politician would cause a scandal if he used the aggressive rhetoric which often characterizes American election campaigns.

But all this does not imply that the members of one nation are themselves culturally homogeneous. Two persons can easily talk the same language, be citizens of the same nation, feel themselves compatriots and have a knowledge of some authors and songs in common, but nevertheless be quite different. The one might be atheist and rationalist, the other deeply religious; the one open-minded, the other xenophobic; the one humanist, the other misan-thropic; the one very erotic, the other afraid of sex. Every European country displays an immense variety of cultural features: many differ-ent religions and confessions, xenophobia and open-integrationist attitudes, hard masculine values as represented by John Wayne and Arnold Schwarzenegger side by side with more balanced attitudes, feminism and traditional female roles, heterosexuality and homo-sexuality, crude materialism and spiritual values, tough industrial-ism and ecologism, and so on. Practically all countries are complex aggregates of cultural features.

It follows that, when writing about cultural features, the use of the definite article (*'the* French', *'the* Germans', *'the* Russians' . . .) is an unmistakable sign of incompetence.

On the other hand, all Western countries have an immense var-iety of cultural features in common. This is due to common tradi-tions such as Christianity or the Enlightenment, but also due to continuous contact and exchange, a process which has been enor-mously amplified during the last decades. For many generations Homer, William Shakespeare and Leo D. Tolstoy have been part of the cultural baggage of the educated strata in Germany, and today John Wayne, Mick Jagger and Agatha Christie are integral parts of German mass culture.

Countries differ from each other not because they are of a different 'nature' but because the components of the cultural aggregates have a different weight. Terms such as 'French culture', 'English cul-ture' or 'German culture' make sense only as labels for different aggregates. As regards Western European societies, the mixture of the components is quite comparable; an empirical social scientist sees a 'similarity of family' among these countries.[14]

Therefore, although the *illusion* of homogeneous nation-states is quite widespread, it is not possible to find a coherent set of cul-tural features which would be 'typical' for one particular nation in the sense that it unites the whole population (or at least the overwhelming majority), and in the sense that the one set of cul-tural features constitutes a, say, French as opposed to German 'na-tional identity'. This is, however, the way many authors use the term national identity.[15] Understood in this way, the 'national identity' is a fiction. To underline the fictive character of *this kind* of 'national identity', it is set in inverted commas. If used without inverted commas, terms of collective identity cover only the group feeling and the symbols by which this group feeling is expressed; it explicitly does not include cultural homogeneity.

Many researchers have found it appropriate to model the components of culture as a kind of onion: the *symbols* of the culture are at the outermost layer, *heroes* and *rituals* are to be found in the deeper layers, and at the centre of the 'culture onion' the *values* are situated, constituting the very core of the culture.[16] Using this model, it follows that language and other symbols which unite nations are on the outside; they are quite superficial. As regards norms and values, the core of culture, nation-states show an immense diversity; conversely, what separates one nation from the other is at the superficial level, whereas most core elements are common across the borders.

Often, however, these onion models have a confusing effect: by modelling symbols, rituals, heroes and values in a suggestive graphic model as *one* onion, they create the misleading impression that that there is *always* an intrinsic connection between values and symbols; people who use the same symbols for communication must have the same heroes and values. This is perhaps a valid assumption for studying the aboriginal cultures on New Guinea or Ashanti culture in West Africa. But this assumption of necessary congruence between symbols, rituals, heroes and values is absurd in connection with modern nations. Here all kinds of evidence show that people who use the same symbols (mainly the language) may have completely different rituals, heroes and values. Models which have been useful in anthropological studies of primitive societies can be very misleading when used on modern societies.

As far as the present writer can see, if 'national identity' is used in an excessive way, implying cultural homogeneity, one mistake is invariably made: material which might be valid to characterize one part of a nation gets over-generalized. The methodology often consists of finding some texts, or some forms of qualitative evidence, and claiming that these texts are characteristic of the 'national identity'. There is, however, one crucial point: how representative are these quotations? In general representativeness is simply stated as fact.

A short review of the characteristics of representative research might be helpful.[17] One method consists of finding a sample of people who are a model of the whole population with regard to several characteristics. This means that the sample must include both men and women, and that age groups, social layers, the different regions, religions and confessions must all be represented in the right proportions.

The other method consists of interviewing a huge sample in which every citizen has the same statistical chance of being included. It requires advanced mathematical methods to establish a selection which really ensures this criterion is fulfilled. Polls in pubs or among the spectators of a football match have to be excluded because many people neither go to a pub nor to a football stadium; also polls where the participants are attracted by prizes are unrepresentative as some people are more inclined to enter than others. This constitutes a difficult problem which requires careful correction. Every sample must comprise at least several hundred people; today many polls in Germany are based on the answers of about 3000 people (2000 in West Germany, 1000 in East Germany). Every opinion poll therefore necessarily requires so much work that it is simply impossible for one person to produce representative results.

Representative opinion polls have rightly been criticized in many respects. The results are often different if the question is altered slightly; election results often prove that predictions were wrong; there have been many opinion polls where the sample was carelessly composed. All this has been a source of constant embarrassment for everyone who uses opinion polls. But in spite of their shortcomings, representative opinion polls are indispensable for those who are interested in learning about the distribution of cultural features. And fortunately at present there is an abundance of representative opinion polls, covering virtually all aspects of life; some, for instance the *Eurobarometer*, even allow for international comparisons.

Certainly it is not possible to study cultural phenomena on the basis of opinion polls alone. When using *quantitative methods*, the questions must necessarily be standardized, and this implies rigidity. One can only count phenomena whose existence is known beforehand, so in order to learn something qualitatively new, to study the richness of cultural phenomena, other sources must be consulted, for instance pieces of literature. There is, however, one barrier which this kind of *qualitative research* cannot pass: the results cannot be generalized. By studying a literary author one can learn about the thoughts of this particular author, but in the first instance, nothing more. Even if the same ideas are repeated by three or ten authors this only means that three or ten authors share the same opinion, not more. Careful *additional* research might establish that the ideas of some authors were influential. All this, however, does not justify promoting them to be representatives of a 'national identity'. No literary author has ever reached a whole nation; without exception their audience has been a fraction only – usually, in relative terms, a very small fraction only. And in modern complex societies for every influential author there have been other influential authors who have been promulgating completely different views.

Unfortunately, the apparent underestimation of the problem of representativeness renders many works about 'national identity', although often stimulating, inconclusive.[18] In other cases they degenerate into crude cultivations of superficial stereotypes.

The dangers which are connected with the construction of 'national identities' can perhaps best be illustrated by studying the book by Liah Greenfeld, *Nationalism. Five Roads to Modernity*.[19] Liah Greenfeld is a scholar of high repute at Harvard University, one of the most prestigious institutions of higher learning in the world, and her book, published by the Harvard University Press, won enthusiastic acclaim.[20] Greenfeld studied an impressive amount of sources.

Greenfeld deals with the emergence of nationalism or 'national identity' (the terms are for her identical). She is aware of 'multiple continuities' in each of the countries she deals with (in fact a recognition of multiculturality), but she insists that it is possible to identify a 'dominant' tradition. In her own words: 'The same tradition, metaphorically, might be a dominant gene in one case, and a recessive in another.'[21] The problem of biological metaphors will be separately discussed below. Unfortunately, she does not explain the term 'dominant': is it the tradition to which the major part of the population has been adhering? Or is it dominant in the sense that it has had the strongest political impact? She seems to see these two aspects as being identical, which in fact they are not (see below). Nor does she state how she found out what the 'dominant' tradition has been, but her procedure can be reconstructed. We concentrate upon the chapter on Germany.

According to Greenfeld German national identity developed between 1806 and 1815 (p. 277), and its two basic characteristics were *ressentiment* against the West and racial anti-Semitism (pp. 371–86). She quotes in this context Fichte, Jahn and other nationalist authors who indeed exhibited an aggressive nationalism and anti-Semitism.

But why was a nationalist maniac like Friedrich Ludwig Jahn a representative of German national consciousness whereas Johann Wolfgang von Goethe, who thought in completely different terms, was not? Why not Friedrich Schiller, or Gotthold Ephraim Lessing, the most important writer of the second half of the eighteenth century and an active partisan for the emancipation of the Jews? Why not the Prussian reformers who in 1812 ended juridical discrimination of the Jews in most fields (and completely in 1848)? Why not the members of the National Assembly in 1848, who proclaimed full emancipation of the Jews? And as to *ressentiment* against the West: what about the admiration of English institutions which many leading German intellectuals of the time expressed, or the enthusiastic reception of Adam Smith's *Wealth of Nations*? The answer is simple: They do not fit into the pattern.

Liah Greenfeld 'solved' the problem of representativeness by implicitly using as axiom number one that the Holocaust was the authentic expression of German identity. She states as axiom number two that national identity is basically constant over time once it has been shaped (p. 22). As axiom number three she introduces the idea that the nationalist anti-French wave after the Napoleonic conquest marked the birth of German identity; this last point allows for disregarding Lessing (he died before). Furthermore, she identified an anti-French, anti-Napoleonic sentiment with an anti-Western sentiment in general, overlooking the widespread admiration for British institutions and concepts.

Unfortunately, Greenfeld's presentation contains severe factual flaws. She writes that *racial* anti-Semitism was a fundamental element of German identity as it was shaped around 1815. But racial anti-Semitism was a phenomenon of the *second* half of the nineteenth century, the thinking in racial categories was completely alien to the period she deals with. This mistake was, however, 'necessary': by becoming aware of the historic development in German anti-Semitism she would have had to give up her axiom number two (constancy of 'national identity' over time) and this axiom was essential for her, otherwise she could not connect the Holocaust with the time around 1815.

According to Greenfeld, the *Bildungsbürger*, the intellectuals who shaped the German identity, were poor writers in a miserable economic position; that's why they were so full of resentment. As a matter of fact, most *Bildungsbürger* held stable positions as ministers, priests, professors and the like, they were 'statalized intellectuals';[22] one just has to think about Goethe (who, however, in Greenfeld's

eyes does not count as a representative of German identity). There
exists much socio-historical research on this subject[23] which Greenfeld
ignores. Her bibliography does not contain one standard work on
German social history, and she states explicitly: 'I tried to rely chiefly
on primary sources, using secondary historical analysis for orientation where my own knowledge of them was insufficient' (p. 26). In
other words, she bypassed the academic research about the topics
she wrote about. 'I was bewildered by the complexity of historical
evidence and periodically discouraged by the sheer quantity of the
material' (p. 26). This complexity she reduced, for five countries,
by axiomatically establishing a rigid pattern which then got projected into a distant past; everything which did not fit into this
pattern was discarded: *Five Roads to Tautology*.

It cannot come as a surprise that authors who try to find out
what the 'national identity' of a given country consists of can come
to completely different results.[24] Given the point that pieces of
modern literary and other texts exhibit an almost endless variety
of cultural patterns, the term 'national identity' can be filled with
whatever content is desired: one just has to choose the 'right' authors.
In German territories, in the short time between 1831 and 1845
161 000 books were newly published;[25] it is certainly not a problem
to find evidence for any kind of 'national identity' at any time.

Some authors resort to political outcomes or institutions and
deduce from these the 'national identity'. Greenfeld did so when
using the Holocaust to 'find' the essence of German identity. And
indeed institutions and political outcomes are often anchored in a
widespread consensus. Often, however, they are not. To mention
one example, in January 1918 the Bolsheviks gained 25 per cent at
the elections to the Russian Constituent Assembly whereas the Social
Revolutionaries, their libertarian, anarchist competitors on the left,
and moderate socialists were elected by 62 per cent.[26] The vast
majority of the Russian population adhered to ideas of liberty, of
social equality, of massive reduction of state power. Nevertheless
it was the Bolsheviks who won the civil war, and they erected an
extremely dictatorial regime. In highly disorderly times where the
traditional authorities and institutions have collapsed, often small
but determined minorities can become dominant, at least for some
time – the Bolsheviks were just one example among many. And
the outcome of the Bolshevik victory – Stalinism – was not intended,
not even by the victors; the Bolshevik leaders thought they fought
for a humane society. Stalinism became the dominant trait in Rus-

sian history, understood in the simple way that the political system became Stalinist, but this tells little about the cultural values to which the Russian population adhered. It requires therefore careful research to establish *whether* institutions or political outcomes correspond to the values of the population. It is not even given that institutions correspond to the cultural values of the ruling groups since institutions often develop a dynamic of their own, and sometimes it is extremely difficult to change them. Therefore, political outcomes or institutions *may* correspond to the cultural values of the population at large or the ruling groups, but they equally may not. Consequently it is not possible to deduce the characteristics of a 'national identity' from the characteristics of political outcomes, institutions or political systems.

As regards cultural phenomena, institutions are, however, essential in another way: cultural phenomena, if they are widespread and stable over time, must be supported by robust institutions. An institution is a complex 'role integrate': many people cooperate in performing a common task, and they are socialized in a particular way, in order to perform their role. If one person dies, another person who is socialized in a similar way can take over his or her role. In this way the lifespan of institutions can be much longer than the lifespan of individuals. And cultural phenomena can only be stable and widespread if certain institutions work as multipliers and stabilizers. Language is a good example. A national language is a set of symbols and standardized rules, and these rules, in an often painful and tedious process, are taught to huge masses of pupils in thousands of schools, which are all united in teaching the same rules; moreover, daily, powerful mass media apply the same rules, thereby stabilizing them. There is hardly any other set of cultural phenomena which receives such massive institutional support. And yet, even standardized national languages show considerable divergence, particularly when spoken, and they are subject to gradual change.

In Europe the Christian religion once had a similar robust institutional buttressing. Once the content of the Bible was canonized, there was a standardized corpus available upon which Christians could be culturally united; hundreds of thousands of clergymen received an intensive training in reading this book, part of its content was expounded to huge masses every Sunday, and after the coming of obligatory schooling, all children were carefully instructed on this ground. This way, for many centuries, Christianity was able to become the cultural basis for most of Europe. And yet, the history of Christianity has also been an endless history of heresies, confessional struggles and disputes. Not even this powerful institutional basis could guarantee cultural homogeneity.

Solid institutions, then, are a necessary condition for stable and widespread cultural phenomena, but they are not a sufficient one. Communist ideology had a massive institutional backing in the GDR, but it did not gain many supporters. After 1989, it practically evaporated. But on the other hand, without a robust institutional setting cultural phenomena cannot be stable and gain quantitative importance. It follows that the study of cultural phenomena in society must incorporate the study of institutions. Authors who claim that the cultural phenomena they deal with are characteristic for huge groups of people must be able to identify the institions which spread and stabilize these phenomena. This is the reason why much of the present book is devoted to institutional arrangements such as schooling or associations.

As mentioned above, to study cultural currents among the population at large, representative opinion polls are indispensable. Their existence dates back to November 1936 when George Gallup on the basis of 6000 interviews predicted Franklin D. Roosevelt's victory at the US presidential elections.[27] In Germany the first representative polls were conducted after 1945 by the US military government. The student who is interested in the strength of cultural currents before 1945 is constrained to use other sources. Several institutions of the Nazi regime compiled reports about the sentiments of the population at large which were based on a dense net of informers, and though they do not fulfil the criteria of representativeness they can at least be used to establish main currents, especially if cross-checked with other sources. In the decades before 1933 the election results show the distribution of political affiliations, and the parliamentary debates are useful qualitative sources. This kind of information in the case of Germany goes back to 1848. The study of the readership of literary output can contribute information about the thoughts of sections of society, and so can the analysis of newspapers and their distribution, or of sports clubs, singing associations or literary societies. But the more we go back in time, the more difficult it becomes to establish even gross magnitudes; and it becomes particularly difficult to say anything about the mental world of the lower, illiterate classes. Even as regards central political events such as the founding of the German

Reich in 1871 'we are simply ignorant what it meant for the Germans underneath the publicist and political top positions' (Hagen Schulze).[28] But whatever the difficulties in establishing the distribution of cultural patterns at a given historical time, every research which does not exclude beforehand *widespread* currents as being irrelevant, shows multiculturality. Nationals have never been identical. Certainly, modern societies could not work if their members were not united by a basic consensus. According to some theorists of modern multicultural societies this basic consensus should comprise: parliamentary democracy, economic pluralism, respect for individual liberty and knowledge of a common language.[29] The problem of the necessary basic consensus will be formulated slightly differently below. At this point, however, the crucial point is that a basic *consensus about a comparatively few items* does allow for multiculturality, and the vast majority of the German population is united by such a basic consensus. But this consensus is common for the Western world (and large parts of the Eastern and Southern too), it does not constitute distinct 'national identities'.

Perhaps the confusion is partly due to the widespread use of biological analogies. In the past two hundred years, thousands of authors have used biological analogies when writing about society. The German philosopher Johann Gottfried Herder made generations of intellectuals regard nations as living creatures, with their own lifecyclus of youth, maturity and decay. Herbert Spencer (*Principles of Sociology*, 1876–96) analysed the complex patterns of the modern division of labour in an explicit analogy to the 'physiological division of labour' of the organs and cells of highly developed organisms. In political rhetoric the use of biological metaphors has been extremely common; the above-mentioned work by Liah Greenfeld also contains numerous biological analogies.[30]

Biological analogies are useful in some respects: modern societies are complex, and people are doing different things. Here it helps to think of the heart, the liver, the kidneys to understand that different functions can be integrated into something coherent. From a pedagogic point of view the organism analogy is aptly chosen since everybody has got a body, so everybody can relate the analogy to their own feelings and experiences.

The analogy is, however, in many aspects extremely misleading. In the biological world the material of the seeds determines the character of the organism which comes out of it down to almost every single detail, allowing for only limited variations. According to the circumstances of soil, of humidity, of sun, a tree might grow to 20 metres or to 35 metres, and it might die after a mere forty years, or after three hundred years, but the seed of a birch tree will never produce an oak. In this sense there is a deterministic relation between seed and fully-developed organism; a prognosis as to the outcome of the development of a seed is, within certain limits, quite safe. But there is no such thing as a 'seed' in human societies. The development of societies depends on a wide range of internal and external factors, even a short-term prognosis is hardly possible. Consequently, in historical analysis the task consists of reconstructing all the major factors, internal as well as external, at every step, which led to a certain outcome. Historical narratives which are instead constructed on the metaphor that someone at a certain time sowed some 'seeds' which then some decades later produced certain 'fruits' are completely fictive.

The biological analogy is also misleading in the sense that a living organism can change only to a limited degree. Therefore it can exist only in certain environments; if a lake dries out, the fish suffocate because they can't convert their gills into lungs. But societies change. One of the basic characteristics of modern societies is exactly social change.

Furthermore, biological organisms, at least the higher ones such as horses or human beings, die if someone cuts them up. But nations can of course be cut up. Divisions of nations can cause much grief, but, for instance, the two parts of Germany functioned much better than the united Germany before 1945. Also South Korea seems to be a society undergoing successful development, more successful than the united Vietnam.

And finally, higher organisms such as human beings have a soul. But nations do not have a soul. The 'soul of the nation' is a poetical metaphor with no hold in reality. Under the name of 'national identity' the old-fashioned metaphor of 'soul of the nation' seems to have experienced a revival.

The idea that nations are culturally homogeneous beings has been very widespread. The success of this idea is partly due to its simplicity: it offers a simple structure for an otherwise highly complex world. But it also reflects a deep-rooted desire of presumably every human being that one's own community should be harmonious. Unfortunately all modern societies are complex systems of cooperation *and conflict*. Fortunately the existence of conflicts is no tragedy. The important point is that conflicts ought not to escalate; and given the appropriate regulations, conflicts do not escalate (see below).

'MAPPING' MULTICULTURALITY IN HISTORICAL
PERSPECTIVE – SOME MODELS OF CULTURAL
DIVERSITY

The present book deals with multiculturality in German history.
Its focus is on different cultural groups which can be traced in German
history, how they became integrated into the German nation, and
which problems originated during the process of integration. The
word 'integration' covers three dimensions here: *national integration* means the process by which a group which did not before regard itself as part of the nation but does so afterwards; *political
integration* means the process by which a group which did not before accept the basic principles of the political system does so afterwards; and finally *social integration* means the process by which a
group which was discriminated against before as to certain social
variables (e.g. income) is afterwards no longer discriminated against
as to those variables. These three types of integration can go together, but they do not necessarily do so. From the context it is
usually clear which type of integration is meant, otherwise it is
explicitly stated. As to processes of integration (all three kinds)
German history is rich in contradictory experiences, spanning from
numerous examples of successful integration and assimilation[31] to
murderous disintegration and genocide.

The present book contains a historical 'map': which cultural groups
can be discerned at a given time, which problems arose in the process
of integration? Were the relations between the cultural groups conflictual or mainly cooperative? In this respect the book is mainly
historical-descriptive. As its main analytical dimension it has the
aim of specifying *under which circumstances* the relations were predominantly cooperative, and under which they turned very conflictual.

The variety of cultural differences has been immense; to 'map'
all of them would have been impossible. The author decided that
cultural divides had to fulfil two criteria in order to be considered
as 'important'. Firstly, the borderline of the cultural group had to
be a multiple one, separating not only one or two isolated cultural
features but coherent sets of many cultural traits. For the second,
the borderline must have been, at least in one period of modern
German history, the front line of political tension. Five cultural
divides passed this test: religion and confession, language borders,
basic differences as to the social order, immigrants versus indigenous people, and region versus centre.

Still the matter remains highly complex. To structure the German material further, as regards the time after 1871, the author has found the concept of *milieu* highly useful. It was originally shaped by classical French sociologists such as Émile Durkheim and Marcel Mauss, but was not used therafter for many decades. As to Germany, in 1966 Mario Rainer Lepsius successfully introduced it into the academic discussion when pointing at the remarkable stability of the German party structure and their connection to, as he called it, four 'socio-moral milieux': Catholic, socialist, urban-liberal, and agrarian-conservative.[32] In this book these will be called the *main milieux* (one could identify many more). There now exists an abundance of research about the historical milieux in Germany.[33]

The present author follows Karl Rohe who proposed to combine Lepsius's milieux with the concept of *cleavage*, a line of long-term political conflict, originally introduced by Stein Rokkan.[34] Rokkan developed a systematization of cleavages which, however, is not used here. In this book, a cleavage is defined as a politicized, long-term cultural divide which has been institutionalized on both sides. For the time after 1871, three cleavages were of particular importance: Protestants versus Catholics, urban liberals against rural conservatives, and socialists against non-socialists.

As Max Weber has already pointed out, it is the conscious opposition to others which above all creates a sense of community. Using the cleavage concept, we can define a (main) milieu as follows: a milieu is a large group of people who share some important cultural norms and values; who share some common experiences; who are united in a cleavage opposition against other groups; who have a much more intensive communication among themselves than with the members of other groups; and who have built up a network of institutions and associations which stabilize their cultural values and their internal communication. In this book the emergence of the cleavages and the development of the four main milieu will be a kind of leitmotiv.

By 1995 the traditional milieux were practically dissolved. New cultural divides have appeared which, however, are no longer institutionalized and politicized. Therefore, the modern milieux will be called 'soft milieux', as opposed to the traditional 'hard' ones divided by cleavages.

The three cleavages and other cultural divides such as German and non-German languages or immigrants versus indigenous people have at different times formed complex patterns of cultural diver-

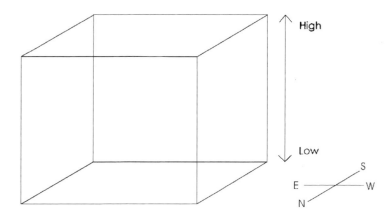

Figure 1.1 Germany by 1900: the national frame.

sity. These can be visualized with the help of some graphic models. In Figure 1.1 we start with the time around 1900 and use a simple cube as a model for Germany.

The cube simplifies the geography – we are looking to Germany, so to speak from the northern tip of Scotland: the nearest side is north, south is in the background, west accordingly on the right and east on the left. The cube also contains a status dimension, 'high' and 'low'. Status is defined as a combination of power, income and prestige. These three features have often not coincided, but we can abstract from this complication in this context.

Into this cube we draw as the first cultural divide the cleavage between Protestants and Catholics, as shown in Figure 1.2. The Protestants are in the north, the Catholics in the south. Rather more than a third of German citizens were Catholics. In reality the geographic boundary between the confessions has been, of course, more curved, and with many islands on both sides. But *most* Catholics have been living in the south and most Protestants in the north. In order not to render the graphical presentation too complex, we have drawn a straight line.

In the third dimension the border is oblique: there are more Catholics at the bottom than at the top. By 1900 the Catholics were a discriminated group who were under-represented in positions of power, economic strength and high culture. They were, however, not completely excluded from high positions, therefore there is a Catholic share even at the highest level of the cube.

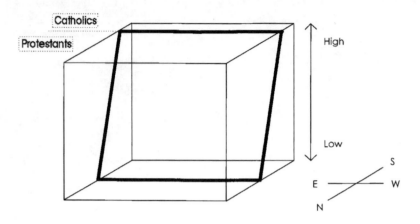

Figure 1.2　Germany by 1900: the Protestant–Catholic cleavage.

The borderline is drawn thickly. It separated two distinct cultural worlds, with practically no intermarriage. Many social scientists have used intermarriage as *the* indicator for the distance or closeness between two cultural groups because intermarriage in the long run will make the two groups merge. As will be explained in more detail in the historical discussion later, the bitter political conflict between the Catholics and the Protestant majority, the *Kulturkampf*, was officially over by 1900, but discrimination, resentments and prejudices were still harsh. By that time the Catholics had built up a dense network of institutions which formed a compact milieu around the Catholic church. Most Catholics – workers, peasants and bourgeois alike – voted for the Zentrum party, the political arm of Catholicism. Most, but not all. To draw the border by only one line/surface is, of course, again a simplification. It is, however, justified because it highlights the *main* aspect in this context.

The next line divides urban Germany from rural Germany as shown in Figure 1.3. West Germany was more urbanized and industrialized than East, and in this model rural Germany is placed in the East. The divide between the urban and the rural world cuts through both the Catholic and the Protestant part of Germany, but the divide was much more marked in the Protestant part. Therefore the line is thicker in Protestant Germany. In Germany's northeastern part we thus find a distinct Protestant agrarian milieu. This was the main basis of the conservative parties, and the Peasants' Association (*Bund der Landwirte*) was a mass organization with many

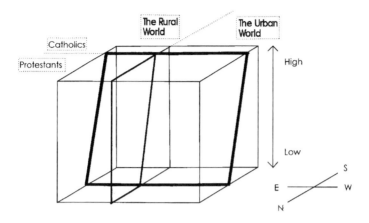

Figure 1.3 Germany by 1900: the divide between the urban and the agrarian world.

ramifications and which often exhorted violent nationalist and anti-democratic agitation. Germany's northeastern parts, east of the river Elbe, were also the territory of the Prussian Junker, the landed gentry, a group with high specific power in the Prussian state apparatus.

For the next line we introduce in Figure 1.4 the class divide between the workers on one side, and the ruling, bourgeois and petty-bourgeois classes on the other side. This divide was most marked in the Protestant urban part; there the line is thickest. In the lower part of Protestant urban Germany there is the socialist working-class milieu. The vast majority of the Social Democrat voters were Protestants – only gradually were the socialists able to gain ground among Catholic workers – and the Social Democrats were a clearly urban party. Also the workers' movement has built up a dense network of associations and institutions of all kinds which formed a compact cultural *milieu*. The workers' movement was politically massively discriminated against: there were no socialists in top positions. Above the workers' movement there is the urban-liberal milieu.

As the next divide, in Figure 1.5 we introduce the border between indigenous linguistic minorities and the German-speaking people. Most people who belonged to a linguistic minority lived in the East, predominantly Poles and Mazurians. There were other minorities, for instance Danes and Frisians on the northern border,

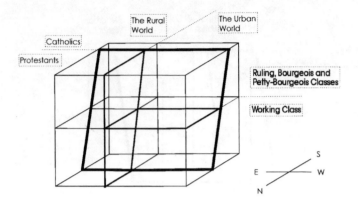

Figure 1.4 Germany by 1900: the divide between the working class and the ruling, bourgeois and petty-bourgeois classes.

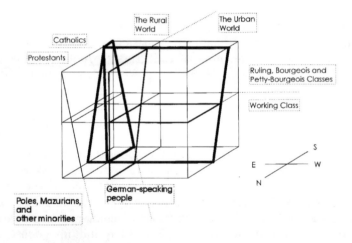

Figure 1.5 Germany by 1900: the linguistic minorities.

but they are omitted here in order not to complicate the drawing. All minorities are placed in the agrarian part of Germany as was indeed the case for most of them. However, one of the most interesting cases in this context was that of the Polish and Mazurian working-class communities in the Ruhr district, but these are also omitted form the drawing for the sake of simplicity. The Poles and other minorities were socially discriminated against, therefore the

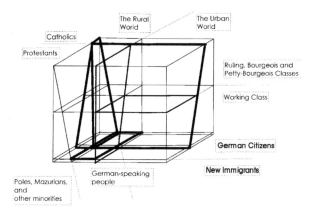

The Rural World

The Urban World

Catholics

Protestants

Ruling, Bourgeois and Petty-Bourgeois Classes

Working Class

German Citizens

New Immigrants

Poles, Mazurians, and other minorities

German-speaking people

Figure 1.6   Germany by 1900: the immigrants.

borderline is again oblique, with most room for the minorities at the bottom.

Poles and Mazurians both spoke Polish, but whereas the Poles were Catholics the Mazurians were Protestants. As will be explained in the historical discussion later, the relations between Germans and Mazurians were fairly unproblematic, whereas there were strong tensions between the Poles and the German authorities which practised a harsh Germanization policy against them. The borderlines around the Catholic Poles are therefore drawn thickly and those around the Mazurians thinly. The drawing could create the impression that there were more Mazurians than Poles; in this respect the model is inaccurate, the Poles were much more numerous, but a correction would involve considerable graphic complication.

Germany was already by 1900 an immigration country, a fact which is visualized in Figure 1.6. Most immigrants had to accept badly paid jobs with heavy work and much dirt. German society became *unterschichtet* ('under-layered'), therefore the immigrants are placed at the bottom of the cube. There were industrial and rural immigrant workers, so the line cuts through the urban and the rural world. Harshest were the conditions for the immigrant rural workers, most of them coming from Russian Poland, against whom the Prussian authorities practised an inhumane policy of strict seasonal employment. Therefore the line is drawn thickest in the German-speaking agrarian part.

Finally, we introduce the Jews in Figure 1.7. The Jews were a predominantly urban community, and they were discriminated against

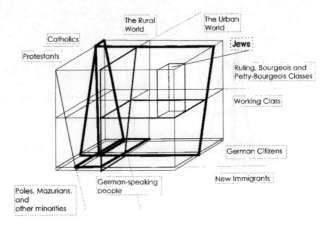

Figure 1.7 Germany by 1900: the Jews.

in a positive way. There were hardly any proletarian Jews any more, and they were highly over-represented in the higher status groups. Many leading politicians were Jews, and they were to be found in the immediate entourage of Emperor Wilhelm II, so their 'box' goes right to the top of the cube. The dividing line around them is rather thin. They had progressed a long way on the road towards assimilation, and the figures of intermarriage were high and increasing, particularly in urban Protestant centres such as Hamburg. Anti-Semitism was a minor political current.

Finally, in Figure 1.8 we highlight the four main *milieux* which were, as we see, differentiated by other cultural divides.

In 1995 the picture has changed considerably. The share of the agrarian population has fallen below 4 per cent, a rural milieu no longer exists, and in comparison to the situation in 1900 we can today regard the whole of Germany as being 'urban'. Furthermore, there are no longer cleavages, only cultural differences of various intensity. They can lead to political polemics, but they are no longer institutionalized, and the party lines go across the cultural divides. Furthermore, only a very few people belong to the indigenous non-German minority (Danes, Frisians and Sorbs – about 0.1 per cent of the population), so we will leave them outside the graphic model. The number of Jews is rising again, due to immigration from the former Soviet Union, but they are still a small minority, so they will be left outside too.

We will apply a similar graphic procedure to that above. In Figure

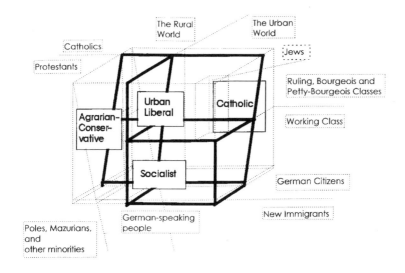

Figure 1.8 Germany by 1900: the four main milieux.

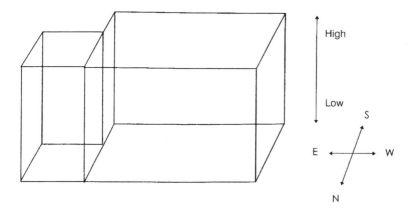

Figure 1.9 Germany by 1995: East and West Germany.

1.9 we again use three-dimensional cubes, but this time one each for East and West Germany. East and West Germans have distinct regional identities, there are many mutual prejudices, and most East Germans feel themselves to be second-rank citizens. They are, however, strongly represented at the political top positions, there-fore their box goes up to the same hight as the West German one.

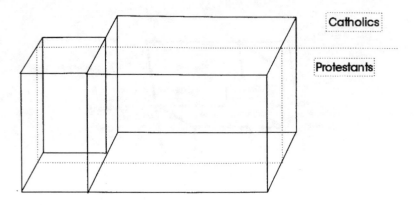

Figure 1.10   Germany by 1995: Catholics and Protestants.

In Figure 1.10 we introduce again the divide between Protestants and Catholics. The divide cuts West Germany roughly in two halves, whereas in East Germany the Catholics are a minority. The Catholics are not discriminated against any more, therefore the divide is drawn vertically, with as many Catholics at the top as at the bottom. And the divide is a soft one by now – it is no longer a politicized cleavage, and since the 1960s there is considerable intermarriage. However, most Germans still declare themselves to be either Protestant or Catholic, and confession is still a relevant factor which influences, for instance, voting behaviour.

Germany has, however, progressed far on the road of secularization, as shown in Figure 1.11. Only about one quarter of the population goes to church with a certain regularity, a figure which was used here to place the divide. Secularization can be measured by many indicators, and in some respects it would be more appropriate to use a broad area with various grey tones to indicate the border. Again the desire to simplify the graphic presentation leads to the use of one line. The border is oblique – secularization has progressed much further in the Protestant part than in the Catholic, – and East Germany is now almost completely secularized.

As the next divide, in Figure 1.12 we introduce Inglehart's division between post-materialist and materialist values. Post-materialists are mostly to be found among people who are well-off, therefore the divide is oblique, placing most persons with a lower status on the materialist part. About 56 per cent of West Germans are post-

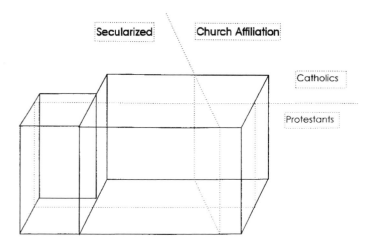

Figure 1.11 Germany by 1995: church affiliation and secularized society.

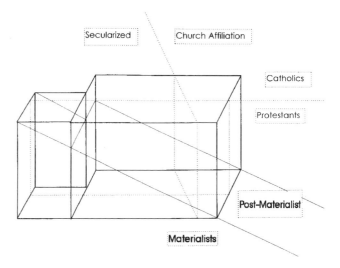

Figure 1.12 Germany by 1995: materialism and post-materialism.

materialists, whereas most East Germans still adhere to materialist values, two points which are expressed by the model. The figure gives, however, the false impression that the West German power elite would belong entirely in the post-materialist side. Correction would again demand considerable graphic complexity.

A significant divide today separates unskilled workers from the

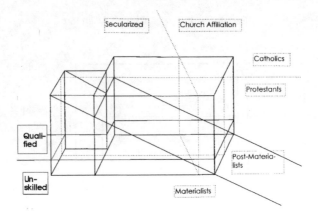

Figure 1.13   Germany by 1995: unskilled and qualified.

rest of society, as shown in Figure 1.13. Many of the unskilled feel culturally marginalized, they carry the heaviest risks with regard to unemployment or criminality, and they have virtually no representation among the political elite. Among them xenophobia is strongest because they see the immigrants, both Turks and ethnic German *Aussiedler*, as menacing competition.

The immigrants finally enter in Figure 1.14. These people are still socially discriminated against, therefore their share is bigger at the bottom of the cube. The process of integration has, however, progressed far, so they are also found in middle-class positions or even high-income levels.

Xenophobia is concentrated among the unskilled workers, therefore the borderline is drawn thickest at the lower segments. This is today the harshest cultural conflict line in Germany and has produced several murders. The attitude of the vast majority of Germans is, however, a completely different one – at the universities Turkish students experience practically no racism whatsoever, and all indicators show a process of social integration. Therefore in the parts above the unskilled workers the borderline is drawn considerably thinner.

There are many more cultural divides in Germany, so the model could be made much more complex or, by highlighting other features, presented differently. For instance, the SINUS institute and a team at Hanover University have developed a very interesting map of German milieux.[35] Following French sociologists such as

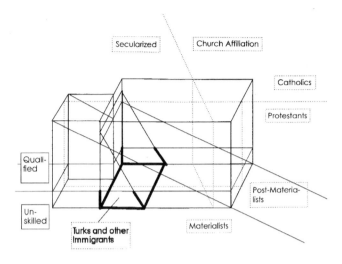

Figure 1.14 Germany by 1995: foreign immigrants.

Pierre Bourdieu, they used the category of *habitus* (lower class, middle classe, upper class) and differentiated further into traditional, partly modernized and modernized, which resulted in nine milieux. Impressive empirical and theoretical research has been done in connection with this milieux map. There are some similarities with the models presented here, but the present author could not follow the SINUS/Hanover team completely. For instance, the confessional gap does not enter their models at all, nor the border between secularization and church affiliation. This is, according to the present author, a disadvantage, given the point that religion is a central cultural factor which structures people's perception to a high extent. The Catholics with church affiliation still form the most faithful constituency for the Christian Democrats, and there the resistance against abortion has been harshest. The difference can perhaps best be explained by the following opposition: the present author deems those cultural divides as most important which have produced conflicts, whereas the SINUS/Hanover team constructed a 'social room' according to the principles of French sociologists and designed – perhaps a bit schematically – a 3 x 3 grid. But, certainly, there are many possibilities to map cultural differences.

And as the models above have perhaps made obvious, cultural divides have formed highly complex, overlapping structures. A complete historical presentation should depict all the different groups

and follow the development of all divides over time but this would
make a very long and complicated text. Most weight has had to be
given to the most important divides of the time in question. Therefore, for instance, the divide between Protestants and Catholics is
more extensively dealt with in the chapter about the Kaiserreich
than that about the time after 1945. By contrast, foreign immigrants occupy much space in the parts concerning the most recent
times, whereas they are only summarily dealt with in the chapters
concerning the time before 1914, and not at all in the passages
about the Third Reich.

An 'anti-logarithmic' scale has been applied to German history:
problems will be treated more extensively the nearer they are to
the present time. The material is basically ordered chronologically,
whereby one chapter covers one period. The borders of the periods
usually coincide with important political events which substantially
changed the political system and thereby the historical context. There
are, however, some important long-term factors and developments
which stretch over several periods, for instance the economic development or the evolution of the educational system. These will be discussed at some points in a more comprehensive form which then
exceeds the border of one period.

The topic of the present book is far too big for primary research.
The main sources for this book had to be published books and
articles written by experts in the different fields. The present author
is as close to the actual research as possible, but only in a few
selected fields has he been able to supplement the existing research
with primary investigations.[36]

COOPERATION AND MULTICULTURALITY: SOME
ABSTRACT CONSIDERATIONS

Cultural conflicts can develop quite differently according to time
and circumstances. A central point for the present book is the author's
contention that cultural differences *as such* do not create severe
conflicts. As long as some essential principles which govern the
relationship *between the cultural groups* are respected, even close
cooperation is possible. Therefore the emphasis of the book is on
the relations between the groups, not so much on the particular
cultural features of the groups.

When different groups have to coexist in one country, the problem of the legitimacy of political power becomes essential. The vast majority of the citizens must accept new laws and new taxes as legitimate, otherwise society gets torn by disastrous conflicts. Today, in Western societies, the source of legitimacy is parliamentary democracy. New laws and new taxes get accepted, albeit sometimes under protest, if they come about through a certain *procedure* (free elections to the parliament, majority vote of the parliament, etc.). Or, in Max Weber's words, legitimacy is based upon 'a positive statute in whose legality one believes'.[37] As long as the different groups accept the decisions of the national parliament, cultural diversity does not endanger political stability.

In history there have been many sources of legitimacy, of which one was religion. St Paul said that all authority comes from God, and as long as this was not questioned, the decisions of kings and dukes were respected. The matter was easier when the subjects belonged to the same religion. But religious homogeneity was not a necessary condition for political stability, as was proved by the Ottoman Empire, whose building blocks were the *Millets*, the four 'religious nations' of Sunnite Muslims, Greek-Orthodox Christians, Jews and Armenians.[38] All groups accepted the Sultan in Istanbul as the legitimate sovereign.

In the fundamentalist version, however, the *content* of the holy scripts is essential for legitimate power; the sovereign has to rule according to the principles which are outlined in the Book. This, indeed, impedes multiculturality.

It has been of crucial importance whether the state in question was embedded in a cooperative international constellation, or whether the relations with other states were conflictual. If one of the internal groups had connections to an external rival, the *external* rivalry usually severely sharpened the *internal* cleavages. When Nazi Germany invaded the Soviet Union in June 1941, the German minority in the Soviet Union was deported to Siberia. When Japanese forces attacked Pearl Harbor, American citizens of Japanese origin were sent into internment camps.

Governments and nationalists have often regarded minorities as collaborators, or at least as *potential* collaborators, although the minority were loyal. The perspective of *potential* collaboration in a future *potential* conflict could already be fatal. Conversely, times of international cooperation have usually been beneficial for the internal relations.

If different groups live together in one state, they must be able to communicate. In the predominantly agrarian world prior to the Industrial Revolution there was not much need for inter-regional communication. The top layers of society – administrators, priests and bishops, generals and merchants – had to be able to communicate over long distances, and they knew languages which allowed for that (for instance Latin), but the vast majority lived in rather isolated rural communities. The members of industrial society, however, as Ernest Gellner put it,

> must constantly communicate with a large number of other men, with whom they frequently have no previous association . . . They must also be able to communicate by means of written, impersonal . . . messages. Hence these communications must be in the same shared and standardized linguistic medium and script. The educational system which guarantees this social achievement becomes large and is indispensable . . .[39]

Gellner went, however, a crucial step too far, writing: 'For a given society, it must be one in which they can *all* breathe and speak and produce; so it must be the *same* culture.'[40]

When different groups come to learn the same standard speech, this is a process of cultural convergence. But it is a process of cultural convergence *as to one feature only*, namely language (let alone the problem that modern languages are divided into many dialects and sociolects, thus exhibiting cultural diversity). Ability to communicate *does not* imply identity of values or norms. Just to give one example, by 1900 many workers in a steel plant in the Ruhr were socialists, others were believing Catholics, a third part were immigrants from Polish-speaking areas, the engineers might have been liberals and the directors extreme nationalists. Despite their cultural diversity they could produce steel together. In modern German car factories the cultural picture is sometimes even more colourful, given the many Turkish or Yugoslav workers.

The education system provides the members of society with the necessary basic command of the standard language and other communicative capabilities. It also strengthens the 'we-feeling' of a nation through subjects like history or literature. No education system has, however, been able to produce pupils who were culturally alike; the system is too heterogeneous in itself, the teachers are very different and of different generations, and there are many cultural competitors such as the family, the media or popular music. The education system has, however, provided everyone with elementary scientific knowledge, and together with the practice of industrial society, it has worked as a great disseminator of rationalist thinking. Rationalist thinking has been one, perhaps the most important, cultural feature of Western societies, irrespective of national boundaries. The education system has also been the main producer of 'human capital', the sum total of knowledge and expertise. The present author regards human capital as the main factor determining long-term economic growth. To put it simply: Germany owes her relative economic successes to her schoolteachers. The education system therefore works in several ways in the context of this book: it provides the necessary means for communication, it strengthens the 'we-feeling' of the nationals, it contributes to the dissemination of rationalist thinking and it produces human capital.

Industrial societies have produced numerous conflicts, but social revolution did not come about. The class struggle lost its previous explosiveness. This was due to a process which sociologists have termed the 'institutionalization of class conflict'. In Theodor Geiger's words:

> The tension between capital and labour is recognized as a principle of the structure of the labour market and has become a legal institution of society ... The methods, weapons, and techniques of the class struggle are recognized – and are thereby brought under control. The struggle evolves according to certain rules of the game. Thereby the class struggle has lost its worst sting, it is converted into a legitimate tension between power factors which balance each other.[41]

Ralf Dahrendorf added:

> Marx displayed a certain sociological naïveté when he expressed his belief that capitalist society would be unable to cope with the class conflict generated by its structure ... Institutionalization assumed a number of successive and complementary forms. It began with the painful process of recognition of the contending parties as legitimate interest groups.

Dahrendorf stressed the importance of collective organization and continued:

Organization presupposes the legitimacy of interest groups, and
it thereby removes the permanent and incalculable threat of guerrilla
warfare. At the same time, it makes systematic regulation of
conflicts possible. Organization is institutionalization, and ... it
invariably has the latent function also of inaugurating routines
of conflict which contribute to reducing the violence of clashes
of interest.[42]

If conflicts become properly institutionalized they get 'defused'.
If they don't get 'defused', they escalate. It is a central contention
of the present book that (as Dahrendorf already hinted at) the
model of institutionalization can also be used for cultural conflicts.
The concrete form of institutionalization must be different according to the character of the conflict, but it is institutionalization
which 'defuses' the conflicts. Institutionalization is the key which
allows for multiculturality in one society. The necessary condition
is, of course, that the different cultural groups accept the principles of the institutionalization, and *to that extent* they must be homogeneous. Otherwise they can be as diverse as they please.
    This is also the reason why it is usually difficult to integrate fun-
damentalist believers. Fundamentalists often refuse to accept the
legitimacy of competing cultures, and therefore it has often been
difficult to reach agreements about viable institutionalization with
them. Rationalism, on the other hand, paves the way for institutionalization, everywhere; with persons who are thinking in rationalist terms it is possible to negotiate the terms of conflict so that
unnecessary damage is avoided, and cooperation in other fields not
impeded.
    In countries with different cultural groups the institutionaliza-
tion of diversity is a necessary condition to stabilize the consensus
about parliamentary democracy. If, for instance, the majority in
parliament decides that a minority language should not be taught
in public schools, the minority will hardly accept this parliamentary decision as legitimate because the disappearance of the language will make the group disappear. Certain minority rights must
be guaranteed, and the parliament must abstain from attempts to
touch them. Only on this basis can the minority develop a feeling
of belonging to the national community.
    Conversely, *destructive* conflicts arise if institutionalization is insuffi-
cient. 'Insufficient' means first and foremost that a group is systematically discriminated against. In this case some members of

the group will highlight the particular cultural features of this group as something sacred, something which must be defended. It was the discrimination of the Catholics in Northern Ireland which brought that conflict about, not their Catholic creed.

The institutional framework which allows for multiculturality must be continuously modernized. The author's polemical stance against 'national identity' is therefore based upon two convictions: (1) that it is untenable from an academic point of a view; and (2) that it renders the political task of modernizing the institutional framework for multiculturality even more difficult that it already is.

Institutionalization and the 'defusing' of conflicts require stable legal systems. Until now legal systems have basically been organized on a national basis. The state and its laws have also provided the basis for organizations such as trade unions, employers' associations, cultural associations and political parties. In fact, all Western European nations have been 'melting pots':[43] they have either made a variety of older cultural identities disappear or have transformed them in such a way that they could be combined with a sentiment of belonging to one nation. But the result has never been homogeneous national cultures, but shifting patterns of multi-culturality. As regards Germany, we will follow this process more closely. We shall go back in time as far as there are written sources.

Part I
The Genesis of a
Melting-Pot

2 From *Germania* to the Holy Roman Empire of the Germanic Nation

ROMANS AND *GERMANI*

Between 58 and 51 BC Caesar conquered Gaul and pushed the borders of the Roman empire to the Rhine. As he wrote in his report about the war, the Rhine was also an ethnic border: Gauls (or Celts) settled on the Western side, Germani on the other. He thereby enriched the Roman world with a new ethnographic category (until then, the people living at the northern fringe of ancient civilization were either Celts or Scythes).[1] But as an ethnographer Caesar was a little inconsistent. As he himself mentioned several times, Germanic tribes had already settled on the Western bank of the Rhine.[2] Additionally, modern archaeologists have established that the whole of southern and central Germany up to the rivers Leine and Lippe was inhabited by Celts.[3]

Roman authors perceived the Germani as a cultural unit, but it is unknown whether the Germani themselves did so. According to modern linguists, at some point before 300 BC the so-called Germanic sound shift had linguistically separated the people living in southern Scandinavia and northern Germany from other Indoeuropeans.[4] Just to mention one feature, 'f' replaced 'p', e.g. Gothic *'fotus'* (foot) instead of Latin *'pedes'*. Unfortunately, the sources of the Germanic languages are scarce. It is very likely that the Germanic tribes spoke a common language which, though divided by dialects, was common enough to allow for communication.[5] Additionally, it is very probable that the Germanic tribes shared identical or at least similar religious concepts. Archaeologists can also identify many common traits in the material culture.[6]

But this linguistic and cultural unity did not create a political unity. According to Roman authors the conflicts among the tribes were endemic, and Roman diplomacy could often only mobilize the support of one Germanic tribe in order to embattle another one. Only in rare cases, such as the battle in the Teutoburg forests, could the Germanic tribes form a short-term alliance. The Germanic tribes were lacking the common interests or the institutions necessary to provide a framework for continuous common action. They had neither a common administration nor generally accepted rules to establish political power.

The Roman presence on the Rhine and Danube had long-lasting effects. In particular the regions on the Rhine underwent a thorough process of Romanization. This was mostly due to the strong Roman army concentrated there. The legions were based in a chain of camps, which developed into proper cities. The craftsmen centred around the military camps became the nucleus of a blossoming industry, and Roman veterans settled in the surrounding countryside. The Romans covered the regions with a dense network of roads and introduced a wide range of new techniques and cultivation, such as vine growing.[7]

Many of their technical and social innovations remained after the collapse of the empire. The cities they founded, like Cologne or Mainz, survived the 'Dark Ages' (although in a very reduced form), thus creating the starting point for town development in Germany. Their language and literacy provided the backbone of the high culture for many centuries. And last but not least, it was through the communication systems of the Roman empire that Christianity came. The first communities date perhaps back to the second century. In the fourth century, Christianity was the dominant religion in the towns of the Rhine Valley. According to some sources, the Germanic tribes of the eastern side of the Rhine were already converted.[8]

Inside the territories which later became Germany, the Roman presence at the Rhine created a marked difference in the level of civilization between west and east. This difference remained a basic feature of German society right into modern times.

The Romans called the vast areas beyond the Rhine *Germania*. But her borders were quite unclear. According to Tacitus, the Rhine and Danube formed the limits in the west and south, but the other parts were 'bordered by the ocean, which comprised large bays and immense islands'; he did not specify whether these islands (presumably Scandinavia) belonged to Germania or not. To Sarmates and Daces the land was separated 'by mutual fear and mountains'.[9] Shortly before Tacitus wrote his *Germania*, Emperor Domitian gave the word a more precise, but quite different, political meaning: Domitian constituted the areas at the *left* bank of the Rhine as two new provinces, naming them Germania Superior and Germania Inferior.[10] Imprecise geographical terms and political units at variance with them are a problem we shall meet frequently.

GENTES AND THE FRANKISH EMPIRE

The Germanic tribes which Caesar encountered converged during the following centuries into larger population units like Saxons, Thuringians and Franconians (mentioned for the first time in AD 258).[11] The causes of this integration are still unclear. It is likely that a growing population pressure urged them to expand geographically, and this could not be done without the additional military strength which the larger units provided. The resulting great migrations led Goths and Vandals to regions as distant as Northern Africa and Spain. In Germany the Alamans gradually occupied the whole southwest and passed around AD 450 over the Rhine into Alsace and climbed up the Alpine valleys. East of them, the Bavarians settled. These expansions were presumably mostly a matter of peaceful osmosis, accompanied, though, by military raids. Organized settlements with the approval of the Roman authorities also played an important role.[12] Alamans and Bavarians could completely assimilate the remainder of the Celtic and Roman populations. The many Celtic loan words in the modern German language (especially in Bavarian dialect) are modern relics of this cultural mélange.

The Germanic people (the sources say *gentes*) had several mechanisms and elements at their disposal to secure a relatively stable integration: each *gens* had its own law and a mythology of common origin. A nobility acted as the core of society and guarded traditions and myths; the *populus* of the sources refers to the nobility, not the people at large. Although relatively stable, the *gentes* were not sharply defined units. There were many examples of groups shifting from one to the other, or of subdued groups which were incorporated into the *gens*.[13]

After the collapse of the Roman empire the Franconians became the strongest *gens*. When their King Clovis died in AD 511, the Frankish kingdom covered most of modern France, Belgium, the Rhine Valley and large parts of southern Germany. The Alamans, Bavarians and Thuringians were subdued, and the same happened in Charlemagne's time (around 800) to the Saxons and Longobards. These Germanic *gentes* conserved their identity within the framework of the Frankish empire, retaining for instance their own laws. When the Carolingian empire eventually collapsed, the *gentes* re-emerged as basic political units.

The political history of the Frankish kingdom is turbulent and chaotic. But in the eighth century, under the kings Pippin and especially Charlemagne, central power was effectively reconstructed. Charlemagne was able to push the border of his empire down to the river Ebro in Spain, conquer northern Italy and, after a long and gruesome war, also northern Germany. In 800 on Christmas Eve he made the Pope in Rome crown him as emperor. At least symbolically, the Roman empire in the West was reconstructed.

The Christian church was an important part of the power structure of the Frankish empire. The Carolingian kings and emperors were able to place reliable lieutenants in the key clerical posts; the church organized a large part of the administration of the empire and was practically the only institution educating personnel with the ability to read and write. The monarchy supported missionary activities among the pagan populations in the north and east. Culturally these parts of the former Germania thereby became effectively linked with the lands west of the Rhine and south of the Alps. The population, or at least part of it, acquired in addition to an ethnic identity a more universal identity as part of Christianity.

TOWARDS LINGUISTIC DIVERGENCE

In France the Romanized majority were able to gradually absorb the Germanic upper class, but the areas on the left bank of the Rhine and in the Mosel valley, in former times thoroughly Romanized, had become Germanic. At around 840, the border separating the Romanic and Germanic languages ran from south of Boulogne on the French Channel coast through modern Belgium to Maastricht, and from there, bending southwards, stretched through east Belgium, Lorraine and Alsace into Switzerland. This border remained relatively stable up to the nineteenth century.

At the same time another linguistic border developed in the east. From about AD 500 onwards, Slavic people migrated into the huge areas of East and East Central Europe. A line stretching roughly from modern Lübeck to Trieste marked the border of their advance.

Meanwhile a number of forces had destroyed the former linguistic unity of the Germanic populations. The most important in this context was the second shift of sounds which, during the fourth and fifth centuries, profoundly transformed the language of the Alamans, Bavarians and, to lesser extent, Franconians.[14] To mention one example, 'p' between two vowels turned into 'ff' (compare the English '*open*' with the German '*offen*'). The Saxons and Frisians in the north were not involved. This second shift of sounds thereby created a deep linguistic barrier, separating for many centuries the High German regions in the south from Low German in the north. Linguists used the term 'Old High German' as a common denominator for the idioms in southern and central Germany transformed by the second shift of sounds, but the texts show a 'hodgepodge of varied and frequently incongruous elements'.[15] A standard written form did not exist, and the spoken language diverged presumably even further. So not even within southern Germany did a common language exist (not to mention the problems between south and north). Inter-regional communication had to be based either on Latin or on the Frankish dialect spoken at the Carolingian court.

Presumably before Charlemagne's time the Germanic language of Scandinavia had already developed into Old Nordic, thereby creating another linguistic border. But this was for many centuries a weak one. Thus, while Saxon peasants from northern Germany could not understand their peers in southern Germany, they did not have many difficulties with their Nordic neighbours. At that time the same was true for the Anglo-Saxons who, originating from northern Germany, settled in England.[16]

This growing linguistic diversity was a consequence of some basic features of early medieval society: most people lived and worked in small units separated from each other, and there was little inter-regional communication. Institutions to secure linguistic continuity or homogenization were weak. Only the church had an educational system at its disposal, and its learned members could use Latin for long-distance communication. There were comparatively few texts written in the popular idioms which, therefore, were able to develop regionally or even locally with relatively few influences from the outer world.

THE EMERGENCE OF A NEW MULTI-ETHNIC UNIT: THE HOLY ROMAN EMPIRE

In the decades after Charlemagne's death (814) the Carolingian empire disintegrated. A series of wars between Emperor Louis the

Pious and his sons, and then among their sons, followed. In 843 the Frankish noblemen, weary of the fratricide, enforced a formal divi-sion of the empire into three parts. According to the Treaty of Verdun, Lothar became emperor and got the central part; Charles the Bold received the western part and Louis II the regions east of the Rhine. The idea of a common Carolingian empire was not yet dead, but the first step to form distinct East and West Frankish political units was taken.[17] These units later developed into the modern states of France and Germany. But it should be empha-sized that the Treaty of Verdun was purely a dynastic compromise, drafted to create three parts of equal economic importance. Cul-tural, linguistic or 'national' considerations did not play a part.

On several occasions the division was redrafted, the last time at Ribémont in 880. With this treaty the border between the West and the East Frankish kingdom was drawn on a line west of the river Maas. There, that is to say to the *west* of the linguistic border between Romanic and Germanic, it remained, except for short inter-vals, throughout the Middle Ages.

In 881 Charles III the Fat was able to re-establish the the united empire for a last time. But when in 887 the nobility of the eastern territories elected Arnulf of Carinthia as Frankish king, the other parts of the empire (Italy, High and Low Burgundy, the West Frank-ish kingdom) did not follow and constituted themselves as inde-pendent units. Only the noblemen of the East Frankish kingdom remained loyal to Arnulf, thereby stabilizing the borders drawn at Ribémont.

Many historians interpreted the establishment of the East Frankish kingdom as the building of a kind of nation-state. According to this interpretation, there existed a German people with at least a rudimentary common identity, and this common identity was an important factor in the decision in 887 to elect Arnulf, and in 911 to elect the non-Carolingian Konrad I. But a German people with a common ethnic identity or common language did not exist; addi-tionally, the East Frankish kingdom included large territories with a Romanic-speaking population. By contrast, many modern histo-rians see the elections as the political moves of noblemen, who were leading large groups tied together by personal bonds. In the case of the East Frankish kingdom, the traditional *gentes* of Franconians, Swabians (Alamans), Bavarians and Saxons, re-emerging as political units headed by dukes, were particularly important.[18] These noblemen saw the necessity of some kind of central power.

So did the church. Grouped around her centres in Mainz and Fulda, the church was a unifying force, being an impersonal institution amidst heterogeneous populations held together by personal bonds. In short, it was not the collective identity of a people that formed the basis of the new political construction. It was culturally rather a heterogeneous core of noblemen and clerics tied together by common interests who erected a new political construction, and it was this new political construction which was to create, in a process of hundreds of years, the German people.

Around 900, devastating invasions by Vikings and Hungarians and murderous struggles between noble families made a strengthening of the royal authority imperative. A decisive move in this respect was the election of Henry I in 919.[19] As Duke of Saxony he was by far the most powerful nobleman, and the church was his effective ally. In 929 Henry I established the principle of the indivisibility of the monarchy. Four years later, in defence against a Hungarian invasion, he was the first East Frankish monarch who managed to mobilize an army composed of all parts of his kingdom. The kingdom could act as an effective political unity.[20]

In 936, his son Otto I was crowned in Aachen with clear Carolingian reminders. Otto enlarged the borders of the monarchy enormously. In Slavic territory he installed special border regions *(Marken)* and extended his sovereignty to the banks of the river Oder; Bohemia became dependent upon his monarchy and gradually became incorporated into it. In 951, Otto conquered northern Italy; four years later he dealt a shattering blow to the Hungarians. And in 962 the Pope crowned him in Rome as emperor. The East Frankish monarchy had symbolically inherited the Carolingian and the Roman empire, and Otto I received the highest form of legitimation conceivable in medieval times.

The strength of the Ottonian empire was to a large extent due to the fact that Henry and Otto could use the church as a powerful administrative organization, which breached traditional regional and personal bonds. The church was the first bureaucracy in the sense of Max Weber. Otto I strengthened the church systematically, providing it with new sources of income and founding new episcopal seats (e.g. Magdeburg and Prague). The bishops were chosen from among the clerics of the royal court, men who were well informed about the lines of Ottonian politics. The church was thus a unified, strong and loyal organization. According to an army list dating from the time of Otto II, bishops and abbots provided

1510 armoured knights, the secular noblemen only 534. The arch-bishops of Mainz and Cologne and the bishops of Strasbourg and Augsburg had to send 100 knights each, the most powerful secular nobleman only 40.[21]

Otto I and his successors were not German, but 'Roman' emperors, governing a huge multi-ethnic entity.[22] They based their legitimation on Christian theory, Christianity (an explicitly supra-ethnic religion) was the uniting ideological bond and the church was the main administrative body.

The political theory reflected itself in the official title of the empire: *Romanum Imperium*, a formula already used under Charlemagne. In 1157, it was enlarged by the adjective *Sacrum*: Holy Roman Empire. It was not until 1442 that the supplement *Nationis Germanicae*, 'of the Germanic Nation', came into use,[23] indicating the change from the concept of a universal monarchy to a partial entity.

THE COLONIZATION OF THE EAST – MULTI-ETHNICITY ENLARGED

In 983 the Slavic population west of the river Oder regained their independence in a great uprising; only in the southern parts of the modern GDR did Otto I's construction survive. But in the twelfth century, the eastbound expansion began again. The initiators were regional princes like Henry the Lion, Duke of Saxony, or ecclesiastical aristocrats. The imperial power was at that time already weakened (see below) and played only a minor role. Sometimes, as in 1149, the military expansion took the form of a crusade. In the central and southern parts of the modern GDR, already conquered under Otto I, the Slavic political structures were annihilated, but in the north, in Mecklenburg and Pomerania, Slavic principalities survived and were incorporated into the empire as such. The ruling dynasty in Mecklenburg, of Slavic descent, governed right up to 1918.

In 1033 the young Christian kingdom of Poland had to recognize the suzerainty of the empire. Although in the following century Poland disintegrated into different duchies, she was eventually able to retain her independence. But the Duchy of Silesia, originally a part of Poland, became incorporated into the Holy Roman Empire for good.

In 1225 the Polish Duke Conrad of Mazovia offered the area around Culm to the Teutonic Order (*Ordo Teutonicorum*), an order of knighthood like the Templars.[24] By this move, the Polish Duke wanted to obtain military protection against the pagan Prussians. The knights dutifully conquered the surrounding areas, but from 1276 onwards, ignoring the reasons they were called for, they also conquered Christian territories. In 1309 their new state ruled over all lands between Pomerania and Livland, and it expanded even further during the following decades. The knights, numbering only about 1000, organized an efficient administration and economy, thereby securing their power.

The fact that the princes, emperors and knights could conquer areas in the east and force Slavic princes to recognize their suzerainty would in itself not have had long-lasting effects. It should be remembered that northern Italy, Provence and Burgundy were for long periods parts of the empire as well. But in addition to the conquest, hundreds of thousands of peasants from the western regions of the empire moved eastwards and dozens of cities were founded. It was this great settlement movement which profoundly transformed the social and cultural pattern of the regions involved. The linguistic barrier between the Germanic and Slavic languages moved several hundred kilometres eastwards.

'Because the country was deserted', a chronicler reported, 'he [the Count of Holstein] sent messengers to all lands, namely to Flanders and Holland, Utrecht, Westfalia and Friesland, that everybody, who had too little arable land, should come with his family, in order to find here the most beautiful, spacious, fertile . . . land.' This settler recruitment in 1143 was one of the first. Other noblemen and princes did likewise in order to strengthen their base for revenues and power. The practical organization of the settlement was often carried out by enterprisers (*locatores*); clerical orders like the Cistercians played an important role as well. All in all, in the twelfth century perhaps 200 000 peasants moved eastwards, and as many did so in the following century.[25] Then the movement lost momentum.

Some areas in the east were devastated by crusades and other wars, but generally the areas were only thinly populated beforehand. Many regions were uncultivated, and between the Slavic populations there were large border woods. It was particularly in these 'pores' in the Slavic settlement that the colonization took place. Gradually the Slavs became culturally and linguistically absorbed,

leaving, however, many loan words in modern German. In Mecklenburg a Slavic language was still spoken in 1521, as there was in the
Wendland (i.e. land of the Vends, the Slavs) *west* of the Elbe even
in the seventeenth century.[26] In Lusatia, southeast of Berlin, a
Slavonic language, that of the Sorbs, has survived until today.

Noblemen and princes systematically founded new towns. The
most successful of them was Lübeck, founded in 1143. Often the
new towns were based on Slavic settlements or castles, but others
were in actual fact built *ex nihilo*. Many of these towns, like Lübeck,
Wismar, Danzig and Riga, became members of the Hanseatic League
and gained for many centuries enormous economic and political
importance. The Baltic Sea and the adjacent land regions, accessible via a series of navigable rivers like the Oder and Vistula, became
firmly linked with the economy of Western Europe.

The 'German' movement eastward belongs to the most hotly
debated subjects in historiography.[27] Some German historians of
the nineteenth century wrote that the 'Germans' brought 'civilization and culture' to uncivilized tribes. For many Eastern European
historians the events were a story of heroic Slavic defence against
German expansionism.

Modern historians underline, however, the following observations.
Firstly, the conquest and colonization described here was but a
part of a general European development. Medieval civilization experienced a substantial population growth which all over Europe
led to inner colonization and territorial expansion (the crusades,
the Spanish *reconquista*, the Norman settlement in southern Italy,
Swedish expansion into Finland, etc.). Secondly, medieval chron-
iclers do report conflicts or mutual resentments between Slavs and
'Germans', but only as a secondary problem. The main line of conflict was the cleavage between Christians and pagans. Rebellions
of vassals against their lords could lead to war as well, but the
question of who supported a rebellion and who stayed loyal was
not decided by language. Often Slavs fought on both sides. Thirdly,
it was in many cases *Slavic* princes and noblemen who organized
the settlement; a famous case in point is Henry I, Duke of Silesia,
calling for settlers from the west in large numbers, and it was the
Polish Duke Conrad of Mazovia who called for the Teutonic knights.

The most important cleavages in feudal society did not run along
nationalist lines, but it was the scholars of the nineteenth and early
twentieth century who projected their nationalist stereotypes into
medieval times.

THE DECLINE OF CENTRAL POWER

The impressive strength of imperial power in the tenth and eleventh centuries rested to a large extent upon the clerical bureaucracy. This point turned out to be fatal when the leadership of the Catholic church endeavoured to tighten its own organization and claimed political power for itself. In 1075 Pope Gregory VII published a decree in which he forbade the appointment of bishops and other clerics by worldly authorities. Insisting that clerical personnel should be subject to Rome and not to the king and emperor,[28] he challenged the central power at a sensitive point. The resulting power struggle between pope and emperor lasted, with interruptions, for decades. On many occasions the Pope could count on the tacit or explicit support of many noblemen of the empire who were also interested in weakening the imperial power. The central power experienced another blow when the blossoming towns of northern Italy, by far the richest part of the empire, rose in revolt.

Emperor Frederick Barbarossa (1152–90), after severe fights with rebellious vassals like Henry the Lion, with the Lombard cities and with the Pope, restored imperial power for the last time, and under his successors central power collapsed. Emperor Frederick II was an able politician, a poet, philosopher and scholar, in short a symbol of the splendour of medieval civilization. But in 1220 and 1232 (*confoederatio cum principibus ecclesiasticis, statutum in favorem principum*), he had to officially acknowledge that it was the clerical and secular princes who governed the territories of the empire, not the emperor; for the first time they were called 'lords of the land' (*dominus terre*). They were the supreme judges within their territories and it was they who coined the money.[29] A group of six powerful noblemen secured for themselves the right to elect the king.

In 1273, after decades with almost non-existent central power (*interregnum*), Count Rudolf of Habsburg became the new king. From then onwards the Habsburg dynasty almost uninterruptedly occupied the throne. But in 1273 they were still weak, and the electors deliberately chose a candidate who could not become dangerous. The title of emperor did not give much power any more, and the emperors had mostly to rely on their own resources (*Hausmacht*).

The empire was transformed into a loose confederation but not completely dissolved. In 1338 at Rhense the six most important princes reaffirmed the concept of the empire, agreed upon the principle of mutual support and declared that the election of the king did not need any papal approval. In 1356, by a lengthy document issued by Emperor Charles IV (*Goldene Bulle*), the empire acquired a kind of written constitution:[30] seven electors, namely the Archbishops of Cologne, Mainz and Trier, the King of Bohemia, the Duke of Saxony, the Margrave of Brandenburg and the Count palatine at Rheine, were to elect the king in Frankfurt; thereafter he was to be crowned in Aachen by the Archbishop of Cologne. It should perhaps be underlined that one of the electors was the Slavonic King of Bohemia. Regional confederations were forbidden. The idea of a common empire survived and could from time to time gain noticeable moral force, especially among knights and town people who resented the often arbitrary rule of the princes and sympathized with a stronger central power. On several occasions treaties of public peace within the empire (*Landfrieden*) were agreed upon.

But in the fifteenth century at the latest the structure of the empire was generally judged to be inadequate. Feuds were frequent, impoverished knights turned into robbers, a state of widespread lawlessness was recorded. This was mostly a consequence of the weak central institutions and the disastrous agrarian crisis at the end of the fourteenth century and onwards. There were some steps towards a constitutional reform of the empire. Representatives of the estates convened regularly and formed an Imperial Diet, the *Reichstag*; from 1489 it was divided into three chambers, one for the duke electors, one for the other princes and one for the cities (i.e. towns not under the authority of princes). In 1495 a general peace was announced again and feuds were forbidden; a supreme court was founded, situated in Frankfurt (from 1527 in Speyer, in 1689 transferred to Wetzlar) and to be financed (in theory) by a general tax.

But the project of a *thoroughgoing* reform of the empire, often and passionately discussed, was not realized.[31]

THE BEGINNINGS OF A COLLECTIVE GERMAN IDENTITY

The Holy Roman Empire never developed into a centralized monarchy. Nevertheless, a slow process of cultural unification, at least among the educated groups of the Germanic-speaking population, is traceable.

The question whether there was in medieval times a collective German identity or not is one which has been discussed for generations.[32] Nevertheless, many problems are still unclear. The following points are, however, quite well established. The modern word *deutsch* (German) stems from early medieval *diutisk*. Its Latin equivalent *theodiscus* is documented for the first time in 786, but as *duitisk* it means 'popular', referring to the spoken non-Romanic languages, including Anglo-Saxon in England and Longobard in northern Italy. The very first source using *theodiscus* is a clerical letter from Mercia, England, referring to the language spoken there.[33] So at least at that time *theodiscus* had nothing to do with the modern notion of German.

From the ninth century onwards *theodiscus* gets a competitor in the word *teutonicus*. From around 1070 it is used in documents to label the empire: *Regnum Teutonicum*. But this was a political category used from the outside, in French or papal texts. These authors thereby denied the universal character of the empire, qualifying it as a partial unit; partisans of the emperor insisted on the formula *Romanum Imperium* or *Sacrum Romanum Imperium*. Within the empire, the 'national' term was not accepted before the fifteenth century, and even then only reluctantly.[34] This might be a reflection of political changes: In the fifteenth century, northern Italy and Burgundy were for practical purposes lost; the empire was more Germanic, less universal in character than before.

The Germanic idioms within the empire were very different from each other for many centuries. It is true that the poetic texts and songs written around 1150 at the courts of knights and noblemen were linguistically rather homogeneous; linguists later grouped them under the term 'Middle High German' (*Mittelhochdeutsch*). But this was a written language, used only in small circles and very much at variance with the spoken idioms.[35] After the collapse of the Staufen dynasty, Middle High German disappeared. Some medieval authors saw the different idioms as dialects of a common language, but even in around 1280 the Bavarian poet Wernher der Gärtner grouped Low German as a foreign language together with Latin, French and Bohemian.[36] During the fourteenth century regional written languages, mostly used by the territorial administrations, developed and stabilized a process of homogenization. The newly colonized areas in the east were of particular importance in this respect because the heterogeneous linguistic heritage of the immigrants favoured a process of linguistic homogenization allowing for communication over longer distances. Within the Low German areas in northern Germany the juridical and commercial texts of the Hanse induced a similar development. The appearance of printed texts (from 1445 onwards) supported this process. Thus around 1500 the lingustic provinces had become larger, but a standard speech still did not exist. At that time, however, the idea that the different idioms were part of a common German language seems to be widespread in educated circles.

The words *Germania*, *Alemania* and *Theutonia* in Latin texts, or *diutsche lant* ('German' lands, plural, later also in singular) and others, were frequently used as geographical terms, but no one before 1500 seems to have had a precise idea about the borders of this country. Many authors referred to the Roman tradition, identifying *Germania* with the regions east of the Rhine;[37] the poet Walther von der Vogelweide, around 1200, uses the Rhine, the Elbe and Hungary as borders.[38] Even at the council at Konstanz (1414–18), the *natio germanica* also comprises Scandinavia, Poland, Bohemia and Hungary.[39]

In the fifteenth century, language enters as a new criterion to define the borders. In the sixteenth century this seems to be the dominant paradigm, as, for instance, dictionaries show: *Germania, Das gantz Teütschland, so weit die Teütsch spraach gehet* (*Germania*, the whole of Germany, as far as the German language is spoken).[40] Some texts show not only language awareness but also language pride (*lingua nobilissima, clarissima et humanissima*, Felix Fabri in 1484). This pride was, however, as this example shows, expressed in Latin.[41]

These processes of linguistic unification, of growing language awareness and language patriotism presumably had common causes. In the High and Late Middle Ages, as a consequence of an increasing division of labour, society became gradually more complex. Especially in the emerging towns, very heterogeneous groups had to live closely together. Essential goods like grain or timber were traded over long distances and inter-regional intercourse became indispensable. And the constant danger of war made the stable organization of power structures necessary; populations who lacked that organization, for instance the Slavs between the Elbe and Oder, succumbed. The structure of power meant the construction of administrative organizations which in turn could not function without literacy.

These processes created together a new and hitherto unknown

demand for literacy; town merchants and the princes of the territories were the main groups to organize measures to fulfil it. The monopoly of the church on literacy crumbled. From about 1250 onwards new schools with new curricula appeared in the towns. In 1348 Emperor Charles IV founded the first university north of the Alps (in Prague). Up to 1477 14 others followed, mostly initiated by the princes,[42] the rivalry between the territories having a positive effect upon the embryonic education system. As regards the number of universities, the empire north of the Alps surpassed Italy, France, and England.

The secularization of education and literacy reflects itself in an enormous increase in the number of documents written in one of the German idioms:[43]

1240–59	:	42
1260–79	:	348
1280–99	:	3169

Many laymen, who often had a critical attitude towards the church, insisted upon the use of the popular idioms instead of Latin, and the growing number of written texts enhanced again the prestige of these idioms.[44]

Among educated people, a common German identity based on language seems to be fairly well established by around 1500 at the latest. But we hardly know anything in this respect about the large peasant population; their world was presumably mostly locally defined. It is also extremely difficult to assess the political importance of this developing common identity. On the one hand, medieval sources do give examples of conflicts in which the antagonists were grouped according to their language, but this seems to be mostly the case in border regions or when enemies from the outside arrived.[45] Furthermore, language was often used in disputes as an ideological argument, for instance to justify territorial claims. But this does not mean that it was the clash of different common identities that created the conflict. Generally, the major lines of conflict did not follow language borders. And it should perhaps be emphasized that, parallel to the process of a growing German language consciousness, a considerable section of *Germania* broke away. In 1291, the inhabitants of three Swiss cantons began their struggle for autonomy, and in 1499 Emperor Maximilian I had to acknowledge the de facto independence of the Swiss confederation.

Thus, around 1500, the Holy Roman Empire of the German Nation was a loosely integrated multi-ethnic confederation. The majority of its inhabitants spoke a German idiom, but many other languages (French, Italian, Czech, Polish and many more) were also strongly represented, while some German-speaking territories (Switzerland, the territory of the Teutonic knights) were outside. Within the German-speaking population of the empire, a process of increasing common identity based on language is traceable, and so is German patriotism. But this patriotism was presumably confined to small groups of educated people. As a political factor it was of minor importance.

3 From Reformation to Enlightenment – Political Fragmentation and Cultural Unification

REFORMATION: A NEW CULTURAL CLEAVAGE

The feeling that change was necessary was widespread at the end of the fifteenth century. Many feuds made it apparent that the worldly order did not function appropriately. The long-lasting agrarian crisis had impoverished large sections of the peasantry; most of the peasants were obliged to work for the noblemen, and their obligations were increasing. The church could not give much consolation – its credibility was ruined. Too obvious were the discrepancies between its preaching and the actual behaviour of its servants, too appalling the instrumentalization of religion in order to accumulate worldly opulence. In large numbers the souls of disappointed believers turned to mystical or heretical movements. Social unrest and subversive conspiracies were frequent.

When in 1517 Martin Luther published his protest against the letters of indulgence, he was at first only one among many clerical dissenters. But within a few years he became the symbol of a new era. He met the desires of many of his contemporaries, showing them in confusing times the way to salvation. His basic message was simple:[1] the Bible, and the Bible only, is God's word, all other texts are but human artifacts. By focusing upon the Bible he stayed perfectly in line with the basic features of the culture of his time – a necessary precondition of his success. But at the same time he came into merciless conflict with the Catholic hierarchy, by labelling its declarations at best irrelevant, at worst anti-Christian. That was much more than a theological dispute: he was challenging the basis of a great institution. The church could only legitimize its privileges by claiming that it knew God's word better than other mortals. Luther found many followers, particularly in the towns. There the cultural monopoly of the Catholic church was already broken.[2]

As regards politics, Luther was conservative, insisting that any secular authority was there because of God (as St Paul said); for him, the field of the church was confined to spiritual matters. This brought him in sharp conflict with other reformers like Huldrych Zwingli, not to mention the theocratic revolutionary Thomas Müntzer, one of the leaders of the Great Peasant Revolt in 1524–5.

By reducing the role of religion, Luther made a strong contribution to the process of secularization of the world, and thereby to its modernization. But at the same time he supplied princes and kings with a new and powerful ideology. Not surprisingly, many of them allied themselves with his cause. Using Luther's theology, the princes could expropriate the goods of the Catholic church and organize new churches under their own supervision. The regulations of Duke-Elector Johann of Saxony became a model in this respect.

Within the empire, the most important adversary of the Reformation was Emperor Charles V. At first glance he was a monarch of breathtaking power: he had inherited the crowns of Spain, Naples, the Burgundian Netherlands and the Habsburg possessions within the Holy Roman Empire, and in 1519, aged 19, he was elected king of the Holy Roman Empire (emperor in 1530). It was symptomatic for the still supra-ethnic character of the empire that the French King François I had for a while the best chance of being elected; Henry VIII of England was also a serious candidate. But the money of the Fugger trading company decided the matter.[3]

After the Spanish conquests in America and elsewhere Charles V reigned over the largest monarchy ever seen in history. But the different parts were only very loosely integrated. In Italy and Spain the Catholic church was still strongly entrenched. Reformation came as a fateful blow to the coherence of Charles's monarchy, and he tried everything to stop it. But in spite of his seemingly enormous resources, he did not succeed.

Within the Holy Roman Empire, Charles V was but one prince among others. And even Catholic princes like Duke Wilhelm IV of Bavaria allied themselves with their Protestant peers if the balance of power seemed to turn too heavily in favour of the Catholic emperor. In addition, power struggles within the Holy Roman Empire were now part of an international political system: in the Southeast the forces of the Ottoman Empire appeared as new dangerous enemies, and to repulse them Charles V needed the support of the Protestant princes. Additionally, the (Catholic) King of France supported the Protestant side in order to weaken the emperor.

In 1555, after several armed conflicts, the Protestant and Catholic parties signed the Peace of Augsburg (*Augsburger Religionsfrieden*). As a basic principle it was established that the rulers of the territories could decide the religion (*cuius regio, eius religio*), dissenting subjects had the right to emigrate, and within the independent towns both religions were guaranteed. The regulations of the Peace of Augsburg contained many inconsistencies,[4] so the struggle continued for decades in a more covert form, with both sides justifying their moves with often doubtful legal arguments. But at least, at a time when France was torn by fierce confessional wars and the Netherlands fought their bitter struggle for independence, the empire was almost an island of stability; with few minor exceptions, all struggles were solved by peaceful means.

Until about 1575 the Protestants were on the offensive, gaining control of almost all the territory east of the Rhine and north of the Danube, and they also had many followers in the Austrian territories and Bohemia. But then, in the course of its Counter-Reformation, the Catholic church became stronger and more dynamic, while Lutheranism evolved into an alliance of dogmatic state churches. Additionally, Calvinism gradually gained in importance, a fact which divided Protestantism. The institutions of the empire (Imperial Diet, courts) were increasingly unable to handle the mounting conflicts. At the beginning of the seventeenth century an atmosphere of cold war reigned within the empire.

Both Catholicism and Protestantism were strongly entrenched within the empire. Both sides were backed by political power centres, and both sides had well-trained spokesmen who preached a highly standardized sermon to large masses of people, an important point in order to maintain the cohesion of the creed. Both sides had their institutions to educate youngsters, to train priests and to modernize and sophisticate the ideology. This strong institutional backing stabilized both Catholicism and Protestantism, and exactly because of this institutional buttressing the confessional gap became for many centuries the main cultural cleavage within the empire.

THE HABSBURG MONARCHY, THE NETHERLANDS, ALSACE – CHANGES IN THE ETHNIC PATTERN

In 1521–2 Charles V passed the government of seven duchies (covering roughly modern Austria) over to his younger brother Ferdinand I.

This was the start of the Austrian line of the Habsburg dynasty. In 1526 Ferdinand I was furthermore elected King of Bohemia and King of Hungary. Thus the Austrian Habsburgs came to rule over a huge geographic area. From the time of Emperor Leopold I onwards, the state was called *Monarchia Austriaca*,[5] later Austria for short. Many of its territories lay inside the Holy Roman Empire, many others (notably Hungary) outside. Thus factually, though not formally, the ethnic composition of the Holy Roman Empire came to be altered by the expansion of the *Monarchia Austriaca*.

Its ethnic composition also came to be changed, in a negative sense, when the Netherlands after decades of war became independent. At the time of Charles V, the 17 provinces of the Netherlands were a heterogeneous conglomerate of territories and towns. Linguistically the northern part belonged to the large family of the Low German idioms. Etymologically, the word 'Dutch' is linked to *deutsch*, German. The Netherlands were one of the richest regions in Europe, with a high population density, prosperous agriculture, blossoming textile industry and profitable trade. The advance of the Reformation (mostly Calvinists and Baptists) led to cultural conflicts, which, however, did not assume dramatic proportions.[6]

The situation changed drastically in 1555 when the Netherlands, after Charles V's resignation, became part of the Spanish empire under Philip II; formally they still belonged to the Holy Roman Empire. Philip II tried to enforce strict control, stationed Spanish soldiers in the provinces, reorganized the church and intensified the persecution of heretics. By doing so he provoked ever fiercer resistance. This began in 1564 as a protest of the estates led by the nobility who were still basically loyal to the monarch. But soon afterwards, Calvinistic preachers and lower noblemen fought openly against the Inquisition and the religious edicts. In 1566, Catholic symbols were burned on a large scale. The Duke of Alba, the king's governor, tried to suppress the rebellion by means of gruesome repression. Dutch noblemen, town patricians and Calvinists organized a common resistance, despite severe differences among them.

By more flexible policies the Spaniards were able to reconsolidate their position in the southern provinces, but the northern provinces declared themselves independent in 1581. Much more fighting followed and eventually, in 1648, the northern Netherlands were formally acknowledged as an independent state. In terms of political, religious and commercial freedom they represented the maximum possible at that time.

Thus, as a consequence of dynastic calculations, harsh attempts at centralization and cultural repression, resistance, escalations and de-escalations, a large territory inhabited by people speaking a German idiom became an independent state whose inhabitants quickly built up a collective identity of their own.

Some decades later, another region inhabited by people speaking a German idiom – the Alsace – broke out of the Holy Roman Empire. From 1667 onwards, under the reign of the 'Sun King' Louis XIV, France embarked upon a policy of systematic expansionism. A French attack upon the Netherlands in 1672 failed, but in the Upper Rhine region French policy was more successful. Bit by bit the Alsace was incorporated into the French monarchy; in September 1681 Strasbourg was occupied. French diplomacy justified the annexations by claiming they were *réunions*: territories which France acquired in 1648 (under the Peace of Westphalia) were in former times linked with neighbouring territories, and these neighbouring territories had to be 'reunited' with the French possessions. As soon as such a claim had been successfully realized with the help of French troops, the whole procedure started again because the new territory had also to be reunited with regions with which it had been linked at some time in history.

In 1688–9 the Holy Roman Empire was able to unite in common defence against Louis XIV, one of the examples where constitutional obligations were fulfilled. At the Peace of Rijswijk (1697), France renounced all further claims but was able to keep the Alsace with Strasbourg. Thus the border of France came to be established considerably to the east of the linguistic border between French and German.[7]

THE THIRTY YEARS WAR

In the second decade of the seventeenth century many lines of conflict ran through the empire. Together they formed an explosive mixture and it was a struggle within the Habsburg monarchy which ignited the compound.

Emperors Rudolf II and Mathias had for decades been engaged in power struggles against the noble estates of the different regions of the Habsburg monarchy. Political and religious matters were closely intertwined because political claims were usually legitimized by theological or juridical arguments. In particular, Emperor

Mathias embarked upon a policy of centralization and counter-reformation, and in 1618 this provoked the uprising of the estates in Bohemia. On 27 August 1619, the estates elected the Calvinist Duke-Elector Frederick V of the Palatinate as King of Bohemia. But the rebellion was soon crushed, and merciless repression followed.[8]

Territories outside the Habsburg empire which had supported the Bohemian revolt were occupied as well with the restitution of former Catholic property. The armies of the emperor and his allies advanced far into northern Germany and encouraged by the emperor's victory the Spaniards renewed their attempts to reconquer the Netherlands. The conflict quickly acquired an international dimension, covertly or overtly involving powers like France, England, Denmark and Sweden.

In 1625 King Cristian IV of Denmark, who was also Duke of Holstein-Gottorp and thereby reigned over a territory within the Holy Roman Empire, let himself be elected Commander-in-Chief of the Protestant territories in northern Germany (*Niedersächsischer Kreis*) and led a Danish army across the Elbe. Cristian IV presented himself as protector of the Lutheran creed but followed at the same time quite worldly ends such as the acquisition of former Catholic bishoprics. At the battle of Lutter am Barremberg his ambitions were crushed. Gradually, the emperor and his allies were able to conquer the whole of northern Germany.

On 6 March 1629, Emperor Ferdinand II issued the *Restititutionsedikt*, a comprehensive order to return former Catholic property to the church.[9] As to the balance of power, the edict would have meant the domination of emperor and Catholicism within the empire. For a short historical moment it looked as if the Holy Roman Empire was to be transformed into an absolutist centralistic monarchy.

This moment did not last. The Catholic princes turned against the emperor and forced him to dismiss his General Albrecht von Wallenstein and to dissolve his army, which weakened the cause of the emperor at a crucial moment. France, under the leadership of the Catholic Cardinal Richelieu, did everything to prevent a Habsburg hegemony, in the beginning mainly by means of financial and diplomatic support for the emperor's enemies but from 1634 onwards by open military engagement. And on 6 July 1630 the Swedish King Gustav Adolf landed with battle-proven troops in northern Germany, officially to defend Protestantism and the German *Libertät*, but also fighting for worldly ends.

The war dragged on, devastating one landscape after another. Alliances changed, and none of the sides could gain decisive supremacy.

THE PEACE OF WESTPHALIA: BALANCING DIVERSITY

After four years of negotiations in the Westphalian towns of Münster and Osnabrück a peace treaty was concluded in 1648. The Westphalian peace was a lengthy and complex set of agreements, settling both international questions and constitutional problems of the Holy Roman Empire.[10]

For the first time in history the international balance of power was consistently regulated. The non-centralist character of the Holy Roman Empire was officially established as an integral part of this balance of power; any attempt to transform Middle Europe into a centralist power block would start an intervention mechanism to prevent it. The Netherlands and the Swiss confederation officially became independent, and Sweden acquired territories within the empire (Vorpommern, Wismar and the bishoprics of Verden and Bremen). The mouths of three rivers (the Weser, Elbe and Oder) and the corresponding customs came under Swedish control; as ruler of these territories, the Swedish crown acquired representation in the Imperial Diet (as did the Danish king, in personal union Duke of Holstein). The borders of the Holy Roman Empire were formally precisely defined, but politically they were quite unclear, because from 1648 onwards there were four major political units which ruled over territories both inside and outside the empire: the *Monarchia Austriaca*, Brandenburg-Prussia (see below), Sweden and Denmark. Two of these states had their centres of gravity within the empire (Austria, Brandenburg), two of them outside (the Scandinavian kingdoms).

Apart from the Swedish acquisitions and other smaller changes, the distribution of territories was restored to the position in 1624. The territories of the empire gained the official right to make alliances with foreign powers as long as they were not directed against other members of the empire. In case of foreign attack the members were obliged to common defence, but it was for the Imperial Diet to decide about war and peace, not the emperor.

As regards religious matters, the basic principles of the Augsburg treaty were reconfirmed, albeit with some modifications. Besides

Catholicism and Lutheranism, Calvinism was also acknowledged and protected; if the ruler changed confession, the inhabitants were no longer obliged to change confession as well. All the institutions of the empire were built upon the principle of parity between Protestants and Catholics. In the Imperial Diet, Catholics and Protestants debated separately when religious matters were to be decided (*itio in partes*); a common solution had then to be found afterwards by an agreement between the two parties.

In many respects, the Peace of Westphalia was an example of the successful institutionalization of cultural diversity, thus making peaceful cooperation possible.

THE RISE OF BRANDENBURG-PRUSSIA

At the beginning of the eighteenth century, the *Monarchia Austriaca* was by far the strongest power in Central Europe. But in the seventeenth and eighteenth centuries a rival appeared in the north. And in the long run this rival had the stronger impact upon what later became Germany.

In about 1600 the electorate of Brandenburg was still a medium-sized territory around Berlin, without direct access to the sea. However, under Prince-Elector Johann Sigismund (1608–19) it was able to more than double its territory by means of dynastic treaties and inheritance. Particularly important was the acquisition of Prussia, the remnant of the former state of the Teutonic knights. Friedrich Wilhelm (the 'Great Elector') made further gains (a part of Vorpommern and Magdeburg) and Brandenburg became the dominant regional power in northern Germany.

In 1701 Prince-Elector Friedrich III let himself be crowned as King *in* Prussia, i.e. outside the Holy Roman Empire. In the Peace of Utrecht (1713) his successor gained international recognition for his status as king. Further acquisitions were incorporated, most importantly in 1720 a part of Swedish Vorpommern with the harbour town of Stettin.

In 1740 King Friedrich II ('the Great') wrested the rich and populous province of Silesia from Austria which led to a bitter and decade-long rivalry. In the Seven Years War (1756–63) Prussia fought for many years against a coalition which was numerically much stronger (comprising Austria, France, Russia, Sweden and most of the German territories). To the surprise of many contemporaries, Prussia survived and retained Silesia. And between 1772 and 1795, when Russia, Austria and Prussia divided Poland among themselves, Prussia was able to construct a land-bridge between her main territory and eastern Prussia and expand deeply into Polish territory. Warsaw became for a while the capital of a Prussian province.

The astonishing rise of Prussia was, of course, to a large extent due to her strong army. No other European society was to such an extent shaped by military demands; more than three-quarters of the budget were devoted to military purposes. By 1740, Prussia could muster an army of 88 000 men, the fourth strongest in Europe, although she lay thirteenth in size of population.[11] But it would be far too simple to attribute Prussia's rise only to militarism. In comparison with France under the 'Sun King', or with the 'systematic aggressiveness'[12] of British policy, Prussia was not characterized by an extraordinary use of military power. To put it simply, the French monarchs maintained powerful armies, but they did not have the money for them, an important factor among the causes of the revolution; on the other hand, the Prussian monarchs organized powerful armies too, but they also provided the necessary political and financial base for them. This process started in earnest under the 'Great Elector' Friedrich Wilhelm (1640–88), who, like many other monarchs of the time, transformed the army from a troop of mercenaries into a regular, permanent body, thereby increasing its efficiency considerably. This made permanent financing imperative. After many conflicts the elector and the nobility concluded a lasting compromise: the landed nobility (the *Junker*) accepted the loss of much of its political power, but as compensation, they got a quasi-monopoly of military and bureaucratic command posts. In addition, the crown stabilized the *Junker*'s position as regards the peasants. The *Junker* served the state, and the state served them.[13] There was presumably no other country in Europe where the integration of the nobility into the state was so successful as in Prussia. Military and agrarian policy was closely integrated, particularly after the introduction of the *Kantonsystem* in 1733.[14] Through this system every regiment was detached to a certain area, and in principle every citizen was obliged to render military service.

It was not infrequently that troops intervened to repress rural unrest,[15] but more than once it was the monarch or the state who also intervened to protect the peasants against arbitrary *Junker* actions.[16] Jurisdiction over severe crimes was eventually taken away from the nobility and placed under independent courts, and in 1763 King Friedrich II tried to abolish serfdom. However, he was only able to realize this idea in the royal domains. Such moves in favour of the peasants were mostly motivated by a desire to protect the recruitment base for the army, but whatever the reasons, the population at large often experienced the state and the monarch as a protective institution. In addition, the army worked for many persons as a channel for social mobility. Serfs for instance, could, become juridically free after military service.

The Prussian monarchy had an important ally in the Lutheran church[17] as the priests preached obedience to the worldly authorities. The clerics also fulfilled many tasks for the state administration. In the villages they were often the only bastions of literacy and high culture. The majority of the population were Lutherans, but in 1613 the royal family converted to Calvinism. After the conquest of Silesia and particularly after the expansion into Polish territory, many of the Prussian subjects were Catholics. A conscious policy of religious tolerance became an effective mechanism to integrate the heterogeneous parts of the monarchy. In 1685, after the revocation of the Edict of Nantes, Prince-Elector Friedrich Wilhelm attracted about 20 000[18] French Huguenots to Brandenburg-Prussia. Something similar happened in 1731 when Archbishop Firmian of Salzburg drove 21 000 Protestants out of his bishopric. Brandenburg-Prussia, originally founded as a colonial territory and mostly inhabited by descendants of Slavic peasants and Germanic immigrants, acquired additional strength through new waves of immigration.

The coexistence of various confessions implied that people were confronted with conflicting religious messages. The 'own' religion could no longer be regarded as something 'natural', something which simply was there, which could not be questioned, or which at least was not allowed to be questioned. Now there were alternatives, and questioning was permitted. This weakened religion in general, and therefore it could not resist the advance of Reason so strongly as it could in many other countries. There were few, if any, states in Europe whose institutions were shaped and reshaped so thoroughly along rationalist enlightened lines. This was mostly an enlightenment from above, but it was able to have important humanitarian consequences, for instance the abolition of torture in 1740.

Friedrich II (1740–86) was a ruthless politician, but he shared an informed interest in enlightened philosophy and had long discussions with Voltaire. He ruled in an authoritarian way, but the intellectual climate was quite free. In principle he accepted the idea that a king had to fulfil a serving role towards society. He supported, partly even initiated, large-scale efforts to systematize legislation. In 1784 the king opened a general public debate about the official draft of a new law code, the *Allgemeine Gesetzbuch für die preussischen Staaten* – quite an unusual, not to say revolutionary, event for an absolutist monarchy.[19] In the climate of stagnation after Friedrich II's death, the *Allgemeine Gesetzbuch* did not come about; instead the much more traditional *Allgemeine Landrecht* was introduced in 1794. But in spite of its severe shortcomings, seen from the perspective of emancipatory enlightenment the *Allgemeine Landrecht* and many other juridical reforms show that Prussia had come far on its way towards a society governed by law.

The juridical reforms were closely linked with the emergence of a relatively efficient state bureaucracy.[20] In the countryside the noblemen ruled, but in the eighteenth century the central administration expanded considerably, becoming more diversified and more efficient. It regulated military questions, nutrition, economic and taxation problems, traffic connections and the Lutheran church. Independent courts grew in importance, guaranteeing a minimum of legal security for the Prussian subjects. 'Prussia showed a double face like the head of Janus: a military one and a philosophical one,' wrote Madame de Staël, attesting Prussian 'civil justice'.[21]

At the end of the eighteenth century the nobility still had access to all key posts, and corruption and nepotism were known phenomena, but the basic loyalties had begun to shift. Prussian bureaucrats thought less in terms of favouring their relatives; instead, they worked increasingly according to rules. This was due to the psychological effects of systematic rewards (career possibilities, decorations, etc.) and sanctions, and due to the professional identity shaped by this special kind of work, and by the increasingly standardized education – to mention just one feature, after 1713 all higher judges had to prove that they had studied law, and from 1737 an *examen* in law was obligatory. Noble birth gradually lost its consequence as qualifications became more important.

A more or less constant flow of reforms secured Prussia an advance in many fields of modernity. Not least because of the political and military rivalry, the other German territories had to do the same, Austria in particular, but it was easy to learn from each other

due to the relatively intense communication within the Holy Roman Empire. Seen from this perspective, the political fragmentation of the Holy Roman Empire and the resulting competition among
the territories was a positive factor as regards modernization.

   In around 1800 the Prussian bureaucracy was quantitatively still
quite small, all in all perhaps 1700 higher civil servants and judges
and about 4000–5000 lower servants out of a population of about
8.7 million.[22] But because of its growing homogeneity, its expertise
and its intense internal communication, the bureaucracy acquired great political strength. A state could no longer be governed
without special political, military, juridical, economic and technical
knowledge. Powerful interest groups like the nobility could delay
or distort the course of events, an unqualified king might confuse
matters considerably, but the initiative had passed over to the
bureaucracy.

EDUCATION AND *BILDUNGSBÜRGERTUM*

Reformation meant a boost to literacy because the Reformers, Luther
in particular, strongly underlined the importance of reading the
Holy Scriptures. Furthermore, the sharp confessional clashes and
ideological disputes fostered an interest in books and literacy, but
after the middle of the seventeenth century this boost faded out.[23]

   In the Protestant territories, the clerical educational institutions
passed under the control of the princes, but at first for many decades they did not seem to pay much attention to them. During the
seventeenth century only some smaller middle German duchies began
some initiatives in this field. Thus, in 1619 the *Weimarer Schulordnung*
established the principle of obligatory schooling, and in the *Gothaer
Schulmethodus* of 1642, elementary schooling was for the first time
regulated as a secular matter, separate from the church. Württemberg
introduced compulsory school attendance in 1649, and Prussia followed in 1717.[24] Nevertheless, illiteracy presumably did not decline
at all between 1618 and 1750.[25] But in the second half of the eighteenth century the pace quickened. The large-scale reform of the
Prussian school system (*General-Landschul-Reglement*, 12 August
1763) was symptomatic. Schooling was declared obligatory for children between 5 and 14 years, and the curricula, organization, education of teachers and supervision were regulated. In 1765 the
Catholic schools in Prussian Silesia and Glatz were regulated on

their own. Other German territories introduced similar reforms. Princes like Friedrich II had understood that schools were powerful instruments in strengthening the loyalty of subjects, and that economic prosperity and military strength depended on knowledge. In addition, many high-ranking bureaucrats were influenced by the ideas of the Enlightenment and saw education as an emancipatory force.

It is extremely difficult to make international comparisons. There is, however, strong evidence that Scotland, England and the Netherlands had the highest standards at that time. In the eighteenth century, literacy grew considerably in England, Scotland, France, the Holy Roman Empire, Switzerland, Holland and Scandinavia, involving the rural population as well. Scandinavia and the German territories were particularly successful in this respect. In the middle of the nineteenth century, when reliable data are available for the first time, Prussia had by far the highest record of literacy among the major European states[26] (see Chapter 5) – achievements which were based on many of the reforms of the eighteenth century.

At the end of the eighteenth century the Holy Roman Empire was the land with most universities (between 42 and 50, depending upon the definition), compared with 22 in France and only two in England. Half of them (24) were founded in the seventeenth and eighteenth centuries, i.e. at a time when only three new universities were founded in France. Due to greater religious tolerance, the quality was considerably higher in the Protestant parts than in Catholic territories. D'Alembert said that, when coming from a Catholic to a Protestant university, he felt as if he had travelled 400 miles in one hour, or passed 400 years.[27]

As to the intellectual climate, the political fragmentation of the Holy Roman Empire was an advantage. The princes had to enter a kind of competition in founding institutions of higher learning. The different institutions produced different opinions, and thus the *polyarchy* led to a *polyphony* of opinions.[28] These opinions were able to circulate almost freely through all the areas inhabited by German-speaking people, for if censorship was applied more strictly in one place, then books and papers were printed in the territory next to it, from which they were then imported. Even so in 1794 conservative hardliners like the Bishop of Passau forbade the works of Klopstock, Schiller and Goethe,[29] but this was a hopeless venture. Willingly or not, the Catholic territories were drawn into the stream of the Enlightenment. To put it very simply: the Spanish inquisitions could burn the heretics, but the German Catholics had to compete with them. And the demand for qualified personnel for the bureaucracy, army and military was as pressing in Catholic Bavaria or Austria as in Protestant Prussia. As in Prussia, the higher bureaucracy and the monarchs became infected by the ideas of the Enlightenment, as the wave of reform in Austria under Maria Theresa and particularly Joseph II shows.

In the eighteenth century the production of books was presumably twice as high as in the seventeenth century, and in the second half of the eighteenth century twice as high again. Book production and selling was still mostly concentrated in the Protestant areas, but the differences became smaller. The first German newspapers were printed in the beginning of the seventeenth century; in the second half of the eighteenth century there were between 200 and 250 papers. The *Hamburgische Korrespondent* was the greatest, with 25 000 sold copies in 1798, three times as many as the London *Times*.[30] The total circulation of all German newspapers was about 300 000, and there were many readers per copy.[31]

By that time most of the German territories had built up quite strong bureaucratic, legal and educational institutions. As a consequence of this development a particular social group had developed, the *Bildungsbürgertum*, i.e. persons with a high level of formal education, such as lawyers, theologians, professors, physicians and pharmacists.[32] They manned the state and church institutions and they formed the bulk of the readership for books and papers. They communicated across the political borders and developed many common standards and values. They often shared a common sense of professional pride and claimed that qualification should be esteemed higher than noble birth. This claim brought many of them into conflict with the social reality of the time, still basically characterized by privileges acquired by birth, by nepotism and by authoritarian political rule from above.

It was mostly the *Bildungsbürger* who entertained the new ideas of the Enlightenment, of individual freedom and of common-German patriotic sentiment (see below). They had a strong impact upon public debate and could thereby influence the higher bureaucracy. But they did not have direct political (or economic) power, and they were scattered all over the country. Because of the political fragmentation there was no centre such as London or Paris which could have led to a bourgeois concentration. In addition, the *Bildungsbürger* depended to a large extent upon the state apparatus, a point which sometimes coloured their intellectual positions. For good or bad, the German intellectual and political climate was shaped by this group to a greater extent than in other countries.

THE EMERGENCE OF A COMMON LITERARY STANDARD

Despite of the many political and confessional cleavages, all the territories inhabited by German-speaking people gradually became united by a common literary standard, based mainly upon the writings of Luther.

In northern Germany, Low German was firmly established as a literary language by about 1500, but Luther's works were not immediately understandable and had to be translated. His New Testament appeared as early as 1522 in a Low German version, and 24 editions of the whole Bible were printed in Low German, the last in 1621. But by around 1600 the Luther-based Middle German had replaced Low German as the dominant literary language, except in Schleswig-Holstein and some Hanseatic cities (and in Lübeck up to as late as 1808).[33] The decisive blow to Low German was perhaps the shift of the Chancery of the Electorate of Brandenburg to Middle German. Even so, in the nineteenth century many texts such as theatre pieces were written in Low German, but its institutional support was too weak. It survived as a predominantly rural dialect and exists still today, but the end seems to be near. The development was, of course, very different with the Dutch version of Low German. In this case, the independence of the Netherlands created the institutions necessary (administration, church, schools, etc.) to secure the survival of the language.

By around 1650 Protestant Swabia had also accepted Middle German as their literary standard. In Switzerland it was at first rejected, but the Swiss printers soon made many compromises towards Upper German (not yet quite Luther's German), mainly in order to secure a greater circulation of their books, notably the Zwingli Bible of 1527. And by around 1700 some literary centres of Switzerland such as Bern and Zürich had been properly converted to the new standard.[34] In 1750 it was accepted in Vienna too. Even so, in 1779 the Bishop of Regensburg rebuked one of his priests for having used 'Lutheran' orthography, but this was a rearguard battle. By around 1800 the educated people of the German areas used the same literary standard. The spoken idioms, however, still differed considerably.

By that time, the German language had spread socially and functionally too. In the sixteenthth century, German was in many respects still an inferior language. It was not until 1681 that German publications outnumbered those in Latin. The use of Latin for theological and scientific purposes declined steadily, but even so in 1801 the mathematician Karl Friedrich Gauss published a treatise under the title *Disquisitiones arithmeticae*.[35] French was another rival. Around 1700 'almost anything French – clothing, foods, social customs and conventions – was adopted wholesale by the upper and middle classes.'[36] In Potsdam, near Berlin, Voltaire had this impression: 'Here I'm in France. They exclusively speak our language. German is only used towards soldiers and horses.'[37] But from about 1750 onwards the influence of French also declined.

The reasons for these developments were numerous. Even before Luther's time the growing literacy of the administration had created regional literary standards. The language used by the Chancery of the Saxon Electorate (*Sächsische Kanzleisprache*) became particularly influential. It was basically this idiom into which Luther translated the Bible and which he used for many of his theological works. But he also adapted his style carefully to the spoken language, modifying it later slightly in favour of southern and western dialects. The tremendous authority he enjoyed in Protestant circles and the vivacity of his style paved the way for his language into other linguistic provinces. It was constantly used in Lutheran churches and for instruction in religion, hymn singing, etc. From there it spread to other teaching.

The process of linguistic unification was considerably reinforced by grammarians and language societies. In 1578, Johann Claius published a very influential grammar, using Luther's language as a standard. Other grammarians sometimes chose other German idioms but they were less successful. In the eighteenth century, after the influential grammars written by Johann Christoph Gottsched and Johann Christoph Adelung, the status of Upper Saxon as the most appropriate variety of German was hardly questioned any longer.[38] The work of the grammarians became the basis for the teaching of grammar in schools, introduced in different German territories from the beginning of the seventeenth century onwards.

In 1617 the first language society, the *fruchtbringende Gesellschaft oder der Palmenorden*, was founded, and counted prominent men of letters such as the poet Andreas Gryphius among its members. Other similar societies followed. Their main purpose was to 'purge' the language of foreign influences. As regards the courts and chanceries, their efforts met with only limited success, but their influence upon the belletristic language was considerable. On some occasions their efforts seem to have been slightly excessive, for instance when they proposed *Entknötelung* ('deknotting') for *Interpretation*, or *Gesichtserker* ('face bay') for *Nase* ('nose'); the latter word was originally borrowed from Latin.[39]

A large number of talented poets, playwrights and novelists like Christoph Martin Wieland, Gotthold Ephraim Lessing and notably Friedrich Gottlieb Klopstock enriched the language and developed it into a multifaceted medium. They thereby considerably contributed to the prestige and proliferation of the language.

INFANT NATIONALISM

Patriotic sentiments are traceable among intellectuals throughout the seventeenth and eighteenth centuries. By about 1750 these feelings had acquired a new ideological quality. The concept of *nation*, based upon the common language, slowly gained an almost religious connotation. The theologian Johann Gottfried Herder, from the 1770s one of the leading language and culture philosophers, became the most influential representative of this new nationalism. For Herder the nations of the world – all equally precious – were natural organisms like plants or persons, with a soul and a definite lifespan.[40] In line with everything in nature they were God's creation and as such emanations of His will.

Herder's ideas were in many respects potentially explosive. 'Nothing seems to be more contrary to the purpose of governments than the unnatural enlargement of states, the wild mixture of human species and nations under one sceptre'.[41] His demand for congruence between nation and state would mean the disruption of multi-ethnic monarchies such as Austria or Prussia. And monarchs in general would become superfluous the more humanity progressed on its way to perfection: 'The human being who needs a lord is an animal; as soon as he becomes human he does not need a proper lord any more. Nature did not name a lord for our species; only animal vices and passions make us need it.'[42]

Nationalism was closely linked to liberalism: patriots who wanted to see the German people united wanted also to see them freed from the burdens of authoritarian government, privileges for the few and 'superfluous' princes. Liberal nationalism thereby closely corresponded to the desires of the *Bildungsbürger* and other bourgeois groups who were excluded from political power and saw their possibilities severely resticted by traditional privileges. German nationalism thus began as an ideology for progressive bourgeois emancipation. It is not surprising that German authors used language as the central criterion to define 'nation' (as, for instance, did Italian or many Slavonic) whereas French authors resorted to citizenship:[43] citizenship presupposes a state, but there was no German or Italian state, in contrast to France.

In Herder's time nationalist ideas were shared by but a small minority, most of them *Bildungsbürger*, and their political importance was practically zero. For political practitioners the territories inhabited by German-speaking people were objects of conquest and barter, just like every other territory. Prussia's policy serves to illustrate this. Between 1772 and 1795 Prussia acquired a huge share of Polish territory, and in 1794 the Prussian army supported Russian troops in crushing a great Polish rebellion. Because of the engagement in Poland, Berlin decided to disengage from the parallel war with revolutionary France and signed the separate Peace of Basel (5 April 1795). By this Prussia agreed that France could push her border right up to the Rhine and annex all German territories on the western bank. In return for Prussian possessions west of the Rhine, France promised support for compensation elsewhere. This Prussia received in 1803.

4 1792–1871: the Shaping of Germany

FRENCH HEGEMONY AND MODERNIZATION

On 20 April 1792 the French National Assembly passed a declaration of war against Emperor Franz II. The war quickly received an all-embracing international character. The French revolutionaries were unexpectedly successful in mobilizing and inspiring large armies. In 1795 they had conquered modern Belgium and the Netherlands and stood firmly along the Rhine. In 1797 (Peace of Campo Formio) the Rhine was officially established as France's eastern border. Huge areas inhabited by German-speaking people passed under French rule.

In return for the Rhine border, France agreed that the larger German states could be compensated east of the Rhine. In November 1801 the emperor and the Imperial Diet set up a commission (*Reichsdeputation*) to draft a comprehensive scheme. In 1803 its results (*Hauptschluß*) were approved by the Imperial Diet and the emperor. Thus the constitutional bodies of the Holy Roman Empire passed a body of legislation which introduced an enormous change of property and sovereignty. The procedure was formally correct, but its content equalled a revolution from above.[1]

All the remaining ecclesiastical territories with 3.2 million inhabitants, roughly one seventh of the population of the empire, were annexed by the larger states. The same happened to 45 out of 51 free towns. Expropriations of ecclesiastical property within the states were also declared to be legal – a possibility thoroughly exploited by Catholic and Protestant states alike. The time of the church as a worldly power had come to an end.

The Peace of Pressburg (1805) initiated a second wave of territorial concentration. Napoleon's allies, Bavaria and Württemberg, were promoted to kingdoms and realized considerable territorial gains. And throughout the empire the *Reichsritterschaften* (imperial knighthoods), 1500 dwarf-units with altogether 350 000 inhabitants, were annexed by the larger states. In 1806 only 2 per cent of the territorial units which existed in 1789 had survived. And in July

1806, under French protection, 16 German princes formed the Rhine League. Franz II declared the empire dissolved; he was now 'only' Austrian emperor. The Holy Roman Empire had come to a rather inglorious end.

Prussia stood aside when Austria and Russia fought against Napoleon at Austerlitz (1805), but in 1806 she entered a war on her own against France. At the battle of Jena and Auerstedt (10 October 1806) the Prussian army was almost annihilated; whole units fled in panic while others deserted with their officers or hastened to surrender. As became apparent, the Prussian state had become hollow. In the Peace of Tilsit (1807) Napoleon reduced Prussia by half. The French emperor was the unquestioned lord over Central Europe and most of the German states were his allies.

French hegemony meant an enormous boost to modernization. In Westphalia, Berg and the regions west of the Rhine, French legislation and the principle of equal rights for all citizens were introduced. Most of the German states embarked on comprehensive reform programmes. In May 1808 Bavaria introduced the first genuine German constitution, abolished serfdom, established the principles of equal rights and equal access to public offices, guaranteed basic rights and freedom of the press, secured the independence of the judges and modernized the bureaucracy. Other Rhine League states introduced similar reforms. These reforms were partly prolongations of the tradition of reforms from above, but they were also introduced to integrate the many heterogeneous regions acquired after the *Reichsdeputationshauptschluß*. And last but not least, the long shadow of Napoleon pushed even reluctant princes along the road of reform in order to mobilize any resource possible.[2]

In Prussia the military disaster of 1806/7 had discredited the old order and opened the way for a group of reform-minded bureaucrats. Of particular importance were Baron Karl von und zum Stein and Count, later Duke, Karl August von Hardenberg. Stein was an expert in administration and economics, a minister since 1804 and a leading Prussian politician between October 1807 and November 1808. He significantly contributed to the modernization of the Prussian bureaucracy and drafted the famous decree of October 1807. Hardenberg, Prime Minister in 1807 and from 1810 to 1822, was a less visionary politician, but it was he who carried out all the major reform projects.

The Prussian reformers saw the possibility 'to expel Napoleon with the help of Adam Smith'.[3] Liberalism seemed to open the way to economic progress and to a revitalization of Prussia, and Smith's *Wealth of Nations* was widely read among the Prussian elite. As Christian Jacob Kraus, professor in Königsberg, put it: 'Since the time of the New Testament no other book has had more blessed effects.'[4]

By the decree of 9 October 1807 all Prussian peasants were declared juridically free, serfdom was to be abolished and all citizens could freely acquire rural estates (formerly only noblemen could); the land used by the village community in common was sold. Later edicts provided that most peasants could free themselves of the obligations to work for the noblemen by ceding one-third of their land to them, or by paying money. The *Junker* thus lost their status as feudal lords, but they could enlarge their estates and start a new career as agrarian capitalists.

The reforms implied heavy economic burdens for the peasants, but only about 2 per cent of them were not able to survive economically; the large masses of agrarian proletarians of later decades were not ruined peasants (as many observers thought) but surplus population. And since the reforms initiated a period of productivity increases and large-scale cultivation of new land (allowing for many new farms), their overall economic and social effects seem to have been beneficial.[5]

Other reform decrees initiated by Stein and Hardenberg introduced the principles of free enterprise and freedom of movement, and the juridical difference between land and town was abolished. The bureaucracy was reorganized and strengthened, and it was established that royal decrees needed the countersignature of the minister to be valid. The *Städteordnung* (town edict) provided for self-administration of the towns. An edict of emancipation (11 March 1812) gave the Jews in most fields the same rights as other Prussian citizens.

Military reformers like August Neidhardt von Gneisenau and Gerhard von Scharnhorst opened the officer's career to ordinary citizens, introduced general conscription, humanized the military disciplinary code and updated the training system. Wilhelm von Humboldt reformed and enlarged the education system. In 1809 Berlin University was founded; the students were not just confronted with lectures, but instead trained in seminars where they discussed research problems with the professors. The grammar schools (*Gymnasia*) became 'academized', with Greek, Latin, German and mathematics as the main subjects, and were socially relatively open, though dominated by the *Bildungsbürger*.

The reforms did not transform Prussia into a democratic state, but they made her a state with a predominantly liberal market economy, a high standard of education, and an efficient juridical and bureaucratic system.

NATIONALISM, PATRIOTISM AND WARS OF LIBERATION

Many German intellectuals and even high-ranking bureaucrats regarded the French Revolution with much sympathy, but after the beheading of King Louis XVI and the Terror, the pro-French enthusiasm declined. Even so, in 1806 the philosopher Georg Friedrich Wilhelm Hegel saw the French victories as the 'triumph of education over hollowness'. Scharnhorst and Gneisenau attributed the strength of the French army to the progressive character of the revolutionary state.[6] The population at large seemed to have registered the French occupation with apathy, but in a few years the realities of Napoleonic occupation, the burdens of housing French troops, the financial contributions, the customs system which blatantly favoured French interests and the occupiers' often arrogant behaviour created widespread anti-French resentment.

In 1812 the *Grande Armée* perished in the snows of Russia. The following spring (16 March 1813) Prussia declared war on Napoleon and an unprecedented outburst of patriotism and hatred of everything French came to the surface.[7] About 45 000 young men volunteered for the Prussian army, a new phenomenon.

There were, however, other voices. Still in December 1813, Johann Wolfgang von Goethe, perhaps the greatest German intellectual of his time, showed 'little patriotic happiness . . . He behaved conspicuously coolly and criticizing and praised even Emperor Napoleon's brilliant qualities in a very eloquent manner.'[8]

The wars of 1813–15 were not one great patriotic outburst as nationalist historians often depicted them. Most volunteers were town craftsmen, civil servants, *Bildungsbürger*, students and pupils, but the countryside, where three-quarters of the population still lived, was represented by only 18 per cent. Patriotism was a sentiment predominantly shared by educated persons and by towns people.[9] Many men liable for military service had to be threatened with punishment before they unwillingly joined the ranks, and there was much shirking.[10] Goethe saw the situation clearly:

You talk about the awakening, about the uprising of the German people . . . But have the people really come awake? . . . Their sleep has been by far too deep . . . We do not talk about the thousands of educated youngsters and young men, we talk about the masses, about the millions.[11]

When war broke out in March 1813, the result was not a common German uprising but a German civil war. The Rhine League states which covered roughly two-thirds of the German-speaking population fought first for many months on Napoleon's side. Bavaria joined the anti-French forces in October 1813, and most of the others did so some weeks later – after Napoleon's defeat at Leipzig. Saxony remained loyal to France even then – Napoleon had given the throne of the Grand Duchy of Warsaw to the Saxon King Friedrich August, thus allying the king firmly to his own cause.

At the Battle of Leipzig, Saxon troops changed sides and fired upon French units, perhaps a sign of German patriotism. But when in 1815 Saxon troops on their way to Waterloo heard that, according to the Congress of Vienna, the northern part of Saxony was to become a Prussian province, they broke out in mutiny. They shouted 'Vivat Napoleon', and Prussian signs were torn down. Thereafter three Saxon battalions were disarmed, their flags burned and seven leading rioters shot.[12]

'Fatherland' or 'nation' often did not mean Germany, but Prussia, or Saxony, or Bavaria; Prussian reformers (like their colleagues in Bavaria) hoped to unite the heterogeneous parts of their state into a strong 'nationality'.[13] In cases of conflict between German patriotism and state patriotism, the latter could be by far the stronger emotion.

The word 'Germany' played an important role in the political rhetoric at the time, but no one could define her borders. Was it the territory of the Holy Roman Empire? Or the area inhabited by people speaking German? And what about regions with a mixed population? In 1813 the question of nationality was still open. Bavaria or Saxony could have developed into 'nations' in the same way as the Netherlands or Switzerland had done before – or as Austria and Luxembourg did afterwards.

THE CONGRESS OF VIENNA AND THE GERMAN LEAGUE, OR THE IRRELEVANCE OF NATIONALITY

In 1814 and 1815 the statesmen of Europe met at Vienna to draft the new peace order. Their guidelines were balance of power and calculation of interests. 'Nation' or the 'uniting band of language' were not relevant categories for them.

Many borders were redrawn, but never in order to make them better follow the linguistic and cultural cleavages. Many patriots demanded the return of Alsace to 'Germany', and Prussia and some southern German states forwarded claims on this province, but Russia, Austria (under the leadership of German-speaking politicians) and Great Britain were not interested in such a weakening of France, so the borders of 1790 were restored.[14] Or, as a result of a complex territorial and financial barter, Denmark was able to retain and even enlarge her possessions in northern Germany.[15] In order to form counterweights to France, the Austrian Netherlands (i.e. modern Belgium) with many regions inhabited by a French-speaking population were handed over to the Netherlands, and large parts of western Germany were incorporated into Prussia.

A dangerous conflict arose when Russia and Prussia jointly demanded that the Grand Duchy of Warsaw should be incorporated into the Russian empire, and Saxony into Prussia. The other powers categorically rejected the demand. In January 1815 Great Britain, France (!), Austria, the Netherlands, Bavaria, Hanover and other German states signed a secret defence alliance against Prussia and Russia. If it had come to war it would have been (again) a German civil war.[16]

German patriots demanded the creation of a united nation. But the emergence of a strong power bloc in the middle of Europe would have been against the interests of most other European powers, and they would have done everything to prevent it. On the other hand, the existing conglomerate of about 40 independent German states was a permanent threat to stability. Some sort of framework had to be found.

Baron von und zum Stein, the Prussian reformer, proposed the division of Germany along the river Main; Austria should dominate the south and Prussia the north. But Austrian diplomacy rejected the idea because Prussia would gain in weight relative to Austria. According to other schemes all German states except Prussia and Austria were to constitute an empire on their own, more loosely connected to Austria and Prussia.[17]

The solution found in the end was the creation of a loose confederation, the *Deutsche Bund* (German League). The German League united almost all the territories of the defunct Holy Roman Empire, the Austrian Netherlands being the main exception. In Frankfurt a parliament of the German League, the *Bundestag*, was installed, but its importance was very limited; only the governments were represented there, not the people. The other few common institutions which came to be erected in later years remained quite uninfluential too. The members – 37 states and four towns – were, however, obliged to common defence.

The German League was an authoritarian construction and most member states were ruled strictly from above. The multiple divisions of 'Germany' continued – a severe disappointment to democratic patriots – but they were far too weak to influence events.

PRUSSIA AND THE POLISH TERRITORIES, OR THE RELEVANCE OF NATIONALITY

Questions of culture and nationality were, however, not completely irrelevant. Thus, although the claims to restore an independent Polish state had no chance of realization, the treaties of Vienna contained at least a paragraph which guaranteed special institutions to the Poles.[18]

As regards Polish territories, there is a discernible development in Prussian policy. In the eighteenth century, Prussia collected all kinds of territories, regardless of their cultural background. The Prussian state apparatus was simply extended to the new provinces. In West Prussia, the region between Pomerania and East Prussia (acquired in 1772), the majority of the population were Kashubes, and there was also a strong German minority. Consequently, Polish culture stood weak and the incorporation into the Prussian state soon became effective. But the territories gained in 1793 and 1795 belonged to the core of Poland, and here the Prussian bureaucracy was perceived as a colonial power. After the Polish uprising in 1794, church land and noble estates were confiscated and the tax level was excessive. Prussian bureaucrats committed psychological blunders such as publishing police regulations exclusively in German. The situation quickly turned explosive, and when, in 1806, French troops entered these provinces, the Prussians were forcefully thrown out.[19]

Prussian politicians learned that Polish territories had to be handled with care. When, in 1815, Prussia again gained a portion of Polish territory (the Grand Duchy of Posen), King Friedrich Wilhelm III promised his new subjects that he would respect their nationality and grant them a provincial constitution, that their religion would be maintained and their language would be used in all public affairs, and that everyone would have equal access to public positions.[20] During the first years Prussian policy towards Posen was, in fact, quite liberal. The Minister of Culture, Karl Baron vom Stein zum Altenstein, precisely formulated the conditions for succesful integration:

> Religion and language are a nation's most sacred possessions, upon which her whole ethical and conceptual world is based. An authority which acknowledges, honours, and appreciates them, can be sure to win the hearts of the subjects, but if it behaves carelessly in this respect or even allows attacks against them, then it embitters or dishonours the nation and creates unfaithful or bad subjects.[21]

The extension of the agrarian reforms into the Polish region had a liberating effect on the peasantry, the nobility profited from the Prussian agrarian credit institutions, and the Prussian administration and the juridical system were superior to the corresponding Polish institutions.

Nevertheless, the relations were not free from friction. Many Prussian bureaucrats showed less respect for Polish culture than Baron v. Altenstein demanded, the agrarian reforms had a greater anti-nobility bias than in the other provinces to weaken the traditional Polish elite, and Polish representatives complained that their language was not on an equal footing with German. This was not so much a result of conscious discriminatory activity: in administrative systems geared to (German-) Prussian principles, mostly staffed by German-speaking experts working along complex laws elaborated in German, Polish was doomed to play a secondary role.

When in 1830 parts of the Polish nobility and the clergy in Posen secretly supported a revolt against Russian rule on the other side of the border, Prussian politicians feared that the revolt might spread. This led to a shift in Prussian politics: the bureaucratic grip was tightened, the rights of the Polish nobility were diminished, the role of German was strengthened, and the agrarian reforms and other economic modernizations were more vigorously implemented. Thus, by a combination of political control and economic and administrative modernization, the Prussian bureaucracy aimed at a cautious but irresistible Germanization.

In 1831 Tsar Nicholas I proposed to Prussia a division of Congress Poland and offered some territories. Berlin said no. This was one of the few occasions in history when a state did not exploit a possibility of expansion. The Poles were seen as unruly – more Polish territory would mean a burden for Prussia, not an asset.[22]

This is the point at which questions of nationality and culture entered the calculations of Prussian political practitioners. They knew from experience that German-speaking regions were easier to integrate than Polish ones. In principle, it was also possible to integrate culturally different regions, but this took longer, absorbed more energy and could lead to long-lasting problems. So, if a state could choose the direction of expansion, it was more appropriate to expand into culturally similar regions. This is what Prussia did some decades later.

THE ZOLLVEREIN

On 1 January 1834 Prussia and 17 other German states formed a customs union, the *Zollverein*. Austria was not among its members. Authors as diverse as nationalist historian Heinrich v. Treitschke and socialist theorist Friedrich Engels interpreted the *Zollverein* as a decisive step towards German unification under Prussian leadership. But there was no one-way road leading from the *Zollverein* to the German Reich of 1871.

In 1818 Prussia introduced a new Tariff Law[23] as part of the wave of reform initiated in 1807. All internal tariffs were abolished and a simplified tariff was established at the enlarged Prussian borders. Thus the administration costs were lowered and the different provinces became better integrated. And as the Prussian bureaucrats knew from reading Adam Smith, the abolition of internal trade barriers also meant a boost to productivity. The efficiency of the tariff system could be enhanced even further by including more states: the borders which had to be guarded became relatively shorter and smuggling could be combated more efficiently. So Prussia entered into negotiations with neighbouring states to form a common customs union and states in southern and central Germany started similar initiatives. Berlin was in a strong position because of the size of the Prussian market, and because Prussia was positioned across vital trade lines of many German states. As William Oscar Henderson put it: 'The States concerned fought for their own narrow interests and many joined the Zollverein only when economic depression and empty exchequers made further resistance to Prussia impossible.'[24]

As a device to fill empty exchequers, the customs union was a success. The *Zollverein* removed barriers (for instance between Prussia and Saxony), but it also erected new ones, for example between Saxony and Austria. The overall effect upon income and productivity was positive, but is difficult to quantify.[25]

In 1834 the Austrian leaders thought it was too risky to open their markets to competition from the outside. From 1849 onwards, Austria tried on several occasions to enter the customs unions, but Prussia blocked the attempts and thereby Berlin deliberately maintained economic walls within the area inhabited by German-speaking people. Only smaller states like Hanover, Oldenburg and Schaumburg-Lippe, unable to weaken Prussian dominance within the *Zollverein*, were allowed to join (in 1853). The two Mecklenburg states entered in 1867; the Hanseatic towns Hamburg and Bremen, dominated by resolute free-traders, did not join the customs union until 1888 – 17 years after the formation of the Kaiserreich.

The forces of production, to use a Marxist term, did not bring about any unification. Trade barriers usually have detrimental effects upon productivity, irrespective of whether they lie within one language community or between two language communities. It was a question of political (mostly Prussian) expediency which borders were removed and which not. From a nationalist point of view the *Zollverein* had the paradoxical result that from 1862/3 onwards (after the trade treaties with France) there was almost free trade between the *Zollverein* and most of Western Europe, but not between the *Zollverein* and the other member states of the German League.

Prussia and the other *Zollverein* members worked together in financial and economic matters but this did not create strong common political interests in other fields. All major political confrontations until 1867 saw the member states of the *Zollverein* on both sides of the barricades (see below). And in 1866 many member states were even at war with Prussia – a fact seemingly completely overlooked by the followers of the idea that the customs union led to the Prussian-dominated Germany of 1871.

The case of Luxembourg is revealing too: the population spoke a German dialect, and the duchy was a part of the German League. In 1842 the country joined the *Zollverein* – and remained within the German tariff system until 1919. But in 1867 it did not become part of the Northern German League, and after a severe diplomatic crisis between France and Prussia, Luxembourg became independent.

This does not, of course mean that the *Zollverein* was irrelevant: the customs union strengthened the economic ties between Prussia and most of the German states; the deliberations about complex matters created stable contacts between the bureaucracies involved; and the negotiations about the distribution of the customs revenues led to fixed exchange rates between the different currencies and finally to the emergence of two large monetary regions (Taler in the north, Gulden in the south). All this eased the functioning of the Reich after 1871, but it did not bring about unification.

LIBERAL PATRIOTISM VERSUS CONSERVATISM: THE EMERGENCE OF A NEW CULTURAL CLEAVAGE

The political order established in 1815 proved to be stable for many decades, but in the end it collapsed. The major reason was a slow but irresistible population increase[26] which in the nineteenth century gained disastrous proportions.[27] Misery grew and many people emigrated.[28]

The authorities were unable to prevent the growth of poverty so they lost much prestige and legitimation. The traditional beliefs, already shaken by the Reformation and the advance of Reason, became even less convincing. Dissatisfaction with the authoritarian political structures became widespread and demands for participation rights and constitutions gained considerable strength. Social demands and the new concepts of socialism and communism appeared. The flow of new ideas was eased by the progress of literacy. In 1770 perhaps 15 per cent of the adult population could read; by 1830 the number had risen to about 40 per cent.[29] And the more educated people became the less they were willing to accept the authoritarian political structures.

In a time of dissolving social structures, the idea of nation gained hitherto unknown force. The 'nation' gave its members the feeling of belonging to something great, something which continued to exist after the individual's death; 'nation' thereby fulfilled a deep-rooted psychological desire. In principle there are many possibilities for such greater 'eternal' groups: tribe, class, Christianity and many more. But in the nineteenth century, it was the 'nation' which had the greatest success. It was easy to understand ('all people speaking the same language belong together'),[30] and it could unite almost all people in the surroundings of the individual; it thereby seemed to fulfil fundamental longings for harmony. Many poets sang about the German mountains and the German oaks, thus creating a dense system of national symbols, and historians were busy finding the 'common roots' of the German nation in the glories of the medieval empire.

In the decades after 1815 the authorities tried to suppress these new ideas. But the citizens could meet in many apolitical societies, and their number was growing. In the 1840s there were over 1100 men's choral societies with at least 100 000 members and about 250 gymnastic societies with perhaps 90 000 gymnasts.[31] Even in the most apolitical cases, just by singing songs of Schubert and Schumann, they contributed to the spread of common-German sentiments. This was potentially explosive because it implied the abolition of many traditional authorities. Many of those organizations, in particular the gymnastic societies of southwest Germany, were strongly influenced by democratic and republican thought. Thus oppositional ideas were stabilized by a dense organizational network.

Brilliant intellectuals such as the poet Heinrich Heine, and the young Karl Marx along with numerous other philosophers, writers and journalists joined in the acrimonious critique of the existing order. In literary history they are usually grouped under the heading *Vormärz*, i.e. prior to March (1848). The spectrum of oppositional opinions was rather diffuse, but, understood in a broad sense, it was the democratic and liberal critique which dominated the cultural scene. According to contemporaty observers, by 1840 the middle classes had become liberal 'thoughout'.[32] Albeit in different forms, the cleavage between conservatism and the forces of the 'movement' (democratic opposition) was to remain a stable feature of German politics for many decades to come.

In the 1840s the situation became untenable. In some bigger towns one-third of the population were on the poor lists, while hunger and diseases were spreading. In 1844 the weavers in Silesia rose in revolt, and grain riots and disturbances caused by high prices became endemic.[33]

1848: ABORTIVE UNIFICATION FROM BELOW

In March 1848 social desperation and political discontent exploded. The countryside became tormented by a revolutionary wave,[34] and almost all German capitals were torn by violent barricade fighting; the princes charged liberal politicians to form governments. King Friedrich Wilhelm IV of Prussia and many other rulers promised liberal changes and a united Germany. 'Prussia will in the future be absorbed in Germany,' the King declared.[35] Citizens formed militia units and the colours of democratic patriotism (black-red-gold) were waved in many places.

The *Bundestag*, the Diet of the German League, accepted that Constituent Assemblies were to be elected in all the member states, and all territories of the German League should participate in the election of a National Assembly. Thereby the German 'nation' was defined in political terms for the first time: it was the territory of the German League. But there were large non-German minorities living within its borders:[36] Poles in Silesia, Czechs in Bohemia and Moravia, Slovenes in Styria, Carinthia, Carniola and the Littorale, Italians in the Trentino, Gorizia and Trieste, Dutch in Limburg. Czech representatives protested, but all influential German politicians insisted that the Czechs belonged to 'Germany'. Even left-wing democrats who for years had vigorously supported Polish independence did the same.[37]

There were many areas outside the League which were inhabited by German-speaking people, notably in West and East Prussia, Posen and Schleswig. Scattered settlements existed all over the Hungarian part of the Habsburg monarchy and in Russia. People in Alsace, northern Lorraine and most of Switzerland spoke German too.

The discrepancy between the language nation and the political borders were somewhat corrected: the *Bundestag* accepted East and West Prussia, two provinces with German majorities, as new members of the League; Posen, inhabited by a Polish majority, was divided. But the dividing line did not correspond to the linguistic border because the Prussian military demanded the fortress of Posen. Thus predominantly Polish-inhabited territories became part of the German League.[38]

The kings of Denmark were also the dukes of Schleswig and Holstein in personal union; Holstein belonged to the German League, Schleswig (inhabited by a German majority) did not. In spring 1848 the two provinces rose in revolt against Denmark and joined the German revolutionary movement. The *Bundestag* accepted representatives from Schleswig as deputies of the National Assembly. The question of the formal incorporation of Schleswig was, however, postponed. But no political decision-maker thought of admitting representatives from Alsace and Lorraine because no one was interested in a conflict with France.[39] Nor did the population of Alsace demand to be represented. They spoke German, but they were integrated into French society.

In May 1848 elections to the National Assembly took place. The regulations differed from state to state, but basically the principle of 'one man – one vote' was adopted.[40] The vast majority of the deputies were liberals working for a constitutional monarchy – republicans were but a small minority, as were conservatives. The German elections thereby showed a remarkably different outcome in comparison to France. There, in the presidential elections of December 1848, about 75 per cent voted for Napoleon's nephew Louis Napoleon, and in December 1851 a vast majority endorsed his *coup d'état* and self-promotion to Emperor Napoleon III.

On 18 May 1848 the National Assembly convened in Frankfurt. The state governments and princes accepted its authority, and on 28 June a provisional government was installed; the work of preparing a common German constitution began. For a short historical moment it looked as if the German liberals could create a united Germany from below.

But it was already a bad omen: on 16 July Eduard v. Peucker, the war minister of the provisional government, ordered all German troops to put on black, red and gold emblems and swear allegiance to Archduke Johann, the head of the provisional government. But only the smaller states complied with this order; Austria, Prussia, Bavaria, Württemberg and Saxony tacitly refused.[41] Similar configurations were frequently to be found during the following two decades: the rulers of the smaller states had given up and were willing to submit to a German central government, whether it was democratic or (preferably) authoritarian. But the ruling groups in the medium-sized states felt secure enough to fight for their sovereignty; only in Baden could the democratic and patriotic forces hold the land on a liberal and unitarian course. In the end the fight of the medium-sized states for their sovereignty failed, but this was not a foregone conclusion.

In summer 1848 the revolutionary movement lost much of its

strength. When, in riots and disturbances, the spectre of a socialist revolution appeared, many better-off members of society took shelter under the protection of the traditional authorities. On the other hand, many radicals became disappointed when the National Assembly seemingly only 'talked' instead of organizing revolutionary action.

The conservative forces received considerable support from abroad because the European intervention mechanism established in 1815 to guarantee the traditional balance of power was still at work. This became overt in connection with the Schleswig-Holstein question: when the Danish crown tried to suppress the uprising by force, the *Bundestag* asked Prussia to help the insurgents. But a massive diplomatic intervention by Russia and Great Britain made Prussia retreat and sign the armistice of Malmö. The Assembly endorsed the armistice afterwards – and made its own political impotence overt.

When debating the new constitution the National Assembly had to define 'Germany' geographically. In October 1848 a large majority of the deputies voted for a constitution whose Article 1 read: 'The German Reich consists of the territory of the hitherto existing German League.' Article 47 of the Basic Rights granted national development to non-German populations, in particular equal rights for their languages within their respective areas in church, education, administration and judicature.[42]

The project of the National Assembly implied the division of the Austrian monarchy; the parts which did not belong to the German League were to be left outside, connected only by a common monarch. The Austrian rulers were – of course – against such a project. For a while it looked as if the Austrian empire would break apart in the storms of revolution and national uprisings. But by the end of 1848 the Austrian monarchy had reconsolidated its position; a *großdeutsch* solution had no chance of realization. In March 1849 and without enthusiasm, with only 267 against 263 votes,[43] the National Assembly accepted a *kleindeutsch* state: unification without Austria under Prussian leadership. On 3 April 1849 a delegation of the National Assembly offered the crown of German emperor to the Prussian king. Friedrich Wilhelm IV refused. He did not want to become a monarch by the grace of the people.

The constitution drafted by the National Assembly provided for a strong Lower House (*Volkshaus*), elected by universal and equal franchise for men, and a *Staatenhaus* (composed of representatives of the state government and state parliaments alike). The Kaiser should have the right to veto laws, but only temporarily.[44] In April 1849 28 German states accepted the constitution but the major states did not. A new revolutionary movement broke out and tried to force the monarchs to accept the constitution (*Reichsverfassungskampagne*). The movement was victorious in many places (Saxony, the Palatinate, Baden), and the regular army of Baden, many volunteers and sections of the Prussian Reserve Guard (*Landwehr*) joined in, but they could not prevail against the regular (mostly Prussian) troops. On 23 July 1849 the fortress Rastatt had to surrender, and this was the end. Many democrats were shot, many thousands driven into exile.

The traditional authorities remained victorious because they were supported by the experienced state bureaucracies, the regular army and the better-off parts of society. In addition they were backed by the foreign powers. Against this set of well-organized political and material interests, the democratic and patriotic movements could not prevail, although they were supported by great numbers and had great cultural influence.

The revolution of 1848–9 was beaten but left many traces. The constitution adopted by the National Assembly remained a constant frame of reference, in the countryside the last remnants of feudalism were abolished, and Prussia became a constitutional state. In November 1848 the king, after having dispersed the Prussian National Assembly by military force, introduced a constitution from above. The lower chamber had the right of budget control and was to be elected on the basis of universal, but unequal, suffrage (*Dreiklassenwahlrecht*), where people were grouped according to the taxes they paid.

By 1848 the German rulers knew that they could only remain in power if their domination was accepted by large segments of the population. This meant that deep-rooted aspirations like those for national unity and democratic participation could not *completely* be ignored. The monarchs began trying to win acclaim by realizing economic and national desires, in order to avoid democratization as far as possible.

THE ROAD TO THE KAISERREICH

As early as in 1849 Berlin tried to engineer a *kleindeutsch* unification from above.[45] Together with other German states Prussia formed a *Union*; its constitution showed many similarities to that of the National Assembly, but provided for authoritarian 'repairs'. By the end of 1849, 26 states had adhered to the *Union*, but again, the larger states of Saxony, Bavaria, Württemberg and Hanover did not participate. In the autumn of 1850 the project was ended by a massive joint Austrian and Russian intervention. Threatened with war Prussia signed the humiliating treaty of Olmütz (29 November 1850). Once again the mechanism of foreign intervention had worked.

But in 1853 the Crimean War broke out and the international system collapsed. Prussia sized the chance to improve relationships with St Petersburg. The collapse of the international system was detrimental for Austria, as became apparent in 1859 when the Habsburg monarchy had to fight against France and Piedmont. Large sections of the German public demanded active support for Austria,[46] but Berlin was not inclined to sacrifice her own interests for alleged German causes. Austria had to cede Lombardy.

The new international configuration was detrimental for Denmark too. At the end of 1863 the parliament in Copenhagen formally incorporated Schleswig into the Danish monarchy. This was a breach of the London protocol of 1852 and gave Prussia and Austria a pretext to conquer Schleswig-Holstein, and this time there was no joint British-Russian intervention to save the Danish position. By the Peace of Vienna (30 October 1864) Denmark had to give up the duchies of Lauenburg, Holstein and Schleswig. Several hundred years of Danish domination in northern Germany had ended. During negotiations in May and June 1864 Prussia and Austria had accepted a borderline near the language border,[47] but Danish diplomacy had refused. In the end the Danes had to accept a border much more to the north, roughly along the historical border of Schleswig. About 170 000 Danes and 30 000 bilingual persons came under Prussian rule,[48] thus the German League acquired a new national minority.

Prussian politics were at that time under the leadership of Count Otto v. Bismarck. He was known as a diehard defender of authoritarian principles, but he was also a flexible tactician. He could coolly analyse complex political configurations and dispassionately choose the best strategy and tactics. He was no warmonger out of passion, but he did not hesitate to start a war when he deemed it necessary. In contrast to some of his successors he always knew when to stop.

In 1862 Bismarck was made Prussian Prime Minister to execute an expensive programme of military reform. The liberal majority in the parliament refused to grant the money, but Bismarck simply raised it without parliamentary consent, thus starting the *Verfassungskonflikt* (constitutional conflict). Bismarck was for many years the most-hated man in German bourgeois and liberal circles, and the cleavage between conservatism and liberalism translated itself into a protracted, bitter political conflict.

Bismarck's reputation deteriorated even further when, in 1866, he escalated the conflict with Austria to the point of war. A reform of the inefficient German League had by then been discussed for many decades, but a solution was impossible as long it was not clear whether Austria or Prussia should be the dominant power. In the 1860s both governments presented reform drafts and both tried to win allies among the princes and the German public. In April 1866 Bismarck signed a secret alliance with Italy against Austria – a blatant breach of the constitution of the German League – and in June of that year war broke out. The smaller northern German states allied themselves with Prussia, but all the bigger states like Saxony and Hanover joined the Austrian camp.

Prussia was by far the more modern state. Her bureaucracy and her economy were superior to their Austrian counterparts, and in the Ruhr district and in Upper Silesia strong agglomerations of heavy industry had emerged. Prussia's dense railway network allowed for quick mobilization, and by 3 July 1866, at the Battle of Königgrätz, Austria was decisively beaten.

Austria had to recognize Prussian hegemony over the German states and had to cede Venetia to Italy, but was otherwise left intact. Prussia annexed Schleswig-Holstein and four states which had fought against her (Hanover, Nassau, Hesse-Cassel and Frankfurt), thereby uniting her two halves. All the other states north of the river Main were united into a new federation under Prussian dominance, the Northern German League (*Norddeutscher Bund*). The constitution of the Northern German League already contained essential features of the Reich of 1871 (see Chapter 5). The four states south of the river Main were left outside as Bismarck saw the risk of a French intervention.

Bismarck concluded defence alliances with the southern German states and agreed with them upon further economic integration. The *Zollverein* was reshaped, and a common parliament of the Northern German League and the southern German states (*Zollparlament*) was installed to provide for common legislation in economic matters. But still there was no automatic development towards further political unity. The elections for the *Zollparlament* in southern Germany showed strong anti-Prussian majorities composed of democratic-liberal, Catholic and pro-Austrian currents.[49] In many cases anti-Prussian resentments were so strong that hopes were expressed that the French army would smash the Northern German League. Loyalists to the dethroned King Georg V of Hanover, whose country Bismarck had annexed, organized a Guelfic legion (700–1000 men) to fight side by side with the French army against Prussia.[50] The process of further unification had come to a deadlock.

French policy changed everything. Emperor Napoleon III had on many occasions tried to stabilize his shaky regime by an aggressive foreign policy. French nationalists had for many decades demanded the Rhine border and they regarded German unification as something which had to be prevented at any cost. After a diplomatic crisis, which Bismarck coolly escalated, the French government, driven by fervent nationalist agitation, declared war on Prussia. On 14 July 1870 Napoleon III said to Prime Minister Ollivier: 'We have no proper reason for war, but we must decide for war to obey the will of the nation.'[51]

The war quickly turned into a series of French disasters. On 2 September Napoleon III had to surrender at Sedan and France became a republic. In Germany the French declaration of war had provoked a national outburst. The anti-Prussian positions in southern Germany evaporated, and in the autumn Bismarck offered to the southern monarchs the opportunity to build a common Reich – in practice this meant the inclusion of southern Germany in the Northern German League, softened by some special rights (and some bribery for the Bavarian king). If the southern monarchs had refused (which the Bavarian king in particular would have preferred), they would have been swept away by a popular movement backed by the army. In November the treaties were signed, and from 1 January 1871 the new Reich was a reality.

When German nationalists (not in the first place Bismarck)[52] demanded the annexation of Alsace-Lorraine, the war changed 'its strictly defensive character' and degenerated 'into a war against the French people', as Karl Marx had already feared in July 1870.[53] By the Peace of Frankfurt France had to cede Alsace-Lorraine, and after demands from the Prussian military the border in Lorraine was pushed over the linguistic barrier. Thus a French-speaking area was incorporated into the Reich.

SUMMARY – THE FORMATION OF THE GERMAN NATION-STATE

In 1871 Germany was at last united – or divided for good. The Germans in Austria and northern Bohemia remained under Austrian rule. The 'hard factors' of power, political hegemony and state-building in Prussia and Austria proved to be stronger than the soft ones of cultural identity.

The new Germany juridically made many people into Germans who did not want to be so – among others, Poles in the east, Danes in the north, and Alsatians and Lorrainese in the west. But at least the word 'German' had from then on a precise juridical meaning. Culturally, however, the new Germany crossed all hitherto existing definitions.

The Germany of 1871 was not the end of an automatic process. There have been many alternatives which could have become reality under different balances of power. One of those alternatives was a division between Austria and Prussia along the Main, an option seriously discussed in 1815. Another possibility was the so-called Trias solution, with the Rhine League states forming a third power besides Austria and Prussia. Unification within the borders of the German League seemed to be at hand in 1848; this would have corresponded to the sentiments of most Germans, and it would have been in line with the long tradition of the Holy Roman Empire.

Even after the erection of the Northern German League, the existence of independent southern German states was not necessarily a short-term phenomenon. And even in the case of a *kleindeutsch* unification, the borders were by no means given. In 1831 Prussia could have expanded deeper into Poland, Danish diplomacy could have realized a more southern border in 1864, and Alsace-Lorraine would have remained French if France had not declared war.

It was a long process with many factors operating with different weights at different times which led to the Germany of 1871. And the dominant trait of this process was the erection of Prussian hegemony. To some extent, Germany showed a parallel to Italy where Sardinia-Piedmont 'unified' the country by annexing the other territories. Italy became, however, a centralized state after the French model, and Germany a federation. The German states were much better consolidated than the Italian and could, if not annexed, continue within a federal structure; the Italian states collapsed.

Cultural bindings alone do not bring about unification, as the case of the Nordic countries and the movement of Scandinavism showed. Only if military powers like Prussia or Sardinia-Piedmont can use these cultural bindings to legitimize their expansion, can 'unification' become a reality.[54]

Finally, the cultural bindings of common language were nothing 'natural'. The German language was, as discussed above, an artefact. In this respect there has been a 'congruence' between language and nation-state: both were artefacts.

Part II
A Melting-Pot Under Pressure

5 Germany after 1871 – Some General Aspects and Trends

POLITICAL SYSTEM AND SOCIETY IN OUTLINE

The Germany of 1871 was a federation of 22 monarchical states and three towns (plus Alsace-Lorraine under special status). The constitution of the Kaiserreich combined federal and unitarian, authoritarian and democratic aspects in a particular way.[1] Foreign policy, customs, trade, communication and economic legislation were to be regulated centrally, but it was for the single states to implement the laws. The Reich had hardly any central administration at all. The states also retained important fields of legislation such as schooling.

Central legislation had to be endorsed by the Reichstag, the national parliament, which was elected according to the principle 'one man – one vote'. The Reichstag had the right of budget control and thereby an indirect control over central government activity, but it was for the Kaiser to appoint and to dismiss the chancellor and the leading personnel, and in the states the procedure was similar. The bureaucracies, diplomacy and army (to be precise: armies) were under no parliamentary control. This lack of sufficient democratic control was the main defect of the political system.

Political power was unevenly distributed. The ruling bureaucracies were powerful organizations in themselves. The Junker, the Prussian landed gentry, were the social group with the highest specific power due to their close contact with the Prussian monarchy; even in 1900 most Prussian generals and 20 per cent of the highest-ranking bureaucrats were *Junker*,[2] and so were chancellors Otto v. Bismarck and Theobald von Bethmann Hollweg (1909–17). Also the commercial and industrial bourgeoisie gained political influence. But large sections of the population such as the working class had little or no direct influence.

The political system was out of harmony with the sentiments of the vast majority of the population, and the parties which advocated

97

further democratization and parliamentarization (the Progressive Liberals, Zentrum, the Social Democrats and also in the beginning the National Liberals) were constantly backed by *at least* two-thirds of the population. This made the Reichstag in most questions a bulwark of liberal and democratic thinking. France offers an interesting counter-example; there, in the 1870s, two-thirds of the deputies of the National Assembly were monarchists.

In Germany the financial requirements of the central government and the amount of central legislation considerably increased. The governments had to cooperate with the majority of the Reichstag in order to have new legislation approved, while control of the budget and of the indirect taxes turned into powerful political tools for the parliament. In the years before the First World War, the Kaiserreich was clearly approaching formal parliamentarization.

Germany was a country ruled in an predominantly authoritarian but not altogether arbitrary way. Germany was, in the tradition of Prussia and most other member states, a *Rechtsstaat*, a state governed by law. Executive, legislative and judicial powers were separated. The Kaiser or chancellor had no say as to court decisions, and every administrative and executive body had to act according to laws. Movements disliked by the authorities were often discriminated against in many ways, but in principle, freedom of the press and of organization were protected by law.

These last aspects are important in the contexts of the present book: political and cultural dissenters of all kinds could organize themselves and forward their claims, and they had basic rights. The constitutional and juridical structure of the Kaiserreich was therefore, in spite of its shortcomings, stable enough to regulate numerous conflicts in an orderly way. This is one of the reasons why the Kaiserreich produced, as we shall see, many cases of successful integration. To these successes the education system, the dynamic economic development and the nascent welfare state also contributed.

From a cultural point of view, Germany was very heterogeneous. A confessional gap ran through the country. Religion still occupied a central part in people's minds, and Protestants and Catholics lived in very different mental worlds. Furthermore, in many regions non-German languages were in use: Polish in Prussia's eastern provinces, Mazurian (a Polish dialect) in East Prussia, Kashubian in West Prussia and Sorbian in Lusatia, southeast of Berlin. At the northern border lived Danes and Frisians, Frisian was also spoken in small areas near the Dutch border, and French was used in parts

of Alsace-Lorraine. The languages were divided into huge continuous spectra of dialects, a point which made the picture of spoken
idioms an absolute Babel. Just to mention one case, in Schleswig
five idioms were competing: German standard speech, Lower German, Southern Jutish (a Danish dialect), Danish standard speech
and Frisian (the latter again fragmented into several idioms).

The majority of the educated urban people adhered to modern
liberal views, whereas most people in the countryside thought in
conservative monarchist terms. But the distribution between town
and countryside and the other features of the social structure changed,
and this had cultural and political consequences.

In 1867 52 per cent of the active population were still engaged
in agriculture.[3] Many peasants in the plains of northwest Germany
and Bavaria were comparatively wealthy, but particularly in the
southwest there were many smallholders. The regions east of the
Elbe were dominated by the *Junker* who ran large estates and often
also controlled the local administration and police. But industry,
although still playing a minor role, was quickly expanding. The Ruhr
district, the Saar region and Upper Silesia were being transformed
into dense agglomerations of the coal and steel industries; in Saxony,
the Rhein/Main region and in Berlin thousands of textile, metal
and optical factories mushroomed; Hamburg and Bremen were
dynamic harbour towns. The process of industrialization was accompanied by the rise of the workers' movement, and this added a
new stable feature to the pattern of cultural currents in Germany.

Four large cultural or social-moral milieux can be discerned: a
conservative, predominantly agrarian and Protestant milieu; a bourgeois-liberal, predominantly urban Protestant milieu; a Catholic
milieu; and a socialist workers' movement. Besides these four main
milieux, there were the linguistic groups and other cultural minorities, for instance the Jews. (For an overview, see the models in
Figures 1.1 to 1.8 in Chapter 1.)

Before we study these milieux and minorities in more detail, we
shall review the education system and the social and economic
development.

THE EDUCATION SYSTEM

By 1871 the German states had already built up efficient educational systems. In quantitative terms the elementary schools were

by far the most important school type. In Prussia in the 1870s clerical influence upon the schools was abolished, the elementary schools were thoroughly modernized, the education of the teachers was improved, and by 1878 31 new training colleges had been founded. New guidelines laid more emphasis upon knowledge and qualification, less upon piety and discipline.

Even so, in 1871 74 per cent of all Prussian schools had only one class and in 1911 this had fallen to 52 per cent. In the towns 68 per cent of the schools had six and more classes. Between 1864 and 1911 state expenditure on elementary schools rose by almost 1400 per cent. The money allowed for the enlargement and modernization of the system as well as for stricter control.[4] The other German states experienced similar developments, but the differences among them were considerable.[5] The church retained a strong influence in Württemberg and in the Bavarian countryside, whereas in Hamburg the school system was almost completely secular.

A small but slightly rising percentage of pupils (5 per cent in 1911) attended a higher school (*Gymnasium, Realgymnasium, Oberrealschule*).[6] These schools opened the way to higher careers. Formally the higher schools were open to every one, but in practice they were mostly institutions for the boys of the upper classes, of the *Bildungsbürger* and the new middle class. The girls were kept in separate higher schools, and they were not allowed to study at universities. But most teachers were women, and feminists vigorously fought against the discrimination in education. In 1900, Baden was the first German state to open the universities to women; Prussia followed in 1908.

In 1866 there were 19 universities; three more were founded in the years to 1914, as were, as embryonic universities, the Academy in Poznań (1903) and the Colonial Institute in Hamburg (1908).[7] Technical universities were a German peculiarity – there were 11 by 1914. There were 14 specialized high schools such as mining or agricultural academies, and after 1898 six commercial high schools were founded. Traditionally, there were strong mental barriers between the high cultural spheres in which the university professors dwelt and the world of industry and commerce. Gradually, however, patterns of cooperation developed, and the rise of the technical universities symbolizes in itself a turn towards industrial problems.

The number of students rose from 18 000 (1869) to 79 000 (1914). The number of institutions and professorships showed similar growth rates. The German universities worked as a model in countries as diverse as the USA and Japan, and in subjects as diverse as physics and history.

The universities worked as powerful agents of integration. The academic discourse (international in principle) was particularly intense within the national borders, and inside Germany, students and professors were mobile across the state borders. Most of the professors came from *Bildungsbürger* homes, had been brought up in a national spirit and shaped the debate in national terms. Many historians made the Prussian-dominated Kaiserreich appear as the logical end point of German destiny.

International comparisons are difficult, but according to estimates, by 1850 illiteracy had fallen to the following percentage levels:[8]

USA, white population	10
Sweden	10
Scotland	20
Prussia	20
England and Wales	30–35
France	40–45
Belgium	45–50
Spain	75
Italy	75–80
Russian Empire	90–95

Practically no European country could match the educational energy of the United States. Within Europe, the Scandinavian countries, Switzerland, Scotland and Germany were at the top. In this respect Germany was several decades in advance of the other great European countries.[9]

The statistics of many European countries show strong regional variations which were quite persistent over time (11 per cent in Italian Piedmont, in Calabria 70 per cent in 1901).[10] But in the case of Germany the figures already show a low level almost everywhere in 1871. By then only in Prussia's eastern provinces, with their Polish, Mazurian and Kashubian populations, was there still some illiteracy.[11] And by 1900 effective elementary schooling had reached even the geographically remote areas between the Mazurian lakes and the countryside of Posen. In 1912 it was regarded as a general standard 'that maid-servants could fluently read, write and – often better than it was desirable – calculate.'[12] By 1900 Prussia's eastern border was a kind of European educational equator: west of it lay the countries with high educational standards, east of it were immense regions with high illiteracy.[13]

The political effects of the Prussian/German school system are not easy to assess. As official regulations specified, the schools should not only teach reading or calculating, but also make the pupils loyal subjects of their monarchs and immunize them against socialist ideas.[14] But the youngsters leaving these schools voted in ever growing numbers for the Social Democratic Party. The Catholic Zentrum party, not favoured by the Prussian bureaucracy, held a strong position.

It is, however, probable that the German schools, by teaching German history (in the new, Berlin-centred version), by instructing in German geography (within the new borders) and by dealing with national themes like the navy stabilized German identity, without the older regional identities such as Saxons or Bavarians vanishing. And the numerous pupils from non-German homes learned at least some basic German. The many thousands of elementary schools prepared the ground for social integration, but they were also a powerful economic motor.

ECONOMY AND INTEGRATION

The first German mechanized cotton mill was installed in 1784, the first steam engine in 1785,[15] but unlike in Great Britain, these early innovations did not at that time signal the beginning of a profound social transformation. But after a preliminary boom in the 1840s, strong industrial growth began in 1852.[16] It lasted almost uninterrupted for more than two decades. The driving force was railway building.[17] Many German firms showed a high capability of catching up with the British standard. To mention one example, in 1835 the locomotive and the driver on the first German railway were English. But from 1854 onwards all German locomotives were produced in German factories.[18]

The social structure changed profoundly. In 1882 42 per cent of the population were still dependent on agriculture, in 1907 only 28 per cent. In the same period the share of industry rose from 35 to 42 per cent, the tertiary sector from 23 to 30 per cent.[19]

By 1914 Germany had reached about the same level as Great Britain in the 'old industries' (coal, iron, steel) and surpassed her in the new branches such as the electrical and chemical industries.

In Great Britain industrial production doubled between 1870 and 1914; in Germany it rose by six times.[20] The reasons for Germany's greater industrial dynamism have been debated for decades.[21] The most important was presumably that Germany possessed more 'human capital', i.e. better educated manpower.

Many economists and economic historians have identified 'human capital' as the most important source for long-term economic growth.[22] It is indeed striking: Great Britain pioneered the Industrial Revolution, and in the centuries before she had an outstandingly high educational standard;[23] likewise the rise of the USA to industrial supremacy was preceded by an unparalleled high educational level. And among the larger European countries it was the one with the most efficient school system – Germany – which was most successful in terms of industrial development.

John Stuart Mill warned his readers as early as 1848, quoting a cotton manufacturer who preferred 'decidedly the Saxons and the Swiss, but more especially the Saxons, because they have a very careful general education, which has extended their capacities beyond any special employment, and rendered them fit to take up, after a short preparation, any employment to which they may be called.' Mill had no doubt: 'The importance, even in this limited [economic] aspect, of popular education, is well worthy the attention of politicians, especially in England …'[24]

Germany's industrial dynamism considerably improved the job creation capacity of the German economy. Between 1867 and 1913 the number of employed people rose from 16 to 31 million. The bulk of the new jobs were created in industry, crafts and mining where employment rose from 4.4 to 11.7 million. The tertiary sector, i.e. transport and services, grew considerably too (from 3.4 to 8.5 million).[25]

As regards job creation, the transition to industrial societies meant a crucial difference. In agriculture, as land was restricted, the 'law of diminishing returns' operated. More employed people meant higher production, but the increase became smaller and smaller. In the end it became too small to support further employment, and the surplus population had to find a living elsewhere. In addition the mechanization of agriculture at first destroyed many employment possibilities. From 1882 to 1907 the number of German threshing machines rose from 0.3 million 1.4 million. During this time the agrarian population shrank from 18.8 to 17.7 million.[26]

But industry could give employment to growing populations. The job creation process was often inadequate, and many jobs were constantly destroyed, but on balance employment rose in every decade. People did not have to emigrate any more. Industrialized countries could even attract immigrants. In the case of Germany the transition from an emigration into an immigration country took place in the 1890s, the same decade that industry became more important than agriculture.

Industrial society brought the Germans in closer contact. The railways, telegraph and telephone made geographic distances shrink, and public transport made it possible to work several kilometres away from home. In agriculture, production was mostly in individual farmsteads, but industry often meant working amidst hundreds or even thousands of people. In 1907, 43 per cent of German industrial workers were concentrated at workplaces with more than 50 employees,[27] and even those large workplaces could only exist because they were integrated into a dense network of suppliers and customers. This created patterns of cooperation and of conflict which ran counter to traditional regional, confessional or ethnic divisions. Closer integration at work, the higher standard of literacy and the spread of newspapers jointly contributed to closer communication.

But industrial occupation was often unstable, and working conditions were often bad, so fluctuation was enormous. To give one example, between 1880 and 1900 the population of Bochum, one of the Ruhr towns, grew from 33 000 to 65 000. During that period the inward migration was 232 000, so about 221 000 persons must have left the town in the same period.[28] In the late nineteenth and early twentieth centuries Germany 'resembled an ant-hill into which a wanderer has pushed his stick'.[29]

The economic policy was basically liberal. In 1879 the Reichstag introduced protective tariffs on grain and steel. But in international comparisons the German tariffs were moderate, and they did not change the predominantly liberal character of the economic policy. The dominant economic philosophy can perhaps be labelled as 'pragmatic market economy'. As a rule, market forces could operate freely, but the state intervened if the markets produced results which were regarded as being socially disruptive. This was also the guideline when in 1883 the Reichstag passed a law concerning obligatory health insurance, thus initiating the era of the German *Sozialstaat*. In 1884 accident insurance followed, and in 1889 old age and invalidity insurance. Bismarck would have preferred it if the state, via taxes, had financed the social security systems. But the Liberals and the Catholic Zentrum jointly resented a strengthening of the central state and insisted upon a solution based on insurances.[30] The new social insurances were obligatory, mainly financed by employers' and employees' contributions, they were publicly regulated with strong elements of self-administration, and their payments depended upon former contributions – they were to give social rights, but they were not to work as income levellers.

Later the social insurances became extended to agricultural workers and family servants. Child labour was forbidden, and from 1878 there was a factory inspectorate throughout the Reich. In Bismarck's time labour protection remained underdeveloped, but after 1890 the Reichstag legislated in this field to a growing extent, for instance by reducing working hours. The sums redistributed by the social legislation were modest when compared with modern welfare states, and many fields were not at that time covered by social security; there was, for instance, no unemployment insurance. But in cases of need, the workers were not dependent upon charity, they had rights. This was one of the reasons why many German citizens identified with 'their' state, even though they were in an inferior social position, or spoke Polish or Sorbian as their mother language.

6 The Four Main Socio-Cultural Milieux

THE GENESIS OF THE MILIEUX

In the 1860s the conflict between liberals and conservatives was still the main cleavage which divided Germany. To recap, a cleavage is a long-lasting conflict line, with institutionalized cultures on both sides of the divide. In 1848/9 the cleavage had produced civil war, and in the 1860s, during the Prussian *Verfassungskonflikt*, both sides stood against each other in a bitter confrontation. The liberals were a predominantly urban movement, the conservatives stood strongest in the countryside, as, for instance, the elections to the Prussian Lower House in 1863 showed.[1] In the countryside the conservatives became the strongest party among the low-tax voters. The fact that the humble people in the countryside had a strong tendency to vote for the conservatives was one of the reasons why in 1867/71 Bismarck conceded the equal franchise at the Reichstag elections.

In 1866 the liberals split: the Progressive Liberals remained in the opposition, whereas the National Liberals began a cooperation with Bismarck. In the 1870s they were the strongest party in the Reichstag, and the legislation which created the unified Germany in the juridical and economic sphere bore a strong liberal imprint. The conservatives also split; the *Freikonservative Vereinigung* (after 1871 the *Deutsche Reichspartei*) supported Bismarck and stood in many matters quite near to the National Liberals. The division between liberals and conservatives gradually lost much of its previous sharpness.

The *rapprochement* between conservatives and liberals was brought about, or at least eased, by the emergence of two new cleavages: against Catholics and against Socialists.

The Catholic world was shaken by the progress of liberalism and the Italian unification in 1860/1. The erection of Protestant Prussia's dominance over Germany was another deep shock to many Catholics, and in 1870 even Rome was incorporated into the new Italy. The Catholic church reacted with a process of 'revitalization' which strengthened its inner cohesion, but also deepened its alienation from other groups. From a liberal perspective, the dogmatization of Mary's immaculate conception (1854) was an insult against rationality, the *syllabus errorum* of 1864 was a comprehensive attack upon all modern principles and institutions, and the dogma of the Pope's infallibility (1870) was a threat to democratic principles and national unity because the Pope seemed to demand loyalty also in political matters.

In Germany, where Protestants held most power positions and where Liberals dominated the public debate, the Catholic revival was doomed to produce political frictions. It was, however, Bismarck's *Kulturkampf*, the attack on the independence of the Catholic church in the 1870s (see below), which transformed the unavoidable frictions into a deep and bitter conflict.

Almost simultaneously another cleavage opened. After 1848 German socialism was for many years only a matter of small sects, but in the 1860s the movement began to grow in earnest, and in 1875 two pioneer parties merged to the *Sozialistische Arbeiterpartei* (SAP), the later SPD. Two years later the party gained 9 per cent of the votes. Many well-to-do Germans were horrified by the spectre of socialist revolution, while the Protestant and Catholic clergy deplored the rise of an openly atheistic party. In 1877 the Reichstag outlawed all socialist organizations. The ban was lifted in 1890, but until 1914 the socialists were systematically discriminated against.

Thus, German society was riven by three cleavages[2] which constituted four distinct socio-cultural milieux: conservative, liberal, Catholic, and socialist. Many cultural values differed fundamentally between the milieux. Catholics and conservatives supported traditional authority; socialists and liberals worked against it. Socialists were partisans of equality in social terms, a position which the other three rejected. Both socialists and Catholics saw themselves as part of an international community; liberals and conservatives did not. Catholics and Protestants had profoundly different conceptions of the world and daily routines which differed in many aspects; marriages across the confessional gap were very rare. The liberals wanted to see religion confined to the private sphere and combated clerical influence in the school system; the socialists were atheists. All four milieux developed comprehensive sets of symbols which were dear to their followers, but which were regarded at best with indifference, if not despised, by the others: the Red Flag;

the picture of the Virgin Mary; the Prussian crown; the Lessing monument.

All milieux created various organizations which united many members in multiple ways. The socialists and the Catholics organized very dense networks and proved to be the most stable milieux; the conservatives and in particular the liberals were more loosely integrated. All milieux had their own newspapers, periodicals and editing houses; communication happened mostly within the milieux. Communication across the cleavages was mostly confined to the elites. The political parties were firmly rooted in the distinct milieux. This is the reason for the remarkable stability of the German party system between 1871 and 1928. About 90 per cent of the German electorate voted for the milieux parties; the remaining 'dissidents' belonged mostly to linguistic minorities.

The conservative and the liberal milieux were politically dominant, while the Catholics and socialists were discriminated against or at times even repressed. If other minorities such as the Jews or Polish-speaking citizens are added to them, then by 1900 a clear majority of the German population belonged to discriminated minorities.

CONSERVATIVES AND LIBERALS

The Conservatives gained 23 per cent of the votes in 1871.[3] After 1887 their share declined (12 per cent in 1912). The appararent numerical stability until 1887 was due to a set of conflicting processes: they lost their remaining influence in the towns and the world of agriculture shrank, but at the same time they were better able to mobilize the countryside. In the 1870s the participation rate in many agricultural provinces was only 40–45 per cent; in 1887 it was 75 per cent, which corresponded to the German average. The conservatives entrenched themselves in their core milieu. They became even more rural and even more Protestant,[4] but could not integrate other sections of the electorate. If measured as share of the people who were entitled to vote, the conservative influence fell from 19 per cent in 1887 to 10 per cent in 1912.[5]

The decline of the agrarian world and the influx of cheap foreign grain induced a sentiment of bitterness in the countryside. This was not only an economic problem, a whole culture had good reason to feel mortally endangered. In the 1870s the *Junker* led a massive campaign for protective tariffs, which were introduced in

1877. In 1893, when Bismarck's successor Leo v. Caprivi concluded trade treaties which implied lower grain tariffs, angry peasants formed the *Bund der Landwirte* (Peasants' League), a mass organization under *Junker* leadership. The Peasants' League organized a massive, often demagogic propaganda; the forces of modernity, of industry, of liberalism and of socialism were perceived as enemies. As long as the *Junker* retained strong positions in the state apparatus, the conservative milieu as a whole could feel protected. But every step towards democracy was seen as a menace; the search for scapegoats (for instance Jews) often replaced sober analysis.

Originally Prussian conservativism was a non-nationalist force, but during the Kaiserreich the conservatists gradually shifted over to a nationalist rhetoric. By the mid-1870s slogans such as the 'protection of national labour' were used to justify grain tariffs. German nationalism, which originally began as an ideology of liberal bourgeois emancipation, became transformed into an ideology of aggressive antidemocracy.[6] In the years before the First World War, the conservatives also supported an aggressive imperialist policy.

The transformation of conservatism had a parallel in the liberal milieu. The Progressive Party remained loyal to democratic ideas, but the National Liberals gradually shifted emphasis from 'liberal' to 'national'. The confrontation with Catholics and socialists made them close ranks with the conservatives, and many National Liberals began to see the authoritarian constitution of the Kaiserreich as an insurance against socialism. Nationalist slogans served to cover privileges and to hide the difficulties in formulating practical solutions for the problems of industrial society. In the years before 1914, the National Liberals also supported an imperialist policy.[7]

In the 1871, the liberals, if grouped together, were still the strongest political force. At the general elections they gained 47 per cent of the votes and an absolute majority of the seats.[8] In the following decades their influence declined and in the years before 1914 they held about a quarter of the seats. But the liberal electorate was numerically more robust than the declining share of the votes suggests. This becomes apparent when it is measured as a percentage of the people who had the right to vote: the liberals entered the Kaiserreich with 20 per cent, climbed to an exceptional 29 per cent in 1887 and received 22 per cent in 1912[9] – almost exactly as much as in 1871. It was mostly the rising participation rate which made their relative share fall. As regards organizations, the liberals stood weakest. German liberalism was based on the prestige of local notables, such as doctors, professors, lawyers or journalists, who stayed in informal contact. It was not until 1890 that the National Liberals formed a central party organization.[10] Unlike the other three milieux, there was no liberal mass organization. By the outbreak of the First World War, the liberal milieu had become fragile.

CATHOLICS AND *KULTURKAMPF*

Of the German population 36.5 per cent were Catholics.[11] Before 1870 many south German Catholics had fiercely resisted incorporation into a united Germany. In 1868 the Bavarian Catholic paper *Volksbote* wrote that many Catholics regarded the Frenchmen as their only protectors against Prussian rape, 'and – God willing – their future liberators from the unbearable yoke of Prussianism.'[12] In 1870 many Catholic deputies voted against the unification treaties. Seen from Berlin, the Catholic church was a force of doubtful loyalty. Bismarck was perhaps also interested in a confrontation in order to prevent cooperation between the Catholic Zentrum party and the National Liberals.

Bismarck initiated the *Kulturkampf* in July 1871 by abolishing the Catholic department in the Prussian ministry of culture, a Catholic stronghold within the Prussian bureaucracy. And in March 1872 the clerical supervision over Prussia's elementary schools was replaced by state supervision. At the request of Bavaria, where state and church had already been engaged for years in a conflict, an article was added to the penal code (*Kanzelparagraph*); it interdicted priests commenting upon public affairs during religious services 'in a way which endangers the public peace'.[13] Civil marriage became obligatory.

Many laws introduced during the *Kulturkampf* were a step in the long development towards the separation of state and church. But others, such as the outlawing of the Jesuits, were downright repression. The laws of May 1873 stipulated that the state had to approve the nomination of the priests; that the priests had to study philosophy, history and German literature at a German university; that Catholic seminars in Prussia were under state supervision; and that no institution outside Germany (i.e. the Pope) had any disciplinary power over German clerics. The scheme of a Catholic state church appeared on the horizon.

Bishops and priests were sentenced to fines or even imprisoned when they did not comply with the May laws. Police officers searched printing houses and confiscated papers. In many Prussian areas Catholics felt like second-rank citizens, and even in normal social or commercial activities they were discriminated against.[14]

But as communities under attack often do, the Catholics closed ranks and became stronger. The votes for the Zentrum party jumped from 18 to 28 per cent at the Reichstag elections in 1874. The party became the umbrella for many forces which resented Bismarck's policy, such as Polish and Alsatian representatives, or (Protestant) Guelfs from Hanover. When Leo XIII became Pope in 1878, Bismarck began to look for a way out of the conflict. Gradually much of the anti-Catholic legislation was repealed.

After 1879 the Zentrum entered the group of 'governing parties'; it supported the budget and legislation in the Reichstag in turn for influence, but the Catholics still had reasons to feel discriminated against. They were under-represented in the Prussian bureaucracy, especially in the higher ranks[15] and among students or university professors. This was also a reflection of the more rural character of their regions, and of the lesser emphasis they placed on education, but it also reflected their pariah position. Many obververs were surprised when, at the elections in 1907, after almost three decades of cooperation in the Reichstag, liberals and conservatives again erupted in a militant dislike of Catholicism.[16]

The Catholics organized many professional associations (craftsmen, peasants), women's associations and educational societies.[17] Other associations did practical charity or distributed literature. In 1912 there were 446 Catholic daily papers and numerous weekly papers, monthly periodicals or calendars. The Catholics were an extremely well-organized minority, a fact which considerably helped to stabilize their milieu.

The share of the votes for the Zentrum party declined from 28 per cent in 1874 to 16 per cent in 1912. But again the picture is much more stable if attention is focused upon the share of the people entitled to vote: 16 per cent in 1877 (the elections in 1874 were extraordinary) and 14 per cent in 1912.[18] At the fringes, however, a gradual process of erosion is traceable. Especially among workers, the church lost influence. In 1914, presumably 800 000 Catholic workers were organized by the socialist trade unions, only 351 000 by the Christian unions.[19] And after the *Kulturkampf* conflicts within the Catholic camp between 'modernists' and 'traditionalists' came to the surface. The slow process towards secularization had its impact also upon the Catholic camp, albeit to a lesser degree than upon the Protestants. Catholic clericals had to make many compromises with new values such as education and rationality. The mystical belief in old rites and the word of popes and priests, which traditionally characterized the Catholic countryside, was less and less tenable.

In 1914, when the First World War broke out, no Catholic editor or politician hoped that French troops would come as liberators. In spite of the *Kulturkampf*, the decades of the Kaiserreich witnessed a process of integration.

THE SOCIALIST MILIEU

Artisan associations or mutual-aid funds were pioneering forms of worker organizations, and in 1848 tobacco workers and printers formed the first nationwide unions.[20] Elementary forms of a labour movement survived the defeat of the revolution. In 1863 Ferdinand Lasalle and his followers on a reformist basis founded the *Allgemeine Deutsche Arbeiterverein* (ADAV), the first German workers' party. Under Marxist inspiration a rival organization, the *Sozialdemokratische Arbeiterpartei* (SDAP), was created in 1869. In the 1860s tobacco workers and printers pioneered again the organization of nationwide trade unions; from 1867 the number of strikes was constantly rising. Mass strikes, like those of the Waldenburg miners in 1869/70 or of the Ruhr coal miners in 1872, had repercussions throughout Germany. Workers joined the unions in hitherto unseen numbers. In 1875 the two workers' parties merged into the united *Sozialistische Arbeiterpartei* (SAP). In 1877 they got 9 per cent of the votes.

In the 1870s fear of socialist revolution was widespread. The German socialists were peaceful men who courageously fought against the annexation of Alsace-Lorraine, but their solidarity with the Communards of Paris made it easy for Bismarck to campaign on the 'Red Scare'. In 1878 the Reichstag, with a majority of National Liberals and Conservatives, outlawed socialist organizations. The repression, however, if compared with twentieth-century standards, was a mild one.

It was one aim of the social legislation of 1884 to immunize the workers against socialist agitation. As such it was a failure. In 1890 their organizations were legalized again. In 1912 the socialist party, officially refounded as *Sozialdemokratische Partei Deutschlands* (SPD) in 1890, gained 35 per cent of the votes and 110 seats in the Reichstag – thereby becoming Germany's strongest party. It was the SPD which profited most from the rising participation rate.[21]

The rise of German socialism was accompanied by the development of a dense network of organizations. Most important were the trade unions. Besides the socialist trade unions – by far the strongest – there were also Christian and liberal unions; in 1914 they counted altogether 2.9 million members. SPD, trade unions and workers', women's and youth associations of all kinds, covering activities such as sports, chess and education, formed a closely connected socialist subculture. Before 1914 the socialist milieu was, however, still in a process of development; not all who voted for the SPD were incorporated into the milieu – the SPD was also a party of protest.

Between 1890 and 1913 the number of strikes rose considerably, and they became more organized.[22] Most of the strikes were local, but some (coal miners in 1905 and 1912, Hamburg dockers in 1896–7) had a nationwide echo. More silent, but perhaps more important in the long run, in more and more cases the unions could successfully organize pressure upon employers by threatening to strike without actually resorting to it. In the last years before the First World War there were twice as many 'strikeless movements' as strikes. In 1873 the first collective agreement was signed, and in 1896 the printers introduced the first nationwide agreement. The 'Ruhr Barons' and other capitalists fiercely resisted collective bargaining, but in branches like printing or the wood industry where the workers were more qualified and more stable, industrial relations became regulated.[23] In 1913 there were 11 526 collective agreements, covering 1.6 million workers (13 per cent of all workers).[24]

In 1891 a new industrial law made written factory statutes obligatory, and the employers had to listen to the workers – a modest but first step on the way towards the 'constitutional factory'. In 1901 local labour courts, where the employers and workers were represented, became obligatory and could decide minor legal controversies. In 1905 the Ruhr miners embarked upon a mass strike and procured a revision of the mining legislation; workers' representatives became entitled to control the registration of the coal wagons – formerly a point of bitter disputes because the pay depended upon it.

By 1913, the Social Democrats were still discriminated against in many ways, and in many branches the unions were without influence. But some groups of workers had strong representation, and mechanisms such as collective bargaining were spreading. Important laws were passed with the help of Social Democratic votes, and as the tactical cooperation between Social Democrats and Progressive Liberals at the elections in 1912 showed – the Social Democrats were on the way out of their political isolation. The growth of the movement meant, however, that the party came to represent groups with different problems and attitudes, and the institutionalization of the movement, with professional trade unionists, editors and members of parliament, also meant bureaucratization.

The Social Democrats indefatigably criticized militarism and imperialism, but on 4 August 1914 the parliamentary group endorsed the war credits in the Reichstag. The SPD lost its innocence by supporting the imperialist war, but it was the decisive last step in making the SPD an integrated part of the political system.

All in all, the Kaiserreich had a history of hard class struggles and discrimination against the working class and its organizations. But the constitutional rights which also protected the socialists, the social legislation which gave the workers social rights, the first steps towards a 'constitutional factory', the beginnings of collective bargaining, and last but not least the first steps towards the incorporation of the SPD in the normal legislative procedures and the imminent parliamentarization of the Reich – all these contributed to the integration of the workers' movement. On 4 August 1914 this integration – yet incomplete, but far-progressed – was made overt.

7 The Uniting Force of Federalism: Southern Germany in Contrast to Alsace-Lorraine

The cultural tension lines gave good potential breeding conditions for separatism, which could become actual in all those cases where a regional dominant culture was in conflict with the main lines of Prussian politics. This was the case with the Polish- and Danish-speaking regions (see next chapter), but also many regions with a German-speaking population were potential candidates. Surprisingly enough, with the exception of Alsace-Lorraine, there was no separatist current of political importance. The integration of the southern German states is one of the successes of the Kaiserreich. Alsace-Lorraine, however, offers an interesting case of unsufficient integration, and will be studied first.

Most of the inhabitants of Alsace-Lorraine spoke German, but in 1871 they opposed incorporation into the new Reich. Alsace-Lorraine was not a state but *Reichslande* directly governed from Berlin,[1] a fact which created much bitterness. In spite of some improvements in 1879 and 1911, the province retained a semi-colonial status. The *Kulturkampf* created further resentment because two-thirds of the population were Catholics.

In the 1880s so-called Protesters gained all the seats of Alsace-Lorraine in the elections to the Reichstag. From 1890 onwards, however, radical protest declined. Hopes for reunification with France dwindled, and in many respects the German administration was felt no longer to be such a burden. In contrast to Prussia's eastern provinces, the language policy was liberal and French was respected. The closer economic integration and a German immigration also strengthened the ties to the Reich.

But German nationalists entertained a deep-rooted mistrust of the Alsatians and Lorrainese and objected to every move towards greater autonomy. Prussian officers often behaved as if in enemy territory, while recruits from the region were usually stationed in garrisons far away. But it was exactly this neglect of equal rights which prevented successful integration. From 1908 tensions grew again. In 1913 the so-called Zabern case led to bitter disputes throughout Germany, when a lieutenant von Forster committed acts of disrespect and brutality against Alsatian civilians.

In 1914, when French troops for a brief time entered the town of Mulhouse, they were cheered by enthusiastic crowds. The German governor Hans v. Dallwitz declared in 1918 that Germany would not dare to hold a referendum in Alsace-Lorraine.[2] In November 1918 French troops arrived and were overwhelmingly greeted by cheering crowds throughout the region. The failure in integration became manifest.

In contrast to Alsace-Lorraine, the southern German states had constitutional rights within a federal framework, and this explains their successful integration. This was not a foregone conclusion. Before 1870, except in Baden, the opponents of a Prussian-dominated Reich were politically on top, and it was the French declaration of war and the subsequent patriotic outburst which pushed them onto the defensive (see Chapter 4, p. 91). When Wilhelm I was proclaimed German emperor (18 January 1871), the Bavarian prince Otto wrote to his brother the king: 'Oh, Louis, I can't describe to you the immeasurable pain and woe I felt during the ceremony ... How sad an impression it made upon me to see our Bavarians bow in front of the emperor ...'[3]

The tighter economic integration and force of habit played a strong role in the process of silent integration. But as circumstances in Alsace-Lorraine and modern separatist movements in Spain or Belgium have proven, habit and economic cooperation alone are not enough.

The southern states had their own laws in most fields, their own bureaucracies, courts, police and educational systems. After 1871 the representatives of the state power did not come from a new distant centre – Bavarian policemen and tax officials were Bavarians. The peasants might have grumbled about them, but the situation would have been much worse if Prussian policemen had been stationed there. Italy after 1860 or Spain form contrasting examples: Southern Italian peasants saw their villages invaded by Piedmontese *carabinieri* whom they could not understand; in Catalonia and the Basque country, the *Guardia Civil* was the hated symbol of Castilian domination, and in Alsace-Lorraine the presence of Prussian troops was a major factor leading to tension.

The educational system was a much disputed battleground for political and cultural struggles throughout Europe. But in Germany the disputes remained within the individual states, otherwise a crisis like the *Kulturkampf* would have meant disaster for national unity. But the *Kulturkampf* hardly took place in southern Germany. Only the regulation of civil marriage, the outlawing of the Jesuits and the *Kanzelparagraph* were federal laws, while the bulk of the anti-Catholic legislation concerned only Prussia and, to a lesser extent, also Baden. Federalism thus meant flexibility; Germany was spared many of the conflicts between centre and periphery which burdened many other European states.

8 The Jews

In contrast to the Catholics, the Jews were socially discriminated against in a positive way. By 1900 there were about 600 000 Jews in Germany, roughly one per cent of the population.[1] But about 4 per cent of the Prussian judges were Jews, so were 3 per cent of the higher Prussian bureaucrats, 2.5 per cent of the professors in ordinary, 6 per cent of the physicians, 15 per cent of the barristers, and 37 per cent of the bank owners and bank managers.[2] Leading liberal politicians such as Ludwig Bamberger and Eduard Lasker were Jews, as was Albert Ballin, director general of the Hapag Lloyd shipping company and intimate companion of Kaiser Wilhelm II, and Walter Rathenau, director general of the electric concern AEG, influential adviser to chancellor Bethmann Hollweg and from 1914 head of the raw material department in the Prussian war ministry.

Throughout the nineteenth century, the history of the German Jews was a success story.[3] Enlightened authors such as Gotthold Ephraim Lessing (*Nathan the Wise*, 1779) had mentally prepared the ground for their emancipation, and in Prussia the major juridical discriminations were abolished in 1812. In 1848–9 the National Assembly proclaimed the principle of equal rights for the Jews, and in 1871 full emancipation was introduced even in the most backward member states. Jews could not, however, become officers in the Prussian army. The army was an organization of its own, to a large extent isolated from the main currents of German society.

The Jews proved to be extraordinarily capable of using the new opportunities. In 1848 65 per cent of the Prussian Jews still lived in miserable conditions, but by 1871, 60 per cent had climbed up into the middle and upper tax brackets.[4] And after 1871 the successes of the Jews multiplied. There were proletarian Jews as well, but these were mostly immigrants from eastern Europe who by 1914 constituted about 13 per cent of the German Jewish population.[5]

Most Jews quickly made the step from emancipation to assimilation.[6] They emphatically adopted German literature, philosophy and music and became active contributors to the development of German high culture. Education was a central value for the Jewish community, a fact which explains their strong presence at the German universities. But this integration also meant a loss of cohesion. About 23 000 Jews let themselves be baptized and mixed marriages became frequent.[7] In 1901–5 there were 18 mixed marriages per 100 Jewish marriages, but 38 in 1911–15 and in urban centres such as Hamburg as many as 73 – an indicator of the willingness for assimilation on the Jewish side, and the openness of German mainstream society. Three-quarters of the children were no longer raised according to Jewish traditions. In 1914 the German Jews were as enthusiastic patriots as the Protestant majority. Jews were nominated to high positions in the war bureaucracy and – for the first time – made officers in the Prussian army. The Jewish-German symbiosis seemed to be perfect.[8]

The Jewish success, however, also provoked envy, and in the 1870s a new wave of anti-Semitism arose. Many anti-Jewish books and periodicals appeared, and in 1893 there were 16 deputies in the Reichstag who had campaigned on anti-Semitism.[9] Some student associations excluded Jews from membership. Anti-Semitic authors like Paul Lagarde reinterpreted the Jewish question in a radically new way: the Jews were not a religious minority but a different race, and as such they were disseminators of decay and decomposition. They could not be assimilated; on the contrary, the deeper they penetrated into German society the more they would spread their 'poison'.[10]

But after 1895 anti-Semitic organizations declined again. German anti-Semitism was too weak to provide a basis for a political movement, and anti-Semitic literature did not seem to be more widespread than in France, where Eduard Drumont saw 100 000 copies of his book *La France juive* sold in only one year. Moreover, unlike their peers in eastern Europe, the German Jews could rely upon the protection of the authorities, the courts and the police. No relevant political force advocated a reversal of the juridical emancipation of the Jews, and as the examples of Ballin, Rathenau and others showed, they were strongly represented even in the entourage of Kaiser Wilhelm II.

9 Native Non-German Minorities

CASES OF CONFLICT: POLES AND DANES

In 1867–71 about one-tenth of Prussia's 24 million inhabitants were Poles. Against the protest of their representatives[1] they were incorporated into the Reich, without any special rights or institutions. Bismarck regarded the Poles as a security problem because they entertained aspirations for a state of their own; in time of conflict they might support the Catholic Austria-Hungary where they enjoyed some autonomy.[2] It is, however, remarkable that Bismarck never tried to find a solution on the basis of mutual understanding.

The *Kulturkampf* law of 1872, which abolished clerical supervision over elementary schools, was mostly aimed at weakening the Polish Catholic church. And on 27 October 1873 it was decreed that all teaching in the provinces of Posen (Poznań) and West Prussia was to be exclusively in German; only religious instruction was exempt.[3] Similar decrees soon followed for East Prussia and Silesia. Seen from a Polish perspective, the schools changed from being an institution of cultural progress into an instrument of cultural oppression. And in 1876–7 German was declared the only language to be used in the courts and for administrative purposes. During the *Kulturkampf* dozens of Polish priests were forcefully evicted from office and imprisoned.

As a response, Polish activists founded educational associations, peasant unions, cooperatives, banks and gymnastic associations. This dense network was additionally stabilized by the Polish Catholic church. Culturally and economically the Poles became stronger. Bismarck resorted to force:[4] between 1885 and 1887 about 26 000 Polish immigrants from Russian Poland, who were not German citizens, were forcibly evicted. This provoked an outraged reaction throughout Germany, and the Reichstag passed a motion sharply criticizing the measures, but this could not directly influence events because they fell into the sphere of Prussian politics.

In April 1886 the Prussian government began subsidizing German settlement in the provinces of Posen and West Prussia. This implied, as the Zentrum politician Ludwig Windhorst pointed out, a breach of the principle of judicial equality of Prussian subjects, a basic principle of the Prussian constitution. The Polish community answered by founding banks which bought land and sold it to Polish small-farmers. Between 1896 and 1904 the Poles organized 36 000 new small farmsteads, with 4.5 hectares on average each; in the same period only 25 000 German settlers began cultivation (on an average 9 hectares per farmstead).[5]

After more conciliatory politics under chancellor Leo von Caprivi the Prussian course was sharpened again. The *Ostmarkenverein* organized an ultra-nationalist agitation. The police forbade many Polish meetings unless German was spoken, declaring it could not control the activities otherwise. This practice collided with basic legal principles, and on several occasions the courts revoked the police decisions. After much wrestling with the Prussian government, as a compromise the Reichstag endorsed the *Reichsvereinsgesetz* (Associations Act, 19 April 1908): the use of languages other than German in public meetings was allowed in districts where more than 60 per cent of the population were non-Germans,[6] otherwise it was forbidden.

When German was declared to be the teaching language even in religious instruction, Polish parents organized school strikes.[7] There were, however, also many tensions within the Polish community. Many peasants and workers no longer accepted their role 'as obedient foot soldiers in the nationalist army commanded by the educated and propertied classes'.[8]

In 1908 a new settlement law provided formally against indemnity for the expropriation of Polish property. It was used in only four cases, but it was a powerful symbol of an anti-Polish policy. Troops, civil servants and railway and postal employees were transferred to the eastern provinces in order to strengthen their German character.

But the Poles were supported by powerful social factors. In the course of industrialization hundreds of thousands of people migrated from the poor eastern provinces to Berlin or to the Ruhr district. It was mostly the German surplus population which was syphoned away. It was easier for Germans to move to a German town, and German rural labourers were less willing to accept the low wages in the eastern countryside. About half a million Polish seasonal workers from Russian Poland (see Chapter 10) contributed to keeping the wages down, thus inducing many Germans to leave. In addition, the Polish birth rate was higher.

This led to a seemingly paradoxical result: in the decades before 1871 the eastern provinces became more German in character.[9] But between 1890 and 1910, at the time of the harshest efforts at Germanization, in West Prussia the share of the German population declined from 64.9 to 64.5 per cent,[10] while in the province of Posen, in 1871 there were 906 000 Poles, but 1.209 million in 1905; their relative share of the population rose from 57 to 61 per cent.

The policy of Germanization destroyed the basis for a full integration of the Polish community. Some integration is, however, traceable: after the First World War a referendum was held in Upper Silesia on whether the region should be a part of the new state of Poland. On 20 March 1921, 707 000 persons voted for Germany and only 479 000 for Poland; this implied that one-third of the Polish-speaking citizens voted for Germany.[11] The high economic and educational standard, the relatively high level of judicial security, the social legislation and the Prussian tradition of local self-government made Germany attractive for a large part of the Polish community. The Poles remembered perhaps also that many German political forces (Zentrum, Social Democrats, left-wing liberals) had supported their struggle for equal rights.

At the Danish border the nationality conflict started in earnest in 1879 when Prussia and Austria jointly cancelled Article 5 in the peace treaty of Prague (1867), which stipulated a referendum in the Danish-inhabited areas.[12] The Danes envisaged a seemingly endless period under Prussian domination and reacted with outrage, while German nationalists blew the trumpet of border defence. At first the Prussian bureaucracy retained its traditional supra-nationalist attitude, but in 1888, after pressure from local nationalists, the Prussian government declared the use of German obligatory in the schools.[13] In 1891 the state gave loans to facilitate German rural colonization, and in 1912 the colonization legislation for the eastern provinces was extended to Schleswig-Holstein. The Danes organized educational societies, sent children on journeys to Denmark, printed newspapers and founded cooperatives and banks. On balance, the amount of land in Danish hands did not decline. The conflict was harshest in around 1900, when many Danes without German citizenship were expelled. The repression policy was sharply criticized by large sections of the German public and the Social Democrats supported the Danish demand for a referendum.[14]

As in the eastern provinces, in spite of the conflicts some integration took place. From 1887 onwards the (Danish) workers in Flensburg voted for the (German) Social Democrats,[15] and class became more important than ethnicity. Most Danes kept a distinct identity, but in 1914 virtually all Danish-speaking recruits in the German army were loyal. This was quite different from the situation in 1870 when there were cross-border flights *en masse*.[16]

On 10 February 1920 a referendum was held in the region north of Flensburg ('1st zone'): 74 per cent voted for Denmark.[17] It was mostly the countryside which voted in this way – the towns Abenrå, Sønderborg and Tønder voted for Germany. And on 14 March 1920 all the districts in the 2nd zone voted for Germany. In Flensburg, clearly a Danish town in 1864, only 25 per cent voted for Denmark – the end of a long decline of Danish support.

RATHER UNPROBLEMATIC COEXISTENCE: FRISIANS, MAZURIANS, KASHUBIANS, SORBS

The Frisians at the northern border[18] became partly intermingled with the German–Danish conflicts. From 1879 onwards there were some organized activities to preserve the tongue and transform it into a literary language, but the Frisian population at large was not involved.[19] In 1909 Frisian activists were to have introduced the Frisian language at a school on the Isle of Sylt, but the Prussian minister of culture intervened to prevent it as a 'dangerous' precedent for the Danes.[20] The loyalty of the Frisians towards Germany remained, however, unshaken. In 1920, 97 per cent of the Frisians on the mainland and 82 per cent on the islands voted for Germany.[21]

The Mazurians were a Slavic ethnic group of about 500 000 people living mostly in the countryside of southern East Prussia.[22] They spoke a medieval Polish dialect with many Germanisms.[23] Because of their geographical remoteness and the introduction of the Reformation in 1525, the ties between Mazurians and Polish culture had practically been cut and their attitudes were marked by a conservative, orthodox loyalty to the Prussian monarchy. After 1871 they did not regard themselves as Germans, but as Mazurian-speaking Prussians. In them some of Prussia's originally supra-national traditions survived.[24]

In contrast to the Poles, the Mazurians were not affected by the

Kulturkampf. And when in 1873 it was decreed that all teaching in Eastern Prussia had to be conducted in German, the Mazurians reacted calmly. At that time the most substantial problem in Mazurian history was the population growth and the subsequent massive migration westwards. Between 1870 and 1908 between one- and two-thirds of all newly-born Mazurians found a new home in the industrial agglomerations of the Ruhr districts, altogether perhaps 200 000 persons. Gradually the combined effects of better schooling, the coming of the railways, the closer market integration and the linkages via the Mazurians in the Ruhr area led to a constant advance of the German language. In 1836 the overwhelming majority in eight districts spoke only Mazurian, as did a substantial minority in three adjacent districts. By 1910, however, the adjacent districts were completely Germanized, in five of the eight core districts the majority had shifted to German, and only in Ortelsburg, Johannisburg and Neidenburg did the majority still speak Mazurian.[25]

The Polish national movement tried to gain ground among the Mazurians, but without success. In the Reichstag elections the maximum for a Polish nationalist candidate was 6147 votes in 1898 (2698 in 1912).[26] The Prussian authorities forbade Polish papers, brought activists to court and financed German papers, associations and Protestant civic centres, small schools and German sports associations.[27] But the failure of Polish nationalism cannot be explained by this harassment (similar measures could not stop Polonism in Posen). The Mazurian echo of Polish initiatives was simply very weak.

On 11 July 1920, under Allied supervision, a referendum was held in southern East Prussia in which 97.8 per cent voted for Germany. In the Mazurian districts the result was even more one-sided; for example, in Oletzko/Treuburg 28 625 voted for Germany, 2 for Poland, in Lötzen the result was 29 378 : 9.[28]

The Kashubians were a Slavonic minority living on the Baltic Coast west of Danzig, numbering about 130 000 in West Prussia and some further tens of thousands in neighbouring Pomerania.[29] Their language represented the last living example of the Elbe and Baltic Coast Slavs.[30] The Kashubians in West Prussia were Catholics, those in Pomerania Protestants. They lived an insular, traditional life.[31] In the nineteenth century the Kashubians produced several authors and their language developed into a 'micro literary language',[32] but it remained split into as many as 70 dialects and no common standard evolved. The Prussian school policy after 1873 led to some discontent, but not to political upheaval.

In Lusatia, southeast of Berlin, lived the Sorbs, numbering perhaps 250 000 by 1800. Like the Mazurians and Kashubians, they
were an almost exclusively agrarian population. Most Sorbs were
Protestants, but near Bautzen there was a Catholic community. The
Sorbian language was split into two dialect groups, and by the end
of the eighteenth century three standardized versions had been
established: Catholic Upper Sorbian, Protestant Upper Sorbian and
(Protestant) Lower Sorbian.[33] The language was used in the churches
and the elementary schools,[34] but there was no Sorbian literature
apart from theological texts. After 1815 the larger northern part,
with about 80 per cent of the population, belonged to Prussia while
the south remained a part of Saxony.

Economic conditions were poor and many Sorbs had to migrate.
But gradually a Sorbian middle-class and a layer of Sorbian
Bildungsbürger developed, and these groups became the bearers of
a movement of growing national consciousness.[35] In the 1840s Sorbian
intellectuals founded newspapers, developed a secular literature and
organized associations of various kinds. Another spelling system
(the fourth) was introduced, close to that of Czech and Polish, in
an attempt to 'purify' the language of German loanwords.[36]
Panslavistic ideas gave the comfort of belonging to a great family.
This did not, however, lead to political revolt. A Sorbian paper
wrote in 1848: 'The Sorbs have always been faithful to their kings
and will continue to be faithful.'[37]

The coming of the railways meant the end of isolation, and by
the 1880s brown-coal mining, iron industries and glass manufacture were well established. Ernst Muka, a Sorbian author, described
the effects: 'Zemicy and Tumicy, which were formerly small Sorbian
agricultural villages, did not begin to be Germanized until after
the founding of the Saxon-Silesian railway (about 1850), changing
gradually into industrial villages and expanding owing to the influx
of many foreigners – Germans, Italians, and Czechs.'[38]

In contrast to the Polish-speaking areas, the German authorities
did not practise a systematic policy of Germanization. One corner
of Sorbian territory was, however, part of the Prussian province of
Silesia, and in that province, as part of the anti-Polish measures,
the use of German was declared obligatory in the schools.[39] But in
the Prussian province of Brandenburg and particularly in Saxony
pupils had to learn to read and write both Sorbian and German.
The churches insisted upon religious instruction in Sorbian, in order
'to reach the pupils' hearts'. In practice, in most Saxon areas even

in 1908 the pupils in elementary schools learnt only a little German.[40] And there was no settlement policy.

The new Saxon school law in 1911 caused some polemics; it provided for teaching in both languages, but gave German priority.[41] Sorbian activists demanded equality, and in 1912 they formed the Domowina, an umbrella organization for 58 associations of various kinds.[42] In 1914, however, the Sorbs were extremely loyal; it had become traditional for many young Sorbs to serve in the Prussian and Saxon armies, and the number of Sorbs who fell in the First World War exceeded by far the figure corresponding to their share of the German population.[43]

10 Immigrants and East–West Migrants

THE TURNING OF THE MIGRATORY TIDE

During the first decades of the nineteenth century, hundreds of thousands of Germans emigrated to Russia and the Habsburg monarchy, and between 1816/17 and 1914 5.5 million Germans crossed the Atlantic.[1] In the early 1880s German overseas emigration reached its peak (857 000 persons within five years),[2] but thereafter the figures steadily declined. The German economy was creating so many jobs that emigration (not internal migration) became widely unnecessary. At the same time millions of people from eastern and southern Europe tried to find employment in Germany.

In 1871, mostly due to the population increase, the social conditions in Prussia's eastern provinces had turned extremely harsh. An eyewitness account from a Polish-speaking region reported:

> On the day of Saint Szcepan all the male farm-hands – the maid-servants the following day – who had received the *terminatka* (notice) from their peasants, gathered at the market place of the nearest town. In long rows these people were standing and timidly expecting the fate which this day would determine for them for all next year. In front of them the fine peasants went to and fro with appraising looks, to find and hire the best and strongest ones. The fear of being 'overlooked' made people bow their heads and press their lips on the backs of the hands which were held 'generously' forward, to be accepted for work.[3]

From such conditions people fled to Berlin or to the Ruhr; others worked seasonally in districts with labour-intensive agriculture such as the sugar-beet farms in Saxony. In order to keep wages down, the proprietors hired farm-labourers from Russian Poland or from Austrian Galicia where conditions were even harsher.

The influx of Polish workers ran counter to the Germanization policy. In 1885 Bismarck ordered the expulsion of 30 000 Polish immigrants (see Chapter 9), but in 1890, the Prussian government came to the conclusion: 'Police provisions are no remedy against imperative economic needs.'[4] Workers from Russian Poland were permitted to work in the four eastern provinces East Prussia, West Prussia, Posen and Silesia, in agriculture and industry, but only seasonally. Between 15 November and 1 April (later between 20 December and 1 February) they had to leave again. This provision was deliberately aimed at making the Polish workers feel like mere 'guests'. In the other Prussian provinces the seasonal workers from Russian Poland were only allowed in agriculture; the aim was to prevent agricultural migration out of the eastern provinces; people were to remain there, keeping wages low. In practice it was, however, not possible to steer migration movements so precisely, for instance because employers asked the authorities for exceptional permits.

The problems of migration and Germanization were also reflected in the citizenship law of 1913. It was based upon the principle of *jus sanguinis* ('law of the blood'): children of German parents had a *right* to German citizenship; all others could only *apply* for it. Children born of Polish seasonal workers thus had no right to German citizenship. During the deliberations in the Reichstag, the Social Democrats, the Progressive Liberals and the National Liberals advocated a law which gave foreigners a right to citizenship after two years of residence.[5] The Prussian government blocked, however, any kind of 'Polonization through the back door'.

Workers from countries such as Austria-Hungary or Italy were not obliged to leave after every season. They worked mostly in road or railway construction, canal digging, brick manufacture and mines, i.e. jobs involving heavy work and much dirt. The economist Wilhelm Stieda already saw them as a kind of 'second-rank workers, like the negroes in the American eastern states, the Chinese in California and Australia, the coolies in British West India, the Japanese in Hawaii.'[6]

For the first time, German society experienced the phenomenon of *Unterschichtung*[7] ('under-layering'): foreign workers usually find themselves at the bottom of society, in jobs which most indigenous workers do not accept. This underprivileged position is not necessarily a sign of racism, just that the differences in the qualifications and the mechanisms of the labour market can bring about this result. But racism and xenophobia usually make things worse.

In June 1907 there were 800 000 foreign workers in Germany: 441 000 in industry and 280 000 in agriculture; 211 000 industrial workers came from Austria-Hungary, 121 000 from Italy and 31 000 from the Netherlands.[8] Before the First World War the number of foreign workers had risen to 1.2 million. Leading Prussian bureaucrats had the – unrealistic – hope that the influx of foreign workers would stop the east–west migration by filling the vacancies in the west.[9] Some bureaucrats and academics feared for the 'purity of the Germanic tribes';[10] others coolly saw them as a reserve which could be quickly pushed out in times of economic slump.

Their precarious conditions forced many foreigners to be very obedient. In this respect conditions were harshest for the rural workers from Russian Poland. A poor educational record additionally contributed to the harshness of their conditions. Bishop Franz Kopp of Breslau wrote: 'When signing the contract something is often read to them which is not written in the contract; often the contracts are invalid because they have not been signed by the workers, and because there was much fraud in connection with the conclusion of the contract.'[11] The supervising personnel often committed acts of corporal ill-treatment.[12]

POLES AND MAZURIANS IN THE RUHR DISTRICT

From 1870 to 1913 employment in the Ruhr mines rose from 52 000 to 409 000; 34 per cent of the miners came from the four eastern Prussian provinces, mostly Poles and Mazurians. As German citizens they could move freely. Eight per cent came from outside Germany.[13] In 1913 there were, relatives included, between 300 000 and 350 000 Poles and 150 000 Mazurians in the Ruhr area; about one-third of them had been born there.[14] They lived in relatively compact settlements, due to the concentration of many miners in company-owned dwellings.

For those coming in, the new jobs in the Ruhr meant a social advance. But the drastic change from rural surroundings to tough industrial work in a foreign milieu entailed heavy stress; work possibilities and social connections were unstable and criminality was high. Among the Mazurians the stress led to 'hectic hyper-nervousness', which a multitude of sects and congregations tried to placate.[15]

The Poles found support in the Catholic church and associations. Polish priests moved to the Ruhr, and the Catholic church trained German priests in Polish.[16] But many German workers regarded the Poles and foreigners as competitors who pressed wages down, so xenophobic resentments flourished which often led to rows and knife-battles. In Herne in 1898 bloody riots broke out which lasted for eight days. Four people were killed and 20 severely injured; 23 young Poles were imprisoned.[17] The echoes from the anti-Polish policy in the eastern provinces made things even worse.

In 1899 the Prussian government issued a regulation that foreign workers could only be employed in mines and adjacent plants if they could understand their German supervisors; in qualified positions such as machine operators or pump attendants, only persons who could speak and read German were admitted.[18] The regulation was justified by safety arguments, but it was in fact a deliberate move to dampen the migration from the eastern provinces.[19]

From 1877 onwards the Poles in the Ruhr began to create organizations of their own,[20] mostly religious associations but also consumer cooperatives or choral, gymnastic, temperance, theatrical and educational associations. In 1912, 875 associations organized 82 000 members (including double-counting); the Poles published several periodicals and two daily papers (*Wiarus Polski* and *Narodowiec*). In 1908 a Polish trade union (ZZP) organized 41 000 miners and metal workers. Polish banks completed the picture of a densely organized Polish subculture. Contacts with the Germans outside working hours drastically declined, as at least the figures of mixed marriages suggest.[21]

Around 1900 many Polish spokesmen condemned membership of German associations and mixed marriages as a 'tomb for Catholicism and Polishness'. In 1907 the *Wiarus Polski* wrote: 'Every German is a hidden Lutheran.' The *Wiarus* also published appeals to boycott German shops.[22] It seems, however, that the very existence of Polish organizations and stable Polish communities helped the Poles to find their place in German society. Police officers observed that criminality among Poles was only half as high in quarters with Polish associations, in particular Polish trade unions.[23]

In 1893 most Poles in the Ruhr district voted for the Zentrum party, but in later elections the picture was less clear.[24] Polish activists usually nominated Polish candidates for the first round and recommended Zentrum or the Social Democrats in the decisive second round. But in 1912, irrespective of these recommendations, the Social Democrats received the bulk of the Polish votes. In the Ruhr as well, class had become more important than language or confession.

There were many signs of integration and assimilation. Again the elementary schools played an important role. In 1912, 149 school-children spoke only Mazurian but 4785 both Mazurian and German, while 26 168 children spoke only Polish but 26 022 Polish and German. The number of bilingual Polish children was increasing sharply. 'What a horrible language these figures speak!' the *Narodowiec* wrote.[25] Between 1908 and 1912 the figures of mixed marriages showed again a slow but systematic increase from 2.8 to 3.2 per cent. The corresponding Mazurian figures were significantly higher (3.8 and 5.3 per cent).[26]

In the great miner strikes of 1905 and 1912, the Polish trade union fought side by side with the Social Democratic union, a fact which considerably increased the prestige of the Polish workers among their German colleagues (and led to severe disputes with Polish representatives in Posen). The majority of the Polish and Mazurian workers were still miners, but in 1912 about 45 000 of them were already working outside the coal industry, and within the mines they were, unlike the Italians, strongly represented in the better qualified job categories.[27] The number of shop owners and other tradesmen was small (about 2000), but they also contributed to the process of social diversification.

11 Some Conclusions: Cultural Conflicts and Integration in the Kaiserreich

Between 1871 and 1914, many cultural groups were discriminated against as an authoritarian regime denied political participation to huge segments of the population. In combination with harsh social problems, this configuration was bound to produce bitter conflicts. Many members of Germany's political and military elite openly advocated an imperialist policy in order to gain economic benefits which could be used to ease internal tensions and to stabilize the position of the ruling classes;[1] substantial sections of the conservative and the liberal milieux actively agitated for such a policy. In July 1914 Berlin deliberately escalated the Sarajevo crisis which resulted in the outbreak of the First World War, and during the war Germany pursued imperialist war aims.[2]

From this perspective the Kaiserreich appears as a construction which produced internal repression and external aggression. But at the time the Kaiserreich was far from the only political system which produced imperialism – even the democratic US and parliamentary Great Britain did so. And if Berlin escalated the crisis in July 1914, it was Austria-Hungary which started the war – Berlin could not force her to do so. In an international system, characterized by multiple imperialisms, unstable balances of power and the permanent threat of potential war, it might be difficult to place the responsibility for the Great War exclusively on one side. The present author follows those many researchers who have regarded the imperfect international system with its multiple imperialisms as the *main* reason for the origin of the the Great War.

There has been an epic controversy in historiography over whether Germany followed a *Sonderweg* ('particular path'), distinct from Western Europe, or not. According to the followers of the *Sonderweg* hypothesis (for instance Hans-Ulrich Wehler), Germany came on the wrong track in 1848–9 at the latest when archaic power structures prevailed. Thereafter Germany was a strange and explosive *mélange* of modern technical elements and backward or outright feudal social and political structures, cut off from the democratic traditions of Western Europe. From this perspective Nazism was not a necessary but a very possible outcome of the *Sonderweg* tradition.

The *Sonderweg* theory has come under severe attack during recent decades, most rigorously perhaps by Geoff Eley. The Germany of the Kaiserreich was not a backward construction, but Europe's most dynamic society. Countries such as Great Britain and France contained so many archaic structural elements that it would be absurd to use them uncritically as the models of modernity. Historical research has dismantled many of the building blocks of the *Sonderweg* theory: there was, for instance, no relative deficit of an urban bourgeoisie, nor was it culturally impotent, nor had the big banks an undue power. The recently published third volume of Hans-Ulrich Wehler's monumental history of German society contains de facto his retreat from the *Sonderweg* theory and presumably marks the end of this paradigm in German historiography.[3]

In any case, the Kaiserreich can be viewed from different perspectives. To highlight repression and conflicts is one possibility, but it is also possible to underline a modern and rather stable juridical system, freedom of the press, freedom of organization, a Reichstag based on equal franchise, an efficient educational system, a pioneer role as regards social politics, a high technological level, a very dynamic economy and some remarkable successes in integration.

Germany's educational system presumably lay at the root of her economic success and also laid a strong basis for cultural integration, which again became supported by closer economic cooperation. The constitutional rights and the juridical system gave a kind of minimum protection to all groups. Neither Catholics nor Danes nor socialists, not even in times of repression, were juridically defenceless. As a rule, all groups could organize themselves and forward their aims collectively. And the regulations of the nascent welfare state gave all citizens social rights. The non-Prussian German states, many of them with a marked regional identity, had strong constitutional rights within a federal framework. All this makes processes of integration and identification with the German state understandable.

The deepest cleavage divided the socialists from the rest of society. The socialists were a very distinct cultural group, but they were

much more than that. They had the ambition to change the whole
of society and they actively threatened the world (and the privileges) of all the others. This explains why the cleavage was so deep.
Furthermore, the socialists defined themselves as part of an international community; they refused to accept national 'solidarity'
(better: obedience) as the supreme value. Whenever a group kept
cultural links across the national borders (in the case of the socialists more imaginary than real links), cultural conflicts became much
sharper than otherwise.

But in the years before 1914 the SPD had become much more
moderate, and it had come a good way out of its isolation. Its
incorporation into the regular political game was imminent. The
trade unions were strong, and the process of collective bargaining
was spreading, as were other forms of working-class representation. The process of the 'institutionalization of the class struggle',
though still incomplete, was well under way.

As to the integration of foreign workers, the picture is ambiguous. In the case of the Polish agricultural immigrants, Prussia followed an inhumane anti-integration policy. Other foreign workers
could at least stay permanently. Poles and Mazures in the Ruhr
were German citizens and had rights, but although there were many
conflicts, signs of assimilation are traceable.

The Catholics had no ambitions to alter German society. The
struggle over the school system was, however, a substantial source
of conflict where the Catholic interest of cultural reproduction and
the political interest of the state collided. Furthermore, the Catholics
had, in a very substantial way, cultural links across the national
border. The vast majority of them were law-abiding citizens, but
for most of them, at least for most of the clergy, the idea of the
nation-state was rather alien. There was material for a conflict, but
it was Bismarck's attack upon the Catholic church which for years
transformed the conflict into a bitter cultural combat. After the
end of the *Kulturkampf* the Zentrum party was able to be integrated into the political system as the political differences between
this party and the majority were much smaller than in the case of
the SPD. But the Catholics remained socially discriminated against
in many ways. Nevertheless, by 1914 the cleavage had considerably
narrowed.

The Jews were discriminated against in a positive way. The many
Jews in leading economic, political and cultural positions, many of
them in the immediate entourage of the Kaiser, and the many mixed
marriages show that the Kaiserreich offered a viable frame, not

only for the integration, but for the assimilation of the Jews. Their success provoked envy, their international character fired suspicions among nationalists, but the dominant trait of German history in the century prior to 1914 was Jewish juridical emancipation, a process which was actively backed and guaranteed by all relevant power centres and all important political parties. If the Kaiserreich had the possibility of continued political evolution without the catastophe of the First World War, anti-Semitism would never have gained political importance.

The linguistic minorities offer interesting cases of conflict and coexistence. Poles and Danes became the victims of a systematic policy of Germanization. Both had strong cultural links across the border. Other groups such as the Frisians and Sorbs were practically left in peace – for them there was no general Germanization policy. But all linguistic minorities were subject to a slow process of erosion due the intensification of schooling, and the coming of the railways and the market economy. This provoked throughout Europe a 'national revival' among these minorities. In some cases such as the Frisians, this was a purely antiquarian movement which only endeavoured to safeguard the language and old traditions. In some cases an active minority forwarded political claims, such as more teaching in the vernacular in the schools. The backbone of these movements were the educated middle classes who had a vested interest in this question.[4] In Germany the Sorbs offered an example of this kind. Every educated Sorb who wanted to occupy a qualified position had to be bilingual, whereas Germans could use their own language. Conversely, the more Sorbian was used in public functions, the better was the 'market position' of Sorbian intellectuals. And although cultural currents cannot be reduced to material interests alone, they have the best breeding grounds when they can also be used to justify material ends. Only in those cases where the state attacked the central values of the minority in question did a mass movement with separatist inclinations develop. This was the case with the Poles and Danes. But even with the Poles and Danes clear signs of integration are traceable.

In this perspective, the Kaiserreich appears as a system which had already developed many mechanisms for successful integration, and where these mechanisms were still incomplete, there were at least substantial beginnings.

It was the catastrophe of the First World War, a process of unparallelled physical, mental and institutional destruction, which brought German history onto a completely different track.

Part III
A Meltdown

In 1914 for Germany a period of disintegration and degradation began which lasted for three decades. At the end of this period stood the Holocaust and other genocides – cases of 'cultural disintegration' which in 1914 nobody would have deemed possible. In the following chapters we shall follow the steps of the process which led to industrialized genocide. Other problems of cultural conflicts will not be forgotten, but they are of minor importance. 'Process' is not to be understood in a deterministic way. At many points there were alternatives, which could have produced completely different outcomes. But as a result of various internal and external factors, the alternatives were not taken.

12 The First World War – The Primary Catastrophe of the Century

When on 1 August 1914 the authorities announced mobilization, the streets of Berlin and other cities quickly filled with jubilating crowds. Three days later the Reichstag unanimously endorsed the war credits, and Kaiser Wilhelm II said: 'I don't know parties any more, I only know Germans.' Millions of workers loyally followed the call to arms, and so did Poles and Danes. It looked as if, after decades of bitter strife, Germany was really united.

But the situation contained elements of deception: the patriotic demonstrations represented only a part of the population. Many people were deeply worried, and at the end of July hundreds of thousands had participated in Social Democratic demonstrations against the war, many of which ended in severe fights with the police. The anti-war demonstrators resigned themselves and left the streets to the war enthusiasts when war eventually broke out.

At the beginning of September 1914, on the Marne the German plans for a quick victory met with fiasco. For four years the Western Front became a continuous line of trenches, barbed wire and fortifications. Offensives moved the front only a few kilometres at the expense of ten thousands of lives. The British navy blocked Germany's overseas connections, food became scarce. In February 1915 rationing was introduced, and malnutrition and hunger spread.

By September 1916 the Prussian war ministry concluded internally 'that the greater part of the people are war-weary'.[1] In Frankfurt (May 1917) there was hope of 'an honourable peace', 'but on the other hand one does not want to continue the war for exaggerated war aims. In particular the lower segments of the population, extending far into the middle classes, reject war aims of this kind.'[2] But the government and the military leadership followed precisely those 'exaggerated war aims' which would have resulted in German domination over Europe. In public, however, the government only spoke about 'guarantees' and 'safety from further attacks'.[3] The war dragged on.

140 *A Meltdown*

In July 1917 the Social Democrats, the Zentrum and the Progressive Liberals in the Reichstag jointly passed a motion which called for a 'peace of understanding' without 'forced annexations': the longing for peace which the vast majority entertained began to gain political weight. The Reichstag resolution was ambiguously formulated,[4] but its text (and the prospect of future democratic cooperation) alarmed the chauvinist minority sufficiently to multiply their propaganda efforts for a 'German peace'. They organized a mass party, the *Vaterlandspartei*, led by Admiral v. Tirpitz and the historian Dietrich Schäfer. In 1918 the party counted 1.25 million members, mostly recruited from the conservative and liberal milieux.

The war, by sending millions of young men into the trenches and spreading hunger at home, politicized German society in a gruesome way. No one could possibly avoid considering problems of 'high politics'. Political and social antagonisms had existed before, but now they had turned into a question of life and death. Most peasants at least had access to sufficient food, but they became the victims of urban aggression and often saw their fields plundered. Many traders and industrialists profited from the war, and the rich had few problems in finding an opulent diet. In July 1918 the military authorities in Magdeburg reported: 'In the poorer layers of the population an almost pernicious hatred against the rich and the so-called war-profiteers has accumulated, and it is to be hoped that it won't come to a dreadful explosion.'[5]

Millions of war-weary workers and petty bourgeois began to see the Kaiser, the generals and the war-profiteers as the decisive barrier to peace. Strikes became frequent. In January 1918 about one million ammunition workers went on strike, demanding a peace without annexations and reparations, the release of political prisoners and an electoral reform in Prussia. Chauvinists attributed the decline of German morale to subversive elements; in their eyes socialist agitators had induced ammunition workers to strike. Older prejudices turned harsher. The Pan-German League agitated against a 'Jewish peace' and equated war-profiteers with Jews.

The war affected the four main milieux in different ways. The socialist milieu began to split. The incorporation of the SPD into the normal political game would have put the socialist milieu in any circumstances under pressure because integration and responsibility has always meant the loss of the utopian counter-culture. But in the concrete case the strain was multiplied because antimilitarism and anti-imperialism belonged to the cultural core of the socialist milieu, whereas the SPD's price for integration was the continued vote for the war credits. The SPD leadership calculated on gains in the form of constitutional reforms, not without reason, as Kaiser Wilhelm II's Easter message 1917 showed when he promised an equal franchise in Prussia. The closer cooperation with Zentrum and the Progressive Liberals increased the weight of the SPD further. And the war bureaucracy recognized the trade unions as workers' representatives, creating some possibilities for co-determination, and in 1916 exempted union officials from military recruitment.[6]

But supporting an imperialist war was a price which many socialists refused to pay. On 2 December 1914 Karl Liebknecht was the first member of the Reichstag to say 'no' to further war credits, and soon there were more. In April 1917 the opponents formed a party on their own, the Independent Social Democratic Party (USPD). The USPD organized both Social Democratic left- and right-wingers, their common denominator being opposition to the war. In 1915 Karl Liebknecht and Rosa Luxemburg founded a revolutionary nucleus (*Spartacus*). Many activists of the extreme left were imprisoned or sent to the front, at a time when leading Social Democrats were collaborating with the Kaiser and the generals. A bitter conflict opened inside the socialist milieu.

The liberal milieu also came under strain. The war-weariness of the urban masses drove the main part of its adherents to the left. But the nationalist tradition of German liberalism also provided some fertile ground for the chauvinist propaganda. The opposite movements of war-weariness and chauvinism weakened the cohesion of the liberal milieu further. In contrast, the Protestant conservative agrarian milieu became radicalized practically *in toto* – towards the right, in hatred against socialists, democrats and Jews.

Imperialism and chauvinism have never been a characteristic feature of the Catholic milieu, but in 1914 the Zentrum party was also gripped by the annexationist mania. In 1917, however, the Zentrum leaders turned sober and, while still voting for the war credits, worked behind the scenes for a peace based on compromise. It was the Zentrum leader Matthias Erzberger who took the initiative for the Reichstag peace resolution.[7] The Catholic milieu came relatively intact through the war.

The war also revived older southern German resentments against Prussia, and relationships with the national minorities became much more tense, especially in the case of the Poles. In 1914 Polish parliamentarians also voted for the war credits, but soon the war placed the question of a Polish state upon the agenda because the belligerents tried to gain Polish support. In November 1916 the German and Austrian emperors jointly proclaimed the resurrection of a new Polish kingdom (comprising, however, only the former Russian territories), and in January 1917 they conceded a Polish state council with advisory competence. In January 1918 US President Wilson incorporated the demand for a Polish state into his Fourteen Points.[8] Three months later the Prussian governor in Posen reported: 'The foundation of the kingdom of Poland and later the widely held doctrine of the people's right of self-determination made the specific Polish national sentiment rise in a way which is profoundly detrimental to German interests.'[9]

In autumn 1918 Germany's military position had turned hopeless. Most German troops were demoralized and about one million deserters were hiding somewhere in Berlin, Brussels or elsewhere. The German army was, however, still basically intact and stood deeply in Belgium when, on 3 October 1918, on pressure of the High Command, the German government sent a request for armistice to President Wilson. The High Command even advocated a partial democratization, hoping that this would soften the Allied peace terms. On 28 October 1918 the Reich officially became a parliamentary constitutional monarchy. But when it had become apparent that the Allied terms implied Germany's de facto disarmament and the political end of the Kaiser and the military leadership, the High Command demanded the continuation of the war, whatever the costs. The navy leadership gave orders to prepare a naval thrust to the Thames estuary. But the war-weary sailors hoisted the Red Flag, and the mutiny quickly spread throughout Germany. On 9 November Kaiser Wilhelm II abdicated. Two days later a German delegation signed the armistice in the forest of Compiègne.

The First World War had caused an immense destruction of life, wealth, and social stability throughout Europe. At its end the Russian empire was tormented by revolution and civil war, Austria-Hungary was breaking apart and Germany was on the brink of civil war. Even the Allied countries were profoundly shaken, particularly Italy. The Allied governments were determined to pass the bill on to Germany. Futhermore, almost all currencies were hopelessly debauched, and this implied the destruction of the international monetary system which had been a prerequisite for the dense network of international trade and cooperation upon which Europe's prosperity had depended before 1914. It was extremely difficult to repair this network.

13 The Weimar Republic

THE BIRTH OF A REPUBLIC

In November 1918 a huge coalition of sailors, soldiers, workers and middle-class people made the power structure of Imperial Germany collapse. Events placed the Social Democrats in a key position. Due to its traditional anti-militarist and oppositional stance, the SPD was the only organization left with authority. On 9 November Prince Max of Baden, the last Imperial chancellor, disregarding the formal rules, named SPD chairman Friedrich Ebert his successor.

The Social Democrats were determined to establish an orderly democracy as quickly as possible, and the provisional government decided that a National Assembly should be elected on 19 January 1919. This National Assembly was to draft a new constitution.

But many workers and soldiers were deeply discontented with the rather superficial character of the revolution. In January 1919 in Berlin, after huge protest demonstrations, left-wing groups proclaimed a general strike and called the masses to overthrow the government. The SPD-led government fell back upon volunteer units, led by former Imperial officers, which quickly suppressed the revolt. The counter-revolutionary troops murdered several prisoners, among them Rosa Luxemburg and Karl Liebknecht, the leaders of the newly-founded Communist Party. In the following weeks civil war flared up again on several occasions.

At the elections for the National Assembly on 19 January 1919, in prolongation of the basic trends of the Kaiserreich, a huge majority voted for a democratic republic. Taken together, the 'Weimar coalition', i.e. the Social Democrats, the Zentrum and the Deutsche Demokratische Partei (DDP, the former Progressive Liberals) received 76 per cent of the vote.

On 6 February the National Assembly convened in Weimar. The place of Goethe and Schiller was regarded as a worthy symbol representing a Germany of peace and culture. Three days later Friedrich Ebert was elected provisional president, and on 11 February the Social Democrat Philipp Scheidemann presented a cabinet with SPD, Zentrum and DDP ministers. The time of revolution was over.

On 14 August the new constitution, one of the most democratic in the world, came into effect: the Reichstag and all the Länder parliaments were to be elected on the basis of universal and equal franchise; the governments were responsible to the parliaments, but the president was to be elected directly. Fifty-seven articles specified a broad range of Basic Rights. The division between central power and Länder competencies basically followed the traditions of 1849 and 1871, but taxation and financial policies were considerably centralized. Juridically Prussia became one Land among others.[1]

Parallel to the constitutional democratization, Germany made further important steps on the way to the 'institutionalization of the class struggle'. 15 November 1918 the leaders of the trade unions and the industrial confederations signed an agreement; in return for union support against working-class radicalism, the employers accepted collective bargaining in all branches, arbitration agreements, workers' representations in all factories with more than 50 employees and an eight-hour working day.[2] Later, in 1925, unemployment insurance was introduced, which closed the most important gap in the *Sozialstaat*.

With the new constitution, the new regulations on the labour market and new rights for minorities, Germany had good institutional preconditions to solve the difficult integration task which lay ahead. But these institutional preconditions were not stable.

It has been quite customary among many researchers to see the Weimar Republic as a kind of still-born child. Generations of academics have deduced from the victory of Nazism in 1933 that Germany was culturally not conducive to democracy. From this perspective, neither the overwhelming electoral support for the republic in 1919 counts, nor the revolution which downed the Kaiser, nor the stable democratic vote of the vast majority of the voters at virtually all elections since 1848.

The hypothesis of a cultural mismatch between Germany and democracy is an unhistorical construction. The Weimar Republic had its burdens and insufficiencies right from the start, but it was by no means a foregone conclusion in 1919 that it would be overthrown in 1933. This was only possible because internal and external factors coincided in a fatal way.

INTERNAL AND EXTERNAL BURDENS

The anti-Republican Opposition and its Strongholds

Weimar's founding fathers made what, with the knowledge of hindsight, must be called important mistakes.[3] Instead of organizing reliable republican units, they completely left the job of restructuring the military forces to Imperial, mostly anti-democratic, officers. As a consequence, the military was not under sufficient political control. A similar omission was committed with regard to the bureaucratic key posts. The necessities of the day and popular sentiment in general forbade far-reaching economic experiments, but the possible socialization of the Ruhr mines would have neutralized the Ruhr barons – a power group with well-known autocratic propensities. Nor was anything done to reduce the economic and social power of the Prussian *Junker*. Important power centres were thereby left in the hands of anti-democratic groups. Anti-republican thoughts were also widespread in the judicial system and among the Protestant clergy.[4]

In 1919, however, public support for anti-democratic opposition on the right was modest. At the election to the National Assembly, the monarchist, anti-republican *Deutschnationale Volkspartei* (DNVP), a merger of former conservative and anti-Semite parties, gained 10 per cent; the *Deutsche Volkspartei*, basically the former National Liberals, which had at least a very cool attitude to the republic, received 4 per cent.[5]

The Germany of 1919 showed some similarities with the France of 1871: an authoritarian regime had collapsed under the impact of military defeat, a new republic was contested by a revolutionary left, and important power centres were still in the hand of the monarchist forces (which in France in the 1870s even had the majority in parliament). But after some years the French republic stabilized itself. The Weimar Republic could not. In this case, in addition to serious internal problems, powerful waves of destabilization came from the outside and interacted with internal ones.

One fatal blow came from the West.

The Non-Peace at Versailles and Reparations

When signing the armistice in November 1918, both sides explicitly agreed upon the Fourteen Points drafted by US President Wilson, supplemented with some other documents, as the basis of the peace terms. The Fourteen Points provided for the return of Alsace-Lorraine to France and for an independent Poland, which implied territorial losses for Germany. Germany also had to restore the destroyed invaded territory and to compensate for 'damage done to civilians and their property', but taken as a whole, the conditions were bearable. 'There shall be no annexations, no contributions, no punitive damages ... Self-determination is not a mere phrase. It is an imperative principle of action which statesmen will henceforth ignore at their peril',[6] as President Wilson said in Congress on 11 February 1918, and this message was part of the armistice agreement. It was under the guarantee of a Wilsonian peace that Germany signed an armistice which rendered her defenceless.

But the peace terms at Versailles did not have much in common with the armistice contract. The financial claims had been inflated about three times.[7] Germany was not treated as a country with whom the Allies wanted to make peace, but as an enemy who had to be kept suppressed. The Versailles treaty forced Germany to cede areas with about seven million inhabitants. Germany had also – in this respect she was lucky – to cede all her colonies.

Many Allied politicians wanted to make Germany pay as much as possible. In addition, the French government coolly aimed at depressing the German economy, calculating that only in this way would there be security for France. Against the background of an disorderly internal system and the fact that Germany was stronger than France, this policy was understandable. But it had dreadful effects. Germany had to hand over all property abroad and most of her mercantile marine; the shipyards had to work for the Allies for many years; the coalfields of the Saar Basin were made French property, and Germany in addition had to deliver about 25 million tons of coal annually – a systematic hit against Germany's coal basis; altogether, as finally fixed in May 1921, Germany had to pay reparations equalling 132 thousand million gold marks (£6.6 thousand million). This was approximately *thirteen times as much*, relative to the size of the economy, as France had to pay after 1871.[8] An Allied reparation commission, seated in Paris, was to supervise Germany's performance and could demand deliveries in specified commodities. John Maynard Keynes, in 1919 official representative of the British Treasury at the Paris peace negotiations, concluded: ' ... little has been overlooked which might impoverish Germany now or obstruct her development in future.'[9]

By disabling the German economy, the treaty dealt a fatal blow to the European economy as a whole. Furthermore, at the Paris peace conference no productive measure was taken to reorganize Europe's shattered network of economic cooperation. As Keynes observed: 'It is an extraordinary fact that the fundamental economic problem of a Europe starving in front of their eyes, was the one question in which it was impossible to arouse the interest of the Four. Reparation was their main excursion into the economic field, and they settled it as a problem of theology, of politics, of electoral chicane, from every point of view except that of the economic future of the states whose destiny they were handling.'[10] And: 'If we aim deliberately at the impoverishment of Central Europe, vengeance, I dare predict, will not limp.'[11]

The fact that the Allied powers first guaranteed a peace on the basis of the Fourteen Points and then imposed a 'Carthaginian Peace' was a procedure as if it was designed to deliver moral ammunition to chauvinist agitators. Furthermore, the economic provisions of the treaty fatally undermined the social stability of the Weimar Republic. What perhaps was even more important, Versailles gave arguments to the chauvinists to sell a *chauvinist interpretation of economic problems*: unemployment or the ruin of farmsteads were not just economic problems which had to be cured by economic means but the consequences of Allied policy. And since the republic was unable to organize the national fight against the Allies, it had to be downed first. This chauvinist interpretation was a gross simplification of reality, but it contained enough elements of reality to become credible to many. It was no coincidence that in 1929/30 the Nazis experienced their propaganda breakthrough in connection with the campaign against the Young agreement. This treaty, in fact, eased Germany's obligations. But it specified also that Germany had to make 37 annual payments of 2.05 thousand million marks, and thereafter 22 annual payments of 1.65 thousand million marks: financial tributes lasting up to the year 1988.

The Spectre of a Bolshevik Revolution

There was never a real danger of a Bolshevik revolution in Germany. But the January uprising in Berlin or the Councils' Republic in Munich in April and May 1919, against the background of the Russian Revolution, could make an armed revolution look like a possibility. Between 1918 and 1923, and again after the onset of

the Great Depression in 1929, the German Communists and the
leaders of the Komintern actually saw Germany at the brink of
revolution. And if the revolutionaries could misjudge the situation
so completely, it is understandable that others could do likewise.
This first had visible results in the elections of June 1920, which
were held shortly after the 'Ruhr War' when large groups of the
Ruhr proletariat formed a Red Army and carried out a military
uprising. The revolt was soon suppressed, but it drove many middle-
class and bourgeois people to the right. Parts of the former progressive
and national liberal electorate drifted to the *Deutschnationale
Volkspartei* (DNVP).[12] The USPD on the left gained 18 per cent
and the Weimar coalition (SPD, Zentrum, DDP) lost its majority –
a severe handicap to the political stability of the Weimar governments.

In 1923 the Communist Party formed a clandestine military organization which was supported by Soviet advisers. This was a new
feature in international relations: in times of peace one state systematically supporting armed movements in another country. This
was, of course, known in Germany.

After the outbreak of the Great Depression in 1929 the Communists again saw revolution as being imminent and talked of armed
rebellion; in 1931 their armed groups committed several murders
of policemen and many more acts of terrorism. The Communists
did not make Nazism, but they contributed to provide a breeding
ground for it.[13]

THE FOUR MAIN MILIEUX AND THE RISE OF NAZISM

At the beginnning of the Weimar Republic the four main milieux
showed a high degree of continuity with the Kaiserreich. The new
parties were basically old parties under new names.[14] But the many
convulsions of the time, in connection with some underlying basic
trends such as progressive urbanization and the beginnings of mass
culture, placed all four milieux under stress. Under this pressure,
the milieux proved to be of quite different character and stability.

The Catholic milieu was the most robust, and political Catholicism was a remarkably stable force. In 1920 Zentrum and *Bayerische
Volkspartei* (a new Catholic party in Bavaria) together received 18
per cent and in November 1932 15 per cent of the vote.[15] And
political Catholicism showed a considerable sense of pragmatism
and flexibility. For 13 years Zentrum was without interruption a

part of the shifting coalitions of the central government, and for 13 years Zentrum, together with the liberals, was a partner in the Social Democrat government in Prussia. There are indications that most Catholics reacted with a kind of reconfessionalization to the crisis of the time, and in the 1920s their network of associations and organizations became even more dense. The Catholic workers' associations became weaker, and so did the *Volksverein*, the biggest Catholic association of the Kaiserreich, but instead the Catholic youth movement and the numerous girls', virgins', womens' and mothers' associations experienced a substantial expansion. Never before was German Catholicism so well organized,[16] and throughout the 1920s the milieu was remarkably stable, its adherents being practically immune to Nazi ideology. There were, however, by then, after long processes of secularization, many Catholics who had no or only weak bindings to the Catholic church; many of them had inherited the centuries-old Catholic anti-Semitism, and here Nazi demagogy could be successful. Adolf Hitler and Heinrich Himmler were themselves secularized Catholics.[17]

The socialist milieu offers, with some modifications, a similar picture. The workers' sports associations counted some 120 000 members before the war; at the end of the 1920s there were 570 000, the workers' singing associations expanded from 100 000 to 230 000, and the youth organization *Naturfreunde* from 12 000 to 60 000. Many new associations were formed, such as the workers' radio association, a Social Democratic teachers' league and the like. There were some 1150 workers' libraries before 1914 and more than double that (2500) at the end of the Weimar Republic.[16] Also this predominantly urban socialist milieu proved to be remarkably stable.

Politically, however, the workers' movement split, and the Communists built up their own network, in aggressive competition with the Social Democrats. From a cultural point of view, the Communist Party, at least in its Stalinist phase, constituted something very unique, an extreme case of cultural disintegration, which should not be confounded with the working-class militancy of other decades: it was a mass party which openly declared war on the central building blocks of the social order and on parliamentarism and the rule of law: it openly proclaimed *and actively prepared* armed insurrection.[19] In practice it declared war on all other German political forces, but voluntarily, in exchange for moral and logistical support, it submitted itself to the detailed instructions of a foreign power. And it enjoyed mass support (16 per cent of the votes in

November 1932), not only among the workers, but also among sections of Germany's cultural elite. Bertolt Brecht was perhaps the most important name in this context.

The Communist Party was a symptom of the severe crisis of German society; the old order was profoundly discredited by the war, and the social conditions often were abhorrent. But the Communist Party substantially contributed to the weakening of the Weimar Republic by dividing the working-class movement and by keeping the spectre of social revolution alive.

In contrast to the socialist and Catholic milieux, the conservative and in particular the liberal milieux were fragile. The liberal milieu was already weakened when the Republic was founded. There were no liberal mass organizations – German liberalism was mostly based on informal contacts. It was already symptomatic that both the National Liberals and the Progressive Liberals did not survive the Kaiserreich; as the *Deutsche Volkspartei* (DVP) and the *Deutsche Demokratische Partei* (DDP) they were founded anew, with a high degree of personal but weakened institutional continuity. The DDP was an integral part of the Weimar coalition, whereas the DVP kept a more distant stance. Many bourgeois and petty-bourgeois circles did not regard Social Democrats and Catholics, the pariahs of the Kaiserreich, as peers, and the fact that socialists and Catholics held leading positions of power in the new state was for those circles difficult to accept.[20]

The liberal clientele, belonging mostly to the segments of the population who were economically better off, was more likely than others to be scared by the spectre of social revolution. And it was mostly these who had saved money who were brutally ruined by the hyperinflation of 1923. Inflation was basically a result of the war, but its final cause was the occupation of the Ruhr district by French troops. The French government formally justified its move by the delay of German reparation deliveries, but its real aim was again, as in 1919, the separation of the regions west of the Rhine and the reduction of Germany's economic potential. Again French policy dealt a severe jolt to German democracy.

The Great Depression of 1929 struck the final blow. Simultaneously it threatened the economic existence of millions of people, it revitalized the spectre of communist revolution, it destroyed faith in economic liberalism, and finally, first by exacerbating the divisions among the democratic parties and then by the rise of extremist votes, it crippled the functioning of German parliamentarism.

A parliamentary Germany had been the aim of liberalism for many decades. In 1918–19 such parliamentary Germany had arrived, but it was accompanied by a humiliating peace, the threat of revolution, the destruction of all savings, weak governments, and Catholics and socialists in power. The liberal political elites became profoundly discredited, and the liberal parties, which in the 1870s united most of the German electorate, practically disappeared (together taking a mere 2 per cent of the votes in 1932). The ideology of German liberalism collapsed, but two of its components, nationalism and anti-socialism, were intact and under the turmoils of the time even inflated to completely new proportions. This made the former liberal milieu one of the best areas for Nazi demagogy.

The other good hunting ground for Nazi demagogues was the Protestant agrarian conservative milieu. Agrarian conservatism already had a long tradition of authoritarian, anti-democratic campaigning and of externalizing economic problems in fighting for protective tariffs. The war meant a further politicization in nationalist terms. The abdication of the Kaiser, parliamentarization, socialists and other urban groups in power and the corresponding decline in political influence for the *Junker*, all this was perceived as one round of catastrophe and decay after another. And from about 1925 onwards, prior to the Great Depression, a merciless agrarian crisis which the Weimar governments proved incapable of curing brought the Protestant countryside to the brink of rebellion. Here the Nazis achieved their first great successes and here they found the basis for their electoral breakthrough in 1930. No other segment of German society was as vulnerable to Nazi demagogy as the Protestant countryside.

At the elections in September 1930, the National Socialist German Workers Party (NSDAP: *Nationalsozialistische Deutsche Arbeiterpartei*) rocketed out of insignificance to a level of 18 per cent. And in July 1932 the NSDAP got 37 per cent of the votes. The Nazis induced in their audiences an almost religious belief in Germany's rebirth and moral righteousness. They named enemies who had to be beaten if Germany was to be reborn: the 'system', i.e the Republic, Versailles and 'Bolshevism'. Anti-Semitism occupied a central position in the minds of Hitler and other Nazis, but in their propaganda it played a less significant role, so even well-informed observers underestimated this point. In 1932 even Paul Silverberg, a leading industrialist and Jew, advocated a government which included the Nazis.

The Nazis were vague as to the solution of concrete problems. What counted most was the symbolic arrangement: the marches in long ranks with flags, the devotion of believers, the military discipline, the brutality in combating the communists in street battles. Their energy and their simple slogans made the Nazis attractive to many who otherwise showed little interest in their ideology. A vote for the Nazis in 1932 was not a vote for the Second World War and Auschwitz.

The Nazi electorate was more diversified than that of any other party, but the borders of the socialist and particularly the Catholic milieu proved to be significant barriers to their advance. In July 1932 only 15 per cent of the Catholics voted for Hitler, but 39 per cent of the non-Catholics.[21] The industrial workers were also relatively immune. And contrary to many popular beliefs, it was the Communist Party which had results above average among unemployed workers, not the Nazis. In November 1932, only 12 per cent of unemployed workers voted for the NSDAP (27 per cent of the population on average).[22]

In those regions, for instance around Leipzig and Dresden, where the socialist milieu was well consolidated and where numerous associations organized many workers in various activities, the workers' movement could hold its position. But further south, for instance around Zwickau and Chemnitz, where the Social Democrats had previously gained impressive election results but where no proper institutionalized milieu had developed, the red strongholds collapsed.[23]

In the autumn of 1932 the Nazi movement began to decline, in November their votes falling from 37 to 33 per cent. For a while it looked as if the NSDAP would go the same way as many other heterogeneous movements with an unclear political basis before had done. A Hitler government was not a foregone conclusion. But in 1932–3 traditional power groups – the army leadership in particular – were, due to the parliamentary stalemate, in a strategic position; they calculated that they could use the Nazi movement as a kind of plebiscitarian pillar for their own anti-republican course.[24] The groups surrounding President v. Hindenburg accepted Hitler as chancellor if he could be placed in a setting of representatives of the traditional elites. On 30 January 1933 Hitler presented his government. Most ministers were conservatives, and those who made Hitler chancellor imagined that the Nazis would remain in an inferior position. This calculation proved profoundly wrong.

But before we enter the history of the Third Reich, some cultural phenomena of the Weimar Republic must be studied in more detail.

NEW UNCERTAINTIES ABOUT 'GERMANY'

Bismarck's construction of 1871 had the advantage of defining what Germany was. But in 1919 Germany's existence as one nation-state was uncertain, the borders came into flux for many years and the term 'Germany' became dangerously imprecise.

In various German regions separatist attitudes spread. When, in December 1918, the new Prussian minister of culture Adolph Hoffmann, an Independent Social Democrat, abolished all religious instruction in the schools, he prepared the way 'for a sentiment of separation of the Rhineland from the Reich in a way which is hard to overestimate', the provincial workers' and soldiers' councils reported.[25] For France, separatist currents in the Rhineland were a potential ally. In June 1919 the Prussian envoy in Karlsruhe, Baden, reported that in case of a French invasion, Baden would secede from Germany within four to six weeks. His impression was that 'Prussia, i.e. in general the northern German hegemony, is hated here in all circles to an extent which I never would have dreamt of'.[26] Also in Bavaria separatist sentiments blossomed. And in Prussia high-ranking officers and conservative politicians elaborated schemes to create a state comprising the territories east of the Elbe (a kind of Old Prussia), to blow up the bridges and fight for the preservation of the eastern provinces.[27] And in October 1923 the French government supported a separatist government in Aachen.

In the end, these separatist tendencies turned out to be weak, but in 1919 the German government had to envisage the risk that the Allies might aim at a dismemberment of Germany, and that they would find German support. This was an important argument in June 1919 when the Scheidemann government had to confront the agonizing question whether it should sign the Versailles treaty.[28]

According to the treaty, in some border districts referenda were to be held. The plebiscites on the Danish border in February and March 1920 produced a stable solution. The campaigns and the details of the border drawing fired nationalist emotions, but once the border was drawn, emotions gradually cooled down. The demands for a revision never had great practical consequences – not even Hitler took steps in that direction. Much of this successful outcome must be credited to the Danish government who asked the Allies for a referendum (not an annexation) and afterwards fully accepted the pro-German result in the southern zone. In 1920 such a policy was far from self-evident.

By contrast, the 'referendum' in Eupen-Malmédy on the Belgian border with a predominantly German population was a farce,[29] and the border drawing in the east was an extraordinarily complex process, often accompanied by gunfire when Polish nationalists tried to establish *faits accomplis*. According to the Versailles treaty, Poland received the province of Posen and most of Western Prussia without a referendum; this implied large areas with solid German majorities. Danzig was made a 'free city' and became economically incorporated into Poland. With regard to Marienwerder, southern East Prussia and Upper Silesia, the Versailles treaty provided for referenda.

At the referenda in Marienwerder and in southern East Prussia in 1920 93 per cent and 98 per cent voted for Germany. Germans and Mazurians voted practically unanimously for Germany. Many Poles did so too – in Upper Silesia about one-third. If this result can be generalized then Poland would not even have won a referendum in the province of Posen.

The referendum in Upper Silesia, on 20 March 1921, showed a majority of 60 per cent for Germany. But this did not mean that the region remained German. Instead the League of Nations decided upon a division. Poland received about three-quarters of the area, with 900 000 inhabitants and about 75 per cent of the Upper Silesian coal production. A town like Königshütte (75 per cent for Germany)[30] came to lie immediately on the Polish side. Thus, although only a minority had voted for Poland, by far the larger part of the population and the industry was assigned to Poland.

The German public, democrats and chauvinists alike, was unable to accept the new border. The question in Germany was *how* it should be revised, not whether. This introduced another element of instability into an international situation which was already shaky. This was detrimental, not least to Germany and the German minority in Poland.

In 1918 the dissolution of Austria-Hungary suddenly put the *großdeutsche* question back upon the political agenda. Before 1914 of the German-Austrian parties only the uninfluential chauvinist, anti-Semitic *Alldeutsche Partei* demanded a unification with Germany.[31] But in the autumn of 1918 all of a sudden the German

Austrians found themselves alone. As Winston S. Churchill formulated it: 'In her miserable plight Austria turned to Germany. A union with the great Teutonic mass would give Austria vitality and means of existence from which she was cut off by a circle of resentful neighbours.'[32] It was thus both rational calculation and a sentimental move when on 12 November 1918 the National Assembly unanimously declared its will for unification with Germany. And in 1921 referenda in Tirol and Salzburg resulted in majorities of almost 100 per cent for *Anschluß* (joining).[33]

The *Anschluß*-enthusiasm was, however, not so much fed by love for Germany as by lack of trust in Austria. Or can it be interpreted otherwise that, in Vorarlberg in 1919, 88 per cent voted for a unification with Switzerland? And in the same Tirol, where in 1921, 98 per cent voted for *Anschluß*, there were in 1919 strong tendencies towards independence, in the hope of avoiding the loss of Southern Tirol.[34]

No one could expect that the Allied powers would allow Germany to enlarge her territory, and in the 1920s *Anschluß* was not a German political aim. Foreign Minister Stresemann, when talking internally about long-term goals, sketched a policy which would intensify German–Austrian cooperation, but by which Austria would remain an independent state.[35] But the question had gained latent importance.

By the treaty of St Germain about 3.3 million German-speaking people in northern Bohemia (Sudeten Germans) came under Czech rule. Czechoslovakia was a democracy where the minorities could organize themselves comparatively freely.[36] The fact remained, however, that a large group of people was forced against its will under foreign domination. Unlike the Slovaks, the Sudeten Germans did not even receive a status of autonomy although they were the second largest group in Czechoslovakia. According to the numerical proportions, the new state should have been called 'Czechogermania'. And when, on 3 and 4 March 1919, many Sudeten Germans demonstrated against the treaty, Czech militia shot and killed 54 civilians, including several children.[37] Among the state officials, the Sudeten Germans were severely underrepresented, the only language in use in the central ministries was Czech, and state orders were mostly contracted with Czech enterprises.[38] In Germany the Sudeten question contributed to fire nationalist emotions, but none of the Weimar governments followed the aim of incorporation of the Sudeten area.

So, as a result of the convulsions of the First World War and the imperfect peace settlement, the cultural categories defining 'Germany' were fluid again. In 1919 there were various separatist movements and a dismemberment of Germany could have counted on some German support. The border struggles and the many blatant violations of the principle of self-determination were food for chauvinist agitators. And finally, all of a sudden the *großdeutsche* question gained new relevance.

IMMIGRANTS AND INDIGENOUS MINORITIES

Foreign immigration played only a minor role during the Weimar Republic because mass unemployment was an almost constant feature. In 1932 there were only 108 000 immigrant workers left. All in all, according to the population census in 1933, there were 757 000 foreigners living in Germany; about half of them were economically active, and 80 per cent of them indicated German as their mother tongue. When the Nazis came to power, foreign employment was a marginal phenomenon, mostly comprising workers from Czechoslovakia, Poland, Holland and Austria who had been living in Germany for a long time.[39]

But in the 1920s judicial and institutional innovations were introduced which had a long-lasting effect. In 1918 the principle of collective agreements became valid for the foreign workers too, and in 1922 the *Arbeitsnachweisgesetz* systematized the existing regulations of the German labour market. The rural proprietors could comparatively freely recruit foreign labour, but in industry the principle of *Inländerprimat* was applied: only in cases where no German applicants were available was the employment of foreigners allowed. Foreigners who since 1913 (land labourers) or 1919 (industrial workers) had been living in Germany received a general residence permit. For *new* immigrants the residence permit was restricted to a period of 12 months; the residence permit for agricultural labourers (most of them Poles) was valid only until 15 December – a reminder of the seasonal employment policy of the Kaiserreich.[40] The new regulations in general considerably eased the situation of those foreigners who were working in Germany, but it was also more difficult to come to Germany.

For the Polish and Mazurian communities in the Ruhr district the years of the Weimar Republic were decisive in many ways. The mining and steel industry underwent a critical period and the Polish and Mazurian groups were no longer rejuvenated by new blood. The Mazurians became practically completely assimilated, but the Polish community was more stable. Some Poles remigrated when Poland was reconstituted as an independent state, but in 1921 there were still between 300 000 and 400 000 Poles in the Ruhr.[41]

The Weimar constitution, Article 113, provided that the ethnic minorities had the right also to use their languages in the schools. The special legislation added, however, that this should not lead to higher expenses, so the article remained theoretical as regards the public elementary schools. But the way was now open for private schools, and in 1921 there were 92 Polish small schools where about 10 000 Polish children received additional teaching in writing and reading Polish, usually twice a week in the afternoon, in a private home or a tavern. Thereafter the number of schools declined, but in principle they continued until 1939.[42]

In 1923 huge waves of dismissals hit the Ruhr workers. Many Polish workers and their families, presumed between 50 000 and 80 000 persons,[43] followed the recruitment appeals of French and Belgian mining companies. The compact Polish settlements became dissolved and the network of Polish associations almost collapsed, but in the following years the Polish associations stabilized again, albeit at a lower numerical level. In 1929 about 150 000 Poles still lived in the Ruhr. The rapid integration of the remainder made itself perhaps even more felt than the migration losses. Those who stayed were presumably those who were most willing to accept German society.

In the eastern provinces according to the population census in 1933 there were 398 000 persons who indicated Polish or German and Polish as their mother tongue; 92 per cent of them lived in German Upper Silesia.[44] Smaller Polish communities existed in Lower Silesia, along the border of the Posen region, and in Berlin. The political atmosphere after the armed fights and referenda of 1921 was in many places very tense. Some of the Poles in Upper Silesia, presumably the most nationalist-minded, migrated to Poland. This and the progress of 'normal' Germanization led after 1921 to steadily falling numbers of voters for the Polish Catholic People's Party. At the national elections in September 1930 its electorate in the eastern provinces had fallen to 42 333 votes,[45] which represented, abstainers and persons not entitled to vote included, at most 100 000 persons – hardly a fourth of the Polish-speaking population.

Most Upper Silesian Poles spoke a dialect which was barely understandable for other Poles (*Wasserpolnisch*), and they felt much more
a regional than a national identity. As in the case of the Ruhr
Poles, their assimilation had already progressed far in the 1920s.
Again the Catholic church played an important role because it could
build a bridge over the national emotions, and it offered religious
services and instruction in both German and Polish. In Upper Silesia
the German government was obliged by treaty to provide public
schooling in Polish, but in the other regions, as in the Ruhr, the
Polish communities had to organize private schools. The demand,
however, was low. In 1927 scarcely 5 per cent of the 116 000 children in Germany with a Polish background received any kind of
instruction in Polish.[46]

In 1928 the Social Democrat-led Prussian government decided
that Polish private elementary schools could receive state subsidies
up to 60 per cent of the teachers' salaries. These schools could be
converted into public schools upon the request of the parents of at
least 40 pupils. Teachers could be hired from Poland. But the vast
majority of Polish-speaking parents met this offer with complete
apathy.

For the conservative rural Mazurians in East Prussia, the revolution and the Polish claims towards their territory were traumatic
events. The strongest party in Mazurian territory was the
Deutschnationale Volkspartei (DNVP). Practically no Mazurian had
any doubts as to which nation he/she belonged to. In this context
the fate of the Mazurians in Soldau is revealing. In 1919 their territory was transferred to Poland without a referendum. The new
administration practised a policy of systematic 'de-Germanization',
new Polish settlers were often hostile, and confessional conflicts
with the Catholic church arose. Most Mazurians left for Germany
and their figure declined from 18 000 (1920) to 6000 in 1931. During the following years the process continued: at a time when Germany was ruled by the Nazis, a Slavonic minority migrated from
Poland to Germany.[47]

In East Prussia the agrarian crisis struck particularly strongly.
As in other Protestant agrarian areas, it was the Nazis who har-
vested the grapes of wrath. The following figures show the votes
for Adolf Hitler at the presidential elections in April 1932 (percentage of people entitled to vote, non-voters and invalid votes
included) in the five districts where the Mazurian language stood
strongest:[48]

Johannisburg	47.7
Lyck	54.4
Neidenburg	51.5
Ortelsburg	51.7
Sensburg	41.5
East Prussia, average	34.7
Germany, average	30.9

In March 1933 the NSDAP received 71 and 70 per cent respectively in Neidenburg and Lyck.[49]

In Lusatia, the inferior role of the Sorbian language in the schools had already before 1914 led to some antagonisms, and the First World War also meant radicalization here. In 1919 Arnošt Bart, the leader of a newly founded Sorbian National Council, travelled to the Paris peace conference with Czech support and claimed independence, with the possibility of a future union with Czechoslovakia; the Allied powers refused to discuss it.[50] Bart had no legitimation for his move, apart from the acclaim of some meetings, but the affair contributed to poisoning German–Sorbian relations. On his return from Paris, Bart and other activists were arrested for 'preparing to commit high treason'.[51]

In 1923 the German authorities organized a special *Wendenabteilung* (Wendish, i.e. Sorbian Department) in Bautzen. It had to monitor the Sorbian press and meetings, but was instructed carefully to avoid the impression of anti-Sorbian policy as such. Sorbian activities which were politically harmless received support.[52]

The network of Sorbian organizations and associations became more dense in the 1920s,[53] but there were also sharp antagonisms among the Sorbs themselves. The Nazis were able to recruit many Sorbian agitators, mostly peasants who had been active in the *Reichslandbund*, but also teachers and Protestant priests. In May 1932 the Nazi press triumphantly wrote that they were able to establish in Guttau 'in the midst of the Wendish population a National Socialist stronghold'.[54] The votes for Hitler at the presidential elections in April 1932 were as follows (again as a percentage of people entitled to vote):[55]

Cottbus town	34.6
Cottbus, land district	43.8
Spremberg	30.5
Hoyerswerda	32.9
Rothenburg (Upper Lusatia)	34.5

Bautzen town	35.2
Bautzen, land district	35.7
Kamenz	35.0
Löbau	29.4
Germany, average	30.9

At the Northern border from about the middle of the 1920s the atmosphere calmed down.[56] In 1920 a private Danish school opened in Flensburg, and six years later the Prussian government opened the way for public contributions to Danish private schools, and for teaching in Danish at German schools, if there were at least 24 Danish-speaking children.[57] Also the districts with the highest concentration of Danish or Frisian inhabitants were good ground for Hitler. At the presidential election in April 1932 he received (in per cent of people entitled to vote):[58]

Flensburg, land district	55.7
Süd Tondern	55.2
Germany, average	30.9

The village of Viöl allows for a more specific test. Viöl constituted a Danish linguistic island northwest of Schleswig town.[59] Here, in September 1930, the votes for the NSDAP reached 52 per cent, making it the seventh best result on the local level in Germany. And in March 1933 the Nazis registered in Viöl 88 per cent: their best result ever in the whole of Germany.[60]

In a negative sense, the successes of the NSDAP document perhaps how much the members of those minorities were already integrated into German society. It was not ethnicity but their position as Protestant agrarian populations which determined their voting behaviour.

Polish, Sorbian, Danish, Lithuanian and Frisian associations formed in 1924 a common umbrella organization, the Union of the National Minorities in Germany (*Verband der Nationalen Minderheiten in Deutschland*). Up to 1928 two members of the Prussian parliament belonged to it.[61] In general the influence of the Union was weak, but it provided a common platform to present claims, and it could attract international attention to the minority problems.[62]

The participation of Frisian activists in the Union and at international minority conferences led to outraged reactions within the Frisian community: German-minded Frisians underlined that the

Frisians were a German 'tribe', not a national minority, and about 13 000 Frisians signed a corresponding proclamation.[63]

1918 FROM A MILITARIST PERSPECTIVE AND ANTI-SEMITISM IN A NEW CONTEXT

In analysing the First World War, senior officers and politicians all over the world came to the conclusion that the home front and its morale was a decisive factor in determining its outcome. According to their reasoning, in preparing for the next war much energy had to be devoted to finding devices to shatter the home front of the adversary, and to stabilize their own. These considerations came to shape the character of the next war to a large extent. In the USA and Great Britain, Generals Billy Mitchell and Hugh Trenchard advocated the organizing of long-range bombing squads to bring the war to the enemy's civilian population. In Germany, militarist thinkers concentrated on their own home front. General Erich Ludendorff wrote that during the First World War Germany's political leadership had been unable 'to collect all layers of the people into the necessary unity'; the weak nature of German politics was due to the existence of democratic parties, and during the war the democratic and Social Democratic press and their anti-militarist agitations completely fell into line with the enemy propaganda. The Social Democrats and their helpers made Germany lose the war because the Supreme Command (i.e. Ludendorff himself) could not prevail over 'the international-pacifist-defeatist part of the nation'. This defeatist part of the nation, according to Ludendorff, constituted a decisive ally for the powers who were aiming at the destruction of Germany; these powers were England, France and 'the leadership of the Jewish nation'. New wars were certainly to come.[64] Many high-ranking officers thought in similar terms. In 1924–5 Lieutenant-Colonel Werner von Fritsch, between 1934 and 1938 commander-in-chief of the army, wrote that 'Pacifists, Jews, democrats, Black-Red-Gold a[nd] Frenchmen were all the same, namely persons who want Germany's destruction.'[65]

Anti-Semitism was nothing new. But after 1918, in many chauvinist eyes, Jewish subversion was responsible for the defeat. It followed that Jews and other defeatists had to be neutralized before the next war started. And the next war would be a Total War – all of civilian society had to be shaped acccording to the needs of warfare.

It was this fusion of anti-Semitic resentment with the concept of Total War which gave these attitudes a completely new quality.

It was no coincidence that militarists and chauvinists concentrated their aversions particularly upon the Jews. The Jews were a minority with international cultural links and, therefore, in the militarist imagination, connected to the enemy. And as a matter of fact, in 1918 there *were* many Jews among the revolutionaries and 'subversives', for instance Rosa Luxemburg. German militarists and chauvinists were certainly not the only persons who have generalized from the example of some individuals to the whole group; this is still quite common today, even in the academic world. Furthermore, the Jews were a politically and culturally influential and rich minority. Among all the minorities only they, in the militarist mind, could possibly undermine German morale successfully – other minorities could not be imagined to have the means for it. On the other hand, the Jews as a minority were so small that they could be 'neutralized' without statistically weakening the German forces very much. To evict all the Catholics or all the socialist workers would cripple the German army substantially. There the militarist solution could only be to 'neutralize' the leaders. And finally, the Imperial German army was an institution which was separated from society to a great extent. No Jews had been made officers before 1914. Traditional anti-Semite stereotypes had, in these circles, much better conditions in which to survive, and therefore, after the convulsions of war and defeat, could become activated and intensified much more than in other places. And it was former officers who formed the backbone of the Nazi movement before 1933.

14 The Third Reich, the Second World War and Genocide

THE THIRD REICH, THE MAIN MILIEUX AND THE *VOLKSGEMEINSCHAFT*

The formation of Hitler's government meant an immediate boost to the morale of the Nazi movement and a severe blow to the spirit of its opponents. The Nazis gained control over strong power instruments such as the Prussian police and, for the first time, could use the radio for their propaganda. This produced a political dynamism which Hitler's conservative allies could not have imagined.

On the night of 27 February 1933, regular police and Nazi stormtroopers jointly started a merciless hunt for communists. Many non-Nazis applauded, but the destruction of the Communist Party tilted the political balance even further to the right. The next day, Hitler presented a decree of emergency which suspended most of the legal guarantees of the Weimar Constitution. His conservative allies accepted it and Hindenburg signed it. This was the 'constitutional document of the Third Reich' (Ernst Fraenkel).[1] The new elections on 5 March, which were held in an atmosphere of massive intimidation of Nazi opponents, resulted in an plebiscitarian affirmation of the new government as a whole (52 per cent of the votes), but did not produce a Nazi majority. On 23 March the Reichstag, partly out of conviction, partly out of intimidation, endorsed a bill which gave Hitler's government unrestricted power. Only the Social Democrats voted against it; the communist deputies had already been arrested or gone underground.[2] During the following months the trade unions and the SPD were forbidden and the other parties dissolved themselves. After a few months Hitler's conservative allies found themselves in a junior position.

The establishment of the Nazi dictatorship would not have been possible if the Nazis had not represented important cultural currents of the time, such as hypertrophical nationalism, anti-Bolshevism and anti-Semitism. But German culture also contained many other

163

currents of quite an opposite character. Most of the leading German authors such as Bertolt Brecht and Thomas Mann saw their books burned by the Nazis and were driven into exile. By then Germany had had a long tradition of constitutional government and rule by law, and it was certainly not in accordance with this tradition that a fanatical minority with a long criminal record was given unrestricted power, freed from constitutional and juridical limitations.

Hitler's regime followed in many fields an unsystematic or pragmatic course which often was at variance with central elements of Nazi ideology.[3] In some central aspects Nazi policy was, however, very consistent. The decisive track of their policy was a programme of large-scale rearmament and aggressive foreign policy which Hitler had already sketched in front of high-ranking officers on 3 February 1933. As to Hitler's aims, Lieutenant-General Kurt Liebmann recorded two alternatives: 'New export possibilities' or, preferably, 'conquest of new *Lebensraum* (living space) in the east and its ruthless Germanization. Certain that present econ. circumstances can only be altered by pol. power and fight.'[4] There is considerable uncertainty about Hitler's precise words and concrete aims,[5] but there is no doubt as to the systematically aggressive character of his policy. He took a new war as being unavoidable, or was at least ready to accept a high risk that his policies would lead to it.

The Nazis and the military leadership had many differences, but they were in perfect harmony as to the view that German society had to be remodelled according to the demands of a coming war, and that the deeply divided German people must be forged into a stable *Volksgemeinschaft*, unity of the people. All means had to be applied to educate the Germans according to that aim and all persons and groups which could endanger the fulfilment of this goal had to be neutralized. Colonel-General Werner v. Fritsch, between 1934 and 1938 commander-in-chief of the army, wrote in 1939: 'Final victory is only possible, as the Führer has underlined, if the *whole nation* stands internally united and firm, ready to stake everything.' And after the anti-Jewish pogrom in November 1938 he wrote:

> Soon after the war [i.e. the First World War] I came to the conclusion that three battles have to be won if Germany is to become powerful again. 1. the battle against the working class, this one Hitler has victoriously fought. 2. against the Catholic church, or rather against Ultramontanism and 3. against the Jews. We are still in the middle of these fights. And the fight against the Jews is the most burdensome one.[6]

Fritsch identified, besides the Jews (see next section), the socialist and the Catholic milieux as the main obstacles on the way to realize *Volksgemeinschaft*. Among the traditional milieux, these were relatively stable and both saw themselves not only as Germans but as part of an international community. During the first years of their dictatorship, Nazis and Gestapo concentrated their repression against the socialist milieu. Thousands of communists and Social Democrats were arrested, hundreds were murdered, all socialist organizations were smashed, all periodicals silenced, all libraries closed. Many communists courageously continued an unequal fight against the regime, and during the first years their clandestine organizations counted about 30 000 adherents, but after tremendous losses many resigned. The rest had to restrict themselves to the policy of keeping superficial contact between loosely organized groups. The Social Democrats never had the ambition of keeping a huge clandestine organization intact, but they formed, among other activities, an informal network which furnished the exiled party leadership with (usually astoundingly reliable) information. These activities could, however, not compensate for the fact that the institutional infrastructure of the socialist milieu was smashed, that it was practically impossible to educate new militants, and that the workers were almost completely exposed to the propaganda of the regime without the possibility of systematic counter-information.

The Nazi leadership was in many respects in a better position than traditional militarism to neutralize socialist internationalist thinking. As a new movement they successfully distanced themselves from traditional authorities, and they took it very seriously to create the impression that *Volksgemeinschaft* was a reality. The first of May became an official holiday, corporations like the *Deutsche Arbeitsfront* and *Kraft durch Freude* initiated noticeable improvements at the workplace and organized cheap holiday travel and numerous spare-time activities. Riding or golf courses demonstratively challenged class privileges, and Nazi propaganda systematically aimed at destroying the link between social prestige and income. The highest propaganda values were given to heroes, workers and peasants. On *Eintopf*-Sundays factory directors had pea soup together with their workers, and Goebbels did this in front of film cameras. Much of this was just show, but some initiatives had real social effects. This gave credibility to the Nazi slogan that the German people were now united in *National Socialism*.[7]

Nazi propaganda could only be so effective because it was supported by a dynamic economic recovery which considerably eased the social burdens of the working class. In 1932 there were (officially) about six million unemployed; in 1938 there was almost full employment. This boom was to some extent a normal recovery. Much, however, was due to the rearmament, which was financed by huge hidden credits: the regime was sitting on a financial bubble which in 1938 only experts worried about but which the general public was not aware of – and could not be made aware of because the Nazis controlled all legal media.

The authors of an illegal opinion survey for the SPD leadership, which presumably better reflected the attitudes within the former socialist milieu than the German people as a whole, concluded in February 1938:

> As far as it is possible at all to express the attitude of a whole people in one formula, one can roughly state the following:
> 1. Hitler has been accepted by a majority of the population in two important questions: he has created jobs and he has made Germany strong.
> 2. There is widespread discontent about the general situation, which, however, only concerns the worries of daily life and has not led until now ... to a principal opposition against the regime.
> 3. There is widespread doubt as to the durability of the regime, but as widespread is the uncertainty about what could be installed instead.
> ... – the regime has until now been unable to eradicate the impression that its rule can only be temporary. This statement is more important as to the question of the inner strength of the regime than the registration of the different fluctuations of satisfaction and dissatisfaction. And it does not contradict the observation that the political apathy of the masses is growing.[8]

The power of the Nazis was unstable, but by a combination of merciless repression and professional propaganda, supported by rapidly falling unemployment and foreign political successes, they were able politically to neutralize the 'defeatist' qualities of the socialist milieu for a crucial length of time.

The Catholic milieu was the only one which existed thoughout the Nazi dictatorship in an – albeit reduced – institutional continuity. Nazism and Catholicism were ideological adversaries, but the Nazis were not interested in a confrontation, and the Catholic church had long accumulated much experience in making arrangements with those who were in power. At the elections on 5 March 1933 the Zentrum and the *Bayerische Volkspartei* still received 14 per cent of the vote and thus exhibited again a remarkable stability. But the leaders of the Catholic clergy had reasons to see their position as being threatened. On 28 March 1933 the Catholic bishops withdrew their previous warnings against the Nazis and declared their willingness to cooperate, and on 20 June 1933 the Vatican signed a concordat with the Nazi government. The Catholic church sacrificed political Catholicism and Christian trade unions, and the Pope even accepted the principle that Catholic priests should completely abstain from political activity; in return the Nazis accepted the existence of non-political Catholic institutions.[9] Like his Italian colleague Benito Mussolini, Hitler had come to terms with the Catholic church. The arrangement stabilized the dictatorship considerably, and in central aspects of propaganda and political loyalty it opened the Catholic milieu for the Nazis. But the church and the adjacent associations, and thus a kind of institutional skeleton for the Catholic milieu, survived.

The liberal milieu was in 1933 practically pulverized as most of its adherents had deserted to the Nazis. Remnants of liberal thoughts survived in small islands in the urban bourgeoisie or at the universities, but these were completely fragmented. The Nazis – correctly – did not expect serious difficulties from that direction.

Ironically, the most serious internal threat to Nazi power came from the remnants of the conservative milieu, i.e. those groups which had brought the Nazis to power. The core of the conservative milieu proved to be more durable than liberalism. In March 1933 the *Deutschnationale Volkspartei* still received 8 per cent of the vote, and, more importantly, traditional conservative elites retained important power positions, notably in the army, higher bureaucracy and diplomacy. Most conservatives shared the Nazi contempt for democracy, and many thought in chauvinist and militarist terms, but many conservatives also retained a sense of rule by law, of order, of elementary justice. The brutality and vulgarity of many Nazis disgusted them, and Hitler's madly risky foreign policy deeply worried them. Hitler was quite aware of the danger and constantly feared a military coup, with good reason. Between 1938 and 1944 groups of senior officers on several occasions planned a coup and finally, on 20 July 1944, attempted one. The Wehrmacht, however, was no longer the traditional Prussian army but a force which in the few years since 1933 had become numerically enormously inflated, with convicted Nazis and opportunists in many leading positions. Traditional Prussian officers were but a minority with reduced power.

The four traditional milieux were not extinguished under the Nazi dictatorship, but their cohesion, in a different degree, was severely weakened. The institutional networks which had stabilized the milieux were forcefully smashed or dissolved, in particular the socialist milieu was hit by huge waves of arrests and murder, and there was no possibility of systematic counter-propaganda. Because the traditional milieux bindings were weakened, most Germans became to quite an extent individualized and incorporated into the new mass organizations of the regime. Nazi mass organizations such as the party or the *Deutsche Arbeitsfront* opened numerous new career possibilities and leading positions for previous social underdogs – during the war there were up to two million of these mini-Führers in Germany.[10] In their propaganda the Nazis could exploit tremendous real successes, internal (abolition of unemployment, re-establishment of 'order') and external. In 1936 German troops occupied the Rhineland (demilitarized according to the Versailles treaty), in March 1938 Hitler realized Austria's *Anschluß*, and in September 1938 he was able to annexe the Sudeten: breathtaking successes which 'General Unbloody' had organized without firing a single shot, just by his geniality. Many observers were deeply impressed, presumably inside and outside Germany. Hitler enjoyed a popularity like no politician had before him.

Nevertheless, his position was shaky, and he knew it. Lacking the primary legitimacy which only orderly elections could provide, he permanently had to reaffirm his power by new 'results'. The feeling that Nazi rule was only temporary was widespread, and their power was founded on a huge financial bubble which one day would burst with disastrous political consequences for them. If Hitler wanted to stay in power, an ever more risky foreign policy was the only way open for him. This way was also in perfect harmony with his social-Darwinistic ideology. But as regards exactly this point, in spite of Hitler's popularity in 1938, his ideology was completely out of touch with the German population at large. Reports by the various information agencies of the Nazi regime, by foreign observers and by German oppositionists all show this. In October 1938 during the Sudeten crisis, the Headquarters of the Armed Forces (*Oberkommando der Wehrmacht*, OKW) reported: 'Any kind of enthusiasm for military entanglements because of the Sudeten

German question does not exist. The insecurity of the political situation lies like a heavy burden upon the population . . . the mood is depressed in many places.' And two months later an OKW report said: 'Everywhere there was great tension and alarm, and everywhere the desire was expressed: if only there will be no war. This desire was particularly sharply expressed by the veterans of the World War.'[11] Hitler himself was said to be 'deeply disappointed that the German people on the brink of war reacted so completely differently than was prescribed in the National Socialist heroes' manual.'[12]

But as regards the political outcome, it did not count what the vast majority of the population thought and wished for, but what the leading group and the leading man did.

THE THIRD REICH AND THE JEWS

In January 1933 there were about 525 000 Jews in Germany. They were strongly represented in the old middle class and among academic professions such as the law or medicine. The big department stores, some sections of the metal trade, clothing/fabrics and the cattle trade were branches with a particularly high Jewish representation.[13] Their presence was in some parts very visible, and that encouraged their treatment as scapegoats.

After Hitler came to power, gangs of NSDAP members and SA troopers attacked Jews physically and smashed windows, and between 1 and 3 April 1933 the SA organized a boycott of Jewish shops. But the Nazi leaders soon intervened against such acts of open physical violence. They had to take into account the strong international reactions, and their conservative allies also protested although many of them were anti-Semites themselves. The *Deutschnationals* advocated measures such as an end to Jewish immigration or the elimination of Jewish influence in politics, but no more. Last but not least, the Nazis realized that the majority of the German population reacted negatively to such treatment.[14]

The Nazis switched to more subtle methods of discrimination. They passed a series of laws which enabled them to dismiss Jews from the public service, or to prevent them from working as lawyers, but after pressure from Hitler's conservative allies, Jewish veterans of the First World War were exempted from this discrimination. As it turned out, however, the majority of the Jews in these professional categories were just such veterans.

Other forms of legal discrimination followed.[15] Many local authorities practised a kind of silent boycott of Jewish firms, and many associations excluded Jews, from the leadership of the federation of German industry to simple card-playing associations. Some did so out of conviction, many more out of opportunism. The Jews experienced a gradual re-ghettoization.[16]

By April 1933 Jewish associations and German institutions – the Gestapo included – began to cooperate to facilitate Jewish emigration, in particular to Palestine. Up to 1939 52 000 Jews had emigrated to Palestine, taking about 140 billion marks with them.[17] But emigration was often very difficult, and most countries were by no means enthusiastic about receiving Jewish immigrants. Furthermore, the majority of the German Jews did not want to emigrate and organized instead a network of mutual aid. Many Jews were convinced that the institutionalized injustice was only a temporary phenomenon. They had had long experience of German society, and the realities of Nazi Germany did not match this experience at all. Most of them felt a deep affection for Germany. Dr Curt Elsbach, member of the leadership of the Jewish union in Germany (*Reichsvertretung der deutschen Juden*), said in 1935: 'We know only one fatherland and one native country, and that is Germany.'[18] Even in January 1942, Curt v. Bleichröder, grandson of Bismarck's private banker, was pleading with the authorities to be once again accepted as an officer in the army.[19]

Given the far-advanced assimilation of the Jews into German society, it was in many cases difficult to determine who was in fact Jewish. In 1936 the Nuremberg laws declared everyone who was descended from at least three Jewish grandparents to be a Jew; special paragraphs regulated the positions of those of mixed parentage. Sexual intercourse between Jews and Germans became a crime. Up to 1940 almost 2000 persons were sentenced under that law, though presumably many more 'crimes' of this kind were secretly committed – an indicator that personal contacts between Jews and other Germans were still at a high level.[20]

In 1938, war could break out at any time. Hitler presumably came to the conclusion that it was high time to expel the Jews as quickly as possible and a process of almost complete expropriation began. Many German businessmen enriched themselves by buying Jewish firms and property cheaply. On 28 and 29 October 1938 about 18 000 Jews with Polish citizenship were driven across the border into Poland.

On the night between 9 and 10 November 1938, SA and SS attacked synagogues and Jewish shops all over Germany. Several hundred Jews were murdered and about 30 000 wealthy Jews arrested. The British chargé d'affaires reported to the Foreign Office that he had

> not met one single German, of whatever class, who in varying measure does not, to say the least, disapprove of what has occurred. But I fear that even the outspoken condemnation of professed National Socialists or senior officers will not have any influence over the insensate gang in present control of Nazi Germany.[21]

It had no effect. In January 1939 Wilhelm Frick, the minister of the Interior, issued an order the first sentence of which reads: 'The emigration of the Jews out of Germany is to be promoted by all means.'[22] By November 1938 the number of German Jews had fallen to about 300 000. Before September 1939 another 115 000 emigrated, and a further 25 000 were able to escape before October 1941.[23] All in all about two-thirds of the German Jews emigrated.

In 1940 the SS leadership was seriously working on plans to deport all Jews to Madagascar.[24] There is not one document from that time which hints at genocide. Even Reichsführer SS Heinrich Himmler still rejected in 1940 the physical extermination of a whole people as 'un-Germanic' and 'Bolshevist'.[25]

THE THIRD REICH AND THE LINGUISTIC MINORITIES

The Nazi policy of genocide has since 1945 often obscured the fact that the linguistic minorities were basically left in peace during the first years of the Nazi dictatorship. The general state of lawlessness in Nazi Germany had a severe impact upon the linguistic minorities, but this was also true for other Germans, and the political repression was much more merciless in communist strongholds than in rural Lusatia or Mazuria. And many members of the minorities were as proud as anyone else of Germany's new strength.

The Polish-speaking communities in Silesia and in the Ruhr often became victims of harassment by local Nazi officials, but during the first years of the Third Reich there was no systematic repression. The Nazi authorities even granted a kind of special status to the Poles (and the other minorities) and let their associations and small schools continue. After the German–Polish treaty of nonaggression and friendship (January 1934), the Gestapo in the Ruhr reported that the 'general mood' of the Poles was 'serene': 'The living together of the Polish minority and the German population develops without friction'.[26] This was presumably an exaggeration. In fact, Polish representatives often complained about cases of harassment by local officials or teachers, but they were also often able successfully to ask higher administrative levels for support. On 5 November 1937 even Hitler received a Polish delegation which presented a list of complaints to him; on the same day the Polish President Mošcicki gave an audience to a representation of the German minority in Poland.[27] For a while it looked as if both states, which at that time closely cooperated on many international affairs, jointly could ease the situation of the minorities. But by the end of 1938 chicanery towards the Poles was increasing again. The Catholic clergy protested several times to Nazi dignitaries, but without success.

In September 1939, after the beginning of the war, religious services in Polish were forbidden, all Polish organizations were dissolved, their fortunes sequestered and their leading functionaries arrested. Most of them were released again in 1940, but some stayed in concentration camps until 1945. After their liberation they returned to their homes which now belonged to Poland; the representatives of the Ruhr Poles returned to Bochum and reorganized their league.[28]

For the Mazurians the first years of the Third Reich were the 'golden era'.[29] They were fully accepted members of the *Volksgemeinschaft*, and the economic recovery meant enormous relief for this remote agrarian area. The use of the Polish Mazurian language was declining after 1933, but this was the result of the 'normal' progress of German. At the population census in 1933, about 40 000 persons indicated 'Mazurian' or 'Mazurian and German' as their mother tongue.[30] In 1938 the Polish/Mazurian language was still used in 113 churches in eight districts, but at the outbreak of war in 1939 it was forbidden.[31]

The fate of the Sorbs was different in some respects. On coming to power, the Nazis arrested some leaders of Sorbian associations and some Sorbian organizations were forced to close down. But in June 1933 those arrested were released again and the umbrella organization *Domowina* and the newspapers were able to continue. Nazi officials assured the Sorbs of the 'friendly and benevolent attitude of the National Socialist leading circles towards the Wendish people', Hitler received a group of Sorbian girls in traditional dresses, and at the great peasants' events such as the *Reichsbauerntag* in Goslar, Sorbs in traditional costume were also present.[32] Sorbian cultural associations and activities, which almost came to an end during the Great Depression, blossomed again as Sorbian culture experienced a revival.

But in 1936 the Nazis gradually began to clamp down. It was presumably local authorities, notably the Wendish department in Bautzen, which took the initiative. They pressed Sorbian associations to join Nazi organizations, often with success, and the *Domowina* received an ultimatum to adopt a statute which defined it as a 'League of Wendish-speaking Germans'.[33] But the Domowina insisted upon the Slavonic character of the Sorbs. In March 1937 the Nazis forbade the *Domowina* and the Sorbian papers, all teaching in Sorbian was discontinued, and Sorbian books were removed from the school libraries.[34] About 30 Sorbian teachers were transferred to other regions. Only Catholic papers, protected by the concordat, were continued until 1939, when they were forbidden too.[35] During the war SS officials developed schemes to 'filter' the Sorbs and resettle 'elements' who could not be 'northernized' in Poland and Alsace, but 'positive' racial studies in Lusatia and the attack on the Soviet Union postponed these projects so they never materialized.[36]

On the northern border, the Danish organizations, their paper and their schools were allowed to continue; in 1935 a new school was even built. Local Nazis tried to press 'non-Danish' members out of the Danish organizations, but German nationalist activists who questioned the border were stopped by the Nazi leadership. In 1940, after the invasion of Denmark and Norway, the Nazis forced the leading editor of *Flensborg Avis*, Ernst Christiansen, out of office, but the paper continued throughout the war.[37] Seen from a Nazi point of view, between 1940 and 1945 there were few problems with Denmark and the Danish minority.

THE BEGINNING OF THE SECOND WORLD WAR, NAZI POLICY IN POLAND AND THE FIRST 'PREVENTIVE' KILLINGS

On 1 September 1939 the German army crossed the Polish border. Two days later, England and France declared war. The regional Nazi leader (*Gauleiter*) in Suebia, Karl Wahl, noted: 'Everywhere you went there was a dejected calmness, not to say depression.

The whole German people seemed to be grasped by a paralysing fright . . .'[38] All available evidence points in the same direction. No enthusiasm, no lust for conquest, just despair. But nevertheless, the overwhelming majority stayed loyal. The strong feeling of belonging to Germany made it almost unthinkable not to be loyal, even for convicted anti-Nazis and many Jews, and the idea was widespread that war was one of the eternal features of the world which had to be endured.[39] For six years an effective repression had almost completely impeded any form of counter-information. The open expression of opposition or non-conformism could only be an individual act at very high personal risk.

Right from the beginning the Second World War was characterized by atrocities against defenceless civilians on a hitherto unseen scale: Nazi policy experienced a new murderous radicalization. In September 1939 special SS and SS-led police formations, the *Einsatzgruppen*, closely followed the armies which invaded Poland. The *Einsatzgruppen* were instructed 'in enemy territory to combat any kind of anti-German elements to the rear of the fighting troops'.[40] The leaders of the *Einsatzgruppen* interpreted their instructions as a *carte blanche* and killed 'suspected' civilians, often Jews, in great numbers. Shortly afterwards the *Einsatzgruppen* were instructed to murder systematically the members of Poland's elite in order to annihilate any Polish national resistance in the future.[41] This was the first *systematic* mass murder which the Nazi leadership organized. Every one behind the German lines, then or in the future, who might have threatened the German position was 'preventively' to be exterminated.

In 1939, however, the huge majority of German society and even most senior officers were not yet willing to accept this 'philosophy'. The army leadership in many instances tried to stop the police and SS terror. Local army officers ordered their troops to load their guns and forced the police units to leave the place.[42] When a police unit murdered several Jews in Mlawa, General Georg von Küchler, commander of the 3rd Army, ordered the immediate disarming and courtmartial of the unit; when a court-martial did not sentence other SS murderers to death, but only to limited terms of imprisonment, he cancelled the sentence and ordered a new trial. General Joachim Lemelsen, commander of the 29th Division, ordered the immediate arrest and court-martialling of an SS trooper who directed the execution of Jewish civilians.[43] Colonel-General Johannes Blaskowitz, commander-in-chief of the military occupation forces, wrote in an official report: 'The opinion of the army concerning the SS and police oscillates between abomination and hatred. Every soldier feels disgust and abhorrence at these crimes which German citizens and state representatives commit in Poland.'[44]

But on 4 October 1939 Hitler issued a general amnesty for all war crimes committed in Poland, and on 17 October he abolished the army jurisdiction over SS and police units; the SS units became responsible only to SS courts. This move was of crucial importance: the SS gained almost complete independence and received its own territory in the east, almost free from supervision. Hitler had made clear where he stood. If the generals had protested jointly, the course of events might have been altered, but the most important in Hitler's immediate entourage had come to the conclusion that nothing could be done about the 'special tasks' of the SS, or they simply did not want to risk their future careers.

The protests were, however, not completely without effect. Hans Frank, Hitler's governor in rump-Poland complained some months later how 'terrible' it was for the men of his administration 'constantly to hear the voices from the propaganda ministry [!], the foreign ministry, the ministry of the interior and even the army that this was a murder regime, that we ought to stop these atrocities etc.'[45]

In October 1939 Hitler ordered that all territories which Germany had lost in 1919, plus huge areas which had never been German before, become formally incorporated into the Greater German Reich. The remaining part of Poland was transformed into a colony (*Generalgouvernement*) under Hans Frank. Hitler's ideas were simple: the annexed parts had ruthlessly to be Germanized, and the Poles in the *Generalgouvernement* should be reduced to a reservoir of cheap labour. Heinrich Himmler, the *Reichsführer SS*, became responsible for the 'strengthening of the German people' in the east.

About 7.8 million Poles and 700 000 Jews lived in the annexed territories. According to Hitler's and Himmler's plans, these people were to be evicted into the *Generalgouvernement* and the space filled with German settlers. Most of the settlers were supposed to come from the Baltic states, Bessarabia, Bukovina or Southern Tirol, and Hitler concluded a series of agreements with the states in question by which the resettlement of the Germans was regulated.

In December 1939, in the annexed territories, a series of organized evictions began. Within 17 days about 90 000 Poles, particularly from the better-off classes, were expelled from the Warthegau (the former province of Posen) and transferred into the *General-gouvernement*. Expulsions of this kind were repeated until spring 1941.[46]

Before spring 1941 about half a million Poles were expelled out of the annexed territories and 350 000 ethnic Germans resettled there. But then massive transport problems and other practical difficulties made the Nazis postpone the programme until after the war. Instead, the Nazi officials intensified the search for Germans among the Poles and began in the spring of 1941 to register every Polish citizen with some connection to the German people in so-called German People's Lists, differentiated into four degrees.[47] In practice, the criteria according to which people were put on these lists were in many cases completely arbitrary.[48]

So, at a time when the German occupation forces in Western Europe and Scandinavia showed a disciplinized conduct and the occupation authorities followed a rather pragmatic course with relatively few interferences in the internal affairs of these countries, in Poland Nazi occupation was characterized by large-scale mass murder of members of the Polish elite, by evictions of huge population groups from their home grounds, by the concentration of Jews into ghettos, by ambitious resettlement schemes and by administratively defining some groups of Polish citizens as Germans of different degree.

'OPERATION BARBAROSSA' AND THE GENOCIDES

On 31 July 1940 – France was beaten, but Great Britain still continued the war – Hitler and some senior officers held a conference near Berchtesgaden. Colonel-General Franz Halder wrote afterwards in his diary:

> England's hope is Russia and America. If belief in Russia disappears, belief in America will also disappear because Russia's disappearance will result in a gigantic revaluation of Japan in East Asia. Russia [is] England's and America's Far Eastern sword against Japan . . . But if Russia is smashed, then England's last hope is extinguished . . . Decision: in the course of this confrontation Russia must be destroyed. Spring 1941.'[49]

It is noticeable that Hitler and the generals did not seriously discuss any alternatives, for instance intensifying the warfare against

Great Britain. But a 'siege of Great Britain', as proposed by Grand-Admiral Erich Raeder, would have shifted the weight of warfare away from the army and towards the air force and navy – a dreadful prospect for the generals. From the logic of their institutional egotism, a land war against the Soviet Union was clearly to be preferred. Furthermore, an invasion of the Soviet Union fitted squarely into stereotypes of *Lebensraum im Osten*, which Hitler and leading generals had held for a long time. Perhaps the formula of 'symbiosis of calculation and dogma' (Jürgen Förster)[50] describes the decision-making process best.

If measured by the number of victims (in the Soviet Union alone perhaps 25 million people – new calculations even say 40 million – the overwhelming majority of them civilians), the assault against the Soviet Union was by far the most monstrous chapter of the Second World War. And this monstrousness was already an integral part of the planning. Hitler declared before the assault that it would result in a 'population catastrophe which will strip not only Bolshevism but also Moscovitism of its centres.'[51] Experts serving under Hermann Göring, the commander-in-chief of the air force, coolly calculated that the campaign after September 1941 could only be continued if the German army was nourished by Soviet resources; and this would 'without doubt' lead to the starvation of 'millions of people'.[52] After the extermination of the Polish elite, this was the second large-scale mass murder which Nazi planners were designing.

As it turned out, *this* mass murder did not become a reality, though the outcome was something similar. By the end of 1941, 60 per cent of the 3.3 million Soviet prisoners who had fallen into German hands were dead. Constantly undernourished, massed together in huge prison camps with abominable sanitary conditions, driven in endless marches on foot through the Russian autumn towards the German border, most Soviet prisoners died before they arrived in regular prison camps. All in all 3.3 million Soviet prisoners did not survive captivity.[53] On 31 October 1941 Hitler ordered that the Soviet prisoners were to be used in the German economy, and that they had to be nourished properly,[54] but by then it was too late for most of them.

In spring and early summer 1941, three million German soldiers and 600 000 Romanian, Hungarian and Finnish troops were concentrated on the Soviet border. This was a gigantic force, but compared with the immense spaces and the huge population of the territory to be conquered, the numerical strength of the German army was rather modest. According to the plans, after only a few weeks dozens of millions of people would be living behind the German lines. In principal neither Hitler nor the generals seemed to regard it as a great problem to rule these masses, if Bolshevism had first been neutralized. In March 1941 Hitler instructed the OKW: 'The whole area must be dissolved into states with their own governments . . . The Jewish-Bolshevist intellectual elite, being the previous suppressor, must be exterminated.'[55] Other instructions specified that the SS would be independently in charge of 'special tasks ordered by the Führer'.[56] Most generals not only tacitly accepted these regulations, they even seemed to regard the SS as a valuable support to secure their communication lines.[57]

Murdering the political elite was still basically the course which was practised in Poland. On 2 July 1941, two weeks after the beginning of the invasion, an order by SS-Obergruppenführer Reinhard Heydrich, director of the *Reichssicherheitshauptamt* and as such leader of the German police, Gestapo and *Sicherheitsdienst* (SD, an internal secret service), specified:

To be executed are all

officials of the Comintern (and likewise all communist professional politicians) . . . Jews who occupy positions in the party and the state [and] other radical elements (saboteurs, propagandists, . . ., instigators).[58]

At that point in time, 'only' the Jews in leading positions were to be executed.[59] There was, however, a guideline, issued on 17 June 1941 by Heydrich, 'not to create any obstacle to the self-purging initiatives of the anti-communist or anti-Jewish groups' in these territories[60] – in other words, to instigate pogroms.

On 22 June 1941 the 3.6 million soldiers invaded the Soviet Union. Behind them four *Einsatzgruppen*, together about 3000 men, crossed the border too. Their first massacre of Jews happened in Kaunas, Lithuania, on 24–29 June 1941. In plain daylight Lithuanian 'partisans', who collaborated with the German forces, slaughtered about 1500 male Jews, most of them with iron bars. There was presumably an agreement between *Einsatzgruppe A* and the command of the 16th Army not to interfere.[61] Other pogroms by local collaborators followed.

In August 1941 the *Einsatzgruppen* in their own 'work' seemed to have dropped all distinctions between Jews in leading positions and other Jews and murdered women and children too. EK 3, a subunit under *Einsatzgruppe A*, reported the following 'result' up to 25 November 1941: 1064 communists, 56 partisans, 653 mentally ill people, 44 Poles, 28 Russian prisoners of war, 5 gypsies, 1 Armenian – and 136 421 Jews.[62] The inclusion of all Jews was only 'logical' from Himmler's and Heydrich's point of view: in their eyes all Jews were born subversives. It is, however, still uncertain when the order to kill all Jews was issued, and who issued it. Some historians even doubt that this order ever existed. Perhaps the various murderous activities simply escalated. An insight into the question is perhaps to be found in a secret speech which Himmler made in October 1943 in front of high-ranking SS officers, and which, as far as the present author can see, has so far been overlooked in this context. Looking back Himmler said:

> The question arose: what is to be done with the women and children? I [!] have decided to find a clear solution also as to this point. I [!] thought I did not have the right to exterminate the men – that is to say, to kill them or have them killed – and to let the children take revenge on our sons and grandchildren. The hard decision had to be taken to have this people disappear from the earth.[63]

This passage was almost literally repeated in another speech.[64]

In many cases army units actively cooperated with the *Einsatzgruppen*.[65] Often such units gave logistic help, and it was often such units which concentrated the Jews in ghettos. Without this active help, or at least tacit acceptance, the genocide could not have taken place. For many, presumably for most, senior officers the words 'Jewish' and 'Bolshevist' meant the same, and the army propaganda had already been spreading this stereotype among the rank and file of the army for a long time.[66] Two years of war had had a brutalizing effect on many minds. In this respect, of quite some importance had been the British aerial bombardments of German living quarters, i.e. of the wives and children of the soldiers, which gave powerful support to the Nazi position that this was a war where traditional rules of warfare were not valid any more. However, the attitude among most German officers seems to have been a different one. In December 1941 the information officer of Army Groups Centre, Major Rudolf-Christoph v. Gersdorff, reported:

In all longer conversations with officers, without having hinted at it, I was asked about the Jewish executions. I gained the impression that the executions of Jews, prisoners and commissars is almost unanimously condemned among the officers ... The executions are regarded as an insult to the honour of the German army ... According to temperament and character of the person involved, in stronger or less strong forms, the question about the responsibility for it was raised. It is to be emphasized that the facts have become known in full, and that they are discussed among the officers at the front to a greater extent than was to be expected.[67]

But the situation was different from that in Poland. In 1939 army officers stopped or court-martialled SS troopers, now SS officers were reporting army officers who made difficulties. And most of those officers who at first were outraged about the executions seem to have decided to turn their full attention to the enemy in front of them. Some began to conspire against Hitler, for instance Captain Axel v.d. Busche, previously an ardent Hitler-believer, who in 1942 witnessed a mass murder of Jews at Dubno.[68]

At about the same time, the policy of extermination had reached its final stage. In summer 1941 – the exact date is unknown – SS Sturmbannführer Rudolf Höß, the commander of the concentration camp of Auschwitz, was told by Himmler that Auschwitz was to play a central role in the 'final solution' of the Jewish question. Höß initiated the necessary building activities, organized experimental killings with the help of Zyklon B poison gas, and from about December 1941 Auschwitz was fully operational.[69] Five similar but smaller camps were also set up. The destruction of human life, organized as an industrial process, began.

From 16 October 1941 onwards railway trains transported German Jews to the ghetto in Łodz.[70] In March 1942 the first transports from France arrived in Auschwitz, and in July 1942 the first trains with Jews left the Netherlands.[71] The industrialized killing continued for almost three years.

Many historians have wondered about the fact that huge numbers of railway carriages and personnel were used to bring Jews to Auschwitz, at a time when the German troops at the front urgently needed transport capacity. But for Himmler this was not a paradox. In October 1943 he said in front of senior SS leaders:

... we know how difficult our situation would be, if there still today in every town – under the bombing raids, under the burdens and sufferings of war – were Jews as secret saboteurs, agitators and instigators. We would presumably have arrived at the stage of the year 1916/17, if the Jews still dwelt within the body of the German people.[72]

The genocide would not have been possible without the existence of an organization such as the SS, which was able to commit any kind of crime. But the SS had first to be 'liberated' from bonds such as army jurisdiction, and the SS needed also 'free space' where it could act 'undisturbed'. The conquest of Poland provided this space. Inside Germany, with its dense network of institutions, the SS did not have this freedom of manoeuvre, as the halting of the 'Euthanasie-Programm' showed.[73]

The number of direct murderers – the *Einsatzgruppen*, the personnel of the six extermination camps – was comparatively small. But the initiators of the Holocaust had numerous helpers and could make use of a large number of German institutions, among them many army units, parts of the foreign ministry, the railroads and the police. The existence of well-established bureaucracies was therefore another condition for the Holocaust. It looks as if the routine of fulfilling instructions from above and the control of the top over career possibilities makes bureaucracies applicable to virtually every purpose.

Himmler and Eichmann also had numerous non-German helpers, for instance the Lithuanian 'partisans'. Romanian army and police units murdered about 350 000 (!) Jews in Bessarabia, Bukovina and, in cooperation with *Einsatzgruppe D*, southern Russia; French policemen arrested about 90 000 Jews and handed them over to the SS; the rapid arrest and transportation of 430 000 Hungarian Jews in 1944 was only possible because of the active collaboration of numerous Hungarian policemen and bureaucrats.[74]

The Holocaust proceeded under the cover of military secrecy, but pieces of information filtered into German society through various channels: soldiers at the Eastern Front heard about or even saw massacres by the *Einsatzgruppen*. Hitler and Himmler openly talked about the genocide in front of generals and admirals (the words were at least twice met with applause).[75] In October 1942, an internal circular of the NSDAP stated that among the population in different regions 'the "very drastic measures" against the Jews particularly in the east' were discussed. 'It is conceivable that not all Germans are able to show the necessary understanding for such measures'; all should be informed that the Jews were to be transported eastward into large camps, where they had to work, or they were to be 'transported even further eastward'.[76] In July 1943 Theophil Wurm, the bishop of Württemberg, sent a letter to Hitler protesting against further 'evacuations to the east'; those events were 'widely discussed' in Germany and 'burden the conscience and the strength of innumerable German women and men'.[77]

But the knowledge did not lead to activity. Many refused to believe what they heard, and if at the end they had to admit to themselves that what they heard was true, they might have felt as sort of accomplices, and to be treated accordingly if the Allies won the war. Up until 1941 Hitler and the Nazis were able to impress most Germans with their successes; thereafter they impressed them with the horrors of defeat.[78] In addition, the hardships of war in which many families had to get along without the father or one or more sons, and the constant threat of Allied bombings, directed their thoughts towards individual problems. Finally, the Gestapo and other agencies of the regime mercilessly clamped down on any sign of opposition or defeatism. To mention just one out of hundreds of similar cases: in February 1944 a railway worker was sentenced to death because he said in a pub that any man who would still enlist in the army was 'stupid', and that the war was being won by the communists.[79]

Efforts to sabotage the Holocaust machine could only take the form of individual initiatives. Some thousand German Jews were hidden by other Germans. This implied many thousand helpers and even more accessories. About ten thousand Jews were secretly transported to Switzerland, every one of them needing, on average, the help of at least eight Germans. Sometimes industrialists were able to save Jewish lives on various pretexts. Oscar Schindler is presumably the best-known example; Berthold Beitz, after the war director general of the Krupp concern, worked in a similar way. In Denmark in September 1943 the German embassy official Georg Ferdinand Duckwitz alerted Danish politicians to an imminent hunt for Jews, organized numerous individual visas and arranged with the German harbour commander in Copenhagen that no German patrol boat would be ready for sailing that night.[80] Many Danes helped the Jews escaping to Sweden.

The murderers themselves often complained about the difficulties which even high-ranking Nazis caused.[81] Or as Himmler put it in October 1943: 'But consider how many – even party comrades – have come to me, or to some office, with their famous petition, arguing that all Jews are swine, of course, but that so-and-so is a decent Jew who should be left alone. I would venture to suggest that the number of petitions and the number of opinions about the matter indicate a greater number of decent Jews than the nominal total of all Jews.'[82]

All in all, more than five million Jews had been murdered.[83]

SUMMARY: WHY IT HAPPENED

To few other subjects of modern history has been dedicated so much research as to the Holocaust. Nevertheless, there is no consensus in the academic world.[84] The argument put forward here is therefore only one among several interpretations. It can be summarized as follows.

Germany was by 1900 a country where the emancipation and assimilation of the Jews had progressed far. They held key posts in the German cultural and economic life and were to be found in the immediate entourage of the Kaiser; intermarriage was frequent. There was an anti-Semite current in German society, but it was not stronger than in, say, France, and it had few political consequences.

But the catastrophe of the First World War fostered a sense of radicalism, brutality and nihilism which was unseen before. Chauvinists and militarists made the Jews responsible for the defeat of 1918. These circles concluded that defeatism of all kinds had to be neutralized before the next war.

It was not inevitable that there would be a next war. In 1919 the Weimar Republic enjoyed the support of the overwhelming majority of the German population but the republic could not stabilize itself. The network of international economic cooperation, on which Europe's prosperity depended before 1914, was not re-established, and the Versailles Treaty was deliberately designed to weaken Germany. The French occupation of the Ruhr was the final straw for the hyperinflation which ruined the German middle classes, and the spectre of a Bolshevist revolution drove many people to the right. The Great Depression in 1929 was the final blow which destabilized German society so much that Nazi demagogy could produce results. But the Nazis could only come to power because some parts of the conservative elites intended to use the Nazis as a plebiscitarian pillar for their own authoritarian plans.

The Nazis followed a policy of massive rearmament and

expansionism; a new war was coolly accepted as a natural risk, or even taken as being unavoidable. The Nazi leadership was determined to neutralize all 'defeatists', and this implied the gradual eviction of the Jews.

Up to 1939 the Nazis had murdered thousands of political adversaries. This is nothing unusual for a dictatorship – the Italian fascists did the same. In autumn 1939, however, the Nazis began murdering people not because they were active adversaries, but because they fell into certain categories, in the first instance members of the Polish elite. If we categorize mass murder according to ethnic membership as 'Nazi-type' mass murder, and mass murder according to social membership as 'Stalin-type' mass murder, then Hitler began with the latter. The plans for 'Operation Barbarossa' also contained systematic 'Stalin-type' mass murders, but initially none of the 'Nazi-type'. This stage was, however, reached in August 1941. As regards Stalin, between 1941 and 1944 whole ethnic groups were deported to Siberia (Volga Germans, Finns, Chechnians, Crimean Tartars). This was not the same as sending them to the gas chamber, but given the low survival probability it came close to it. These we must call 'Nazi-type' deportations.

The Holocaust was the result of a long chain of factors and circumstances. A necessary condition for this outcome was the existence of an anti-Semite current in Germany, but authors who see German anti-Semitism as the *cause* of the Holocaust[85] confuse a necessary condition with a sufficient condition. Many more factors had to work jointly; for instance, without the Versailles Treaty there would have been no Holocaust. One of the most striking aspects of the Holocaust is precisely that it originated in a country which only three decades before had offered much better conditions for Jews than most others.

The Holocaust was a product of the Second World War. More specifically, it was the particular circumstances of 'Operation Barbarossa' with huge areas to be conquered and long lines of communication which made the Nazis cross the border to genocide. The connection between 'Operation Barbarossa' and the Holocaust was not only one of time, but of substance too.

Moreover 'Barbarossa' was the cause of several genocides. The Holocaust of the Jews was unique in the sense that it was organized as an industrial process, but the Jews were not the only victims of Nazi genocides, nor were they the first. Most victims, by far, were Slavonic.

Part IV
A Melting-Pot Modernized

15 The Integration Miracle

DIVISION AND THE RETURN TO NORMALITY

In 1945 the Allies had actually given up any plans for division: Germany was to be disarmed and placed under strict control, but kept intact. The four military occupation zones (American, British, French, Soviet) were not intended as preconfigurations of future states. As to the eastern borders no decision had at that time been reached, but by May and June of 1945 Polish and Czech militia had begun to evict the German population from the East German territories and the Sudeten. At the Potsdam Conference in July–August 1945 the eastern border was drawn along the rivers Oder and Neisse ('provisionally', until a proper peace treaty was signed), and the Western Allies consented to the principle of 'ethnic cleansing' of the former East German and Sudeten territories.[1] It was the outbreak of the Cold War between the Western Allies and the Soviet Union which led to the division of Germany. In September 1949, under Western Allied supervision, the Federal Republic of Germany was founded, and in October 1949, under Soviet control, the GDR (which will be left outside the following presentation).

West Germany's constitution, the *Grundgesetz* (Basic Law), was constructed strictly according to the principles of representative democracy: the central and the Länder governments are responsible to freely elected parliaments which also have to endorse all legislation, but there is no direct possibility of the people introducing or altering legislation through referenda. In this sense, the *Grundgesetz* is less democratic than the Weimar Constitution. Also the president is not elected directly, as was the case in the Weimar Republic, but through a representative body. And in contrast to Weimar, the president is not a powerful political actor but mainly a representative figure – the key political post is the chancellor.

In conformity with German traditions, West Germany was constructed as a federation. Important fields of legislation such as schooling became the prerogative of the Länder, which were to implement the laws; only a few administrative bodies are steered centrally. The *Bundesrat*, the representative body of the Länder, has to endorse all legislation which affects the Länder (roughly half of all legal acts), and by a two-thirds majority it can block any piece of legislation. West Germany has been considerably more federal than Weimar, due to the configuration imposed in 1948/9, when the Allies saw a decentralized power structure in particular as an insurance against dictatorship and insisted on a more federal solution.[2]

Separatism and sharp regional conflicts have been virtually absent since 1949. Due to her federal construction, West Germany has been able to balance regional conflicts much more smoothly than Italy, France or Great Britain, all of which have been troubled by regional disputes of various kinds, including terrorist separatism (as in Corsica) and strong separatist feelings over a huge region (as in Scotland).

There has been a long and often bitter debate over whether the foundation of the Federal Republic meant severing the traces in German history which produced Nazism, or whether it was basically a restoration of the old power structures and the re-establishment of continuity, which implies the danger of a new 1933.[3] The followers of the continuity interpretation point to the fact that Germany's industrial elite occupied its previous position again, that the bureaucratic personnel was to a large extent the same as under Hitler, and that most judges served under Hitler too. And as regards the population at large, many observers feared the existence of widespread anti-democratic propensities. Among others, practically a whole generation of American social scientists was convinced that the German population simply did not accept democracy's basic values.[4] In this perspective, the new German democracy was in permanent danger of being overthrown, as had happened to its Weimar predecessor.

The historical experience points in quite another direction. Ever since the local elections in the American Zone on 20 January 1946, the first democratic elections after the war, the overwhelming majority of the population has constantly voted for democratic parties. There were three short-term waves of election successes for right-wing extremists on regional levels but none of these parties ever passed the threshold of 5 per cent to be represented in the *Bundestag*, the national parliament, the NPD in 1969 coming closest (with 4.3 per cent). In many cases the *past* of persons occupying high positions gave reasons to doubt the sincerity of their democratic sentiments, but there has been no case of active anti-democratic sensibilities among the leading players in society, and there has not been a single power centre in German society which has come under the control of anti-democratic forces. Never has West German democracy been in danger – no dissolution of civil authority and the threat of a military coup as in France 1958; no penetration of the democratic state by organized crime and organized corruption as in Italy.

Many observers have attributed the stability of West German democracy to its successful economic development. Certainly the 'economic miracle' of the 1950s and 1960s contributed to the stabilizing of German institutions. But after 1973 German society again experienced mass unemployment, though this did not reinforce right-wing extremism, if compared, for instance, with the NPD in the 1960s.

Twelve years of Nazi indoctrination had left its traces, and many components of Nazi ideology were still widespread. For many Germans (including the Mazurians – see above) the years between 1933 and 1939 were the best they had experienced, and consequently, after the war many Germans had an idealized idea about the 'good years' of Nazi rule before 1939.[5] But this did not imply any sympathy for right-wing extremism. According to opinion research organized by the US military government, between 15 and 18 per cent had to be classified as 'unreconstructed Nazis'.[6] About as many were 'hard anti-Semites' (18 per cent in 1946 and 14 per cent 1948).[7] This implied that even by that time about 85 per cent were non-Nazis. During the second half of the war, Nazi propaganda had completely lost its previous fascination,[8] never to gain it again.

The mental state of the majority after the war can perhaps be labelled as confusion and delusion. They were not convinced democrats, but neither were they convinced anti-democrats. Thereby the West German democracy had already better starting conditions than the French republic in the 1870s, where the majority voted for monarchist parties. Gradually among the German majority the sceptical and confused attitude became replaced by proper democratic convictions and a decided position against right-wing extremism. In 1965, 9 per cent wished more influence for the extremist NPD, but 72 per cent were against it.[9] Since 1951 the proportion of Germans with a decidedly anti-right-wing position has grown from one-third to almost three-quarters.

None of the factors which crucially weakened the Weimar Republic were operative in West Germany. Many authors have wondered why the harsh peace conditions of 1945 did not cause political upheavals in Germany, whereas the much milder ones of Versailles did.[10] This is partly a misunderstanding. As regards the territorial aspects, the Versailles Treaty was milder, but its economic provisions were deliberately designed to obstruct the development of German society, and this under the conditions of a disrupted international economic network. By contrast, West Germany was basically left in peace, and even received aid from the American Marshall plan. The difference to the 1920s could hardly be greater. Furthermore, under American hegemony the network of international economic cooperation was repaired, to the benefit of all. And there was no danger of communist revolution. West German communism had some strength in the immediate postwar years, but the practice of Soviet occupation and the realities of the GDR quickly profoundly discredited this ideology. The Soviet Union was perceived as a threat, but this was an external menace, and the logical reaction to this perception was a strengthening of the ties to Western Europe.

In addition, West Germany had much better starting conditions than Weimar on the institutional level. Weimar was a republic which had no proper control of its armed forces, but when the West German armed forces became organized, several years after the foundation of the new republic, it happened under strict political control. Furthermore, the Prussian *Junker*, an anti-democratic power centre, no longer existed, their estates being situated in territories which, after 1945, belonged to Poland, the Soviet Union or the GDR.

In many respects, after 1945 Germany simply returned to 'normality'. This can perhaps best be explained by discussing the 'economic miracle' first. The Gross National Product in real terms (i.e. after inflation) grew as follows:[11]

1950	:	100
1950	:	157
1960	:	213
1965	:	270

No other European economy showed such dynamism at this time. By the middle of the 1960s, however, West German growth rates slowed to more 'normal' levels, i.e. rates which were nearer to those of her neighbours, or to the German rates before 1914. The reasons for the 'economic miracle' during the first two postwar decades have been the subject of much debate among economists and economic historians.[12]

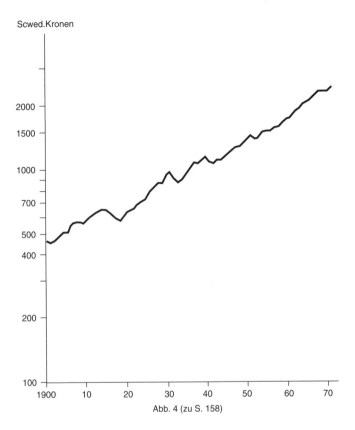

Scwed.Kronen

Abb. 4 (zu S. 158)

Figure 15.1   Real national income per inhabitant: Sweden 1900–70.

(*Source*: Borchardt, 1977: 157.)

Many factors contributed – of course – to this outcome, but the *essential* element can perhaps best be explained by the 'Theory of Reconstruction' which owes much to a book by the Hungarian economist Ferenc Jánossy.[13] His starting point was the observation that economic growth, in the long run, has been remarkably stable. For countries such as Sweden or the United States whose economies have only to a limited extent been disturbed by wars it resembles a straight line on diagrams with a logarithmic scale, such as Figure 15.1.

In those cases where wars or other severe disturbances led to a sharp decline in production (as in Germany) the economy seemed to catch up again comparatively quickly, not only to the prewar

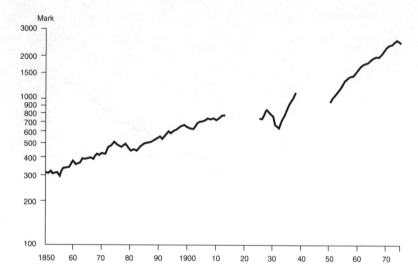

Figure 15.2   Real national income per inhabitant: German Reich and West Germany.

(*Source*: Borchardt, 1977: 147).

level, but to the point where production reaches the long-term trend line again. In the case of Germany, if one uses economic growth between 1871 and 1914 to establish a trend line of 'normal growth' and this line is extended into the twentieth century, as shown in Figure 15.2, then the West German economy after 1945, from a deep low, rapidly catches up, until it reaches 'more or less'[14] the long-term trend line at the middle of the 1960s. Thereafter it continues with 'normal' growth.

What makes long-term growth so stable? According to Jánossy, it is the qualification of the labour force, the aggregated knowledge of millions of people. To put it simply, it is usually much easier to build a new factory than to educate the workers, engineers and employees to run the factory. Because the creation of new 'human capital' is such a burdensome process, it works as a kind of 'chain' which in 'normal' times impedes any 'great leaps forward'. But after 1945, the 'chain' was loose: Germany's labour force was well-educated, and to a large extent it had the structural composition suitable for an efficient modern economy; Germany's

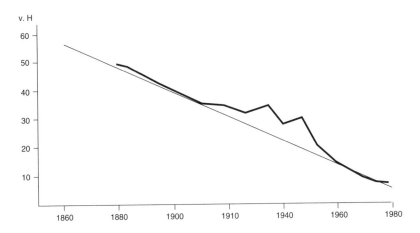

Figure 15.3 People employed in agriculture, as share of all people gainfully employed, and long-term trend: German Reich and West Germany, 1860–1977.

(*Source*: Abelshauser, 1983: 127.)

'human capital' was far ahead of the actual level of production. Therefore, exceptionally, 'supergrowth' was possible. It ended when the level of production was again so high that it corresponded to the qualifications of the labour force. Thereafter only 'normal' growth was possible.

Seen in this perspective, the 'economic miracle' after 1945 was essentially due to the same factor which explained Germany's economic success in the nineteenth century. Germany had economically surpassed Great Britain before 1914, so it is not surprising that she did so again after 1945.

Another indicator which shows the return of German society to a long-term trend line is the share of the population employed in agriculture. Over a period of many decades, this share has been falling in all countries, practically as a linear trend. In Germany, however, after the First and in particular after the Second World War, an unusually large number of people again lived in the countryside. This 'rerurization' was due to the air raids and the destruction of the towns which forced people out into the countryside. But after some years people moved back to the towns and the number of persons employed in agriculture fell rapidly – until it reached a level which corresponded to its long-term trend, as shown in Figure 15.3.

In the light of these graphs, German society experienced 'normality' before 1914 and after about 1965. The years between 1914 and 1945 were a series of profound disturbances, and the years after the Second World War until about 1965 witnessed the return to normality. 'Normality' is here defined as a point on a trend of long-term development.

Many authors who often have been categorized under the heading of 'modernization theorists' have postulated that there is a connection between the level of economic development and the political and judicial institutions, and that the liberal-democratic state is an essential element accompanying the transition from tradition to modernity.[15] The Germany of the Kaiserreich had in many respects institutions which were more modern than its Western European neighbours, and in the years before 1914 the parliamentarization of government was imminent. On average, Germany was on a trend line of 'modernization theory', and in many aspects was even more modern than her Western neighbours.[16] Since the Second World War Germany has had a high level of economic development and stable democratic and judicial institutions; in this respect she has perfectly fitted the models of modernization theory.

The transition to democratic normality would not have been so smooth if it had not been possible to build the new state upon some strong traditions which could give the political actors some points of orientation in an otherwise confusing reality. To these belonged Germany's tradition of a state ruled by law. After 1945 many were painfully aware of what could happen if one abandoned this tradition. Furthermore, from the Weimar times West Germany had inherited a huge body of qualified democratic political personnel, people who in 1933 had either been 'cleansed' out of political office by the Nazis (as happened to Konrad Adenauer, West Germany's first chancellor), sent to concentration camps (as was Kurt Schumacher, the chairman of the postwar SPD) or driven into exile (as was Erich Ollenhauer, his successor). After 1945 these people filled almost all the key political posts; those with a Nazi past were automatically disqualified for the top political positions. Only on levels which were subordinate to the democratic top, for instance among leading civil servants, were there former Nazis in significant numbers – and most of them were *former* Nazis who fell back after 1945 into a tradition of bureaucratic routine. The population at large, with few exceptions, followed the democratic elite and voted basically as they had before 1930 (the political scientist Jürgen

Falter has characterized the Bundestag election in 1949 as 'the last Reichstag election of the Weimar Republic').[17] It is not the Germany after 1945 which has been unusual, nor the Kaiserreich before 1914. It was the period in between, with its profound convulsions caused by the First World War, which was unusual.

THE END OF THE OLD *MILIEUX* AND THE 'SOCIETY OF CHANGING VALUES'

In 1945 the traditional agrarian-conservative milieu and the urban liberal milieu were practically destroyed, whereas the Catholic and the socialist milieux still showed considerable cohesion. But gradually social development made them dissolve too.

In 1950, due to the 'reruralization' and the settlement of refugees and expellees in the countryside, about a quarter of the West German population was employed in agriculture, but this was no longer a homogeneous milieu. The refugees and expellees, in rural Schleswig-Holstein 40 per cent of the population, were regarded as newcomers, if not foreigners, and the same was true as regards the town people who temporarily had moved to the countryside. Because of the influx of refugees and expellees, there was practically no local community left where the inhabitants belonged to one confession only. Furthermore, the agrarian conservative milieu had lost the *Junker*, and thereby its social top and influential political representation near the German power centres. And last but not least, nationalism was profoundly discredited and could no longer fulfil its previous role as an ideological integrator. Anti-democratic sentiments were still widespread in the countryside during the 1950s, but they did not become concentrated into a milieu of compact political opposition as in the 1920s. Instead, the overwhelming majority of the peasants gradually rallied behind the Christian Democrats.

In the 1950s the share of the agrarian population was rapidly declining. The peasants became quite effective as regards lobbying for their economic interests, but this could not prevent the continuous decline of their sector. In the 1980s, when the share of the agrarian population fell below 4 per cent, researchers encountered 'passive resignation' and a 'consciousness of belonging to a dying culture' in the countryside.[18]

In 1945–6 liberal politicians began reorganizing political liberalism, and after some effort, in 1948 were able to found a united liberal party, the *Freie Demokratische Partei* (FDP). They were able to build upon the fragments of the traditional urban bourgeois-liberal milieu, and in some respects they were remarkably successful. Throughout the history of West Germany the FDP has been a political factor of importance, and it has had a stable electoral base in the segments of the urban population who were economically better off. In this sense the FDP became again an almost classical milieu party. But the FDP came to represent only a segment of the urban bourgeois population, and political and economic liberalism have become broad currents which are firmly represented in the other parties too. The FDP has been in many respects more a kind of economic lobby for wealthier people who are tired of high taxes than a political liberal force. As a rather homogeneous milieu with marked borders against other milieux, the urban-liberal milieu had already ceased to exist in the postwar years.

The socialist and the Catholic milieux, however, still enjoyed a considerable cohesion after the war. The Catholic church (and the charity organization Caritas) provided an institutional backbone of unbroken continuity through the time of Nazism, and in the late 1940s and early 1950s the previous dense network of associations became almost completely reconstructed.[19] Ideologically, Catholicism became strengthened at that time because the mental jolts of Nazism and defeat made many previously lukewarm adherents once again believers, and the church had no problems in explaining the catastrophe as the result of missing obedience to God. Of all Catholics 55 per cent went regularly to service in 1963; in 1958 800 000 believers participated at the final manifestation of the Catholic lay convention in Cologne. The Christian Democrats were seen as the authentic representation of the Catholic milieu (61 per cent of the Catholics voted for them in 1957). Never were Catholics able to identify so much with a German state as in the 1950s when the chancellor, many ministers and many deputy ministers had close ties to the Catholic milieu, when the capital was not the distant and Protestant Berlin but Catholic Bonn, and when Catholics were no longer a minority but quite exactly half the population.

In the 1960s, however, signs of massive erosion became apparent.[20] This was partly the result of success: the Catholics no longer had a real enemy. Furthermore, the massive expansion of education in those years contributed to open the minds to secular values, the electronic media reached the villages, and the beginning of the sexual revolution dealt an almost mortal blow to the authority of the Pope. Between 1967 and 1973 the share of regular churchgoers among the Catholics fell dramatically from 55 to 35 per cent, a trend which, after a temporary stabilization, continued in the 1980s. And figures of intermarriage between Catholics and Protestants rose significantly. However, in the 1990s German Catholicism could still mobilize some political strength, for instance in the debate about abortion, but as a closed milieu it exists at best in a few pockets.

In 1945 the Social Democrat working-class milieu was more damaged than the Catholic. Not one socialist institution could continue between 1933 and 1945, no systematic ideological work could be organized, and for 12 years the induction of new militants had been practically impossible. But nevertheless, in 1945 the SPD became reorganized as the traditional working-class milieu party, and retained this character of milieu party until the end of the 1950s. Many milieu associations, such as the youth organizations *Falken* and *Naturfreunde*, many choirs and the *Arbeitersamariter*, a kind of socialist Red Cross, were also refounded.[21] The socialist network, however, did not regain the same strength as before 1933; there were, for instance, no longer many workers' sports associations.

During the 1950s the class divide lost most of its previous sharpness, strikes became a rare phenomenon and the rapid improvement in the standard of living worked, in relative terms at least, as a leveller of social differences. Furthermore, the Cold War and the profoundly discrediting effect which the GDR exerted over socialist symbols such as the Red Flag or Marxist rhetoric, caused severe semiotic difficulties for the traditional milieu. The SPD could enlarge its electoral basis and attract sections of the urban middle classes, but this implied again an ideological dilution. Electronic media and commercial mass culture began to have a substantial impact on the working class. Furthermore, by the 1960s many traditional industries such as the shipyards, steel plants and the coal mines in the Ruhr and Saar had reduced their workforce, and this process led to the dissolution of many traditional working-class communities; after 1970 even the general share of people employed in industry began to shrink (from a maximum level of 48 per cent).[22] Germany began to move out of industrial society.

The working class shrank and changed character. In the 1960s most Germans belonged to families where the breadwinners were unqualified or semi-qualified labourers; in the 1980s the members of the un- or semi-qualified fell to 16 per cent.[23] The general level of qualification has risen considerably, a fact which has brought workers closer to other urban groups. But the un- and semi-qualified have come under severe stress. They have the highest unemployment risk, and practically not one is to be found among the political elite, not even among the leadership of the unions. And it is they who have experienced the influx of immigrants as massive competition (see below). Not surprisingly, in the 1980s and 1990s xenophobic parties were able to register remarkable successes in rundown working-class areas which previously were red strongholds. At the end of the 1980s, the socialist milieu also existed only in small pockets.

By the 1950s, when the Catholic and socialist milieux were still in existence, their borders had mostly lost their character as politicized cleavages.

In contrast to the Zentrum, the Christian Democrats were founded in 1946 as an inter-confessional party (which in practice, however, during the first years was primarily based upon the Catholic milieu). After the catastrophe, no one among the German elite was interested in politicizing the confessional gap again. Instead the party founders aligned themselves along the divide between Christian religion and secularization. In fact, in 1953 the CDU gained a clear majority among those Protestants who had a church affiliation.[24] But the CDU was not only a Christian party, but also a kind of bourgeois catch-all party to the right of the Social Democrats. In that respect, the results in the 1950s were uneven. The CDU seemed to be particularly attractive in those regions where Bismarck's solutions of 1866–70 had been met with reluctance, if not severe protest, i.e. the Catholic regions, Hanover, and Schleswig-Holstein.[25]

Furthermore, the CDU incorporated the traditions of Christian trade unionism. Therefore, in Bonn ever since 1949 trade union representatives have held important ministries. And the unions themselves merged in 1948 into large, non-partisan organizations each covering whole branches of industry, and which are united under one umbrella organization. The unions have had a strong position on the labour market, they have organized collective bargaining which has effectively regulated industrial relations, they have been represented on the boards of all bigger companies, and they have had an important voice in political decision-making. The class struggle has become effectively institutionalized.

Most trade union leaders have been Social Democrats, but the Christian Democrats have not been a negligible force. Because of the character both of the unions and the CDU, the class divide has only to a limited extent become translated into the political sphere. There has not been one party which is *the* union party, and the CDU has not been anti-union. These structural features of unions and parties substantially contributed to the de-ideologizing of the union question and the class divide in general. As to industrial relations, postwar Germany has had a more flexible political system than Great Britain. Ironically, the West German trade union structure was to a great extent the result of the intervention of the British military government.[26]

Academic researchers agree that the traditional four milieux are gone, but there is no consensus as to what characterizes modern German society after their demise. In the 1980s the cultural picture of West Germany was highly complex and sociologists talked of *Neue Unübersichtlichkeit*, perhaps best translated by New Confusion. The only constant feature is that values have been changing, so some use the term *Wertewandelgesellschaft*, a society of changing values.

According to the present author, the following 'soft' cultural divides can best be used to structure the picture. First, the difference between Protestants and Catholics has not disappeared completely, even among those who are not religious believers. In 1992 about 84 per cent of the population declared themselves to be either Protestant or Catholic[27] and therefore felt themselves as part of those communities. Religious convictions are still an important cultural factor: 56 per cent believe in God, a further 17 per cent in a Higher Being.[28] Negative stereotypes as regards other confessions are still quite widespread,[29] and although intermarriage has become frequent, statistically there is still a barrier. And the confessional divide is still a factor which strongly influences voting behaviour; in 1987, 59 per cent of the CDU voters were Catholics and 'only' 37 per cent Protestants; by contrast, 56 per cent of those who voted for the SPD were Protestants and 37 per cent Catholics.[30]

If religious convictions are measured by the activity of the persons in question, then Germany has largely become a secular society. Only 12 per cent declared in 1992 that they went to church at least once a month. In particular, Catholic churchgoers are the most faithful CDU voters, and there the resistance against abortion is strongest, there the bishops have authority. The border between secularization and church loyalty has therefore been another important cultural divide. In East Germany the process of secularization has been almost completed.

A third divide which has been progressing through West German society has been the border between 'materialists' and 'post-materialists'. According to Ronald Inglehart who introduced these categories, Western societies exhibit a general trend: the more basic material needs are fulfilled, the more important become post-material values such as protection of the ecological environment. At a given point in time people with higher education and higher incomes show significantly stronger attachment to post-materialist values than low-paid workers – their basic material needs are fulfilled. According to surveys, in 1990 most West Germans were post-materialists (56 per cent, as opposed to 41 per cent 'materialists'), whereas most East Germans, who lived under harder economic conditions, still adhered to materialist values (62 to 41 per cent).[31] The rise of the Greens has partly translated the divide between materialist and post-materialist into the party structure.

As a subgroup of the 'materialists', the defensive milieu of the un- and semi-qualified workers can be discerned. They are discriminated against in many ways (high unemployment risk, no representation at the political top, high criminality risk), and here, more precisely in the unqualified groups with no church loyalty, xenophobic aggression has been widespread. And it has been xenophobia which has produced the harshest incidents of cultural conflict in German history since 1945 (see below).

The cultural divides of Protestant–Catholic, secularization–church loyalty, materialism–post-materialism and unqualified–qualified separate new milieux. These milieux are, however, soft – they are no longer separated by stable political cleavages, and therefore are of a weaker quality than the four traditional milieux. We can say the borders between the old milieux have melted.

EXPELLEES AND REFUGEES

West Germany has been a stable society, although she has had to integrate huge waves of immigrants. The first were the refugees and expellees from the former eastern German territories and the Sudeten area. West Germany had to integrate about eight million, the GDR four million. Many had endless traumatic experiences behind them.[32] Including those civilians who were killed by Red Army soldiers (not as a result of combat, but in revenge acts and other atrocities); including those who succumbed while being deported to labour camps in the Soviet Union; including those who died during the flight in front of the Red Army; including those civilians who did not survive the many months of internment in overcrowded former POW-camps or former Nazi concentration camps; including those who were murdered during the expulsions; and finally including those who died during transport, for instance in open railway carriages without proper food, calculation of the number of deaths range between 1.8 and 2.4 million.[33] This was Europe's largest 'ethnic cleansing' so far.

In the immediate postwar years, Allied occupation officers and German politicians were deeply worried about the political risks which the expellees might represent because they seemed to form an almost natural basis for a revival of revanchism. But the integration happened with astounding smoothness.

After their arrival, the expellees had to be distributed throughout the countryside. As a consequence, the Länder which were mostly agrarian in character bore the brunt of the integration. Bavaria received most, followed by Niedersachsen and Schleswig-Holstein. In relative terms Mecklenburg-Vorpommern in the Soviet zone carried the heaviest burden, with 869 000 expellees in 1946, or 41 per cent of the population.[34] Under the special postwar conditions when many vital items were rationed and when money (and thus salaries) were of little importance, surprisingly many expellees were able to find a job. But when after the currency reform in July 1948 money became important again, many were sacked. In February 1950 in Bavaria only 472 000 refugees and expellees had a job; 201 000 were unemployed.[35]

In summer 1948 the Western Allies instructed German politicians to elaborate a scheme of burden-sharing between the indigenous population and the migrants. In November 1948 the CDU/CSU and SPD jointly passed a provisional law (*Soforthilfegesetz*, in effect from August 1949), which granted a monthly payment of 70 DM to the refugees and expellees.[36] This was no more than they had received before in social assistance, but the law represented an important psychological change: they no longer depended on charity but now had a legal right. The payment was supplemented by grants for furniture, house building, education and starting their own businesses.

On 16 May 1952, after tough political controversies with expellee representatives, the West German parliament passed the *Lastenausgleich* (burden-sharing) legislation.[37] The refugees and expellees were granted a so-called 'main compensation' for lost property, which varied between 95 per cent (losses up to 5000 DM) and 6.5 per cent (losses above one million DM). This restitution was supplemented by special compensation for pieces of furniture and lost savings accounts. To old people and people unable to work who could not document the loss of property, a monthly payment was granted. The legislation also opened up the possibility of special housing grants and credits.

The burden sharing was financed by a special tax upon the remaining fortunes in West Germany (in general 50 per cent, on agricultural fortunes 25 per cent) as they had been fixed in July 1948.[38] The tax was distributed over a period of 30 years. Much additional legislation was necessary to regulate details. By 1979 about 22 per cent of the property lost had been restored; up to the average loss (4800 DM) the restitution was complete.[39]

The *Lastenausgleich* and other social legislation substantially eased the entry of the refugees and expellees into West German society, but the most important integrative agent was the economic recovery. By the late 1950s unemployment among expellees had fallen to the average level among the West German population as a whole. The most important step to social integration had been taken. In 1971, however, the expellees were still in some respects socially discriminated against. For instance, of those expellees who were unemployed in 1950, 45 per cent were by 1971 occupied in unskilled jobs while the corresponding figure among the indigenous population was 37 per cent; 52 per cent of the expellee pensioners earned less than 600 DM a month (indigenous pensioners 41 per cent).[40] The influx of the expellees had meant a process of *Unterschichtung* which in 1971 was still traceable.

As regards the process of political integration, the party *Bund der Heimatvertriebenen und Entrechteten* (BHE), the League of Expellees and Those Deprived of Rights, serves as a kind of political thermometer.[41] At the election to the Schleswig-Holstein parliament in 1950, it gained 23 per cent of the votes, whereafter it spread to the other Länder. The party concentrated its agitation upon the expellees and refugees and aggressively forwarded social demands on their behalf. Although the party leadership condemned right-wing extremism, many of the voters were former Nazis who also felt deprived of their rights. At the national elections in 1953, under the extended name *Gesamtdeutscher Block/Bund der Heitmatvertriebenen und Entrechteten (GB/BHE)* the party gained 5.9 per cent and passed the threshold for parliamentary representation. Thereafter its voters, the Catholics in particular, gradually shifted over to the CDU/CSU. In 1957 the GB/BHE was unable to renew its parliamentary representation (receiving only 4.6 per cent of the vote). And the 1961 elections were a fiasco (2.8 per cent), although it had merged with a smaller conservative party in the meantime. And in the 1960s when the right-wing extremist party NPD (*Nationaldemokratische Partei Deutschlands*) gained some electoral successes, its share among the expellees and their descendants was no higher than among the population at large:[42] Most expellees had become fully politically integrated. There were still special expellee organizations which made revisionist claims, but they represented only about one per cent of the expellees and their descendants.

The success of integration had many causes: the *Lastenausgleich* was a powerful symbol of solidarity; in purely financial terms the ordinary *Sozialstaat* was even more important. Furthermore, the expellees were German citizens, and those who had been expelled from non-German territories were granted citizenship. In this respect the immigrants could feel at home, and they could act successfully in the field of politics and make politicians respect their interests. And last but not least: the German economy was quickly recovering and showed a remarkable job-creating capacity.

REFUGEES FROM THE GDR AND ADDITIONS TO WEST GERMANY'S HUMAN CAPITAL

By the late 1940s people were migrating in great numbers from East to West Germany.[43] But in the late 1940s, at a time of severe social problems and much unemployment, the West German authorities looked with an unsympathetic eye upon most people who came from the Soviet zone. Qualified workers were welcome, but most others were regarded as 'asocial elements'; German administrators and Allied occupation officials even discussed the possibility of closing the border,[44] but gradually Western attitudes changed. In 1950 the Bundestag passed a law which regulated the accommodation of GDR refugees (*Notaufnahmegesetz*); the idea was to help

persons who came for political reasons, but at the same time not
to encourage migration out of the GDR. The GDR should not be
'emptied', and especially housing was still a severe problem. The
regulations did not, however, prove a great deterrent. In practice,
the Western authorities abandoned their restrictive position in 1953.[45]

From 1952 onwards it was practically impossible for a GDR citizen to cross the border between East and West Germany, but West
Berlin was still open. A refugee just had to travel to East Berlin
and take a subway train to West Berlin. Between September 1949
and August 1961, the Western authorities registered 2.7 million GDR
refugees. The real figure was presumably about one million higher
because those people who did not enter a refugee camp but went
directly to relatives or other acquaintances were not counted.[46] Among
the refugees were at least 20 000 engineers and technicians, 4500
doctors and 1000 university lecturers; the younger generation was
greatly overrepresented.[47] According to a survey in 1971, only one-
tenth of the GDR refugees had no professional education; among
the indigenous population and the expellees it was one-fifth. Also
the percentage of people with a high school or university degree
was twice as high among the GDR refugees as among the indigenous or expellees.[48]

At a time of economic super-growth the integration of these
migrants did not create lasting social problems, and the cultural
and judicial conditions for a quick integration were also fulfilled:
the migrants spoke German and felt themselves to be Germans,
and according to West German legislation all GDR-inhabitants were
German citizens. Seldom in history was a mass immigration integrated so smoothly.

In the night between 12 and 13 August 1961 GDR troops and
working brigades erected the Berlin Wall. For the Germans in the
GDR it meant the abolition of the human right to emigrate, but it
also implied problems for the Federal Republic because it blocked
a source of precious human capital.[49] During the 1950s West
Germany's reserves of human capital were so great that the Federal Republic could neglect her education system. Then, however,
severe signs of deficiencies accumulated and the German public
began debating an 'educational catastrophe'. Given the tradition
of education, a diagnosis of this kind hit a nerve in politicians,
administrators and business executives. Within a few years schools
and universities experienced a remarkable expansion, and the system also became socially more open.

The integration of the expellees and then the GDR refugees were great tasks which often occupied public debate and the agendas of the top politicians. But parallel to that, on a much smaller scale, both German states had to solve another integration task.

SORBS AND DANES: TWO PROBLEMS PASS INTO NEAR OBLIVION

After 1945 Sorbs and Danes (and Frisians and some Poles in the Ruhr) were the only indigenous linguistic minorities left on German territory. Numerically they were rather small, but for some time the situation on the northern border and in Lusatia was potentially explosive.

In 1945 the Sorbian and the Danish organizations experienced a spectacular boom. The *Sydslesvigsk Forening*, the association of the Danish minority, counted 2700 members at the end of the war; in 1948 they were 75 000. In Flensburg in April 1947 about two-thirds of the voters put their cross on the Danish list.[50] The number of Danish schools and other institutions showed a similar increase. Obviously Danish organizations had also become very attractive for Germans who had had no relation to Danish culture before. In Lusatia something similar happened where the refounded Sorbian *Domowina* was backed by many non-Sorbian Germans.[51] In both cases material factors were of some importance: the Danish minority received food parcels from Denmark, and this made their organizations very attractive in a time of malnutrition. *Speckdänen*, Bacon Danes, was the German name for these ethnic converts. In Lusatia, belonging to the Sorbian minority could mean protection against undisciplined Soviet soldiers (a severe problem in those years), and perhaps also food ration privileges. But in addition to this, being a German in 1945 meant belonging to a defeated community which often in total was declared guilty of genocide. One solution was mentally to leave the German community, for instance by tracing one's Danish or Sorbian roots. A corresponding phenomenon could be noticed in Austria where, after 1945, most people insisted that they were Austrians, not Germans.

Both at the northern border and in Lusatia there was a revival of separatism. In southern Schleswig some Danish spokesmen advocated a new referendum, while others wanted to move the border without a referendum. The Danish government, however, did not support revisionist border claims, correctly doubting the durability of the re-Danification of Flensburg. By stressing the validity of the border of 1920, the Danish government made a substantial contribution to the peaceful evolution of the situation.

In 1945 in Lusatia, Serbian activists demanded unification with Czechoslovakia. Their claims comprised an area which was inhabited by about 900 000 people[52] (of whom perhaps one-eighth spoke Sorbian). The Soviet leadership left the matter undecided for years. Behind the scenes there was an intense struggle between Sorbian activists who in Upper Lusatia were backed by the Soviet military government, and the SED, the East German communist party.[53]

The beginning of the Cold War finally decided the matter both in Lusatia and on the northern border. From a Western point of view, interest in stabilizing West Germany was paramount, and Schleswig-Holstein was very important as a new home for refugees and expellees; a revision of the border would have impeded the reconstruction of the western zones. Correspondingly, the Soviet Union could not be interested in a further weakening of her occupation zone. Both occupation powers used their influence to initiate and monitor negotiations for a *modus vivendi*.

In November 1947 the *Domowina* and the SED leadership signed an agreement, according to which the *Domowina* would receive state support for cultural activities. Between 1948 and 1950 the SED introduced special articles into the Länder constitutions of Sachsen and Brandenburg and into the GDR constitution which guaranteed Sorbian minority rights. Special measures and legislation followed, and throughout the history of the GDR many Sorbs were mayors and members of parliament. The price was the tacit acknowledgement of the 'leading role' of the SED.

In Schleswig-Holstein, under British leadership, negotiations between representatives of the Danish minority and the regional government in Kiel resulted in September 1949 in a declaration by the Kiel government which the Landtag thereafter endorsed. The general democratic rights of Danes and Frisians were guaranteed. No one who belonged to one of the minorities should be discriminated against, and everyone was free to declare his or her adherence to the minority; the authorities were not to object or control this[54] – a response to the experiences of the Third Reich when the Nazis tried to press 'non-Danish' persons out of Danish associations. In 1955 the Danish list at the regional elections in Schleswig-Holstein was exempt from the rule of 5 per cent; it thereby gained representation in the Landtag in Kiel, if there were votes enough for one seat. Parallel to that the Danish government gave the right of examining to the German schools north of the border.

Ever since, Danes, Frisians and Sorbs have had rather generous conditions as to schooling and cultural activities. In the GDR by the end of the 1960s there were seven 'A' schools where Sorbian was the main teaching language, and 85 'B' schools where Sorbian was taught as a foreign language. There were 'A' and 'B' kindergartens, a Sorbian Teachers Training Institute at Bautzen and a Sorbian Institute at Leipzig University. By 1967 more than 1000 Sorbian books had been printed, a daily paper and several other periodicals were being published, and there were five hours of Sorbian radio programmes a week.[55] The Danish minority has been able to use generous funding from both Germany and Denmark for its schools, and as for book production, radio or TV, the Danes south of the border have had the solid backing of Danish production north of the border. Danish universities have provided opportunities for further education in Danish. Frisian was taught at 30 schools (in 1989), though most pupils have had to learn it almost as a foreign language.[56]

In all three cases, however, a process of cultural erosion and acculturation is traceable. In 1880–4 there were about 166 000 Sorbs; by 1970 the figure had fallen to 70 000.[57] At the end of the 1980s, all Sorbs were bilingual, and in most parts of Lusatia the younger generations no longer understood Sorbian. Most people in Lusatia were German monoglots, and not more than half of those who spoke Sorbian defined themselves as Sorbs. Only in a small Catholic rural area west of Bautzen was there still in 1989 a Sorbian community of a certain stability where all generations spoke Sorbian, where there were few German monoglots, and where there were regular religious services and comprehensive school teaching in Sorbian. The Catholic resistance against intermarriage rendered this 'hard core' relatively stable.[58]

The Danish culture and language has proven more durable than the Sorbian because the Danish minority has been stabilized by the country at the other side of the border. Many German words and grammatical transferences show, however, a strong cultural pressure from the German surroundings.[59]

In both regions the questions of language and ethnicity have completely lost their previous political explosiveness. In Lusatia the atmosphere seems to be more melancholic, due to the apparent decline of Sorbian culture.[60] This outcome can be ascribed to the combination of stable borders, special minority rights, generous founding of schools and cultural activities, and equal citizen rights in general. In addition, Danes and Sorbs have been stable minorities who have been around for a long time. Things turned out to be much more complex when it was not a question of already existing minorities, but of newly arrived minorities.

FROM 'GUESTWORKERS' TO NEW ETHNIC MINORITIES

On 22 December 1955, West German representatives signed a labour recruitment treaty in Rome, the first of its kind.[61] At that time there were still more than one million Germans unemployed, but the labour market showed many regional and sectoral imbalances; southwest German farmers in particular had severe problems in recruiting manpower. According to the treaty the German labour market administration should collect the requirements of Germans firms and, in cooperation with the Italian authorities, find suitable applicants. The contracts with the Italians contained specific regulations about payment, housing and length of the contract and reflected to a large extent the position of the German trade unions; the collective labour market agreements were also valid for the newcomers. If the workers could find suitable housing, the German authorities were to react positively to requests from family members to move to Germany too. Compared with the situation of the Polish farm labourers before the First World War, the progress was remarkable.

During the first few years the quantitative importance of the new migration was limited. In 1959 there were less than 50 000 Italian workers in West Germany, most of them in agriculture. By the end of the 1950s, however, massive shortages on the labour market had made themselves felt, and in March 1960 Theodor Blank, the German minister of labour, signed recruitment treaties with Spain and Greece. More contracts followed: Turkey (October 1961), Portugal (March 1964), Yugoslavia (October 1968). The continuing economic expansion and the abrupt ending of the influx from the GDR made the demand for foreign workers almost explode. In 1964 the first million was reached.[62] The influx led to an increase of xenophobia, which at this time was mostly directed against the Italians, the most numerous group among the immigrants.

By that time, all parties involved were in perfect agreement about one point: this was a temporary migration. German firms wanted workers for a few years, the foreign workers wanted to earn money and then return home, and the governments of the home countries were interested in transfer payments in DM. The demographic and social features of the immigrants reflected this short-term character: most of the migrants were men between 20 and 40, they often lived in modest – sometimes very modest – accommodation and kept in general a low level of consumption in order to transfer as much money as possible homewards.

In 1966–7 the West German economy experienced its first noticeable set back, and the number of foreign workers briskly fell from 1.314 million to 991 000.[63] New migrants were not recruited, contracts were not extended, and in this way the foreign population functioned as a business cycle buffer. But shortly afterwards the demand for foreign labour rose again steeply. In 1973, when the first oil crisis heralded the coming of a new economic age, the West German statisticians counted almost 4 million foreigners; 2.6 million of them were gainfully employed.[64] On 23 November 1973 the Bonn government banned further recruitment of foreign labour.

But the number of foreigners continued to rise, predominantly due to the arrival of family members and higher birth rates. And their national composition changed. In 1970 Yugoslavs were the most numerous group, but in the following year the Turks took the lead. In 1981, of about 4.5 million foreign residents, one-third were Turks. The Turks also took over from the Italians the role of the main target group for xenophobia. On balance, and quite contrary to the intentions behind it, the recruitment stop contributed to the increase in foreign residents: Turks and Yugoslavs had to take into account that they could not go back to Germany once they had left, so many workers stayed more years than previously planned and instead asked their families to join them.[65]

Gradually the foreign population changed its demographic character – there were more women, children, and old people among them. There was still much coming and going – between 1961 and 1987 about 15 million came and 11 million left – but the fluctuation decreased considerably. In 1980 about a quarter of the foreigners said that they intended to stay in West Germany for 'a long time'; in 1988 half of them said so. In 1980 about one-third of the foreigners had already lived in Germany for ten years; in 1987 the fraction has risen to two-thirds. The 'guestworkers' became new ethnic minorities.

The German political system reacted slowly and inconsistently to the new development. The illusion that the foreigners were only 'guests' proved to be quite durable. During the 1970s, however, the first signs of a growing awareness were visible. In 1979 Heinz Kühn, the first government commissioner for aliens (*Ausländer-beauftragter der Bundesregierung*), demanded a consistent policy of integration, the first time that such a demand had been stated in an official document. Kühn's demands remained, however, mostly a dead letter, and in 1980 the government formulated for the first time the contradiction which was to dominate German politics for many years to come. On the one hand, the government asked for an integration which covered all aspects of life; at the same time, the ties to the countries of origin were to be strengthened, explicitly in order to reinforce the propensity to return.[66]

This contradiction left its mark, especially on school policies. The German school authorities agreed upon the principle that foreign children should be integrated into the German school system, even if they were to stay only for a limited period. Children with sufficient knowledge of German should be taken directly into German classes; children with a deficient knowledge should first go to preparatory classes. But the effects were often limited because the foreigners lived concentrated in certain quarters, and this led to very high percentages of foreign children in the classrooms. In addition, the countries of origin received permission to organize a supplementary national education programme. In general, Länder with a Social Democrat government laid more emphasis upon integration into German society whereas CDU- or CSU-led governments supported ties with the countries of origin.[67] Throughout Germany teachers with a foreign background entered the schools – in the 1970s in Berlin alone some 300 Turkish teachers were engaged.[68]

In 1983 the new CDU-led government published a law package to encourage the foreigners to return home. To the workers from countries outside the European Community, i.e. in particular the Turks, the German state offered special bounties – the repayment of their contributions to the pension system and technical advice – if they moved back to their country of origin with all their relatives. This had a positive effect of about 3–4 billion DM for the German pension system (the employers' contributions were not paid out), whereas the overall effect upon the number of foreigners in Germany was quite limited. The initiative had, however, a symbolic content of non-integration.[69]

In practical terms, however, integration made considerable progress. Xenophobia among West Germans significantly declined. In 1980 52 per cent were of the opinion that foreigners should be sent home if there was a shortage of jobs; by 1988 the share had fallen to 36 per cent. In 1980 44 per cent of Germans were against marriages between Germans and foreigners; in 1988 only 33 per cent.[70] Other surveys showed other – lower – values for xenophobic attitudes, but confirm the same tendency of significant decline during the 1980s.[71]

The following figures illustrate the changing attitudes towards Turks and Italians:[72]

Attitudes towards Italians (in per cent)

	1982	1993
'Italians are friendly and courteous'	26	47
'They are industrious people'	23	42
'They take away our jobs'	32	3
'They are not so intelligent as we are'	13	2

Attitudes towards Turks

	1982	1993
'Turks are friendly and courteous'	13	36
'They are industrious people'	29	44
'They take away our jobs'	39	15
'They are not so intelligent as we are'	20	8

In both cases the positive answers have considerably increased. Negative stereotypes of Italians, still at a considerable level in 1982, have become insignificant. Anti-Turkish resentments have strongly declined too, but they have not yet disappeared. The fact that the attitudes towards Italians were more friendly than towards Turks is easy to explain: the Italians came much earlier, and their number had stopped increasing in 1974, whereas the number of Turks continued to rise throughout the 1970s and, to a lesser extent, during the 1980s. Practically all Germans have become used to Italians, and in 1993 the Italians were no longer seen as competitors for jobs, whereas 15 per cent of the Germans still regarded the Turks as a threat. But as the figures also show, in 1993 attitudes towards the Turks were already considerably more friendly than towards the Italians in 1982.

The integration was more marked in the younger generation. Among the Yugoslavs, 59 per cent of the parents and 83 per cent of the youngsters had German friends; among the Turks the figures were 30 per cent (parents) and 57 per cent (youngsters).[73] Other surveys show that the contacts have often been rather superficial,[74] but the tendency over time is well established. In general, the Turks were the group which was most reluctant to integrate, perhaps due to their Islamic religion, many Turkish children being educated in special Turkish schools. Additionally – and this perhaps also explains their slower integration – the Turks were the group against which most xenophobia was directed; 37 per cent of southern European immigrants said that xenophobia was a substantial problem (which implied that for two-thirds it was not), but among the Turks the proportion was 49 per cent. The xenophobia was more generally felt – 'only' 27 per cent reported concrete experiences at the workplace.[75]

By 1987 85 per cent of the younger Yugoslavs and 42 per cent of the younger Turks spoke fluent or good German.[76] In addition, besides the schools, many organizations, associations and institutions actively contributed to integration. At the end of the 1970s throughout West Germany a huge number of intercultural associations developed. As Cem Özdemir, the first native Turk to become a member of the Bundestag, put it:

> Whether the matter was language courses, emancipation of women, the formulation of political demands or just meeting and the celebration of festivals: here a great part of the non-German young generation for the first time gained access to German society, here possibilities opened for personal development, here they made transnational friendships, had a platform for their interests and were regarded as persons.[77]

Also the bigger firms organized many activities. The car manufacturer BMW trained German workers or foremen to work as 'language foremen' in special 'language workshops' where the lesson was closely workplace related.[78] Foreign workers have always had the right to vote for the workers' representation (*Betriebsrat*); since 1972 they can also be elected. The trade unions too have been an important integrating agent.

The progress in integration was, however, a relative one. Many foreigners were still connected to the 'home village' in their minds, in particular the older generation, whereas the youngsters often found themselves split between the cultures. Only a minority of them wanted German citizenship (after ten years of residence they could apply for it). And although their schooling showed consistent improvement, in 1988 there were still only about 30 per cent of foreign youngsters taking a professional qualification (German youngsters: 73 per cent).[79] Most foreigners worked in unskilled or semi-skilled jobs, the average income of the southern European immigrants being about 22 per cent lower than the German average. German society became again *unterschichtet*. The immigrants usually lived in flats of lower standards in older industrial quarters.[80] In many of these quarters they became the majority. It was the cheaper rents, not a sense of common ethnicity, which made them concentrate.

In *social* matters the foreigners had equal rights. Their wages were regulated by collective agreements which covered both Germans and foreign workers, they contributed to the German social security insurances and gained rights accordingly. They were, however, juridically discriminated against because they were not German citizens. They had no voting rights, even in local elections. As a consequence of the Maastricht Treaty, immigrants from EU member countries received that right, but not others, including the Turks.

Political parties for aliens are explicitly forbidden, and other organizations can be outlawed if they endanger the interests of the Federal Republic. This happened in 1993 to the Kurdish PKK after a series of attacks against Turkish offices. These juridical differences are presumably not very important for daily life in the short run, but they imply a serious drawback for the political system. Foreigners are not voters, and as such are not of interest to the strategists of the German parties. This is an important factor in explaining why the political system reacted so slowly towards the new problems. Officially, the German government stuck to the fiction that Germany was not an immigration country (perhaps out of anxiety not to encourage further immigration and not to stir xenophobic emotions). But this fiction considerably delayed the development of a constructive policy to tackle the new problems.

To become German citizens, foreigners used to have to apply for it. Unlike the French tradition (*jus soli*) which used to grant an automatic right of citizenship to every person born on French soil, only persons with German parents had such a right (*jus sanguinis*). Foreigners who could prove knowledge of German, basic knowledge of the political system and cultural affinity to Germany could apply for citizenship after ten years of residence. On deciding these applications, the authorities had room for discretion (*Ermessensspielraum*).[81] However, the regulations were eased in 1990;

foreigners who had stayed more than 15 years and youngsters between 16 and 23 born in Germany received a legal *right* of citizenship. Certain conditions being fulfilled, the authorities were obliged
to grant citizenship, with no room for discretion. Since that reform, practically all former 'guestworkers' and their relatives living
in Germany have not only had the possibility of but the right to
German citizenship.[82]

But comparatively few foreigners have applied. In 1987 only about
14 000 applications were approved.[83] A serious barrier to integration has been the fact that Germany, like most other European
states, has not been allowing dual citizenship. Applying for German citizenship implied giving up the old one, and many foreigners,
Turks especially, felt that to be cutting off their roots and the life
lines which connected them with their families of origin.

The question of German citizenship has been one where the
speculations about 'national identity' have sometimes produced the
most absurd outcomes. Whatever the reason, the misunderstanding has spread, even in academic literature, that German legislation did not contain the possibility for foreigners to become German
citizens. This cartoon of German legislation has then often been
connected with a 'closed', 'biology-based' 'national identity'. As a
matter of fact, in 1993 61 per cent of all Germans were in favour
of dual citizenship for foreigners who have been living in Germany
for more than five years, and 70 per cent were advocating dual
citizenship for Turks who have been living in Germany for a longer
period.

But in spite of the shortcomings of German legislation, during
the 1980s the new ethnic minorities were rather unspectacularly
on their way to integration. A number of additional waves of immigration, however, added new explosiveness to the situation.

'VOLUNTARY GERMANIZATION' AND THE INFLUX OF *AUSSIEDLER*

By 1950, after the end of the expulsions, there were still about
four million ethnic Germans and former German citizens living in
Eastern Europe. Until 1956 they experienced outright repression,
thereafter until the end of communism massive discrimination.[84]

Many wanted to emigrate. Throughout the postwar decades several thousand *Aussiedler* came to West Germany per year, altogether

1.6 million between 1950 and 1988.[85] For many years their arrival was a rather unspectacular process. In absolute terms Poland experienced the greatest loss of human capital. All in all, between 1950 and 1992 1.43 million persons migrated to Germany; Poland lost most 'indigenous' population, i.e. those who in 1945 had at least some command of Polish and therefore were not expelled, mostly Mazurians and Silesians. The higher standard of living in West Germany was one factor, but as experiences from other countries show, higher wages *alone* do not make people migrate. If there isn't hopeless unemployment (which was not the case in Poland), ties to the place of origin, to family members and to friends are too strong. According to the Polish sociologist Jan Korbel about 70 per cent of the migrants were ethnic Poles, or at least people who were only partly Germanized. There were many families among the emigrants who during the war successfully resisted Germanization. In psychological terms it was, in Korbel's words, a re-Germanization, or, according to the Polish author in exile Tadeusz Folek, 'a voluntary Germanization'.[86]

The repression of ethnic minorities in the immediate postwar years left many bitter traces, and even in the 1980s Mazurians and Silesians felt systematically treated as second-class citizens.[87] A kind of 'snowball effect'[88] made itself felt: once some members of a minority emigrate, they make the situation of the remainder even more difficult, and they also act as pioneers by setting an example.

Unlike people from other countries outside the European Community, the *Aussiedler* could freely emigrate to Germany because juridically they were Germans. The West German legislation defined 'German' in this context quite generously. Every person who was a German citizen before 1939 was accepted as German. The people whom the Nazis made Germans by writing them into their *Volkslisten* were recognized as Germans too – if they came from Eastern Europe; however, similar documents from Alsace-Lorraine and Eupen-Malmédy were invalid after the war, nor did the descendants of German emigrants to the USA have a right to a German passport. People in Eastern Europe could also be recognized as German if they could 'prove' their attachment to German culture, but these 'examinations' were rather tame. And if a person was recognized as German, then his or her spouse and their children also had the right to German citizenship.[89]

The West German policy can to some extent be explained by humanitarian motives. However, they were also in harmony with economic and political interests: until the mid-1970s, the *Aussiedler* were valuable additions to the labour force, and in the time of the Cold War migrants seemed to testify against the Eastern European regimes.

The situation of the *Aussiedler* in West Germany was often very difficult. About 80 per cent had such a bad command of German that they had to take language courses. This was partly a result of the ban against the German language in Eastern Europe, but perhaps also an indicator that the process of 'voluntary Germanization' had spread to people with no previous contacts with German culture.[90] Their basic professional education was usually of a comparatively good standard, but the specific qualifications often did not match the demands of the West German labour market.[91] More than 50 per cent participated in retraining and qualification courses. Furthermore, the attitudes and values of most *Aussiedler* were much more traditional than those of their new neighbours in Germany, which often made the parents retreat into privacy, as they tried to 'protect' their children against the vices and temptations of West German society.[92]

Many of these difficulties were, however, of a temporary character. The *Aussiedler* were usually highly motivated to learn German, a fact which profoundly distinguished them from many Turks. In addition, the German authorities organized quite an efficient integration policy, by giving passports to the newcomers and by providing housing facilities, language courses and labour market training programmes. Employers reported good experiences with them, and once the *Aussiedler* found a job, their position seems to have been rather stable.[93]

In the second half of the 1980s the Polish authorities, later also the Soviet/Russian authorities, began to apply a much more liberal attitude towards emigration than before. The number of *Aussiedler* considerably increased:[94]

1985	:	39 000
1986	:	43 000
1987	:	79 000
1988	:	203 000
1989	:	377 000
1990	:	397 000
1991	:	222 000
1992	:	231 000

The sum total of *Aussiedler* who arrived after 1950 rose to 2 850 000. And the rapid increase in around 1988 made xenophobic sentiments blossom. *Aussiedler* competed for jobs and cheap housing in the same way as Turks or Portuguese, and the support which the authorities granted to the *Aussiedler* evoked envy. In addition, only 38 per cent of West Germans regarded the *Aussiedler* as Germans; about as many (36 per cent) saw them as Poles or Russians in disguise. In November 1988 only 22 per cent of the West German population thought that the arrival of the *Aussiedler* was 'a good thing' while 61 per cent had 'doubts'.[95] Xenophobic aggression against *Aussiedler* could be much stronger than against Turks.

The political changes in Eastern Europe and the rise of xenophobia in Germany induced a marked shift in German policy. The *Aussiedleraufnahmegesetz* of 1990 stipulated that potential *Aussiedler* had to send applications to be recognized as such from their home countries before they migrated. This procedure allowed for a stricter bureaucratic control to see whether the potential *Aussiedler* really fulfilled the legal requirements, and it opened the possibility of a numerical quota. In 1992 the Bundestag decided that future *Aussiedler* immigration should be kept at the average level for the years 1991 and 1992, which meant between 200 000 and 250 000 people per year.[96] And the Supreme Court decided in November 1996 that applicants had to prove factual attachment to German culture and a sufficient command of German.[97]

The *Aussiedler* problem has thus constituted the only field so far where Germany has developed an overt and precise immigration policy: the criteria for people who were allowed to immigrate were defined, their number was determined, and measures to support their factual integration were organized. In addition, the German government initiated measures to make the Germans in Eastern Europe stay. The influx of *Aussiedler* became regulated and the subject lost much of its dramatic aspect.

By the end of the 1980s, however, the by then rising aversion to *Aussiedler* converged with the (declining) xenophobia against Turks and other foreigners. And by that time yet another influx – that of asylum applicants – made this cocktail potentially dangerous.

THE INFLUX OF ASYLUM SEEKERS AND THE REVIVAL OF XENOPHOBIA

Article 16 of the West German Basic Law stated: 'Persons who are persecuted for political reasons have the right of asylum.' The German legislation was very liberal on this point, if compared with other European countries – many of the legislators who drafted the Basic Law in 1948/9 had themselves been in exile.

During the first few decades after 1949 most asylum seekers came from Eastern Europe, usually some thousands a year. The German asylum legislation was fairly uncontroversial at that time. In the 1970s, however, the ethnic composition of the asylum seekers changed; the majority came from the Third World. For them, the application for asylum was the only legal way to migrate to Germany. Getting to West Germany was easy at that time – in West Berlin there was no passport control as the Western authorities wanted to underline the fact that they did not regard the border in Berlin as an international border. In 1972 there were only 5000 asylum seekers; by 1986 the figure was up to 11 000, and in 1980 the total of 100 000 was reached for the first time.[98] Parallel to that, the percentage of people who eventually were recognized as political refugees fell from 57 per cent in 1971 to 12 per cent in 1980. At that time the investigations were still quite scrupulous, and the applicants had the choice of going to court if they were not recognized. There were thus indications that the asylum regulations were developing into an unregulated door for non-political immigration.

Throughout the 1980s the subject remained on the political agenda. In large sections of the population xenophobic reactions against *Scheinasylanten* ('fake asylum seekers') were strong. In vain in 1986 the trade union confederation DBG warned of an agitation against asylum seekers, Amnesty International cautioned against a 'hollowing out' of the right of asylum, and representatives of the churches, human rights organizations and charity associations formed an umbrella organization 'Pro Asyl'. But these initiatives were doomed to failure when in 1987 the figures for asylum seekers steeply rose again:[99]

1987	:	57 000
1988	:	103 000
1989	:	121 000

```
1990  :  193 000
1991  :  256 000
1992  :  438 000
```

Between 1988 and 1992 1.1 million people came as asylum seekers. Of those coming in 1992, only 4 per cent were eventually recognized as political refugees. In spite of several adjustments of the German regulations the basic principles of individual examination and the possibility of going to court in case of non-acceptance were still applicable. A particular feature of the German situation was the fact that only about 3 per cent of those asylum seekers whose applications were eventually turned down actually had to leave again.[100] The reasons for this de facto permission to stay for everyone were provisions in the German legislation against overhasty expulsions, humanitarian considerations and the fact that German groups were hiding many asylum seekers.

The integration of the asylum seekers was often very difficult because the cultural differences were great. Most of them had no knowledge of German, and many lacked interest in learning it. During the long time during which their applications were being examined they had to stay in special centres, and that implied few possibilities of coming into contact with German society. These centres, which quickly increased in number at the end of the 1980s, made the influx visible. And at a time when the relations between most Germans and immigrants like the Turks became markedly more relaxed, the influx of asylum seekers, which came on top of the *Aussiedler* immigration, provoked some outright paranoic reactions. The seemingly endless and uncontrolled character of this immigration was a crucial factor in this context. According to an opinion survey, in 1989 almost three-quarters of the West German population, twice as many as six years before, were of the opinion that the asylum regulations were too generous. At the same time, 70 per cent of the population were still *in favour* of a right of asylum for political refugees, but there was very little support for the acceptance of persons who claimed political asylum without actually being political refugees.[101]

In January 1989 the *Republikaner*, a right-wing party with a diffuse ideology and outspoken xenophobic resentments and which systematically campaigned with anti-asylum slogans, gained a sensational 11 per cent at the regional elections in West Berlin. In the same year the *Republikaner* shook the German political establishment by winning 8.8 per cent at the elections to the European parliament. At the same time a growing number of acts of xenophobic violence were recorded. It became obvious that xenophobia, from being a diffuse sentiment in the underground, was about to gain political strength, with potentially far-reaching consequences. German society was approaching a dangerous stage.

Before this became really overt, unexpected events in Eastern Europe completely altered the political agenda.

16 Unification and Current Problems

NATIONAL SENTIMENTS AND UNIFICATION

In autumn 1989 the GDR imploded. The Berlin Wall fell on 9 November, and less than a year later, on 3 October 1990, the new Länder of the GDR became members of an enlarged Federal Republic of Germany. Many obervers interpreted the German unification as the natural outcome of history. To divide a nation was seen as 'unnatural', so it was 'natural' to unite it again. Ex-Chancellor Willy Brandt expressed this in a classical way after the fall of the Berlin Wall: 'Now what belongs together, grows together.' Again the German nation was seen as kind of organic being.

But as discussed in Chapter 1, nations are not organic beings, and biological analogies only confuse the matter. A necessary condition for German unification in 1990 was the fact that the GDR did not work. It was a repressive system with inefficient institutions with which the majority of the population never could properly identify. In 1990 the repression was gone and only the inefficiency was left. The GDR was simply bankrupt. Churchill's remarks, quoted in Chapter 13 with regard to the Austrian vote of 1918 for unification with Germany, can be used again almost verbatim, only *the GDR* has to be substituted for *Austria*: 'In her miserable plight the GDR turned to Germany. A union with the great teutonic mass would give the GDR vitality and means of existence ...' But as the example of Austria shows, division can become a case of a new normality. In 1918 the Austrians felt themselves to be Germans, and in 1938 the majority approved Hitler's *Anschluß*. But since 1945 most Austrians have been insisting that they were an entity on their own. Austrian society and Austrian democracy worked, and the Austrians could identify with it. Their German identity largely disappeared and is hardly of political relevance any more.

This process of gradual identification with a new political unit was also traceable in West Germany. During the 1980s about 80 per cent of West Germans were in favour of unification, but only about 9 per cent thought they would witness it. And among the younger generation aged between 14 and 29 there was a strong minority of about 35 per cent who regarded East and West Germany as two different nations.[1] A process of mental separation was clearly under way. It would have been only a question of time before the majority of West Germans would have been marked by it. The situation in the GDR was different because the GDR did not work, so it could not provide the basis for a new stable collective identity.

But in the autumn of 1989 the majority of the GDR citizens were *not* in favour of unification; instead they shared hopes for a better GDR. Gradually, however, the atmosphere shifted, and at the Monday demonstration in Leipzig on 20 November 1989, some people demonstratively shouted the last verse of the original GDR anthem (which for decades had not been sung but only played by instruments): 'Germany, united fatherland.'[2] Slogans like this gained increasing popularity.

According to opinion polls conducted by a GDR institute, the slide towards unification can be quantified as follows (in per cent):[3]

'*What is your opinion about a unification of GDR and FRG?*'

	Strongly positive	More positive than negative	More negative than positive	Strongly negative
20/11–27/11/89	16	32	29	23
29/1–9/2/90	40	39	15	6
26/2–6/3/90	43	41	13	3
18/4–27/4/90	49	36	12	3

As the table shows, by November 1989 the majority were still against the idea of unification. But in December 1989 and January 1990 a landslide towards unification occurred, bringing the numbers in favour of unification close to 80 per cent. The following weeks saw a continuation and consolidation of this trend.

This was by no means a euphoric or blind trust in the blessings of the Free West (as it often was depicted in the Western press). In April 1990 about 49 per cent regarded the possibility of unemployment as a personal threat, 80 per cent feared an increase in aggression and violence, 78 per cent felt threatened by a potential increase in selfishness and 83 per cent dreaded an increase in criminality.[4] According to another opinion poll, conducted by a West German institute in March 1990, most people preferred a slow progress towards unification; only 35 per cent advocated unification as quickly as possible.[5] But all in all, West Germany seemed to be an acceptable model, and unification seemed to be a realistic way towards a higher living standard and an orderly democracy. The concept of a 'Third Way' which the oppositional groups of the GDR advocated remained nebulous, and the vast majority of the GDR population seem to have been very sceptical about the idea of new social experiments with unknown consequences. Everyone knew about the miserable state of the GDR economy, and only with unification could the GDR citizens count upon substantial economic help, only with unification could they *claim* assistance from West Germany.

Under these circumstances, Chancellor Kohl's CDU and his allies in the GDR best met public feelings. Under the short election campaign – the first free GDR elections were to be held on 18 March 1990 – their message was simple: unification as quickly as possible. And they could already present one concrete step towards that aim: monetary union. Kohl and his partners systematically played down the difficulties of the transition period ahead, but given the many uncertainties among the GDR population, these election campaign illusions alone cannot explain the CDU success.

The Social Democrats and the former opposition groups had no easy message; they stressed the many difficulties ahead (being on this point more realistic than the CDU), and according to them, unification was a problem for a distant future. The SPD was, as a matter of fact, divided. Willy Brandt and other Social Democrats worked with great commitment for unification, but Oscar Lafontaine, the West SPD's candidate for the chancellorship, more than once hinted that this was not what he most desired. Many spokesmen of the German political left felt uneasy about the prospect of Germany as a new Great Power and dreaded spectres of the past. But this made them fail to meet the problems and sentiments of the GDR population.

On 18 March 1990 the CDU and its allies, together forming the *Allianz für Deutschland*, got 48 per cent of the votes. The liberals gained some 5 per cent, and this meant a stable majority for a centre-right coalition. For the SPD the result was disappointing: 22 per cent. *Bündnis '90*, a party where most members of the GDR opposition were active, scored only 3 per cent. Obviously the voters did not value the courage shown during the peaceful revolution, but voted instead according to what they thought would be best for the future. The post-communist PDS (*Partei des Demokratischen Sozialismus*), the successor of the SED, scored a respectable 16 per cent.

Also in West Germany the majority was for unification, but it should be a cheap one. Only 27 per cent accepted the view that the West Germans should accept economic burdens in order to help their eastern compatriots; 55 per cent explicitly did not consent.[6] So, German patriotism was at best lukewarm. If in the autumn of 1990 there had been a referendum, and if the population had received realistic pieces of information about the coming financial burdens, it is more than doubtful whether the majority of the West Germans would have endorsed unification. Nationalist hubris, at least, was nowhere to be found, and most members of the intellectual elite, obviously fearing nationalist outbursts, did their best to spread ill-humour.[7]

When it became apparent that unification did imply burdens for them too, many West Germans reacted with outrage. The opening of the Wall in November 1989 was not just a source of joyful sentiments. The *Ossies*, as many came to call the East Germans, formed long queues in front of the cashiers of the supermarkets, many shelves were emptied, and particularly in West Berlin the mass influx created traffic jams. Many came to stay permanently. It was often very difficult to find housing for them, so many had to be billeted on camp sites, in sports halls or swimming-baths. The West German housing market was already under stress due to the other immigration waves. In November 1989 the Hamburg Senate diagnosed a 'strong competition for housing among the various homeless groups'.[8] Statisticians counted 234 000 *Übersiedler* in the fourth quarter of 1989, and another 184 000 during the first three months of 1990.[9]

Yet another mass immigration wave washed into West Germany, and as in the case of the Turks, the *Aussiedler* and the asylum seekers, people particularly in the lower income groups, who felt the competition, reacted xenophobically. In Essen, allegedly not a unique case, East Germans heard: 'GDR swine.' Some West Germans were envious because East Germans received 100 DM as 'welcome money' when they crossed the border, and in Erlangen it came to a brawl when some West Germans in a bus had to pay a fine after a ticket inspection whereas an East German could travel freely without a ticket.[10] Hermann Heinemann, minister of labour in North-Rhine Westphalia, received numerous letters like the following:

> There are six million people dependent on social help who live at the margin and receive little attention. But *Aussiedler* and

Übersiedler get the first priority, they receive tax advantages beyond imagination. The dynamite is there. Just wait. This is going to explode.[11]

In Berlin the tyres of numerous East German cars were slashed and in Hanover unknown perpetrators threw bottles filled with gasoline at parked East German cars – three cars were burned out.[12] In February 1990, twice within a short time, arson was reported from a temporary home for *Übersiedler* near Cologne. In Stuttgart one such home was burned down completely.[13] It was sheer good fortune that no one died.

All in all, German unification occurred at a time when the majority of the West Germans *still* adhered to the idea of one German nation, when a West German government, out of ideological reasons but also because it implied more power for themselves, skilfully exploited the opportunities of the international situation in which the Soviet Union was about to disintegrate, and when the East Germans realized that their society was bankrupt so they had to accept all West German conditions.

'INNER UNIFICATION' AND THE 'WALL IN THE MINDS'

Most Germans in the East and West approved the unification, and unification day on 3 October 1990 passed in an atmosphere of serene delight. In December 1990 Chancellor Kohl's centre-right coalition won the first general election in the united Germany, and the CDU consolidated its position as the strongest party in East Germany. But already at this time it had become apparent that the process of unification had produced many frustrations and many mutual resentments between East and West Germans. In January 1991, 86 per cent of East Germans felt that they were treated as second-class citizens.[14] When East Germans were asked to write down their opinion about their Western compatriots in key words, some wrote as follows: 'Arrogant like occupational troops – ... – they regard us former GDR citizens as the idiots of the nation – think they are the victors – they think they are the greatest, do not accept other opinions.' For some West Germans who began to dread the expenses of unification, the economic difficulties in East Germany were mostly due to lack of initiative: 'That's a lazy people – ... – they just want to have everything served – they are not as industrious as we Germans [!] are – they simply have not learned how to work – ...'[15] Jokes flourished, and German intellectuals had a new topic for debate: after the fall of the Wall, a new wall in the minds?

The mutual resentments, however, did not reflect profound cultural differences. East Germans were usually less extrovert, less used to 'selling themselves'; these qualifications are often necessary in the context of a market economy, but they were not needed or even suppressed in the GDR. In the beginning many East Germans made mistakes, for instance when applying for a job. But they could learn and adapt to new demands – often they just needed a second chance.[16]

According to mass psychological tests[17] the behaviour of most East Germans was more controlled; they were less spontaneous, they followed principles and norms more strictly; they were more reliable. These differences can be explained by the cultural change which had taken place in West Germany since the 1960s, not least under American influence. Under the impact of this cultural change the West Germans placed less emphasis upon values such as 'duty', more emphasis on 'self-realization'. In a way, by 1990 the East Germans were the 'more German' Germans. Other researchers spoke of the 'refrigerator function' which the GDR had with respect to cultural change.

As discussed in Chapter 15, in 1990 most West Germans were post-materialists (56 per cent, as opposed to 41 per cent 'materialists'), whereas most East Germans still adhered to materialist values (62 to 41 per cent).[18] This difference could also be interpreted as a sign of retarded cultural change, but it presumably mostly reflected the fact that the East Germans had to live under harder economic conditions. They simply could not yet 'afford' to have post-material positions to the same extent as the West Germans.

In one important cultural aspect the East Germans were more *advanced* than their Western compatriots: secularization. In 1992 only 27 per cent of East Germans believed in the existence of God (West Germans: 56 per cent), and two-thirds were not members of a Christian church (30 per cent were Protestants and 5 per cent Catholics).[19] There was no religious instruction in the GDR schools, the state did not collect the church tax and in general did not support the churches, and this disruption of traditional continuity and institutional backing was sufficient to make the process of secularization accelerate in East Germany.

All in all, however, most psychological differences between East and West Germans were not too substantial, and many of those mental differences can be seen, not as something qualitatively different, but as the result of differences in the speed of the processes of cultural change. Changes started earlier in the West and developed faster there, so although East and West Germans differed in 1990, it was qualitatively the same patterns of change which affected West and East Germany. East and West Germans had had common experiences until 1945, and the GDR was, after all, an industrial society where living conditions, apart from many differences, also showed many similarities with West Germany, and where rationality was a determining feature of daily life. Furthermore, throughout the history of the GDR the media of the West have played an important role, in particular radio and television; moreover, after the erection of the Berlin Wall there were still many personal contacts between East and West Germans, when West Germans came to visit relatives in the East, and through letters and parcels.[20] The Berlin Wall was not a cultural Chinese Wall between the two societies.

The mutual resentments between 'Ossies' and 'Wessies' were not due to the clash of incompatible cultures, but due to the concrete circumstances of the unification process. The Bonn government had strictly engineered the unification as an entry of the GDR into the Federal Republic, according to Article 23 of the Basic Law. The other possibility – Article 146, by which East and West Germans might draft a new constitution in common – was rejected. Bonn's course implied that West Germany to a large extent could go on as it was. The burdens of adapting were almost exclusively placed on the East Germans. Even on the symbolic level Bonn's negotiators left no doubt about the procedure. When GDR Prime Minister Lothar de Maizière proposed a modified national anthem (the words of one stanza of the GDR anthem should be incorporated into the West's hymn, to be sung to Haydn's tune), and when he also proposed a new name for the new state: *Deutsche Bundesrepublik* or *Bund Deutscher Länder* (League of German Länder), Wolfgang Schäuble, the Bonn minister of interior and Bonn's chief negotiator, used a kind of standard reply:

> Dear friends, we are talking about an accession of the GDR to the Federal Republic, not the other way round. We have got a good Basic Law which has proved a success. We shall do everything

for you. You are cordially welcome. We don't want cynically to
neglect your wishes and interests. But this is not the unification
of two equal states. We don't start from scratch from equal starting
positions. There is the Basic Law, and there is the Federal Republic of Germany. Let's start from the premise that you have
been excluded from both for forty years. Now you have a right
to participate, and we respect that.[21]

Bonn's course implied that the East Germans had to accept the
West German conditions as a 'take it or leave it' offer; they could
say 'no' to the whole project (which the East German representatives were not willing to do), but otherwise they had hardly any
possibilities of influence. They had to listen to what Western experts told them. In fields such as administration or the police the
East German civil servants had to make themselves familiar with
West German legislation and organization. Many GDR employees
were not used to modern technology. Their equipment was usually
outdated and adapting to Western standards usually meant learning a lot. Practically every East German was placed in the position
of a pupil who had to learn from West Germans. Many key posts
in East German enterprises and administrations were taken over
by West Germans. To some extent at least, East Germany became
überschichtet ('over-layered') by West Germans.

Many East Germans experienced this process as a profound moral
injustice: they, the heroes of the peaceful revolution of autumn
1989, had to accept the inferior position of pupils.

Furthermore, East German society experienced a process of profound transformation which implied much social hardship. After
the monetary union with West Germany on 1 July 1990, the East
German economy was pushed into near collapse. Even after one
month, industrial production had fallen to 60 per cent compared
to the first half-year of 1990. At the end of 1990 it was down to 49
per cent and by 1991 it fell to one-third of the former level. Other
sectors such as administration or trade were less severely hit, but
nevertheless the whole Gross Domestic Product fell by 35 per cent.[22]
Never in peacetime had a modern economy experienced such a
disaster. A direct consequence was an explosion in the number of
unemployed:[23]

1990	:	240 000
1991	:	912 000
1992	:	1 170 000

To these figures must be added each year several hundred thousand East Germans who were employed via work provisions, who participated in labour-market retraining programmes or who were engaged only in part-time work.[24] Until the summer of 1993 the impact of the economic transformation upon the East German employment situation can be summarized as follows: in 1990 about 78 per cent of the population above 18 years of age were gainfully employed; in 1993 the proportion was down to 54 per cent. Of those employed almost 30 per cent reckoned to lose their job in the near future. By 1993 every fifth ex-employee had involuntarily left the labour market altogether, every fourth experienced temporary, often long-lasting unemployment, every fifth had to change workplace, and every tenth had to change profession.[25] Only gigantic monetary transfers from West Germany (in 1992 alone 218 billion DM, private investments not included) prevented total collapse and helped bring East Germany back onto the growth path.

The collapse of the East German economy dissolved millions of meshes within the social networks. In many cases even basic social institutions disappeared. In GDR times many kindergartens were organized at factory level, but when the plants ran into economic difficulties the social institutions were the first to be closed. Thousands of female workers were forced back to their place in the kitchen, and dense networks of workplace-based companionships were cut into pieces. In GDR times life was restricted, but in many repects orderly and safe; students knew what kind of work they were to do after their examinations, there were jobs for all, and there was no risk of unemployment. Criminality was at a low level, and there were no tabloid media to spread insecurity by noisily publishing horrible crime cases. After unification, society became much more complex, and even most of those who gained in material terms experienced their job situation becoming uncertain.

Against this background it is hardly surprising that many East Germans expressed profound disappointment with unification. A kind of GDR nostalgia had developed by 1993. Only 41 per cent said they formerly had had a critical stance towards the GDR system, while 43 per cent said they had been, albeit critically, in favour of the system. Obviously, after its collapse, the GDR was more attractive than at the time of its existence.

By 1993, however, many signs of a cultural *détente* between East and West were traceable. Sixty-six per cent of East Germans agreed with the statement: 'It is noticeable that we have been living in two different systems for many years, but by and large we get along well.' And almost nine out of ten agreed with the sentiment: 'There are communication problems, but they are solvable as time passes by.'[26] East and West Germans still saw themselves as different groups, but the construction of a 'wall in the minds' appeared to be highly exaggerated. It has perhaps been a fence which kept people at a distance, but which nevertheless allowed for communication.

The characteristics of the unification process have often (and often very polemically) been debated, and many political mistakes have been highlighted. As practically all German experts pointed out in 1990, it was economic madness to convert the East German salaries which were paid in GDR marks at a rate of 1:1 into DM salaries, and this in conjunction with rapidly rising nominal wages. This procedure simply destroyed the remaining competetiveness of the East German industry. In addition, by establishing the principle 'restitution, not indemnity' Bonn had created an artificial investment barrier: according to West German law many former owners had property rights in houses or factories which had been expropriated by the GDR regime. Many experts advocated paying an indemnity, but instead the unification treaty stated that property had to be compensated in kind. There were, however, many conflicting property claims, and it was a cumbersome task to clarify their validity, but as long as the property rights were not clarified, no investor was motivated to invest money in the objects in question. In March 1991 the Bundestag passed a law to remove some of these investment obstacles.[27]

Furthermore, the *Treuhand*, the gigantic holding which took over GDR industry, had no consistent strategy. It proved to be fatal that the unification process was carried out so hastily, a factor which at least was partly due to electoral tactics. Kohl and his strategists knew that they would lose an election in the spring of 1991 because of exploding unemployment, so elections had to be held in 1990, which again implied a swift unification. Furthermore, many Western politicians and experts committed psychological blunders when dealing with East Germans, thereby providing food to their feelings of being colonized.

In spite of all these shortcomings, it must, however, be underlined that there were no *principal* alternatives. It was the GDR which was bankrupt whereas the structures of West German society had been basically proven to be robust. Many participants in the German debate sharply criticized the one-sided character of the unification and demanded a procedure where two equal partners in common would elaborate a new constitution. But this would have implied substantial instability for West Germany, and no one in East or West could have been interested in that. Under any circumstances, it was the East Germans who had to adapt to a Western type of society. Their fate of coming into the inferior position of pupils having to catch up was unavoidable. And although many mistakes were committed in the field of economic policy, no one could have spared the East Germans a painful process of economic restructuring and mass unemployment. In this perspective, the delusions and disappointments and the emergence of the *Ossi-Wessi*-conflict were unavoidable.

Furthermore, Germany's economic and political structure proved capable of balancing the new cultural conflict. The East–West divide did not develop into a long-lasting and bitter cleavage with institutionalized political forces on both sides of the divide. This was mainly due to Germany's federal system. The East Germans had little to say as regards the details of the unification, but once the unification was implemented, it gave the East Germans a share in the German power structure. Five new Länder were created (and Berlin united), and this meant that important policy fields fell under East German legislation – most federal laws were to be executed by the East German administrations. Because of their representation in the Bundesrat, the new Länder had immediate influence upon central policy. The East Germans also became represented in the leading groups of the Bonn parties, usually as vice-chairmen, and in the parliamentary groups in the Bundestag. By 1994 the organization of the new Länder administrations was to a large extent completed. On 1 January 1995 the Länder became integrated into the scheme which provides for money transfers from the richer to the poorer Länder (*Länderfinanzausgleich*): an important factual and a symbolic step towards real equality.

In spite of many public and private investments, in 1996 the East German economy was still weak, and there was still a long way to go to achieve parity with West Germany. The many transfers meant, however, that the gap was narrowing. Those who were employed experienced a marked increase in real wages. The average salaries in East Germany developed, as a percentage of the West German average, as follows:[28]

$$1991 \quad : \quad 46$$
$$1992 \quad : \quad 62$$
$$1993 \quad : \quad 70$$

Average real income increased by about 50 per cent after 1990.[29] In comparison to West Germans many East Germans may still feel discriminated against, but their standard of living is much higher than what their own production would allow. In this perspective, their decision for unification in 1990 proved to be rational. And the point that the difference in the standard of living has been shrinking continuously means that the cultural divide has lost much of its sharpness. 'Us versus them' attitudes have usually been much more persistent if they have coincided with persistent social barriers.

All in all, unification meant for Germany a new regional divide and substantial economic problems, but not a cultural cleavage. The Germany of the 1990s had much better possibilities for integrating the new region than the Kaiserreich had in the case of Alsace-Lorraine.

THE XENOPHOBIC WAVE AND THE NEW IMMIGRATION POLICY

In 1990 unification overshadowed all other problems. But when unification increasingly turned into day-to-day business, other issues once more gained considerable attention. In particular the questions of immigration and xenophobia quickly gained dramatic proportions. The immigration of *Aussiedler* and asylum seekers continued at a high level:

	Aussiedler[30]	*Asylum seekers*[31]	*Total*
1989	377 000	121 000	498 000
1990	397 000	193 000	590 000
1991	222 000	256 000	478 000
1992	231 000	438 000	669 000

It was in particular the seemingly ever increasing stream of asylum seekers, on top of the influx of *Aussiedler* and GDR *Übersiedler*, which brought German society to the brink of its integrative capacity. There was no mechanism to regulate the number of asylum seekers, and given the fact that most other countries had practically closed their borders to them, Germany became a kind of magnet.

In 1990 Germany received *twice* as many asylum seekers as France, Great Britain, Spain and Italy *together*.[32] Right-wing extremism grew. In 1992 the *Republikaner* clamorously entered the regional parliament in Baden-Württemberg with more than 10 per cent of the votes, and at the local elections in Hesse in March 1993 they scored 8.3 per cent. Xenophobic resentments and an ardent agitation against asylum seekers formed the core of their election campaigns.[33] Eighty per cent of their voters declared they were deeply worried that 'simply nothing gets done about the flood of asylum seekers'. Among the population at large other themes (unemployment, rising right-wing extremism) caused more concern, but 41 per cent were still deeply worried about the 'flood' of asylum seekers.

The leadership of the *Republikaner* endeavoured to present the party as a moderate, conservative force, firmly loyal to the constitution; as regards foreigners, the official programme only called for a stop to the influx of asylum seekers who did not have a real political motive. But the 'unwritten programme', the parlance of the speeches by leading officials, the slogans, the articles in the party paper, etc., gave many hints (without, however, providing proof) that they were a right-wing extremist, anti-constitutional party.[34] This was certainly the case with the *Deutsche Volksunion* (DVU). The DVU also ran its election campaigns predominantly on anti-asylum and other xenophobic slogans – and gained surprising successes in northern Germany: 6.2 per cent in Bremen in 1991, 6.3 per cent in Schleswig-Holstein the following year.

The election successes of *Republikaner* and DVU were accompanied by a steady increase in membership numbers of right-wing extremist and outright neo-Nazi organizations. In 1992 the German authorities counted 82 right-wing extremist organizations and associations with 42 000 members.[35] This was almost twice as many as in 1986. For a while it looked as if right-wing extremists might establish themselves, as in France, as a stable political force.

In 1992 the German authorities classified 6200 persons as 'violent right-wing extremists or extremist skinheads'. This number among a population of 80 million is not many from a statistical point of view, but for a while these 6200 gained crucial importance. During the second half of the 1980s the authorities registered a gradual increase in acts of violence with a xenophobic or right-wing extremist background. But in 1991 and 1992 the figures exploded:[36]

          1985 : 123
          1990 : 306
          1991 : 1489
          1992 : 2639

Most of these were xenophobic acts (2277 in 1992);[37] among the latter were 585 bodily injuries and 656 acts of arson. Two crimes gained particular importance: in Mölln during the night of 22–23 November 1992 a 51-year-old Turkish women, her grand-daughter (10 years) and her niece (14) died when two skinheads (aged 23 and 18 years) set their house on fire.[38] And in a similar case in Solingen on 29 May 1993 two Turkish women and three children died. The police arrested a 16-year-old boy as main instigator; his accomplices were another 16-year-old boy, a 20-year-old soldier and a 23-year-old unemployed man.[39] Many observers feared that Germany was on the brink of a fatal escalation of xenophobic violence and counter-violence.

Three-quarters of the persons who committed acts of xenophobic violence were under 20 years of age. Only 10 to 15 per cent acted out of political conviction or were organized in right-wing extremist groups. About 30 per cent were social losers with no ideological ties who were aiming at drawing attention to their own problems; another 30 per cent were youngsters with a criminal background, usually from socially disadvantaged families. A further 30 per cent were followers, often from middle-class homes who hoped to find the emotional warmth which they lacked at home in skinhead groups and the like. The perpetrators usually acted on spontaneous impulse, almost always under the influence of heavy alcohol consumption. Those few who belonged to the organized right-wing extremist scene acted on their own initiative, with no organized steering or coordination of the assaults.[40]

There was, however, a mutual encouragement among the groups because the German media extensively reported the assaults. Many journalists rang the alarm bell 'before it once again was too late', while others just exploited the sensationalism. They therefore gave much publicity to events – and triggered off copycat crimes. This effect was particularly noticeable after xenophobic outbursts in Hoyerswerda and Rostock. In September 1991 a home for asylum seekers in Hoyerswerda, in eastern Saxony, was attacked five nights in a row with petrol bombs, signal flares and stones. Large crowds of 'ordinary citizens' stood by and applauded.[41] In Rostock in August

1992 the gravest riots of this kind took place: under cover of a demonstration against a home which was overfilled with asylum seekers, most of them gypsies, many people threw petrol bombs and stones. The extensive media coverage attracted right-wing extremist activists from a large area and many bystanders. Altogether the police counted 1200 people who were actively committing acts of violence, and about 3000 bystanders who often goaded on the violent activists.[42]

In particular Rostock set a wave of copycat crimes in motion. 'Seen from their perspective the accused could easily gain the impression that they were the radical spearhead of a broad movement', the court in Schleswig wrote about the two men who committed the deadly arson in Mölln.[43] This was, however, a deception; the xenophobes were in a minority. In October 1992 a large-scale opinion poll produced the following results:[44]

'How would you react if Germans attacked foreigners in front of you?'

	West	East
'I would participate'	1	2
'I would watch but not intervene'	9	8
'I would go away, not want to be involved'	56	65
'I would, if possible, try to help the foreigners'	31	22

The majority of Germans preferred to look the other way, and among those who had an active opinion, the pro-foreigners outnumbered the xenophobes by far. After Mölln the pro-foreigner sentiments gained in strength even further:[45]

'Supposing that in your town there were two demonstrations, one against the hatred of foreigners and one against the influx of foreigners. How would you react?'

'I would demonstrate against the hatred of foreigners'	40
'I would demonstrate against the influx of foreigners'	11
'I would not participate in any of these demonstrations'	44

The wave of xenophobic violence gained momentum at a time when the general attitude of the German population, apart from the widespread irritation about asylum seekers, was more friendly towards foreigners than ever. In 1992 there was, for the first time, on average a *positive* attitude towards Turks. On a scale which ran from −5 ('very unsympathetic') to +5 ('very sympathetic') they were on average placed on 0.2; as regards Turks in Turkey the average value was 1.4.[46]

For the sake of completeness it should perhaps be added that anti-Semitism has also had a systematically falling trend since 1945. Research initiated by the US military government in 1946 quantified the percentage of 'hard anti-Semites' at 18 per cent; a further 21 per cent were anti-Semites in a broader sense. In 1989, according to an EMNID poll, the proportion of anti-Semites in a broader sense had fallen to 14 per cent, while only 4 per cent were 'hard' anti-Semites.[47] The absolute figures vary according to the formulation of the question or the indicators used, but all opinion polls where the same questions were asked over time show a decline.[48] On the above mentioned sympathy scale ranging from –5 to +5, in December 1991/January 1992 the Jews were on average placed at +1.0.[49]

The murder in Mölln set a huge wave of anti-racist demonstrations in motion. In Munich on 6 December 1992 about 350 000 people formed a candlelit chain as a symbol of solidarity with the foreigners, and one week later 300 000 people formed a candlelit chain around Lake Alster in Hamburg; on the same day, 13 December 1992, 150 000 persons attended an anti-racist rock concert in Frankfurt.[50] Between 2 and 3 million people participated in solidarity demonstrations. They had an important function because they signalled to the xenophobes that they were but a small minority.

Football associations and other sports clubs organized solidarity activities, in the larger firms trade unions and industrialists intensified their anti-racist schooling activities, theatres and musicians contributed with cultural performances. Even many people who watched the influx of asylum seekers with uneasiness were disgusted by right-wing extremism. In 1992, 77 per cent of West Germans (79 per cent in East Germany) said they did not want to have right-wing extremists as neighbours (France, 1990: 33 per cent). Right-wing extremists were by far the most unpopular minority in Germany, in this respect clearly surpassing alcoholics, drug-addicts or other misfits. The proportion of people who did not want to have right-wing extremists as neighbours was ten times higher than the percentage of those who did not want Jews as neighbours (7 per cent).[51]

In combating xenophobic violence, German society received much help from the outside. Criticism has always been a scarce and precious resource, but Germany was in a position to exploit the critical resources of other countries. Events like Rostock gained worldwide publicity, and pictures of German right-wing extremists covered the front pages of international magazines. Experts of the Washington-based Center for Media and Public Affairs, after having analysed the programmes of the US television chains, concluded that in the second half of 1993 the transmissions were dominated by reports about the Nazi era and neo-Nazism, xenophobia, HIV-infected donor blood and asylum legislation.[52] Many observers (Germans and foreigners alike) drew parallels with the Nazi era; the eminent scholar Gordon Craig was quoted for the judgement that these criminal acts were symptoms of a general German disease called xenophobia which time and again had broken out.[53]

From a comparative perspective it is, however, noticeable that right-wing extremism and xenophobic violence had been at much higher levels in many other European countries. In Great Britain in 1992 ten people were killed because of the colour of their skin,[54] or as *The Independent* put it in 1992: 'There are some 70 000 racial incidents a year in Britain – one every five minutes . . . These, unlike those in Germany, rarely make it past the local papers.'[55] *The Observer* collected some cases:

. . . **Norbury**: Afghan refugee Ruhullah Aramesh murdered after attack by 15 white youths wielding iron bars and clubs. **Eltham**: Asian youth, Rohit Duggal, 16 stabbed to death by white youth. **Plumstead**: Asian man, a mosque elder aged 60, seriously assaulted outside his front door. **Charlton**: Mosque set on fire, second time in two years. **Tower Hamlets**: Murder of Tamil refugee Panchadcharan Sahitharan after attack four days earlier by white youths wielding baseball bats. **Newham**: Somali boy stabbed; Bengali family fired at by white neighbour armed with sawn-off shotgun; Nigerian refugee woman, 24, punched and kicked. Graffiti sprayed on car . . .[56]

In Brixton in 1981 13 immigrants died when their house was set on fire.

In France Jean-Marie Le Pen and his *Front National* collected 13 per cent of the vote at the *national* elections in 1993. And Le Pen and his followers have proved to be a stable political force, with a growing trend over time (15 per cent of of the vote at the first round of the presidential elections in 1995). In France also xenophobic violence has been at a high level, with many murders every year and some very dramatic incidents. In 1992 four policemen were sentenced, two of them to life imprisonment, because they had systematically tortured two immigrants; one of the victims died, the other was mutilated.[57] In April 1993 a youngster from Zaïre was shot in a police station while being interrogated. Shortly afterwards an Arabian boy was shot in the head while being arrested. These cases were unusual because the perpetrators were policemen.[58] In July 1994 at Dreux, west of Paris, four Frenchmen fired with automatic guns at a group of immigrants, wounding 12.[59]

In Italy right-wing extremism has also been a stable political force for many decades. Acts of xenophobic violence have been very frequent,[60] some of outstanding brutality: two gypsy girls, aged 3 and 13, were severely wounded when a doll which they received as a gift exploded.[61] In 1994 it became known that a group of policemen had, among many other acts of criminality, assaulted a gypsy camp (two dead) and killed two Senegalese by submachine gun fire.[62] In Belgium in Antwerp the right-wing extremist party *Vlaams Blok* got 28 per cent of the votes at the local elections in 1994, a result which made Antwerp a kind of capital of European right-wing extremism. In the Netherlands in 1992 two mosques, several immigrant meeting places, a radio station and several foreign-owned restaurants were destroyed by bombs or arson.[63] In 1994 the extremist Center Democrats received 8 per cent of the vote in Amsterdam and 10 per cent in Rotterdam.[64] Austrian society has repeatedly been shocked by murderous xenophobic assaults, and the right-wing politician Jörg Haider gained a stable political base.

All in all, although the impact of immigration – and of asylum seekers in particular – was much higher on German society than on most others, the xenophobic reaction in Germany was *weaker* than in most other countries. But most international (and German) media perceived the situation differently. This was perhaps a factor which positively contributed to making German politicians act. The police intensified their fight against xenophobic groups, several extremist groups were forbidden, and the activists experienced an almost constant police pressure.[65] It was perhaps of crucial importance that the police both in Mölln and in Solingen after a few days were able to arrest the persons who had committed the deadly arson – and the escalation of violence which many feared did not take place.

In 1993 xenophobic and right-wing extremist violence declined again. In 1992 17 people died (ten Germans, seven foreigners), in 1993 'only' six. The number of acts of arson decreased from 656 to 284, while the total number of violent xenophobic acts fell from about 2300 to 1600.[66] The decline was particularly marked after the summer of 1993. Gradually the problems of immigration and xenophobia again lost their explosiveness. This was clearly noticeable in the opinion polls: in the beginning of 1993 more than 75 per cent of the Germans still indicated 'foreigners' as one of the political fields where there were most problems, but thereafter the figure constantly fell, and by early 1995 it was below 50 per cent. By that time 'the labour market' and 'taxes' had become more important.[67] The *Republikaner* and the DVU began to decline. At the national elections in 1994 they had no chance of passing the 5 per cent marker (*Republikaner*: 1.9 per cent).

The massive anti-racist mobilization after Mölln played an important role in bringing the xenophobic parties down again. The main factor was, however, the changing of the German asylum legislation. In December 1992 the government and the SPD agreed upon a legislative package which became effective in July 1993. All persons who originated from 'countries without political persecution', or persons who came to Germany via 'secure countries' could no longer get asylum. Since all neighbouring countries were declared 'secure', an asylum seeker had to come by plane or by boat; in all other cases he or she was to be sent back. The number of asylum seekers fell drastically[68] and the xenophobic wave calmed down. But the price was high: Germany had adapted herself to the illiberal practice of her neighbours.

The new asylum regulations did not mean the end of immigration. There were still many *Aussiedler* to accommodate, and asylum was given to those who came as UN refugees and from the former Yugoslavia. There has been Jewish immigration from the Soviet Union, many foreigners have been working in Germany on a contract basis, and there has been illegal immigration from Eastern Europe. But before 1993 immigration seemed endless and therefore threatening to many. After July 1993 it was precisely this aspect of seeming endlessness that was overcome.

CONTRADICTORY INTEGRATION

In 1992 about 6.5 million foreigners were registered in Germany, the highest figure since 1945 so far.[69] To this number must be added more than a million immigrants who have acquired German citizenship,[70] *Aussiedler* not included. In principle, there are good possibilities for progress on the road to integration. The German economy is one of the strongest in Europe, large parts of the labour market are organized and the education system is quite strong. And all minorities are just minorities. There is no group which could be suspected as a kind of 'Fifth Column' for an external enemy, simply because after the end of the Cold War Germany has no external enemies.

On the other hand, there are several features which weaken the integrative capacity of German society. One obvious flaw is the German legislation concerning citizenship and voting rights. In local elections citizens from EU countries are entitled to vote, but otherwise foreigners do not have any rights. This means that immigrants have a very weak representation in the political system, and they hardly count in the calculations of the politicians – at least not directly, unless, for instance, negative reports in the international media endanger German exports.

However, immigrants do get the right to vote and the right to be elected when they become German citizens. Citizenship is an important symbol of belonging to the country of immigration, and it also removes many barriers to the labour market, for instance as regards the public sector. In addition, Turkish policemen and other state officials mean an immense reinforcement of the credibility of the German institutions as regards the Turkish or other minority communities. Foreigners can become German citizens after ten years of residence, and after 15 years they have a legal right to citizenship.

It has been a substantial problem in this context that German legislation, as in most other European countries, does not allow for dual citizenship (see Chapter 15, p. 214). In 1995 practically all Turks in Germany had the right to German citizenship, but most of them did not take it up because for many giving up the old citizenship meant cutting off their 'roots'. These problems would have been removed with dual citizenship; the construction of an 'active' and a 'resting citizenship', according to the country in which the person lives, could have solved many juridical complications which a dual citizenship otherwise might entail.

In practice, however, the German regulations have been flexible enough to allow for some exemptions, for instance when the Turkish authorities have refused to release young men who are liable to military service out of Turkish citizenship. In 1995 there were 25 000 Turks with a dual German-Turkish citizenship.[71]

In June 1993 about 61 per cent of the German population advocated granting dual citizenship to foreigners who have resided for longer than five years in Germany.[72] The German legislation is therefore much more restrictive than the sentiments of the population at large. Among the political forces the Greens, the Social Democrats, the liberal FDP and some sections of the CDU are in favour of dual citizenship, but the conservative wing of the CDU and in particular the Bavarian CSU have blocked the Kohl government in this respect.

However, an increasing number of foreigners do become German citizens:[73]

1989 : 69 000
1990 : 101 000
1991 : 142 000
1992 : 180 000

Particularly among many Turks in 1994 a kind of mental change towards German citizenship was noticeable. There were Turkish-German policemen, and in 1994 the first former Turkish citizen became a member of the Bundestag. Another has been a member of the Hamburg regional parliament, and yet another became deputy mayor in the town of Bielefeld.

The process of integration has also become mirrored in a growing social diversification of the Turkish community. Turkish entrepreneurs, engineers, physicians, dentists, social workers and teachers form a new Turkish middle class; in North Rhine-Westphalia alone there were in 1994 about 1000 full-time teachers of Turkish origin in the public schools and 128 Turkish social workers.[74]

On the other hand, there has also been a building up of an almost closed Turkish society whose members communicate with German society at large as little as possible. A very dense network of various institutions has emerged, ranging from religious associations to Turkish discos and Turkish media. To mention just a few figures: in 1994 there were some 1200 mosque communities;[75] 87 per cent of the Turks in Germany read a Turkish paper;[76] and most of them only watch Turkish television and Turkish video films.

Many observers have interpreted this development as a failure in integration. It is perhaps too early to formulate definitive conclusions, but if the historical experiences of the Poles in the Ruhr in 1900 can be used, then a network of immmigrant associations is nothing negative from a point of view of integration. Stable immigrant communities can provide a secure basis from which to progress into German society. And German society has proven to have a high capacity of melting down cultural barriers, so it is unlikely that in the long run the outcome as regards the Turks will be different from those of the Ruhr Poles.

(For a graphic representation of Germany in 1995, see again Figures 1.9 to 1.14 in Chapter 1.)

17 Summary: How a Melting-Pot Works

According to an encyclopedia definition, the model of the melting-pot

envisions an assimilation process that operates on cultural and structural plans. One outcome is a culture that contains contributions from numerous ethnic groups and is adopted by their members. A parallel outcome on a structural plane is a pattern of widespread marriage across ethnic lines, in which the members of all ethnic groups participate, leading ultimately to a population made up of individuals of quite mixed ancestry.[1]

That is what has happened in Germany.

Ethnically, the Germans of today are of Celtic, Roman, Saxon, Frankish, Alaman, Danish, Frisian, Obodrite, Polabic, Pomeranian, Kashubian, Sorbian, Old-Prussian, Mazurian, Polish, French Huguenot, Jewish, Czech, Italian, Spanish, Portuguese, Yugoslav and Turkish origin. In most cases, the languages of these people are extinct by now, or still exist only outside Germany. Through a long process German standard speech has almost completely covered the whole area of Germany, with German dialects and non-German idioms as relics mostly in the private sphere. Germany's long tradition of strong educational institutions is one essential factor which has produced this outcome. And her relatively successful economic development, which in turn to a large extent has been due to her education system, has likewise produced complex patterns of co-operation, communication and thus cultural exchange.

On the other hand, parallel to the process of linguistic homogenization, numerous new cultural divides have been appearing. Reformation, which meant a strong boost to the development of German standard speech and education and thus to cultural homogenization, has at the same time produced the most persistent cultural cleavage of German history. The rise of the *Bildungsbürger* and the urban middle classes brought about the cleavage between liberalism and conservatism. And industrialization opened the cleavage between socialists and non-socialists. Furthermore, Prussian expansionism

243

has made numerous regions with non-German populations parts of Germany, and ever since about 1890 Germany has been an immigration country.

There has been an almost endless number of cultural divides within Germany – only a few of them have been treated in this book – and here have been numerous conflicts. But German history also contains numerous cases where different cultural groups have been able to peacefully cooperate, or at least coexist side by side. Coexistence is not so exciting as conflict, and that is perhaps the reason why the cases of conflict usually have attracted much more attention than the cases of coexistence.

Cooperation and coexistence have been possible whenever a set of institutionalized regulations existed which were accepted by the sides involved. One of the most important set of regulations of this kind was the Peace of Westphalia in 1648, by which the conflict between Catholics and Protestants lost its murderous character. The policy of religious tolerance which the Prussian kings and other rulers followed was of a similar character; they concentrated their demands for loyalty on worldly matters but left religious matters to the individuals. This was implicitly the recognition of some basic human right, and it made Brandenburg-Prussia attractive for qualified immigrants.

The principles of rule by law, of equality before the law, of constitutional government, of freedom of speech, of freedom of organization and of representation were introduced in several stages from the end of the eighteenth century. Before 1918 Germany was not a state of parliamentary government, but the Kaiserreich, in spite of cases of repression, was already ruled by the above mentioned principles to a great extent. This is one factor which explains the gradual disappearance of the liberalism–conservatism cleavage, and in general many integration successes. In particular the Jews were very successful in using the new possibilities, and as the high and rising figures of intermarriage and their strong representation in economic and political top posts show, they were progressing rapidly on their way towards assimiliation. Anti-Semitism was a politically inferior phenomenon.

The federal structure of Germany made it possible to balance many regional conflicts. It was much more difficult to find regulations for the many problems which appeared as a consequence of industrialization; consequently the Kaiserreich witnessed the emergence of a solid socialist counter-culture, and was torn by many hard class struggles. By 1914, however, many elements of the 'institutionalization of the class struggle' were already a reality; a strong working-class party, trade unions, the beginnings of collective bargaining and the nascent social state were not burdens for Germany but part of her economic success.

Conflictual international configurations have always produced severe burdens for those minorities who had cultural links across the border to potential enemies. It was therefore no coincidence that Poles, Danes, the Catholic church and the socialists were those minorities who experienced the harshest repression. The repression against the socialists in 1877–90 was the strongest, much stronger than the repression against the Danes or Poles who were protected by many legal provisions and additionally had the support of important sections of German society (Zentrum, Progressive Liberals, Social Democrats). Minorities who just were minorities, with no links across the border, were basically left in peace.

The catastrophe of the First World War and its aftermath brought German society onto the wrong track. Defeat in the Second World War and Western occupation brought (West) German society back onto the right track.

After 1949, a stable legal, constitutional and federal framework gave all groups a representation in the power structure and allowed for the balancing of most conflicts. The divide between Protestants and Catholics lost its character as a cleavage, while German political Catholicism lost its enemy and even became for some time the strongest political force. But the Social Democrats have also held an influential position, the trade unions have been strong actors in the labour market, and collective bargaining and social legislation have smoothed many social antagonisms. The class divide also lost its cleavage character.

Successive waves of immigration have repeatedly created new potential conflict lines. The most dangerous case was presumably the influx of 12 million refugees and expellees (8 million in West Germany). They could have become the reservoir of a new revanchism and of massive social unrest. Their successful integration was due to the 'economic miracle', the general social legislation, special regulations such as the *Lastenausgleich*, the rather orderly labour markets with equal wages for the same type of work regardless of the origin of the employee (though not regardless of the sex), and the skill of politicians such as Chancellor Konrad Adenauer.

The coming of *Gastarbeiter*, *Aussiedler*, GDR *Übersiedler* after

November 1989 and asylum seekers have on several occasions produced xenophobic reactions. The harshest problems arose in context with the seemingly endless influx of *Aussiedler* and in particular asylum seekers at the end of the 1980s and the beginning of the 1990s. There is presumably no society on earth which, with virtually open borders, could stand an economically motivated mass immigration; Germany at least could not. The immigration of *Aussiedler* became regulated quantitatively, and in practice asylum seekers can only come as UN quota refugees, or as a special case, as Jews from the former Soviet Union. The quantitative restrictions, in combination with massive anti-racist activities by large segments of the German society, brought the xenophobic wave down again.

As to the integration of the foreigners who have arrived, the record is uneven. Many groups, such as the Italians, have progressed far on their way towards assimilation, and the same can be said of the Mazurians and Silesians who came as *Aussiedler*. These also receive substantial public support in the form of labour market training programmes, language courses and housing assistance. Other groups such as the Turks, however, live to a large extent on their own, and have built up dense institutional networks. But also in their case there are many unmistakable signs of integration and assimilation. As regards the external configuration, Germany's conditions are favourable because no minority could be suspected of being the Fifth Column of an external enemy.

For the Turks, German legislation with regard to citizenship has proven inadequate. Virtually all Turks in Germany have a legal right to German citizenship, but the provision that they have to give up their Turkish citizenship prevents most of them from doing so. This implies a systematic drawback for Germany's political system. As to this point there is an obvious demand for reform. The point that this reform has been blocked, in spite of the fact that the partisans of reform enjoy a strong majority in parliament and among the population at large, constitutes an interesting case for political scientists.

German history can be interpreted as a series of challenges and responses to the problems of cultural conflict. Many reponses have proven to be adequate. But it has always taken much time before an adequate response has been introduced. This time lag has often been fatal, in the sense that it has meant harsh conflict, sometimes even bloodshed, before the new regulation has been properly introduced. One lesson for the future should be that it is important to make the time lag as short as possible. If reforms drag out, old problems might converge with new, and the point that in the past many regulations have proven to be adequate is no guarantee that they will be so in the future.

Notes

CHAPTER 1   INTRODUCTION

1. In 1992 there were 6496 million foreigners registered in Germany. To this figure must be added those who have acquired German citizenship, roughly one million (between 1972 and 1992 1 035 000 immigrants received German citizenship (Cornelia Schmalz-Jacobsen et al., *Einwanderung – und dann? Perspektiven einer neuen Ausländerpolitik*, Munich, 1993, pp. 311 and 317; *Statisches Jahrbuch für die Bundesrepublik Deutschland 1994*, Wiesbaden, 1994, p. 74).

2. In 1990 the German government, after an agreement with the Central Council of the Jews in Germany, decided to grant the right of immigration, without restriction, to Jews coming from the Soviet Union. According to Ignatz Bubis, the chairman of the Central Council, until May 1996 118 000 persons have applied for permission to immigrate; by that time 86 000 permissions had been granted; 45 164 persons had immigrated, about 25 000 to 28 000 had become members of the Jewish communities in Germany ('Eine gewisse Unsicherheit', *Der Spiegel*, 22/1996, p. 24).

3. Reiner Hans Dinkel and Uwe Lebok, 'Demographische Aspekte der vergangenen und zukünftigen Zuwanderung nach Deutschland', *Aus Politik und Zeitgeschichte*, B 48, 1994, p. 27–36, esp. p. 31.

4. The so-called net immigration rate (immigrants per 1000, emigrants subtracted) was in Germany 9.7, in the United States 3.5, in Great Britain 0.5. Dinkel and Lebok, 1994: 28.

5. In East Germany the figure was down to 27 per cent *Spiegel Spezial*, 1/1991, p. 76.

6. In 1992 56 per cent believed in God, a further 17 per cent in a Higher Being, while 25 per cent indicated 'neither-nor' (only 10 per cent did so in 1967). *Der Spiegel*, 25/1992, p. 41.

7. See, for instance, the discussion between a group of some critical historians and journalists and, on the other side, some veterans, among them the former chancellor Helmut Schmidt: '"Wir hatten geglaubt, wir könnten anständig bleiben"', *Die Zeit*, 3 March 1995, p. 14–20.

8. Ronald Inglehart, *The Silent Revolution – Changing Values and Political Styles Among Western Publics*, Princeton, 1977.

9. 'Homosexuelle Subkultur', 'das gutbürgerliche Schöneberg', 'die Drogenszene', 'die Punks', 'die erste New-Wave-Generation', 'die linksalternative Szene', 'die Alternativszene', 'die sogenannten neuen Mittelschichten', 'Altlinke'. Stefan Hradil, 'Die 'objektive' und die 'subjektive' Modernisierung. Der Wandel der westdeutschen Sozialstruktur und die Wiedervereinigung', *Aus Politik und Zeitgeschichte*, B 29–30, 1992, pp. 3–14, esp. p. 11.

10. The concept of a 'multicultural society' has been intensely debated in

Germany since the beginning of the 1980s. The term has been used both to describe the actual situation and, in a normative way, to formulate a political aim. Here it is used descriptively. An older but related concept is the 'pluralist society'. But whereas pluralist theories highlight the diversity of social and political interests and their organization in Western societies, the term 'multicultural society' stresses the diversity of norms, values and other cultural features (see Axel Schulte, 'Multikulturelle Gesellschaft: Chance, Ideologie oder Bedrohung', *Aus Politik und Zeitgeschichte*, B 23–4, 1990, pp. 3–14, esp. p. 11). The difference between the two categories is, however, more of emphasis than of substance because different social groups and interest organizations are also characterized by different cultural features; class struggles have also been struggles between different cultures.

11. Petra Bauer and Oscar Niedermayer, 'Extrem rechtes Potential in den Ländern der Europäischen Gemeinschaft', *Aus Politik und Zeitgeschichte*, B 46–7, 1990, pp. 15–26, esp. p. 26.
12. *Der Spiegel*, 6/1991, p. 46.
13. Eric J. Hobsbawm, *Nations and Nationalism Since 1780. Programme, Myth, Reality*, second edition, Cambridge, 1992, p. 91.
14. 'Familienähnlichkeit in Europe': Erwin K. Scheuch, *Wie deutsch sind die Deutschen? Eine Nation wandelt ihr Gesicht*, Bergisch-Gladbach, 1991, pp. 229–48.
15. 'In other words, nations must have a measure of common culture and a civic ideology, a set of common understandings and aspirations, sentiments and ideas, that bind the population together in their homeland ... In the Western model of national identity nations were seen as culture communities, whose members were united, if not made homogeneous, by common historical memories, myths, symbols and traditions.' Anthony D. Smith, *National Identity*, Reno/Las Vegas/London, 1991, p. 11.
16. See, for instance, Geert Hofstede, *Interkulturelle Zusammenarbeit. Kulturen–Organisationen–Management*, Wiesbaden 1993, p. 22.
17. See, for instance, Klaus Allerbeck, 'Repräsentativität', in Günther Endruweit and Gisela Trommsdorff (eds), *Wörterbuch der Soziologie*, Stuttgart, 1989, pp. 543–5.
18. See for instance Harold James, *A German Identity 1770–1990*, London, 1989. 'The analysis selects, in an inevitably and admittedly personal way, certain ideas and figures important to German reflection about Germanness' (p. 2).
19. Liah Greenfeld, *Nationalism. Five Roads to Modernity*, Cambridge, Mass., 1992.
20. See the quotations from reviews printed at the back of the paperback edition in 1993.
21. Greenfeld, 1992: 25; see also p. 493, n4.
22. See, for instance, Hans-Ulrich Wehler, *Deutsche Gesellschaftsgeschichte. Erster Band: Vom Feudalismus des Alten Reiches bis zur Defensiven Modernisierung der Reformära 1700–1815*, 2nd edn, Munich 1989, pp. 210–17.

23. See Wehler's comprehensive references in Wehler, 1989: pp. 607–9.
24. Compare, for example, Liah Greenfeld and Harold James (see note 19. Harold James sees a 'cycle of national doctrines from cultural to political and economic and then back all the way, becoming ever more radical in the course of this progression' (p. 3).
25. Hans-Ulrich Wehler, *Deutsche Gesellschaftsgeschichte. Zweiter Band. Von der Reformära bis zur industriellen und politischen 'Deutschen Doppelrevolution' 1815–1845/49*, 2nd edn, Munich, 1989, p. 524.
26. William Henry Chamberlain, *Die Russische Revolution 1917–1921*, Vol. 1, Frankfurt-am-Main, 1958, p. 337.
27. Peter Förster and Günther Roski, *DDR zwischen Wende und Wahl. Meinungsforscher analysieren den Umbruch*, Berlin, 1990, p. 11.
28. 'Was die Reichsgründung eigentlich für die Deutschen unterhalb der publizistischen und politischen Spitzenplätze bedeutete, wissen wir ganz einfach nicht.' Hagen Schulze, *Der Weg zum Nationalstaat. Die deutsche Nationalbewegung vom 18. Jahrhundert bis zur Reichsgründung*, second edition, Munich, 1986, p. 180.
29. Axel Schulte, 'Multikulturelle Gesellschaft: Chance, Ideologie oder Bedrohung?', *Aus Politik und Zeitgeschichte*, B 23–4, 1990, pp. 3–15, esp. p. 13.
30. See, for instance, Greenfeld, 1992: 25, or p. 494, note 4.
31. Assimilation is here defined as a process by which a group takes over the cultural norms and values of another group.
32. M. Rainer Lepsius, 'Parteiensystem und Sozialstruktur: zum Problem der Demokratisierung der deutschen Gesellschaft', in Gerhard A. Ritter (ed.), *Die deutschen Parteien vor 1918*, Cologne, 1973, pp. 56–80.
33. For a recent overview, with many references, see Franz Walter, 'Milieus und Parteien in der deutschen Gesellschaft. Zwischen Persistenz und Erosion', *Geschichte in Wissenschaft und Unterricht*, vol. 46, 1995, pp. 479–93.
34. Stein Rokkan, 'Nation building, cleavage formation and the structuring of mass politics', *Citizens, Elections, Parties. Approaches to the Comparative Study of the Processes of Development*, Oslo, 1970, p. 73–144. Karl Rohe, *Wahlen und Wählertraditionen in Deutschland*, Frankfurt-am-Main, 1992, p. 22. Rohe merged, however, Lepsius's liberal and conservative milieux into one national camp, a procedure which is not followed here.
35. Michael Vester et al., *Soziale Milieus im gesellschaftlichen Strukturwandel. Zwischen Integration und Anpassung*, Cologne, 1993.
36. The author thereby followed principles which Theda Skocpol formulated many years ago (Theda Skocpol, 'Emerging agendas and recurrent strategies in historical sociology', in Theda Skocpol (ed.), *Vision and Method in Historical Sociology*, Cambridge University Press, 1984, p. 356–91, esp. pp 382f.).
37. Max Weber, *Wirtschaft und Gesellschaft*, Cologne/Berlin, 1964, p. 26.
38. These were the four original *Millets*. As a consequence of the Western penetration of the Empire, a Protestant, a Catholic and other *Millets* were also introduced. Dimitri Kitsikis, *L'Empire Ottoman*, second edition, Paris, 1991, pp. 20f. and 109.

39. Ernest Gellner, *Nations and Nationalism*, Oxford, 1983, p. 35.
40. Gellner, 1983: 38.
41. Theodor Geiger, *Die Klassengesellschaft im Schmelztiegel*, Cologne and Hagen, 1949, p. 184, as quoted by Ralf Dahrendorf, *Class and Class Conflict in Industrial Society*, London, 1972, p. 65.
42. Dahrendorf, 1972: 65.
43. Regarding the case of the United Kingdom, Hugh Kearney uses the term 'The Britannic melting pot' (Hugh Kearney, *The British Isles. A History of Four Nations*, Cambridge, 1989, p. 149). The present author thanks Professor Ulf Hedetoft, Aalborg University, for this piece of information.

CHAPTER 2   FROM *GERMANIA* TO THE HOLY ROMAN EMPIRE OF THE GERMANIC NATION

1. Rolf Hachmann, *Die Germanen*, Munich, 1971, pp. 31ff.
2. Caesar, *De bello gallico*, II, 3 and VI, 32.
3. Hachmann, 1971: 67.
4. John Waterman, *A History of the German Language*, Washington, 1966, pp. 24ff.
5. Bruno Krüger et al., *Die Germanen. Geschichte und Kultur der germanischen Stämme in Mitteleuropa. Ein Handbuch in zwei Bänden. Band II: Die Stämme und Stammensverbände in der Zeit vom 3. Jahrhundert bis zur Herausbildung der politischen Vorherrschaft der Franken*, Berlin (East), 1983, p. 327.
6. Hachmann, 1971: 69ff.
7. Rigobert Günther and Helga Köpstein et al., *Die Römer an Rhein und Donau. Zur politischen, wirtschaftlichen und sozialen Entwicklung in den römischen Provinzen an Rhein, Mosel und oberer Donau im 3. und 4. Jahrhundert*, Vienna-Cologne Graz, 1975 (Akademie-Verlag, Berlin, DDR, 1975), pp. 137ff.
8. Charles-Marie Ternes, *Die Römer an Rhein und Mosel. Geschichte und Kultur*, Stuttgart, 1975. French original: *La Vie quotidienne en Rhénanie Romaine (Ier–IVe siècle)*, Paris, 1972, pp. 178ff.
9. Tacitus, *Germania*, I ('. . . a Sarmatis Dacisque mutuo metu aut montibus separatur; cetera Oceanus ambit, latos sinus et insularum immensa spatia complectens').
10. Günther and Köpstein, 1975: 51.
11. Krüger et al., 1983: 16.
12. Krüger et al., 1983: 549ff.
13. Joachim Ehlers, 'Mittelalterliche Voraussetzungen für nationale Identität in der Neuzeit', in Bernd Giesen (ed.), *Nationale und kulturelle Identität. Studien zur Entwicklung des kollektiven Bewusstseins in der Neuzeit*, Frankfurt-am-Main, 1991, pp. 77–99, esp. pp. 80f.
14. Krüger et al., 1983: 332ff.
15. Waterman, 1966: 77.
16. Otto Jespersen, *Growth and Structure of the English Language*, Oxford 1967, p. 60.

17. Josef Fleckenstein, *Grundlagen und Beginn der deutschen Geschichte*, Göttingen, 1974, pp. 125ff.
18. Ehlers, 1991: 93ff.
19. Fleckenstein, 1974: 135ff.
20. Fleckenstein, 1974: 170.
21. Fleckenstein, 1974: 152.
22. Ehlers, 1991: 97.
23. Gerhard Taddey (ed.), *Lexikon der deutschen Geschichte. Personen, Ereignisse, Institutionen. Von der Zeitenwende bis zum Ausgang des 2. Weltkrieges*, Stuttgart, 1977, p. 501.
24. Charles Higounet, *Die deutsche Ostsiedlung im Mittelalter*, Munich, 1990, pp. 228ff.
25. Higounet, 1990: 99.
26. Joachim Herrmann (ed.), *Die Slawen in Deutschland. Geschichte und Kultur der slawischen Stämme westlich von Oder und Neisse vom 6. bis 12. Jahrhundert. Ein Handbuch – Neubearbeitung*, Berlin (East) 1985, pp. 448ff.
27. Higounet, 1990: 13ff.
28. It should perhaps be emphasized that constitutionally it was the kings of the East Frankish kingdom who in addition were crowned as emperors. Not all kings became emperors – many rulers remained 'only' kings.
29. Joachim Leuschner, *Deutschland im späten Mittelalter*, Göttingen, 1975, p. 85.
30. Leuschner, 1975: 179ff.
31. Karl Bosl, Staat, 'Gesellschaft, Wirtschaft im deutschen Mittelalter', in Herbert Grundmann, (ed.), *Gebhardt. Handbuch der deutschen Geschichte*, Vol. 1, ninth edition, Stuttgart, 1970, pp. 694–835, esp. p. 833.
32. For an overview, see Joachim Ehlers, 'Die deutsche Nation des Mittelalters als Gegenstand der Forschung', in Joachim Ehlers (ed.), *Ansätze und Diskontinuität deutscher Nationsbildung im Mittelalter*, Sigmaringen, 1989, pp. 11–58. A recent overview is to be found in Reinhard Stauber, 'Nationalismus vor dem Nationalismus? Eine Bestandsaufnahme zu 'Nation' und 'Nationalismus' in der Frühen Neuzeit', *Geschichte in Wissenschaft und Unterricht*, vol. 47, 1996, pp. 139–65.
33. Watermann: 77. Peter Wiesinger, 'Regionale und überregionale Sprachausformung im Deutschen vom 12. bis zum 15. Jahrhundert unter dem Aspekt der Nationsbildung', in Ehlers, 1989: 321–43, esp. pp. 324f.
34. Rüdiger Schnell, 'Deutsche Literatur und deutsches Nationsbewusstsein im Spätmittelalter und Früher Neuzeit', in Ehlers, 1989: 247–320, esp. pp. 282ff.
35. Wiesinger in Ehlers, 1989: 322.
36. Wiesinger in Ehlers, 1989: 335.
37. It is therefore extremely misleading, as Higounet points out (Higounet: 65), when the ninth-century king *Ludovicus, rex Germaniae* is called *Ludwig der Deutsche* (Louis the German) in modern historical texts

(as still, for instance, in the authoritative handbook Grundman, 1970: 197ff).
38. Schnell in Ehlers, 1989: 266.
39. Wiesinger, in Ehlers, 1989: 336.
40. Schnell, in Ehlers, 1989: 269.
41. Schnell, in Ehlers, 1989: 303.
42. Leo Stern and Erhard Voigt, *Deutschland in der Epoche des vollentfalteten Feudalismus von der Mitte des 13. bis zum ausgehenden 15. Jahrhundert*, Berlin (East), 1976, pp. 242ff.
43. Schnell, in Ehlers, 1989: 301.
44. Schnell, in Ehlers, 1989: 302f.
45. Schnell, in Ehlers, 1989: 295ff.

CHAPTER 3   FROM REFORMATION TO ENLIGHTENMENT –
POLITICAL FRAGMENTATION AND CULTURAL UNIFICATION

1. Luther's theological works are complex and often contradictory. The interpretation presented here follows closely Richard van Dülmen, *Reformation als Revolution. Soziale Bewegung und religiöser Radikalismus in der deutschen Reformation*, Frankfurt-am-Main, 1987, pp. 23ff.
2. Bernd Moeller, *Deutschland im Zeitalter der Reformation*, Göttingen, 1977, p. 83.
3. Moeller, 1977: 69ff.
4. For an overview of the peace regulations and their ambiguities, see Martin Heckel, *Deutschland im konfessionellen Zeitalter*, Göttingen, 1983, pp. 33ff.
5. Gerhard Taddey (ed.), *Lexicon der deutschen Geschichte. Personen, Ereignisse, Institutionen. Von der Zeitenwende bis zum Ausgang des 2. Weltkrieges*, Stuttgart, 1977, p. 896.
6. Richard van Dülmen, *Entstehung des frühneuzeitlichen Europa 1550-1648*, Frankfurt, 1982, pp. 370ff.
7. Walter Hubatsch, *Deutschland zwischen dem Dreißigjährigem Krieg und der Französischen Revolution*, Frankfurt-am-Main–Berlin–Vienna, 1973, pp. 88ff.
8. Heckel, 1983: 134.
9. Heckel, 1983: 145ff.
10. Heckel, 1983: 181ff.
11. Hans-Ulrich Wehler, *Deutsche Gesellschaftsgeschichte. Erster Band. Vom Feudalismus des Alten Reiches bis zur Defensiven Modernisierung der Reformära 1700-1815*, second edition, Munich, 1989, p. 246.
12. Eric Hobsbawm, *Industry and Empire*, Harmondsworth, Middlesex, 1979, p. 49.
13. Francis L. Carsten, *Geschichte der preußischen Junker*, Frankfurt-am-Main, 1988, p. 36.
14. Manfred Messerschmidt, 'Preussens Militär in seinem gesellschaftlichen Umfeld', in Hans-Jürgen Puhle and Hans-Ulrich Wehler (eds), *Preussen im Rückblick*, Göttingen, 1980, pp. 43–88, esp. pp. 48ff.
15. Carsten, 1988: 68ff.

16. Carsten, 1988: 55ff.
17. Wehler, 1989, I: 270ff.
18. Taddey, 1977: 954.
19. Horst Möller, 'Wie aufgeklärt war Preussen?', in Puhle and Wehler, 1980: pp. 176–201, esp. p. 195.
20. Wehler, 1989, I: 254ff.
21. Möller, H. in Puhle and Wehler, 1980: 192.
22. Wehler, 1989, I: 261f.
23. Dülmen, 1982: 294.
24. Wehler, 1989, I: 285.
25. Rolf Engelsing, *Analphabetentum und Lektüre*, Stuttgart, 1973, p. 43.
26. Carlo M. Cipolla, *Literacy and Development in the West*, Harmondsworth, 1969, esp. pp. 64ff and 116f.
27. Wehler, 1989, I: 292f.
28. Wehler, 1989, I: 50f.
29. Wehler, 1989, I: 306.
30. Engelsing, 1973: 60.
31. Wehler, 1989, I: 307f.
32. Wehler, 1989, I: 210ff.
33. John Waterman, *A History of the German Language*, Washington, 1966, p. 133.
34. Waterman, 1966: 134 and 146.
35. Waterman, 1966: 127.
36. Waterman, 1966: 137.
37. 'Je me trouve ici en France. On ne parle que notre langue. L'allemand est pour les soldats et pour les chevaux...' Waterman: 138.
38. Waterman, 1966: 143.
39. Waterman, 1966: 141f.
40. Georg Iggers, *Deutsche Geschichtswissenschaft. Eine Kritik der traditionellen Geschichtsauffassung von Herder bis zur Gegenwart*, Munich, 1971, p. 51.
41. 'Nichts scheint also dem Zweck der Regierungen so offenbar entgegen, als die unnatürliche Vergrösserung der Staaten, die wilde Vermischung der Menschen-Gattungen und Nationen unter Einem Szepter.' Johann Gottfried Herder, *Ideen zur Philosophie der Geschichte der Menschheit*, ed. Martin Bollacher, Frankfurt-am-Main, 1989, pp. 369f.
42. '... der Mensch, der einen Herrn nötig hat, ist ein Tier; sobald er Mensch wird, hat er keines eigentlichen Herrn mehr nötig. Die Natur nämlich hat unserem Geschlecht keinen Herrn bezeichnet; nur tierische Laster und Leidenschaften machen uns desselben bedürftig.' Herder: 369.
43. Hobsbawm, 1992: 19f.

CHAPTER 4   1792–1871: THE SHAPING OF GERMANY

1. Hans-Ulrich Wehler, *Deutsche Gesellschaftsgeschichte. Erster Band: Vom Feudalismus des Alten Reiches bis zur Defensiven Modernisierung der Reformära 1700-1815*, second edition, Munich, 1989.
2. Wehler, 1989, I: 368ff.

3. Reinhart Koselleck, *Preußen zwischen Reform und Revolution. Allgemeines Landrecht, Verwaltung und soziale Bewegung von 1791 bis 1848*, Munich, 1989, p. 14.

4. 'Seit der Zeit des Neuen Testamentes hat kein Werk segensreichere Wirkungen gehabt', in Wehler, 1989, I: 405.

5. Wehler, 1989, I: 407.

6. Wehler, 1989, I: 523f.

7. Hagen Schulze, *Der Weg zum Nationalstaat. Die deutsche Nationalbewegung vom 18. Jahrhundert bis zur Reichsgründung*, second edition, Munich, 1986, p. 66.

8. '... seine geringe patriotische Freude... Er verhielt sich auffallend kühl und kritisierend dagegen und pries sogar die vielen glänzenden Eigenschaften des Kaisers Napoleon auf eine sehr beredte Weise.' Eckart Kleßmann (ed.), *Die Befreiungskriege in Augenzeugenberichten*, Düsseldorf, 1966, p. 216.

9. Schulze, 1986: 67f.

10. Wehler, 1989, I: 525.

11. 'Sie sprechen von dem Erwachen, von der Erhebung des deutschen Volkes... Ist denn wirklich das Volk erwacht... Der Schlaf ist zu tief gewesen... Wir sprechen nicht von den Tausenden gebildeter Jünglinge und Männer, wir sprechen von der Menge, von den Millionen.' Kleßmann, 1966: 218.

12. Kleßmann, 1966: 173f and 298ff.

13. Koselleck, 1989: 210.

14. Karl Griewank, *Der Wiener Kongress und die europäische Restauration 1814/1815*, Leipzig, 1954, pp. 305ff.

15. By the Treaty of Kiel (14 January 1814), it was decided that Denmark (Napoleon's ally) had to cede Norway to Sweden; as partial compensation, the Swedish possessions in northern Germany (Vorpommern with the isle of Rügen) were promised to Denmark. Sweden encountered, however, massive resistance in Norway, claimed that Denmark stood behind it, and refused to cede her German possessions. After complex negotiations Prussia acquired Vorpommern and Rügen; Denmark received instead the Duchy of Lauenburg from Hanover, and financial contributions from Prussia (Griewank, 1954: 260f).

16. Peter Burg, *Der Wiener Kongreß. Der Deutsche Bund im europäischen Staatensystem*, Munich, 1984, p. 9ff.

17. Burg, 1984: 74ff and 144ff.

18. Martin Broszat, *Zweihundert Jahre deutsche Polenpolitik*, Frankfurt-am-Main, 1972, p. 82.

19. Broszat, 1972: 69ff.

20. Broszat, 1972: 85.

21. 'Religion und Sprache sind die höchsten Heiligtümer einer Nation, in denen ihre ganze Gesinnungs- und Begriffswelt gegründet ist. Eine Obrigkeit, die diese anerkennt, achtet, und schätzt, darf sicher sein, die Herzen der Untertanen zu gewinnen, welche sich aber gleichgültig dagegen bezeigt oder gar Angriffe dagegen erlaubt, die erbittert oder entwürdigt die Nation und schafft sich ungetreue oder schlechte Untertanen.' Broszat, 1972: 90.

22. Broszat, 1972: 96.
23. William Oscar Henderson, *The Zollverein*, third edition, London, 1984, pp. 39ff.
24. Henderson, 1984: 95.
25. Rolf H. Dumke, 'Der Deutsche Zollverein als Modell ökonomischer Integration', in Helmut Berding (ed.), *Wirtschaftliche und politische Integration in Europa im 19. und 20. Jahrhundert*, Göttingen, 1984, pp. 71–101.
26. Schulze, 1986: 49ff.
27. In 1816 about 23.5 million people lived in Germany (borders of the Kaiserreich of 1871); in 1865 there were 38 million. Prussia and Saxony doubled their population in that period. Between 1816 and 1825 the population rose by 15 per cent, which equals an annual rate of 1.6 per cent, about double the rates known in the eighteenth century. Peter Marschalck, *Bevölkerungsgeschichte Deutschlands im 19. und 20. Jahrhundert*, Frankfurt-am-Main, 1984, p. 27.
28. Even in the eighteenth century about 200 000 people emigrated to overseas destinations, with perhaps 100 000 going to southeast Europe and Russia as colonists. Between 1816 and 1844 about 303 000 persons emigrated to overseas destinations. Marschalck, 1984: 21f and 177.
29. Schulze, 1986: 75.
30. As explained above (Chapter 3), most German authors used language as the central criterion to define 'nation'.
31. Dieter Düding, 'The nineteenth-century German nationalist movement as a movement of societies', in Hagen Schulze (ed.), *Nation-Building in Central Europe*, Leamington Spa/Hamburg/New York, 1987, pp. 19–50, esp. p. 38.
32. Hans-Ulrich Wehler, *Deutsche Gesellschaftsgeschichte. Zweiter Band. Von der Reformära bis zur industriellen und politischen 'Deutschen Doppelrevolution' 1815–1845/49*, 2nd edn, Munich, 1989, p. 431.
33. Wehler, 1989, II: 652ff.
34. Wehler, 1989, II: 706ff.
35. 'Preußen geht fortan in Deutschland auf.' Schulze, 1987: 87.
36. Harm-Hinrich Brandt, 'The revolution of 1848 and the problem of Central European nationalities', in Schulze, 1987, pp. 107–34, esp. p. 115.
37. The position of Friedrich Engels was perhaps symptomatic in this respect. As regards Poland he coined the fine words: 'A nation cannot become free and at the same time continue to suppress other nations. Germany's liberation cannot come about without the liberation of Poland from the suppression by Germans.' But 'Bohemians, Carinthians, Dalmatians etc.' were in his eyes just 'dying nations', doomed by history to be absorbed into the German nation, a process which at the same time brought Western European civilization to Eastern Europe. ('Eine Nation kann nicht frei werden und zugleich fortfahren, andere Nationen zu unterdrücken. Die Befreiung Deutschlands kann also nicht zustande kommen, ohne daß die Befreiung Polens von der Unterdrückung durch Deutsche zustande kommt.' (Karl Marx and Friedrich Engels, 'Reden über Polen' (on 29 November 1847), *Marx Engels Werke*,

vol. 4, Berlin (East), 1974, pp. 416–18, esp. p. 417; Friedrich Engels, 'Revolution und Konterrevolution in Deutschland', in Marx and Engels, 1974, vol. 8: 3–108, esp. p. 81.
38. Engels, in Marx and Engels, 1974, vol. 8: 118f.
39. Engels, in Marx and Engels, 1974, vol. 8: 116f.
40. Women had no right to vote, nor had 'dependent' persons, e.g. servants. The definition of 'dependency' differed. All together about 80 to 90 per cent of the adult male population had the right to vote (Wehler, 1989, II: 738).
41. Schulze, 1986: 88.
42. Brandt, in Schulze, 1987: 125.
43. Wehler, 1989, II: 751.
44. Wehler, 1989, II: 750.
45. Wolfram Siemann, *Gesellschaft im Aufbruch. Deutschland 1849–1871*, Frankfurt-am-Main, 1990, p. 27ff.
46. Siemann, 1990: 171ff.
47. During negotiations in London several projects for the division of Schleswig were discussed. Denmark presented a line near Schleswig town, Prussia one at Åbenrå. In the end Great Britain, backed by France and Russia, proposed that a neutral power should draw a line between those above mentioned. This would have resulted in a line very close to the one established in 1920. The German powers accepted, Denmark did not (Lorenz Rerup, *Slesvig og Holsten efter 1830*, Copenhagen, 1982, pp. 202ff.).
48. Rerup, 1982: 207.
49. Michael Stürmer, *Die Reichsgründung. Deutscher Nationalstaat und europäisches Gleichgewicht im Zeitalter Bismarcks*, Munich, 1990 (first edition, 1984), pp. 65ff.
50. Ernst Engelberg, *Bismarck. Urpreuße und Reichsgründer*, Munich, 1991, (first edition, 1985), pp. 577ff.
51. Siemann, 1990: 298.
52. Siemann, 1990: 305.
53. Karl Marx, 'Erste Adresse des Generalrates über den Deutsch-Französischen Krieg', in Marx and Engels, 1974, vol. 17: 3–8, esp. p. 6.
54. The present author owes this aspect to the Danish historian Uffe Østergaard, 'Hvornår opstod Norden?', *Information*, 15 June 1993, p. 2.

CHAPTER 5   GERMANY AFTER 1871 – SOME GENERAL ASPECTS AND TRENDS

1. Hans Boldt, *Deutsche Verfassungsgeschichte, Band 2. Von 1806 bis zur Gegenwart*, second edition, Munich, 1993, pp. 168ff.
2. Francis L. Carsten, *Geschichte der preußischen Junker*, Frankfurt-am-Main, 1988, pp. 128 and 149.
3. Thomas Nipperdey, *Deutsche Geschichte 1866–1918. Erster Band. Arbeitswelt und Bürgergeist*, third edition, Munich, 1993, p. 35 and 269.
4. Nipperdey, 1993: 538f.
5. Nipperdey, 1993: 536f.

258   *Notes*

6. Nipperdey, 1993: 547ff.
7. Nipperdey, 1993: 568ff.
8. Carlo M. Cipolla, *Literacy and Development in the West*, Harmondsworth, 1969, pp. 94 and 115.
9. Cipolla, 1969: 89 and 118.
10. Cipolla, 1969: 16 and 19.
11. Cipolla, 1969: 86f.
12. 'Von den Dienstmädchen galt es 1912 als selbstverständlich, daß sie "heute fast durchgängig geläufig lesen und schreiben und, oft besser als wünschenswert, rechnen"' (G. v. Schönthan, 'Kinder und Dienstboten', *Gartenlaube Kalender 1912*, p. 91, as quoted in Rolf Engelsing, *Analphabetentum und Lektüre*, Stuttgart, 1973, p. 105).
13. See the statistics in Cipolla, 1969: 16 and 128.
14. Nipperdey, 1993: 537.
15. Knut Borchardt, 'The Industrial Revolution in Germany 1700–1914', *The Fontana Economic History of Europe*, vol. 4 (1), Glasgow, 1973, pp. 76–160, esp. p. 76; Hubert Kiesewetter, *Industrielle Revolution in Deutschland 1815–1914*, Frankfurt-am-Main, 1989, p. 33.
16. Hans-Ulrich Wehler, *Deutsche Gesellschaftsgeschichte. Zweiter Band. Von der Reformäru bis zur industriellen und politischen 'Deutschen Doppelrevolution' 1815–1845/49*, second edition, Munich, 1989, p. 613.
17. Wehler, 1989, II: 614ff.
18. Wehler, 1989, II: 628.
19. Wehler, 1989, II: 269.
20. Wehler, 1989, II, 278.
21. See, for instance, Eric J. Hobsbawm, 187ff; Richard H. Tilly, *Vom Zollverein zum Industriestaat. Die wirtschaftlich-soziale Entwicklung Deutschlands 1834 bis 1914*, Munich, 1990, p. 108.
22. As one example of the abundant literature about the subject the small book by Carlo M. Cipolla, often quoted here, may be mentioned.
23. Lawrence Stone even spoke of an 'educational revolution' in England; Lawrence Stone, 'The educational revolution in England 1560–1640', *Past and Present*, vol. 28 (1964), pp. 41–80.
24. John Stuart Mill, *Principles of Political Economy with some of their Applications to Social Philosophy*, edited with an introduction by Sir William Ashley, London, 1904, reprinted 1987, Fairfield, NJ, p. 109.
25. Nipperdey, 1993: 269.
26. Nipperdey, 1993: 194.
27. Nipperdey, 1993: 297.
28. David Crew, *Bochum. Sozialgeschichte einer Industriestadt 1860–1914*, Frankfurt-am-Main/Berlin/Vienna 1980, p. 71. There must be a calculation mistake in Crew's figures: if, as he writes, 10 807 of the population increase can be attributed to net immigration, and if the inward immigration was 232 092, then the outward migration must have been 221 285 (not 194 836).
29. ' . . . einem Ameisenhaufen, in den der Wanderer seinen Stock gestoßen hat': Werner Sombart, *Die deutsche Volkswirtschaft im 19. u. im Anfang des 20. Jh.* (1903), Berlin, seventh edition 1927, p. 408, as quoted by Klaus J. Bade, 'Politik und Ökonomie der Auslanderbeschäftigung im

preußischen Osten 1885–1914. Die Internationalisierung des Arbeitsmarkts im "Rahmen der preußischen Abwehrpolitik"', in Hans-Jürgen Puhle und Hans-Ulrich Wehler (eds), *Preußen im Rückblick*, Göttingen, 1980, pp. 273–99.
30. Nipperdey, 1993: 342ff.

CHAPTER 6   THE FOUR MAIN SOCIO-CULTURAL MILIEUX

1. Karl Rohe, *Wähler und Wählertraditionen in Deutschland. Kulturelle Grundlagen deutscher Parteien und Parteiensysteme im 19. und 20. Jahrhundert*, Frankfurt-am-Main, 1992, pp. 46f.
2. For definitions, see Chapter 1.
3. M. Rainer Lepsius, 'Parteiensysteme und Sozialstruktur: zum Problem der Demokratsierung der deutschen Gesellschaft', in Gerhard A. Ritter (ed.), *Die deutschen Parteien vor 1918*, Cologne, 1973, p. 63.
4. Technically speaking, from 1893 to 1907, the correlation between agricultural occupation and conservative votes rose from 0.31 to 0.54; as to Protestant confession, the figures are 0.41 and 0.44 (Rohe: 272).
5. Rohe, 1992: 270.
6. For a short account of this process with references, see Heinrich-August Winkler '1866 und 1878: Der Liberalismus in der Krise', in Carola Stern and Heinrich-August Winkler, *Wendepunkte deutscher Geschichte 1848–1990*, Frankfurt-am-Main 1994, pp. 43–70.
7. The *rapprochement* between the liberals and the conservatives and their common front against Catholics and Socialists lend support to Karl Rohe's procedure which merged them into one 'national camp'. A 'camp', a concept created by Adam Wandruszka, is more based upon a confrontation against others than upon internal cohesion (Rohe: 21f). The concept of a 'national camp' blurs, however, the important differences which nevertheless existed among liberals and conservatives.
8. Hans Boldt, *Deutsche Verfassungsgeschichte, Band 2. Von 1806 bis zur Gegenwart*, second edition, Munich, 1993, p. 375.
9. Rohe, 1992: 270.
10. Lepsius, 1973: 71.
11. Thomas Nipperdey, *Deutsche Geschichte 1866–1918. Erster Band. Arbeitswelt und Bürgergeist, third edition*, Munich, 1993, p. 450. The figure relates to the year 1907.
12. '... daß viele in den Franzosen ihre einzigen Schützer gegen preußische Vergewaltigung ... und – wenn Gott es will – ihre dereinstigen Befreier von dem unerträglichen Joche des brutalen Preußentums ersehen.' Ernst Engelberg, *Bismarck. Urpreuße und Reichsgründer*, Munich, 1991, p. 583.
13. Ernst Engelberg, *Bismarck. Das Reich in der Mitte Europas*, Munich, 1993, p. 107.
14. See the report by Eduard Hüsgen, a leading Catholic journalist, in Gerhard A. Ritter (ed.), *Das Deutsche Kaiserreich 1871–1914. Ein historisches Lesebuch*, fifth edition, Göttingen, 1992, p. 199ff.
15. Nipperdey, 1993: 450.
16. Rohe, 1992: 117.

17. Nipperdey, 1993: 439ff.
18. Rohe, 1992: 270.
19. Rohe, 1992: 463 and 465.
20. Klaus Schönhoven, *Die deutschen Gewerkschaften*, Frankfurt-am-Main 1987, pp. 20f.
21. Rohe, 1992: 98–102.
22. Nipperdey, 1993: 329f.
23. Schönhoven, 1987: 89.
24. Nipperdey, 1993: 332.

CHAPTER 7   THE UNITING FORCE OF FEDERALISM: SOUTHERN GERMANY IN CONTRAST TO ALSACE-LORRAINE

1. Hans-Ulrich Wehler, *Krisenherde des Kaiserreiches 1871–1918. Studien zur deutschen Sozial- und Verfassungsgeschichte*, Göttingen, 1979, p. 32.
2. Wehler, 1979: 64.
3. 'Ach, Ludwig, ich kann Dir gar nicht beschreiben, wie unendlich weh und schmerzlich es mir während jener Zeremonie zumute war, . . . Welchen wehmütigen Eindruck machte es mir, unsere Bayern sich da vor dem Kaiser neigen zu sehen . . .' Ernst Deuerlein, *Die Gründung des Deutschen Reiches in Augenzeugenberichten 1870/71*, Düsseldorf, 1977, p. 308.

CHAPTER 8   THE JEWS

1. From 1871 to 1910, the number of Jews grew from 512 000 to 615 000; this meant an increase in absolute numbers, but a relative fall from 1.25 to 0.95 per cent of the population (Thomas Nipperdey, *Deutsche Geschichte 1866–1918. Erster Band. Arbeitswelt und Bürgergeist*, third edition, Munich, 1993, p. 396).
2. Nipperdey, 1993: 399.
3. Hermann Graml, *Reichskristallnacht. Antisemitismus und Judenverfolgung im Dritten Reich*, Munich, 1988a, pp. 44ff.
4. Graml, 1988a: 45f.
5. Nipperdey, 1993: 397.
6. Graml, 1988a: 46ff.
7. Nipperdey, 1993: 396.
8. Nipperdey, 1993: 412.
9. Graml, 1988a: 81.
10. Graml, 1988a: 68.

CHAPTER 9   NATIVE NON-GERMAN MINORITIES

1. See the declaration of the Polish group in the Reichstag, 1 April 1871, Hans Fenske (ed.), *Im Bismarckschen Reich 1871–1890 (Quellen zum politischen Denken der Deutschen in 19. und 20. Jahrhundert. Freiherr vom Stein Gedächtnisausgabe, Band VI)*, Darmstadt, 1978, pp. 43ff.

2. Ernst Engelberg, 1993: 364.
3. Martin Broszat, *Zweihundert Jahre deutsche Polenpolitik*, Frankfurt-am-Main, 1972, p. 135.
4. Broszat, 1972: 146ff.
5. Broszat, 1972: 166.
6. Broszat, 1972: 162ff.
7. Broszat, 1972: 161.
8. William W. Hagen, *Germans, Poles, and Jews. The Nationality Conflict in the Prussian East, 1772–1914*, Chicago and London, 1980, p. 264.
9. There are no language statistics for that time, but the number of German Catholics was constantly rising. This was not due to the immigration of German Catholics, but because Polish Catholics became German. In 1910 only 54 per cent of the Catholics in West Prussia were Poles; 32 per cent were German. See Stefan Hartmann, 'Zu den Nationalitätenverhältnissen in Westpreußen vor dem Ausbruch des Ersten Weltkrieges', *Zeitschrift für Ostforschung – Länder und Völker im östlichen Mitteleuropa*, vol. 42. no. 3, 1993b, pp. 391–405, esp. p. 394.
10. Hartmann, 1993: 392.
11. Broszat, 1972: 210.
12. Oswald Hauser, 'Obrigkeitsstaat und demokratisches Prinzip im Nationalitätenkampf. Preußen in Nordschleswig', *Historische Zeitschrift*, vol. 192, 1961, pp. 318–61, esp. p. 321.
13. Lorenz Rerup, *Slesvig og Holsten efter 1830*, Copenhagen, 1983, pp. 209ff.
14. Rerup, 1982: 259.
15. Rerup, 1982: 269.
16. Rerup, 1982: 301.
17. Rerup, 1982: 338.
18. There were also small Frisian communities near the Dutch border. Their problems will not be treated here due to lack of space.
19. Thomas Steensen, *Die friesische Bewegung in Nordfriesland im 19. und 20. Jahrhundert (1879–1945)*, Neumünster, 1986, pp. 42ff.
20. Steensen, 1986: 97ff.
21. Steensen, 1986: 146f.
22. Hans-Ulrich Wehler, *Krisenherde des Kaiserreiches 1871–1918. Studien zur deutschen Sozial- und Verfassungsgeschichte*, Göttingen, 1979, pp. 238ff.
23. Joachim Rogall, 'Die Tragödie einer Grenzlandbevölkerung – polnische Forschungen über die Masuren', *Zeitschrift für Ostforschung – Länder und Völker im östlichen Mitteleuropa*, vol. 41, no. 1, 1992, pp. 102–11, esp. p. 104.
24. Wehler, 1979: 239.
25. For detailed statistical evidence, see L. Wittschell, *Die völkischen Verhältnisse in Masuren und dem südlichen Ermland*, Hamburg, 1925, p. 23, as quoted in Stefan Hartmann, 'Zur nationalpolnischen Bewegung und zur preußischen Politik in Masuren vor dem Ersten Weltkrieg', *Zeitschrift für Ostforschung*, no. 1, 1993a, pp. 40–83, esp. p. 43.
26. Wehler, 1979: 243.
27. Hartmann, 1993b: *passim*.

28. Rogall, 1992: 105.
29. Broszat, 1972: 144f; Hartmann, 1993b: 392.
30. Dietrich Gerhardt, 'Das Elb- und Ostseeslavische', in Peter Rehder (ed.), *Einführung in die slavischen Sprachen*, Darmstadt, 1986, pp. 103–10.
31. Hagen, 1980: 7.
32. Rehder, 1986: Chapter 7.
33. Gerald Stone, *The Smallest Slavonic Nation. The Sorbs of Lusatia*, London, 1972, pp. 99–120.
34. Herrmann, 1985: 469
35. Stone, 1972: 18–23.
36. Stone, 1972: 28f, 128–31.
37. Stone, 1972: 24.
38. Stone, 1972: 18.
39. Hartmut Zwahr, *Sorbische Volksbewegung. Dokumente zur antisorbischen Staatspolitik im preußischen Reich, zur Oberlausitzer Bauernbewegung und zur sorbischen nationalen Bewegung 1872–1918*, Bautzen, 1968, p. 8, and documents no. 1 and no. 2, pp. 24–6.
40. Zwahr, 1968: 49, document no. 28.
41. Zwahr, 1968: 189, document no. 179.
42. Hans Lindemann, 'Stichwort: Domowina', *Deutschland-Archiv*, no. 10, 1987, pp. 1025f.
43. Stone, 1972: 31f.

CHAPTER 10 IMMIGRANTS AND EAST–WEST MIGRANTS

1. Klaus J. Bade, *Homo Migrans – Wanderungen aus und nach Deutschland*, Essen, 1994a, p. 23.
2. Peter Marschalck, *Bevölkerungsgeschichte Deutschlands im 19. und 20. Jahrhundert*, Frankfurt, 1984, p. 178.
3. Christoph Kleßmann, *Polnische Bergarbeiter im Ruhrgebiet 1870–1945. Soziale Integration und nationale Subkultur einer Minderheit in der deutschen Industriegesellschaft*, Göttingen, 1978, p. 44.
4. 'Gegen zwingende wirtschaftliche Bedürfnisse komme man mit polizeilichen Maßregeln nicht auf.' Klaus J. Bade, 'Politik und Ökonomie der Auslanderbeschäftigung im preußischen Osten 1885–1914. Die Internationalisierung des Arbeitsmarkts im "Rahmen der preußischen Abwehrpolitik"', in Hans-Jürgen Puhle und Hans-Ulrich Wehler (eds), *Preußen im Rückblick*, Göttingen, 1980, p. 283.
5. Cornelia Schmalz-Jacobsen et al., *Einwanderung – und dann? Perspektiven einer neuen Ausländerpolitik*, Munich, 1993, p. 71.
6. '. . . Arbeiterschicht zweiten Grades, wie etwa die Neger in den nordamerikanischen Oststaaten, die Chinesen in Kalifornien und Australien, die Kulis in Britisch-Westindien, die Japaner in Hawai.' Johann Woydt, *Ausländische Arbeitskräfte in Deutschland. Vom Kaiserreich bis zur Bundesrepublik*, Heilbronn, 1987, p. 15.
7. The term was created by the Swiss sociologist Hoffmann-Nowottny. Rainer Geißler, *Die Sozialstruktur Deutschlands. Ein Studienbuch zur*

Entwicklung im geteilten und vereinigten Deutschland, Opladen, 1992a, pp. 161ff.

8. Woydt, 1987: 11.
9. Bade, 1980: 286f.
10. Woydt, 1987: 17.
11. '... beim Kontraktabschluß wird ihnen vielfach vorgelesen, was im Kontrakt gar nicht steht. Vielfach sind die Kontakte ungültig, weil sie von den Arbeitern nicht unterschrieben sind und viel Betrug beim Abschluß vorliegt.' Woydt: 23.
12. Woydt: 31.
13. Kleßmann, 1978: 263ff.
14. Kleßmann, 1978: 22.
15. Hans-Ulrich Wehler, *Krisenherde des Kaiserreiches 1871–1918. Studien zur deutschen Verfassungsgeschichte*, Göttingen, 1979, p. 227.
16. Kleßmann, 1978: 56ff.
17. Kleßmann, 1978: 77.
18. Kleßmann, 1978: 63.
19. Bade, 1980: 287.
20. Kleßmann, 1978: 94ff.
21. See Kleßmann, 1978: 72 and 280.
22. Kleßmann, 1978: 93 and 110.
23. Kleßmann, 1978: 82.
24. Kleßmann, 1978: 125ff.
25. Kleßmann, 1978: 68.
26. Kleßmann, 1978: 280.
27. Kleßmann, 1978: 71.

CHAPTER 11 SOME CONCLUSIONS: CULTURAL CONFLICTS
AND INTEGRATION IN THE KAISERREICH

1. See Volker Berghahn, 'Flottenrüstung und Machtgefüge', Michael Stürmer (ed.), *Das kaiserliche Deutschland. Politik und Gesellschaft 1870–1918*, Kronberg/Ts, 1979, pp. 378–96, esp. p. 383, or Hans-Ulrich Wehler, *Bismarck und der Imperialismus*, fourth edition, Munich, 1976, *passim*, for instance, p. 151.
2. The share of Berlin's responsibility for the outbreak of the First World War and the character of the German war aims were the subject of the most famous controversy in modern German historiography, the *Fischer-Kontroverse*, started by Fritz Fischer's book published in 1962, *Griff nach der Weltmacht. Die Kriegszielpolitik des kaiserlichen Deutschland 1914/1918* (newer edition: Kronberg/Ts., 1977). Fischer and his followers were able to document that the German government followed a policy of imperialist madness during the war, and that imperialist ambitions were already widespread among parts of the political elite and some segments of German society before the war. The 'Fischerites' were, however, not succesful in their efforts to show that the German government systematically aimed at war in the years before 1914. For a recent contribution to the subject, with many references, see Gregor

Schöllgen (ed.), *Flucht in den Krieg? Die Außenpolitik des kaiserlichen Deutschland*, Darmstadt, 1991.
3. Hans-Ulrich Wehler, *Deutsche Gesellschaftsgeschichte. Dritter Band. Von der 'Deutschen Doppelrevolution' bis zum Beginn des Ersten Weltkrieges 1849–1914*, Munich, 1995.
4. See Eric J. Hobsbawm, *Nations and Nationalism since 1780: Programme, Myth, Reality*, second edition, Cambridge, 1992, pp. 117–20.

CHAPTER 12 THE FIRST WORLD WAR – THE PRIMARY CATASTROPHE OF THE CENTURY

1. '... daß das Volk in seinem überwiegenden Teil kriegsmüde ist.' As quoted in Jürgen Kocka, *Klassengesellschaft im Krieg. Deutsche Sozialgeschichte 1914–1918*, Frankfurt-am-Main, 1988, p. 63.
2. 'Sehnsucht nach einem 'ehrenvollen Frieden'. 'Andereseits will man aber den Krieg nicht fortgeführt wissen, um übertriebene Kriegsziele zu erreichen. Ganz besonders lehnen die unteren Volksschichten bis weit in den Mittelstand hinein derartige Kriegsziele ab.' Kocka, 1988: 63.
3. Fritz Fischer, *Griff nach der Weltmacht. Die Kriegszielpolitik des kaiserlichen Deutschland 1914/1918* Kronberg/Ts., 1977, *passim*.
4. Fischer, 1977: 341–4.
5. 'In den ärmeren Bevölkerungsschichten hat sich gegen die Reichen und namentlich gegen die sogenannten Kriegsgewinnler ein geradezu schädlicher Haß aufgestapelt, von dem man nur wünschen kann, daß er nicht doch einmal zu einer furchtbaren Entladung kommt.' Kocka, 1988: 66.
6. Klaus Schönhoven, *Die deutschen Gewerkschaften*, Frankfurt-am-Main, 1987, p. 105.
7. Klaus Epstein, *Matthias Erzberger und das Dilemma der deutschen Demokratie*, Frankfurt-am-Main/Berlin/Vienna, 1976, pp. 129–37 and 204–36.
8. Martin Broszat, *Zweihundert Jahre deutsche Polenpolitik*, Frankfurt-am-Main, 1972, pp. 189–94.
9. 'Die Gründung des Königreiches Polen und später die überall verbreitete Lehre vom Selbstbestimmungsrecht der Völker hat das spezifische polnische Nationalgefühl in einer die deutschen Interessen schwer schädigenden Weise wachsen lassen.' Broszat, 1972: 198.

CHAPTER 13 THE WEIMAR REPUBLIC

1. Hans Boldt, *Deutsche Verfassungsgeschichte, Band 2. Von 1806 bis zur Gegenwart*, second edition, Munich, 1993, p. 234.
2. Klaus Schönhoven, *Die deutschen Gewerkschaften*, Frankfurt-am-Main, 1987, p. 124.
3. The argumentation on this point follows Heinrich-August Winkler, *Von der Revolution zur Stabilisierung. Arbeiter und Arbeiterbewegung in der Weimarer Republik 1918 bis 1924*, second edition, Berlin/Bonn, 1985, pp. 68–96.

4. Wolfram Wette, 'Ideologien, Propaganda und Innenpolitik als Voraussetzungen der Kriegspolitik des Dritten Reiches', in Wilhelm Deist et al., *Ursachen und Voraussetzungen des Zweiten Weltkrieges*, Frankfurt-am-Main, 1989, pp. 25–208, esp. p. 65.
5. Boldt, 1993: 375.
6. Quoted in John Maynard Keynes, 'The economic consequences of the peace', *Collected Writings*, vol. II, London, 1971, p. 39.
7. Keynes, 1971: 101.
8. According to Keynes (Keynes: 128) an indemnity of £500 million was roughly comparable to the sum paid by France in 1871. The exchange rate in 1919 was 20 gold mark for £1 (ibid.: 103). 132 billion gold marks thus equalled £6.6 billion.
9. Keynes: 70.
10. Ibid.: 143.
11. Ibid.: 170.
12. Karl Rohe, *Wähler und Wählertraditionen in Deutschland. Kulturelle Grundlagen deutscher Parteien und Parteiensysteme im 19. und 20. Jahrhundert*, Frankfurt-am-Main, 1992, p. 136.
13. The fear which Bolshevism and the international communist movement induced in large masses of citizens was one among many factors explaining the rise of Nazism. This point was, however, exaggerated by the historian and philosopher Ernst Nolte (*Der Europäische Bürgerkrieg 1917–1945. Nationalsozialismus und Bolschewismus*, fourth edition, Frankfurt-am-Main, 1989). Nolte depicted Nazism as a reaction to Bolshevism, an 'over-shooting' and exaggerated reaction, but a reaction nevertheless. Nolte's well-written book contains numerous fascinating insights, but the few pages about the genesis of the Nazi party (pp. 116–23) which, being at the core of his argument, should be very solidly documented, are speculations with hardly any source material. He does not mention the fact that the organizational beginnings of the NSDAP are to be found in the chauvinist campaigns during the First World War; he mentions the point that the main subject of Nazi propaganda between 1919 and 1921 was the fight against Versailles (p. 117), but he writes nevertheless that Hitler's 'moving impulse' was somewhere else, and that 'much points in the direction that' this was the Bolshevist atrocities. Nolte's book provoked the so-called '*Historikerstreit*', – as often in Germany, a quite polemical historical debate.
14. Rohe, 1992: 121.
15. Boldt, 1993: 377f.
16. Many authors have placed the peak of the German milieux at the time before 1914. Newer research has shown, however, that the Catholic and the socialist milieux had their greatest density in the 1920s. See, Franz Walter, 'Milieus und Parteien in der deutschen Gesellschaft. Zwischen Persistenz und Erosion', *Geschichte in Wissenschaft und Unterricht*, vol. 46, 1995, pp. 479–93, esp. pp. 486f.
17. Many authors who interpret the Holocaust as the authentic expression of German 'national identity' have tried to connect Nazi anti-Semitism with Luther's anti-Semitic pamphlets, Luther being given the

role of a kind of ideological grandfather of German 'national identity'. This interpretation heroically abstracts from the fact that many building blocks of Nazi ideology were fabricated in Austria-Hungary, that Hitler himself was a Catholic Austrian, and that Austrians were strongly overrepresented in the SS murder machine.

18. Walter, 1995: 482.
19. There has been a tendency in West German historiography to underestimate the seriousness of the military preparations of the German Communists in the early 1930s. It is true that the Communists, in contrast to 1923, had not (yet) taken decisions to start an armed uprising, but they made, to the best of their ability, military preparations for the revolution to come in the near future. According to police information, the Central Commitee decided in September 1930 to transform the illegal *Rote Frontkämpferbund* into a clandestine military organization which was to be ready within six months, and which was to serve as the skeleton for a Red Army. The Communists organized clandestine armed groups and trained them and they made preliminary preparations for an attack upon the police stations. In this way they intended to get access to more weapons, as with the Hamburg uprising in 1923 (Organisation und Tätigkeit des verbotenen Rotfronkämpferbundes in Deutschland, Juli 1931, Brandenburgisches Landeshauptarchiv, Potsdam, Pr. Br. Rep 30 Bln, tit. 90 Nr. 7572, Blatt 239–250; unfortunately the present author does not know a more easily accessible source). Reliable Communists received intensive military training in the Soviet Union; the first of these military courses was held in 1924, the sixth (42 participants) in 1932. Lists of the names of the participants are kept in the former SED archives (Archiv der Parteien und Massenorganisationen der DDR im Bundesarchiv, Berlin, I 2/3/ 81). The Communist Party illegally distributed instruction manuals about the art of armed uprising (reprinted in 1971 as A. Neuberg et al., *Der bewaffnete Aufstand. Versuch einer theoretischen Darstellung. Eingeleitet von Erich Wollenberg*, Frankfurt-am-Main, 1971), and, likewise illegally, a periodical named *Oktober* where military problems were debated. In 1931 the paper advocated a theory of a kind of guerrilla warfare against police and right-wing paramilitary organizations (Paul Heider et al., *Geschichte der Militärpolitik der KPD 1918–1945*, Berlin (East), 1987, p. 216); this was presumably the background for the series of murders of policemen which Communist groups committed in that year. The Communists also endeavoured to organize clandestine groups inside the army and the police; according to police information, in October 1931 the Communist leadership decided to replace the agitation 'from the outside' by a systematic effort to infiltrate army and police (Bericht über den illegalen 'Am'-Apparat [Antimilitaristischer Apparat] der K.P.D., 30. September 1932, Brandenburgisches Landeshauptarchiv, Pr. Br. Rep. 30 Bln C, Nr. 197, Blatt 2–11). As it turned out, the military force of the German communists remained weak, but there can be no doubt about the seriousness of their intentions.
20. Rohe, 1992: 161.
21. Jürgen W. Falter, *Hitlers Wähler*, Munich, 1991 p. 184. The figures

are calculated as a percentage of all people entitled to vote (non-voters and invalid votes included).

22. Falter, 1991: 311.
23. Walter, 1995: 485.
24. Martin Broszat, *Die Machtergreifung. Der Aufstieg der NSDAP und die Zerstörung der Weimarer Republik*, second edition, Munich, 1987, p. 175.
25. '... die Stimmung für eine Loslösung der Rheinlande vom Reich in einer nicht leicht zu überschätzenden Weise vorbereitet hat'. Winkler, 1985: 93.
26. '... daß Preußen, d.h. überhaupt die norddeutsche Hegemonie hier in allen Kreisen in einem Maße verhaßt ist, das ich mir nie hätte träumen lassen.' Report from Schmidthals, 22 June 1919, *Akten zur auswärtigen Politik 1918–1945. Aus den Archiven des Auswärtigen Amtes.* Series A: 1918–1923, Volume II, Göttingen, 1984, p. 135.
27. 'Aufzeichnungen General Groeners vom 18. bis 20. Juni 1919', in Herbert Michaelis and Ernst Schraepler (eds), *Ursachen und Folgen. Vom deutschen Zusammenbruch 1918 und 1945 bis zur staatlichen Neuordnung Deutschlands in der Gegenwart*, Volume 3, Berlin, 1960, pp. 373–6.
28. See the memorandum written by Matthias Erzberger, the chairman of the Zentrum party, outlining the consequences of a German refusal to sign the treaty, in Klaus Epstein, *Matthias Erzberger und das Dilemma der deutschen Demokratie*, Frankfurt-am-Main/Berlin/Vienna, 1976, pp. 356–8.
29. Helmut Heiber, *Die Republik von Weimar*, nineteenth edition, Munich, 1990, p. 105.
30. Gerhard Taddey (ed.). *Lexicon der deutschen Geschichte. Personen, Ereignisse, Institutionen. Von der Zweitende bis zum Ausgang des 2. Weltkrieges* Stuttgart, 1977, p. 5.
31. Ernst Nolte, *Der Faschismus in seiner Epoche. Action française – italienischer Faschismus – Nationalsozialismus*, eighth edition, Munich/Zürich, 1990, p. 367.
32. Winston S. Churchill, *The World Crisis, The Aftermath*, London, 1929, pp. 222–31, as reproduced in I. Lederer (ed.), *The Versailles Settlement. Was It Foredoomed to Failure?*, Boston, 1965, pp. 78–85, esp. p. 84.
33. Taddey, 1977: 46.
34. Taddey, 1977: 46.
35. Note by secretary of state von Schubert, 16 July 1927, in Peter Krüger, *Versailles. Deutsche Außenpolitik zwischen Revisionismus und Friedenssicherung*, Munich, 1986, pp. 194f.
36. Rudolf Jaworski, 'Die Sudetendeutschen als Minderheit in der Tschechoslowakei 1919–1938', in Wolfgang Benz (ed.), *Die Vertreibung der Deutschen aus dem Osten. Ursachen, Ereignisse, Folgen*, second edition, Frankfurt-am-Main, 1985a, pp. 29–38, esp. pp. 30f.
37. Alfred M. de Zayas, *Die Anglo-Amerikaner und die Vertreibung der Deutschen Vorgeschichte Verlauf, Folgen*, Munich, 1980, pp. 49 and 204 note 19.
38. De Zayas, 1980: 50.
39. Ulrich Herbert, *Die Geschichte der Ausländerbeschäftigung in Deutschland*

1880–1980. Saisonarbeiter, Zwangsarbeiter, Gastarbeiter, Berlin/Bonn, 1986, pp. 118f.

40. Herbert, 1986: 116.
41. Herbert, 1986: 157.
42. Herbert, 1986: 172f.
43. Herbert, 1986: 166.
44. Theodor Schieder et al. (eds), *Dokumentation der Vertreibung der Deutschen aus Ost-Mitteleuropa*. Bonn, 1954, reprinted Munich, 1984, Band I/1, p. 6 E.
45. Schieder, 1954: 6 E.
46. Edward D. Wynot, 'The Poles in Germany, 1919–1939', *East European Quarterly*, vol. 30, no. 2, June 1996, pp. 171–86, esp. p. 176.
47. Rogall, 1992: 106.
48. *Statistik des Deutschen Reiches. Neue Folge, Band 427*, Berlin, 1932 (reprint Osnabrück, 1978), pp. 6–9 (henceforth referred to as StDR 427). Election results are usually reproduced as the percentage of valid votes. This procedure eliminates the 'party of the non-voters' and thereby overstates the importance of the other parties. Therefore the figures shown here are calculated as percentages of persons entitled to vote (non-voters and invalid votes included). Presented in this way, they are also comparable with Falter's tables, which are also quoted in this context (Falter, 1991).
49. Falter, 1991: 161.
50. Zwahr, 1968: 17 and 276f.
51. Stone, 1972: 32.
52. Stone, 1972: 34.
53. Herrmann, 1985: 475f.
54. Martin Kasper, *Geschichte der Sorben, Band 3. Von 1917 bis 1945*, Bautzen, 1976, p. 113f.
55. StDR 427: 13–17, 44–5.
56. Steensen, 1986: 154f.
57. Rerup, 1982: 368.
58. StDR 427: 22–23.
59. Ellen Andersen et al., *Sønderjylland med Vadehavet og Rømø. Gyldendals Egnsbeskrivelser*, second edition, Copenhagen, 1977, p. 171.
60. Falter, 1991: 159 and 161.
61. Thomas Steensen, *Die friesische Bewegung in Nordfriesland im 19. und 20. Jahrhundert (1879–1945)*. Neumünster, 1986, p. 229.
62. Kleßmann, 1978: 170; G. Stone, *The Smallest Slavonic Nation. The Sorbs of Lusatia*, London, 1972, p. 33.
63. Steensen, 1972: 226–79.
64. '... alle Schichte des Volkes zur notwendigen Geschlossenheit zusammenzufassen ...', '... den internationalistisch-pazisitisch-defaitistisch denkenden Teil des Volkes ...', '... die Leitung des jüdischen Volkes'. Nolte, 1990: 400f.
65. '... Pazifisten, Juden, Demokraten, Schwarzrotgold u(nd) Franzosen alles das Gleiche, nämlich Leute, die die Vernichtung Deutschlands wollen.' Quoted by Karl-Heinz Janßen und Fritz Tobias, *Der Sturz der Generäle. Hitler und die Blomberg-Fritsch-Krise 1938*, Munich, 1994, p. 143.

CHAPTER 14   THE THIRD REICH, THE SECOND WORLD WAR
AND GENOCIDE

1. 'Verfassungsurkunde des Dritten Reiches', as quoted in Norbert Frei, *Der Führerstaat. Nationalsozialistische Herrschaft 1933 bis 1945*, Munich, 1987, p. 45.
2. Martin Broszat, *Der Staat Hitlers*, eleventh edition, Munich, 1986, pp. 105–13.
3. See Broszat, 1986: *passim*.
4. 'Vielleicht Erkämpfung neuer Export-Mögl., vielleicht – und wohl besser – Eroberung neuen Lebensraumes im Osten u. dessen rücksichtslose Germanisierung. Sicher, daß erst mit pol. Macht u. Kampf jetzige wirtschaftl. Zustände geändert werden können.' Bernd-Jürgen Wendt, *Großdeutschland. Außenpolitik und Kriegsvorbereitung des Hitler-Regimes*, Munich, 1987, p. 187.
5. Major v. Mellenthin recorded 'colonies' instead of 'living space in the east' as Hitler's favourite aim, and at the Nüremberg trial, Grand Admiral Erich Raeder gave a third version of the meeting. Aage Trommer, 'Program eller ej? Om udforskningen af Tyskland i den anden verdenskrig', *Historisk Tidsskrift*, vol. 87, no. 2, 1987 pp. 318–34, esp. p. 325.
6. 'Bald nach dem Krieg kam ich zu der Ansicht, daß 3 Schlachten siegreich zu schlagen seien, wenn Deutschland wieder mächtig werden sollte. 1. die Schlacht gegen die Arbeiterschaft, sie hat Hitler siegreich geschlagen. 2. gegen die katholische Kirche, besser gesagt gegen den Ultramontanismus u. 3. gegen die Juden. In diesen Kämpfen stehen wir noch mitten drin. Und der Kampf gegen die Juden ist der schwerste.' In Karl-Heinz Janßen and Fritz Tobias, *Der Sturz der Generäle. Hitler und die Blomberg-Fritsch-Krise 1938*, Munich, 1994, pp. 253f.
7. Frei, 1987: 93–100.
8. 'Soweit sich überhaupt die Einstellung eines ganzen Volkes auf eine Formel bringen läßt, kann man etwa folgendes feststellen:
   1. Hitler hat bei einer Mehrheit des Volkes Zustimmung in zwei wesentlichen Fragen: er hat Arbeit geschaffen und er hat Deutschland stark gemacht.
   2. Es besteht weitgehend Unzufriedenheit über die herrschenden Zustände, die aber nur die Sorgen des Alltags betrifft und bis jetzt . . . nicht zu grundsätzlicher Gegnerschaft gegen das Regime führt.
   3. Weit verbreitet ist der Zweifel in den dauernden Bestand des Regimes, ebenso weit verbreitet aber auch die Ratlosigkeit darüber, was an seine Stelle treten könnte.
   . . . – es ist dem Regime bisher nicht gelungen, die Vorstellung auszurotten, daß seine Herrschaft nur ein Übergangszustand sein kann. Diese Feststellung ist für die Beurteilung der Frage nach der inneren Kraft des Regimes wichtiger als die Registrierung der jeweiligen Schwankungen von Zufriedenheit und Unzufriedenheit. Sie steht auch nicht im Widerspruch zu den Beobachtungen darüber, daß die politische Teilnahmslosigkeit der Massen wächst.' In Wolfgang Michalka, *Das Dritte Reich. Band 1: 'Volksgemeinschaft' und Großmachtpolitik 1933–1939*, Munich, 1985, p. 110.

9. Broszat, 1986: 115 and 123–5.
10. Frei, 1987:107.
11. 'Irgendwelche Begeisterung für kriegerische Verwicklungen wegen der sudetendeutschen Frage besteht nicht. Unsicherheit der politischen Lage liegt drückend auf der Bevölkerung ... Stimmung vielfach gedrückt.' 'Überall herrschte große Spannung und Beunruhigung, und überall wurde der Wunsch laut: nur keinen Krieg. Besonders scharf wurde dieser Wunsch von den Frontkämpfern des Weltkrieges ausgesprochen ...', Wolfram Wette, 'Ideologien, Propaganda und Innenpolitik als Voraussetzungen der Kriegspolitik des Dritten Reiches', in Wilhelm Deist et al., *Ursachen und Voraussetzungen des Zweiten Weltkrieges*, Frankfurt-am-Main, 1989, pp. 165f.
12. This was the observation by Paul Schmidt, the chief interpreter in the foreign ministry. 'Der deutsche Diktator war tief enttäuscht, daß das deutsche Volk angesichts des Krieges so ganz anders reagierte, als es im nationalsozialistischen Heldenhandbuch vorgeschrieben war.' Paul Schmidt, *Statist auf diplomatischer Bühne 1923–1945. Erlebnisse des Chefdolmetschers im Auswärtigen Amt mit den Staatsmännern Europas*, Bonn, 1950, p. 418.
13. Avraham Barkai, *Vom Boykott zur 'Entjudung'. Der wirtschaftliche Existenzkampf der Juden im Dritten Reich 1933–1943*, Frankfurt-am-Main, 1987, pp. 11–15.
14. Hermann Graml, *Reichskristallnacht. Antisemitismus und Judenverfolgung im Dritten Reich*, Munich, 1988a, pp. 108–14.
15. Graml, 1988a: 122.
16. Graml, 1988a: 124–6.
17. Barkai, 1987: 63.
18. 'Wir kennen nur ein Vaterland und eine Heimat, und das ist Deutschland.' Graml, 1988a: 128.
19. Graml, 1988a: 129.
20. Graml, 1988a: 156f.
21. *Documents on British Foreign Policy 1919–1937*, third series, vol. 3, p. 277, as quoted in Hermann Graml, *Antisemitism in the Third Reich*, Oxford, 1992, p. 141.
22. 'Die Auswanderung der Juden aus Deutschland ist mit allen Mitteln zu fördern.' Graml, 1988a: 182.
23. Barkai, 1987: 168.
24. Graml, 1988a: 202f.
25. Graml, 1988a: 204f. The version in Graml 1992: 164 ('un-German') is based on a translation mistake.
26. The 'allgemeine Stimmung' was 'gehoben'. 'Das Zusammenleben der polnischen Minderheitsangehörigen mit der deutschen Bevölkerung wickelt sich reibungslos ab.' Christoph Kleßmann, *Polnische Bergarbeiter im Ruhrgebiet 1870–1945. Soziale Integration und nationale Subkultur einer Minderheit in der deutschen Industriegesellschaft*, Göttingen, 1978, p. 179.
27. Kleßmann, 1978: 182.
28. Kleßmann, 1978: 184–6.
29. According to the Polish sociologist Bożena Domagala – see Joachim Rogall, 'Die Tragödie einer Grenzlandbevölkerung – polnische

Forschungen über die Masuren', *Zeitschrift für Ostforschung – Länder und Völker im östlichen Mitteleuropa*, vol. 41, no. 1, 1992, p. 109.

30. Theodor Schieder et al. (eds), *Dokumentation der Vertreibung aus Ost-Mitteleuropa*, vol. I, no. 1, p. 6E, Bonn, 1954, reprinted Munich, 1984.
31. Rogall, 1992: 105.
32. Martin Kasper, *Geschichte der Sorben, Band 3. Von 1917 bis 1945*, Bautzen, 1976.
33. Jan Foitzik, 'Domowina, Zwjazk luziskich Serbow' ['Heimat, Verband der Lausitzer Sorben'], in Martin Broszat and Hermann Weber (eds), *SBZ-Handbuch. Staatliche Verwaltungen, Parteien, gesellschaftliche Organisationen und ihre Führungskräfte in der Sowjetischen Besatzungszone Deutschlands 1945–1949*, Munich, 1990, pp. 802–11, at p. 804.
34. Kasper, 1976: 176.
35. Gerald Stone, *The Smallest Slavonic Nation. The Sorbs of Lusatia*, London, 1972.
36. Foitzik, 1990: 804.
37. Lorenz Rerup, *Slesvig og Holsten efter 1830*, Copenhagen, 1982, pp. 369 and 372.
38. 'Überall, wohin man kam, herrschte eine bedrückende Ruhe, um nicht zu sagen Niedergeschlagenheit. Das ganze deutsche Volk schien von einem lähmenden Entsetzen gepackt zu sein ...' Wette, 1989: 25.
39. Wette, 1989: 66.
40. 'Bekämpfung aller reichs- und deutschfeindlicher Elemente im Feindesland rückwärts der fechtenden Truppe.' Helmut Krausnick, *Hitlers Einsatzgruppen. Die Truppen des Weltanschauungskrieges 1938–1942*, Frankfurt-am-Main, 1985, p. 29.
41. Krausnick, 1985: 51.
42. Graml, 1988a: 197.
43. Graml, 1988a: 66.
44. 'Die Einstellung der Truppe zu SS und Polizei schwankt zwischen Abscheu und Haß. Jeder Soldat fühlt sich angewidert und abgestoßen durch diese Verbrechen, die in Polen von Angehörigen des Reiches und Vertretern der Staatsgewalt begangen werden.' Krausnick, 1985: 84.
45. 'Furchtbar', 'immer wieder die Stimmen aus dem Propagandaministerium, aus dem Auswärtigen Amt, aus dem Innenministerium, ja sogar von der Wehrmacht vernehmen zu müssen, daß das [hier] ein Mordregime wäre, daß wir mit diesen Greueln aufhören müßten usw.' Krausnick, 1985: 81.
46. Martin Broszat, *Zweihundert Jahre deutsche Polenpolitik*, Frankfurt-am-Main, 1972, pp. 286f.
47. Wolfgang Benz, 'Fremde in der Heimat: Flucht – Vertreibung – Integration', in Klaus J. Bade (ed.), *Deutsche im Ausland – Fremde in Deutschland. Migration in Geschichte und Gegenwart*, Munich, 1992, pp. 374–86, esp. p. 376.
48. Broszat, 1972: 289.
49. 'Englands Hoffnung ist Rußland und Amerika. Wenn Hoffnung auf Rußland wegfällt, fällt auch Amerika weg, weil [dem] Wegfall Rußlands eine Aufwertung Japans in Ostasien in ungeheurem Maß folgt. Rußland [ist] ostasiatischer Degen Englands und Amerikas gegen Japan ... Ist

272 *Notes*

aber Rußland zerschlagen, dann ist Englands letzte Hoffnung getilgt . . .
Entschluß: Im Zuge dieser Auseinadersetzung muß Rußland erledigt
werden. Frühjahr 1941.' Jürgen Förster, 'Hitlers Entscheidung für den
Krieg gegen die Sowjetunion', in Horst Boog et al., *Der Angriff auf die
Sowjetunion*, Frankfurt-am-Main, 1991, pp. 27–68, esp. p. 38.

50. Förster, in Boog et al., 1991: 41.
51. 'Volkskatastrophe, die nicht nur den Bolschewismus, sondern auch das
Moskowitertum seiner Zentren beraubt.' Krausnick: 96.
52. Krausnick, 1985: 96.
53. Rolf-Dieter Müller, 'Das Scheitern der wirtschaftlichen "Blitzkriegstrategie"', in Boog et al., 1991: p. 1116–226, esp. pp. 1195–202.
Alexander Werth, *Rußland im Krieg 1941–1945*, Munich/Zurich, 1965,
p. 477.
54. Müller, 1991: 1197.
55. 'Das ganze Gebiet muß in Staaten aufgelöst werden mit eigenen
Regierungen . . . Die jüdisch-bolschewistische Intelligenz. als bisheriger
Unterdrücker, muß beseitigt werden.' Förster, in Boog et al., 1991:
499.
56. 'Sonderaufgaben im Auftrage des Führers'. Förster, in Boog et al.,
1991: 500.
57. Krausnick, 1985: 104f.
58. 'Zu exekutieren sind alle Funktionäre der Komintern (wie überhaupt
alle kommunistischen Berufspolitiker schlechthin) . . . Juden in Partei
und Staatsstellungen . . . sonstigen radikalen Elemente (Saboteure,
Propagandeure, . . ., Hetzer usw.).' Krausnick, 1985: 135.
59. This point has been debated for a long time among researchers. Many
have held that the *Einsatzgruppen* were instructed to murder all Jews
indiscriminately, but such an order was never found. Only oral evidence given *after* the war, for instance by Otto Ohlendorf in front of
the Nüremberg trial, where this was part of the defence strategy, supported this view. But the original documents from summer 1941 mention only Jews in leading positions, alongside other specified groups.
See Albert Streim, 'Zur Eröffnung des allgemeinen Judenvernichtungsbefehls gegenüber den Einsatzgruppen', in Eberhard Jäckel and Jürgen
Rohwer (eds.), *Der Mord an den Juden im Zweiten Weltkrieg. Entschlußbildung und Verwirklichung*, Frankfurt-am-Main, 1987, pp. 107–19.
60. 'dem Selbstbereinigungsbestrebungen antikommunistischer oder
antijüdischer Kreise . . . kein Hindernis zu bereiten.' Streim, in Jäckel
and Rohwer, 1987: 112.
61. Krausnick, 1985: 179f.
62. Graml, 1988a: 214f.
63. 'Es trat an uns die Frage heran: Wie ist es mit den Frauen und Kindern?
– Ich habe mich nun entschlossen, auch hier eine ganz klare Lösung
zu finden. Ich hielt mich nämlich nicht für berechtigt, die Männer
auszurotten – sprich also, umzubringen oder umbringen zu lassen –
und die Rächer in Gestalt der Kinder für unsere Söhne und Enkel
groß werden zu lassen. Es mußte der schwere Entschluß gefaßt werden,
dieses Volk von der Erde verschwinden zu lassen.' Speech, 6 October
1943, in Graml, 1988a: 264 and 266.

64. Speech, 24 May 1944, in Graml, 1988a: 266.
65. Krausnick, 1985: 104–214.
66. Krausnick, 1985: 104f.
67. 'Bei allen längeren Gesprächen mit Offizieren wurde ich, ohne darauf hingedeutet zu haben, nach den Judenerschießungen gefragt. Ich habe den Eindruck gewonnen, daß die Erschießung der Juden, der Gefangenen und der Kommissare fast allgemein im Offizierskorps abgelehnt wird . . . Die Erschießungen werden als eine Verletzung der Ehre der Deutschen Armee . . . betrachtet. Je nach Temperament und Veranlagung der Betreffenden wurde in mehr oder starker Form die Frage der Verantwortung hierfür zur Sprache gebracht. Es ist hierzu festzustellen, daß die vorhandenen Tatsachen in vollem Umfang bekannt geworden sind und daß im Offizierskorps der Front weit mehr darüber gesprochen wird, als anzunehmen war.' Krausnick, 1985: 226f.
68. Joachim Fest, *Staatsstreich. Der lange Weg zum 20. Juli*, Berlin, 1994, p. 227.
69. Graml, 1988a: 228f.
70. Graml, 1988a: 232.
71. Graml, 1988a: 284f.
72. '. . . wir wissen, wie schwer wir uns täten, wenn wir heute noch in jeder Stadt – bei den Bombenangriffen, bei den Lasten und Entbehrungen des Krieges – noch die Juden als Geheimsaboteure, Agitatoren und Hetzer hätten. Wir würden wahrscheinlich jetzt in das Stadium des Jahres 1916/17 gekommen sein, wenn die Juden noch im deutschen Volkskörper säßen.' Graml, 1988a: 263.
73. In October 1939 Hitler ordered the killing of mentally disturbed people. The killings quickly became known and led to widespread unrest among the German population, and even to some cases of courageous protests. The bishop of Münster, Hans Graf v. Galen, publicly denounced the mass murder in his Sunday sermons. In August 1941 Hitler, being worried about the morale of the home front, ordered the programme stopped, but only for Germany. In eastern Europe the programme continued (Karl A. Schleunes, 'Nationalsozialistische Entschlußbildung und die Aktion T 4', in Jäckel and Rohwer, 1987: 70–83).
74. Graml, 1988a: 243.
75. Rudolf-Christoph v. Gersdorff described in his memoirs (*Soldat im Untergang*, 1977) a situation where Himmler on 26 January 1944 openly talked about the genocide in front of generals and admirals. In his original manuscript (the printed version has been modified) Gersdorff wrote: ' . . . I became the witness of a deeply shameful scene: with a few exceptions the generals and admirals jumped up and broke out in frenetic applause.' (' . . . wurde ich Zeuge einer mich zutiefst beschämenden Szene: mit wenigen Ausnahmen sprangen die Generale und Admirale auf und brachen in brausenden Beifall aus.' Bodo Scheurig, 'Zu einer Himmler-Rede im Januar 1944: Kaum einer schämte sich', *Das Parlament*, 28.1./4.2.1994, p. 17.) Also the protocol of Himmler's speech on 24 May 1944 in front of generals records 'Applaus'. Graml, 1988a: 266.

76. ' . . . werden neuerdings innerhalb der Bevölkerung in verschiedenen
Teilen des Reichsgebietes Erörterungen über 'sehr scharfe Maßnahmen'
gegen die Juden besonders in den Ostgebieten angestellt . . . Es ist
denkbar, daß nicht alle Volksgenossen für die Notwendigkeit solcher
Maßnahmen das genügende Verständnis aufzubringen mögen . . . werden
die Juden laufend nach dem Osten in große . . . Lager transportiert,
von wo sie entweder zur Arbeit eingesetzt oder noch weiter nach dem
Osten verbracht werden.' Michalka, 1985, vol. 2: 250f.
77. Diese in Deutschland 'viel besprochenen' Geschehnisse belasteten 'das
Gewissen und die Kraft unzähliger Männer und Frauen im deutschen
Volk auf das schwerste.' Graml, 1988a: 251.
78. Graml, 1988a: 252.
79. Ralph Angermund, *Deutsche Richterschaft 1919–1945*, Frankfurt-am-
Main, 1991, pp. 214f.
80. Jørgen Hæstrup, . . . *Til Landets Bedste – Hovedtræk af departementschefsstyrets virke 1943–45*, vol. 1, Copenhagen, 1966, p. 148.
81. SS-Sturmbannführer Strauch bitterly reported about Wilhelm Kube, a
former *Gauleiter* and in 1943 *Generalkommissar* in Whiteruthenia, who
said that the acts of the SS would be unworthy of the Germany of
Goethe and Kant. Michalka 1985 2: 254–6.
82. ' . . . bedenken Sie aber selbst, wie viele – auch Parteigenossen – ihr
berühmtes Gesuch an mich oder irgendeine Dienststelle gerichtet haben,
in dem es hieß, daß alle Juden selbstverständlich Schweine seien, daß
bloß der Soundso ein anständiger Jude sei, dem man nichts tun dürfe.
Ich wage zu behaupten, daß es nach der Anzahl der Gesuche und der
Anzahl der Meinungen in Deutschland mehr anständige Juden gegeben
hat als überhaupt nominell vorhanden waren. Graml, 1988a: pp. 263f.
83. Graml, 1988a: p. 253.
84. For an overview, see for instance Saul Friedländer, 'Vom Antisemitismus
zur Judenvernichtung: Eine historiographische Studie zur nationalsozialistischen Judenpolitik und Versuch einer Interpretation', in Jäckel
and Rohwer, 1987, pp. 18–60.
85. The latest contribution to this kind of explanation is Daniel J.
Goldhagen, *Hitler's Willing Executioners. Ordinary Germans and the
Holocaust*, New York, 1996.

CHAPTER 15 THE INTEGRATION MIRACLE

1. See Alfred M. de Zayas, *Nemesis at Potsdam. The Anglo-Americans
and the Expulsion of the Germans. Background, Execution, Consequences*,
London/Henley/Boston, 1977, passim.
2. Hans Boldt, *Deutsche Verfassungsgeschichte, Band 2. Von 1806 bis
zur Gegenwart*, second edition, Munich, 1993, p. 312.
3. See, Jürgen Kocka, '1945: Neubeginn oder Restauration?', in Carola
Stern and Heinrich-August Winkler (eds), *Wendepunkte deutscher
Geschichte 1848–1990*, Frankfurt-am-Main, 1994, p. 159–92.
4. Erwin K. Scheuch, *Wie deutsch sind die Deutschen? Eine Nation wandelt
ihr Gesicht*, Bergisch-Gladbach, 1991, p. 23.

5. Scheuch, 1991: 186f.
6. Werner Bergmann, 'Die Reaktion auf den Holocaust in West-deutschland von 1945 bis 1989', *Geschichte in Wissenschaft und Unterricht*, 1992(6), p. 327–50, esp. p. 329.
7. Werner Bergmann, 'Sind die Deutschen antisemitisch? Meinungsum-fragen von 1946–1987 in der Bundesrepublik Deutschland', in Werner Bergmann and Rainer Erb (eds), *Antisemitismus in der politischen Kultur nach 1945*, Opladen, 1990, pp. 108–30, esp. p. 113.
8. See, for instance, the reports of SD, the internal Nazi secret service, on the German population, reproduced in Norbert Frei, *Der Führerstaat. Nationalsozialistische Herrschaft 1933 bis 1945*, Munich, 1987, pp. 216–25.
9. Scheuch, 1991: 121.
10. Eric J. Hobsbawm, *Nations and Nationalism since 1980: Programme, Myth, Reality*, second edition, Cambridge, 1992, p. 144.
11. Calculated after Brian R. Mitchell, *European Historical Statistics 1750–1975*, second revised edition, London and Basingstoke, 1981, p. 829.
12. For a recent overview, see Costanza D'Elia, 'Miracles and mirages in the West German economy: a survey of the literature of the 1980s', *Journal of European Economic History*, vol. 22, no. 2, 1993, pp. 381–401.
13. Jánossy, Franz [Ferenc] (with contributions by Maria Holló), *Das Ende der Wirtschaftswunder. Erscheinung und Wesen der wirtschaftlichen Entwicklung*, Frankfurt-am-Main, 1966.
14. The statistical picture is somewhat ambiguous, not the least depend-ing upon which measure is chosen. See Rolf H. Dumke, 'Reassessing the *Wirtschaftswunder*: reconstruction and postwar growth in West Germany in an international context', *Oxford Bulletin of Economics and Statistics*, vol. 52, no. 2, 1990, pp. 451–92.
15. For a short overview, see, for instance, Anthony Giddens, *Sociology. A Brief but Critical Introduction*, London and Basingstoke, second edition, 1986, pp. 25–33.
16. See Chapter 11 above.
17. As quoted in Karl Rohe, *Wähler und Wählertraditionen in Deutschland. Kulturelle Grundlagen deutscher Parteien und Parteiensysteme im 19. und 20. Jahrhundert*, Frankfurt-am-Main, 1992, p. 164.
18. Rainer Geißler, *Die Sozialstruktur Deutschlands. Ein Studienbuch zur Entwicklung im geteilten und vereinten Deutschland*, Opladen 1992a, pp. 111f.
19. Franz Walter, 'Milieus und Parteien in der deutschen Gesellschaft. Zwischen Persistenz und Erosion', *Geschichte in Wissenschaft und Unterricht*, vol. 46, 1995, pp. 490f.
20. Walter, 1995: 492.
21. Walter, 1995: 488f.
22. Geißler, 1992a: 22.
23. Geißler, 1992a: 146f.
24. Rohe, 1992: 171.
25. Rohe, 1992: 168.
26. Klaus Schönhoven, *Die deutschen Gewerkschaften*, Frankfurt-am-Main 1987, pp. 212f.

276 *Notes*

27. *Der Spiegel*, 1992/25, p. 38.
28. *Der Spiegel*, 1992/25, p. 41.
29. *Der Spiegel*, 1992/25, p. 53.
30. Rohe, 1992: 300.
31. Scheuch, 1991: 392.
32. See, for instance, de Zayas, 1977: *passim*.
33. Rüdiger Overmans, 'Die Toten des Zweiten Weltkrieges in Deutschland. Bilanz der Forschung unter besonderer Berücksichtigung der Wehrmacht- und Vertreibungsverluste', in Wolfgang Michalka (ed.), *Der Zweite Weltkrieg. Analysen, Grundzüge, Forschungsbilanz.* Munich/Zürich, 1989, pp. 858–73, esp. p. 865.
34. Wolfgang Zank, *Wirtschaft und Arbeit in Ostdeutschland 1945–1949. Probleme des Wiederaufbaus in der Sowjetischen Besatzungszone Deutschlands*, Munich, 1987, p. 145.
35. Franz J. Bauer, 'Aufnahme und Eingliederung der Flüchtlinge und Vertriebenen. Das Beispiel Bayern 1945–1950', in Wolfgang Benz (ed.), *Die Vertreibung der Deutschen aus dem Osten. Ursachen, Ereignisse, Folgen*, second edition, Frankfurt-am-Main, 1985a, pp. 158–72, esp. p. 168.
36. Reinhold Schillinger, 'Der Lastenausgleich', in Benz, 1985a: 183–92, esp. p. 184.
37. Schillinger, in Benz, 1985a: 188.
38. Schillinger, in Benz, 1985a: 189.
39. Schillinger, in Benz, 1985a: 190.
40. Paul Lüttinger, 'Der Mythos der schnellen Integration. Eine empirische Untersuchung zur Integration der Vertriebenen und Flüchtlinge in der Bundesrepublik Deutschland bis 1971', *Zeitschrift für Soziologie*, vol. 15, no. 1, 1986, p. 20–36, esp. p. 24.
41. Hermann Weiß, 'Die Organisationen der Vetriebenen und ihre Presse', in Benz, 1985a: 193–208, esp. p. 199.
42. Weiß, in Benz, 1985a: 206.
43. For a detailed discussion, see Zank, 1987: 37–9 and 164–7.
44. Falk Wiesemann, 'Flüchtlingspolitik in Nordrhein-Westfalen', in Benz, 1985a: 173–82, esp. p. 179.
45. Helge Heidemeyer, *Flucht und Zuwanderung aus der SBZ/DDR 1945/ 1949–1961. Die Flüchtlingspolitik der Bundesrepublik Deutschland bis zum Bau der Berliner Mauer*, Düsseldorf, 1994, p. 331.
46. Klaus J. Bade, *Deutsche in Ausland – Fremde in Deutschland. Migration in Geschichte und Gegenwart*, Munich, 1992, p. 402.
47. Werner Abelshauser, *Wirtschaftsgeschichte der Bundesrepublik Deutschland 1945–1980*, Frankfurt-am-Main, 1983, p. 96.
48. Lüttinger, 1986: 30.
49. For a quantitative estimation, see Abelshauser, 1983: 95.
50. Lorenz Rerup, *Slesvig og Holsten after 1830*, Copenhagen, 1982, p. 406.
51. Jan Foitzik, 'Domowina, Zwjazk luziskich Serbow' ['Heimat, Verband der Lausitzer Sorben'], in Martin Broszat and Hermann Weber (eds), *SBZ-Handbuch. Staatliche Verwaltungen, Parteien, gesellschaftliche Organisationen und ihre Führungskräfte in der Sowjetischen*

Besatzungszone Deutschlands 1945–1949, Munich, 1990, pp. 802–11, esp. p. 804.
52. Foitzik, in Broszat and Weber, 1990: 805.
53. Foitzik, in Broszat and Weber, 1990: 806.
54. Rerup, 1982: 412–14.
55. A. Stone, *The Smallest Slavonic Nation. The Sorbs of Lusatia*, London, 1972, pp. 175–7.
56. Alastair Walker, 'Nordfriesland als Sprachenkontaktraum', *Germanistische Linguistik*, 101–3. 1990, pp. 407–26, esp. p. 411.
57. Stone, 1972: 184.
58. Siegfried Michalk, 'Deutsch und Sorbisch in der Lausitz', *Germanistische Linguistik*, 101–3, 1990, pp. 427–44, esp. p. 428.
59. Mogens Dyhr, 'Hybridisiertes Südjütisch', *Germanistische Linguistik*, 101–3, 1990, pp. 25–47, esp. pp. 36–8.
60. Ivar Hoekstra, 'From father to Sorbs. Slavonic traditions live in Eastern Germany', *Euroviews*, no. 4, 1994, p. 31; Ivar Hoekstra, 'Dying to rise again. Slavonic minority threatened with extinction in Eastern Germany', *Euroviews*, no. 4, 1994, pp. 32–3.
61. Ulrich Herbert, *Die Geschichte der Ausländerbeschäftigung in Deutschland 1880–1980. Saisonarbeiter. Zwangsarbeiter, Gastarbeiter*, Berlin/Bonn, 1976, pp. 191f.
62. Hartmut Esser, 'Gastarbeiter', in Wolfgang Benz (ed.), *Die Bundesrepublik Deutschland. Geschichte in drei Bänden. Band 2: Gesellschaft*, Frankfurt-am-Main, 1985, pp. 127–56, esp. p. 133.
63. Esser, in Benz, 1985b: 133.
64. Esser, in Benz, 1985b: 133.
65. Klaus J. Bade, *Ausländer Aussiedler Asyl. Eine Bestandsaufnahme*, Munich, 1994b, p. 46.
66. Esser, in Benz, 1985b: 147f.
67. Esser, in Benz, 1985b: 149.
68. Hans-Michael Bernhardt, Heide Heimpel and Leylâ Schulzke, 'Minderheiten in der Mehrheit: Schulalltag in Kreuzberg', in Wolfgang Benz (ed.), *Integration ist machbar. Ausländer in Deutschland*, Munich, 1993, pp. 132–44, esp. p. 138.
69. Bade, 1994b: 55–60.
70. Geißler, 1992a: 160.
71. Scheuch, 1991: 170.
72. Surveys by the Institut für Demoskopie, Allensbach, IfD-Umfragen 4005, 5082, quoted for instance in *Frankfurter Allgemeine Zeitung*, 18 August 1993, p. 5.
73. Scheuch, 1991: 172.
74. Ursula Boos-Nünning, 'Einwanderung ohne Einwanderungsentscheidung. Ausländische Familien in der Bundesrepublik Deutschland', *Aus Politik und Zeitgeschichte*, B 23–4, 1990, pp. 16–26, esp. p. 19.
75. Geißler, 1992a: 160.
76. Geißler, 1992a: 160.
77. 'Ob es um Sprachkurse ging, um Frauenemanzipation, um die Formulierung politischer Forderungen oder auch nur um Begegnung

und das Feiern von Festen: Hier fand ein großer Teil der nicht-deutschen jungen Generation erstmals Eingang in die bundesdeutsche Gesellschaft, hier erschlossen sich ihnen Möglichkeiten der persönlichen Entfaltung, schlossen sie nationalitätenübergreifende Freundschaften, hatten sie eine Plattform für ihre Interessen und waren als Personen gefragt.' Cem Özdemir, '"Die stürmischen Zeiten sind offenbar vorbei"', *Das Parlament*, 10–17 February 1995, p. 3.

78. Juliane Wetzel, 'Integration im Großbetrieb – Das Beispiel BMW', in Benz, 1993: 93–108, esp. p. 98.
79. Boos-Nünning, 1990: 22.
80. Geißler, 1992a: 158.
81. *Die Zeit*, 6 August 1993, Dossier, p. 10; Bade, 1994a: 88.
82. Cornelia Schmalz-Jacobsen et al., *Einwanderung – und dann? Perspektiven einer neuen Ausländerpolitik*, Munich, 1993, p. 317.
83. See, for instance, Hans-Werner Rautenberg, 'Deutsche und Deutschstämmige in Polen – eine nicht anerkannte Volksgruppe', *Aus Politik und Zeitgeschichte*, B 50, 9 December 1988, pp. 14–25.
84. Klaus Leciejewski, 'Zur wirtschaftlichen Eingliederung der Aussiedler', *Aus Politik und Zeitgeschichte*, B 3, 1990, pp. 52–62, esp. p. 53.
85. As quoted in Rautenberg, 1988: 22 and 25.
86. Rautenberg, 1988: 22.
87. Bade, 1994b: 155.
88. Silke Delfs, 'Heimatvertriebene, Aussiedler, Spätaussiedler. Rechtliche und politische Aspekte der Aufnahme von Deutschstämmigen aus Osteuropa in der Bundesrepublik Deutschland', *Aus Politik und Zeitgeschichte*, B 48, 1993, pp. 3–11, esp. p. 6.
89. Barbara Koller, 'Aussiedler in Deutschland. Aspekte ihrer sozialen und beruflichen Eingliederung', *Aus Politik und Zeitgeschichte*, B 48, 1993, pp. 12–22, esp. pp. 14f.
90. Leciejewski, 1990: 56.
91. Koller, 1993: 15–20.
92. Koller, 1993: 21.
93. Leciejewski, 1990: 53; Koller, 1993: 13.
94. Scheuch, 1991: 181.
95. Delfs, 1993: 7–9. In 1993 the authorities registered 219 000 *Aussiedler*, in 1994 220 000. *Statisches Jahrbuch für die Bundesrepublik Deutschland 1994*, Wiesbaden, 1994, p. 92, and (as regards 1994) *Frankfurter Rundschau*, 13 June 1995, p. 4.
96. *Morgenavisen/Jyllandsposten*, 14 November 1996.
97. Schmalz-Jacobsen, 1993: 318.
98. Schmalz-Jacobsen, 1993: 319.
99. Rudolf Wassermann, 'Plädoyer für eine neue Asyl- und Ausländer-politik', *Aus Politik und Zeitgeschichte*, vol. 9, 1992, pp. 13–20, esp. p. 15.
100. Scheuch, 1991: 174.
101. Scheuch, 1991: 174.

CHAPTER 16 UNIFICATION AND CURRENT PROBLEMS

1. Heinrich-August Winkler, '1989/1990: Die unverhoffte Einheit', in Carola Stern and Heinrich-August Winkler (eds), *Wendepunkte deutscher Geschichte 1848–1990*, Frankfurt-am-Main, 1994, pp. 193–226, esp. at p. 194.
2. 'Deutschland, einig Vaterland'. Winkler, in Stern and Winkler, 1994: 205.
3. 'Wie stehen Sie zu einer Vereinigung von DDR und BRD?' 'Ich bin sehr dafür – eher dafür als dagegen – eher dagegen als dafür – sehr dagegen'. Peter Förster and Günther Roski, *DDR zwischen Wende und Wahl. Meinungsforscher analysieren den Umbruch*, Berlin, 1990, pp. 8 and 53.
4. Förster and Roski, 1990: 86.
5. Matthias Jung, 'Parteiensystem und Wahlen in der DDR. Eine Analyse der Volkskammerwahl vom 18. März 1990 und der Kommunalwahlen vom 6. Mai 1990', *Aus Politik und Zeitgeschichte*, vol. 27, 1990, pp. 3–15, esp. p. 12. According to this opinion poll 91 per cent were in favour of unification, some percentage points more than according to the above quoted poll.
6. Erwin K. Scheuch, *Wie deutsch sind die Deutschen? Eine Nation wandelt ihr Gesicht*, Bergisch-Gladbach, 1991, p. 436.
7. Scheuch, 1991: 319–28.
8. '. . . einen erheblichen Verdrängungsprozeß unter verschiedenen wohnungslosen Personengruppen . . .' Klaus J. Bade, *Ausländer Aussiedler Asyl. Eine Bestandaufsnahme*, Munich, 1994b, p. 172.
9. Rainer Geißler, 'Die ostdeutsche Sozialstruktur unter Modernisierungsdruck', *Aus Politik und Zeitgeschichte*, vol. 29–30, 1992b, pp. 15–28, esp. p. 26.
10. 'Ossi go home', *Der Spiegel*, 1989, 48, p. 69.
11. 'Wir haben sechs Millionen Sozialfälle, die am Rande leben und wenig beachtet werden. Aber Aussiedler und Umsiedler haben den Vorrang, bekommen Steuervorteile, daß es nur so kracht. Der Zündstoff ist da. Abwarten. Das explodiert noch.' Bade, 1994b: 171.
12. 'Ossi go home', *Der Spiegel*, 1989, 48, p. 69.
13. '"Wieso kommen die noch"', *Der Spiegel*, 1990, 8, pp. 29–32, esp. p. 30.
14. *Der Spiegel*, 1991, 6, p. 46.
15. 'Arrogant wie Besatzer – . . . – Sehen in uns ehemaligen DDR–Bürger die Deppen der Nation – Fühlen sich als Sieger – Wissen alles besser – Denken, sie sind die Größten, lassen keine andere Meinung gelten – . . .' – 'Es ist ein faules Volk – . . . – Wollen nur bedient werden – Sie sind nicht so fleißig wie wir Deutsche – Arbeiten haben die nicht gelernt – . . .' *Der Spiegel*, 1991, 30, p. 27.
16. Ingrid Stratemann, 'Psychologische Bedingungen des wirtschaftlichen Aufschwungs in den neuen Bundesländern', *Aus Politik und Zeitgeschichte*, vol. 24, 1992, pp. 15–26, esp. pp. 24f.
17. Peter Becker, 'Ostdeutsche und Westdeutsche auf dem Prüfstand psychologischer Tests', *Aus Politik und Zeitgeschichte*, vol. 24, 1992, pp. 27–36, esp. pp. 32–5.

18. Scheuch, 1991: 392.
19. *Der Spiegel*, 1992/25, pp. 38 and 44.
20. Scheuch, 1991: 251–61.
21. 'Liebe Leute, es handelt sich um einen Beitritt der DDR zur Bundesrepublik, nicht um die umgekehrte Veranstaltung. Wir haben ein gutes Grundgesetz, das sich bewährt hat. Wir tun alles für euch. Ihr seid herzlich willkommen. Wir wollen nicht kaltschnäuzig über eure Wünsche und Interessen hinweggehen. Aber hier findet nicht die Vereinigung zweier gleicher Staaten statt. Wir fangen nicht ganz von vorn bei gleichberechtigten Ausgangsposition an. Es gibt das Grundgesetz, und es gibt die Bundesrepublik Deutschland. Laßt uns von der Voraussetzung ausgehen, daß ihr vierzig Jahre von beiden ausgeschlossen wart. Jetzt habt ihr einen Anspruch auf Teilnahme, und wir nehmen darauf Rücksicht.' Wolfgang Schäuble, *Der Vertrag. Wie ich über die deutsche Einheit verhandelte*, München, 1993, p. 131.
22. Gerda Sinn and Hans-Werner Sinn, *Kaltstart. Volkswirtschaftliche Aspekte der deutschen Vereinigung*, second edition, Tübingen, 1992, p. 30.
23. Jürgen Kühl, 'Arbeitslosigkeit in der vereinigten Bundesrepublik Deutschland', *Aus Politik und Zeitgeschichte*, vol. 35, 1993, pp. 3–15, esp. p. 5.
24. For a detailed table for each category, see Kühl, 1993: 6.
25. *Die Zeit*, 1 October 1993, p. 18.
26. 'Man merkt zwar, daß wir viele Jahre in unterschiedlichen Systemen gelebt haben, aber im großen und ganzen kommen wir gut miteiander aus.' 'Es gibt zwar Verständigungsprobleme, aber die sind mit der Zeit lösbar.' *Die Zeit*, 1 October 1993, p. 21.
27. Sinn and Sinn, 1992: 100f.
28. *Das Parlament*, 1–8 July 1994, p. 6.
29. *Die Zeit*, 1 October 1993, p. 17.
30. Barbara Koller, 'Aussiedler in Deutschland. Aspekte ihrer sozialen und beruflichen Eingliederung', *Aus Politik und Zeitgeschichte*, vol. 48, 1993, pp. 12–22, esp. p. 13.
31. Cornelia Schmalz-Jacobsen et al., *Einwanderung – und dann? Perspektiven einer neuen Ausländerpolitik*, Munich, 1993, p. 319.
32. 193 000 came to Germany, 56 000 to France, 25 000 to Great Britain, 7000 to Spain and 5000 to Italy. *Der Spiegel*, 40/1991, p. 33.
33. Bundesministerium des Innern (eds), *Verfassungsschutzbericht 1993*, Bonn, 1994, pp. 137–41.
34. Bundesministerium des Innern, 1994: 137; Claus Leggewie, 'Aus Anti-Effekten Zustimmung mobilisieren', *Frankfurter Allgemeine Zeitung*, 19 April 1993, p. 11. The *Verfassungsschutz*, the authority in charge of the surveillance of anti-constitutional activities, originally did not observe the *Republikaner*. At the end of 1992 the *Verfassungsschutz* was, however, ordered to do so by the federal minister of the interior, Rudolf Seiter. Seiter's order came after three Turks were burnt to death in the town of Mölln. There were, however, no direct links between the *Republikaner* and the men who set fire to the house in Mölln.
35. This figure does not include the 23 000 members of the *Republikaner*

(who cannot in total be qualified as right-wing extremists). Bundesministerium des Innern, 1994: 74.
36. Bundesministerium des Innern, 1994: 84.
37. Bundesministerium des Innern, 1994: 79.
38. Bundesministerium des Innern (eds), *Verfassungsschutzbericht 1992*, Bonn, 1993, p. 75.
39. Bundesministerium des Innern, 1994: 85.
40. The figures were produced by a research team at Trier University which scrutinized 1400 police documents and 41 court decisions against 131 perpetrators. *Der Spiegel*, 17/1993, p. 91.
41. Hoyerswerda created an immense echo in the media, inside and outside Germany. As *Der Spiegel* (40/1991, p. 41) put it: 'In Hoyerswerda the ugly German experiences his coming out.' ('In Hoyerswerda hat der häßliche Deutsche sein Coming-Out.') This was perhaps an example of negative cultural imperialism, given the fact that Hoyerswerda is situated in the midst of Sorbian territory, a point which not one journalist seemed to have noticed (or pretended not to have noticed). See, for instance, the lengthy report by Matthias Matussek, 'Jagdzeit in Sachsen', *Der Spiegel*, 40/1991, pp. 41–51.
42. Bundesministerium des Innern, 1993: 77.
43. 'Aus ihrer Sicht hätten die Angeklagten durchaus den Eindruck gewinnen können, die radikale Spitze einer breiten Bewegung zu sein.' Bade, 1994b: 188.
44. *Der Spiegel*, 44/1992, p. 65. The survey was conducted by the EMNID-Institut and was based on 3000 interviews (2000 in West, 1000 in East Germany). 'Wie würden Sie sich verhalten, wenn Deutsche vor Ihren Augen Ausländer angreifen? – Würde selbst mitmachen – Würde selbst zuschauen, aber selbst nicht eingreifen – Würde mich entfernen, will damit nichts zu tun haben – Würde, wenn möglich, versuchen, den Ausländer zu helfen.'
45. *Der Spiegel*, 50/1992, p. 65. 'Angenommen, es gibt in Ihrem Ort zwei Demonstrationen, eine gegen Ausländerhaß und eine gegen den Zustrom von Ausländern. Wie würden Sie sich verhalten? – Würde mit gegen Ausländerhaß demonstrieren – Würde mit gegen den Zustrom von Ausländern demonstrieren – Würde an keiner Demonstration teilnehmen.'
46. 'Jeder achte Deutsche ein Antisemit', *Der Spiegel*, 4/1992, pp. 41–50, esp. p. 41.
47. Gisela Dachs, 'Jüdisch und Deutsch', *Die Zeit*, 18 December 1992, p. 9f.
48. Werner Bergmann, 'Sind die Deutschen antisemitisch? Meinungsomfragen von 1946–1987 in der Bundesrepublik Deutschland', in Werner Bergmann and Rainer Erb (eds), *Antisemitismus in der politischen Kultur nach 1945*, Opladen, 1990, pp. 108–30, esp. p. 113.
49. *Der Spiegel*, 3/1992, p. 56.
50. *Das Parlament*, 25 December 1992, p. 3.
51. Allensbacher Archiv, IfD-Umfragen, 5074, November/December 1992.
52. 'Alle kennen Mölln', *Der Spiegel*, 22/1994, pp. 27–8.
53. Renate Köcher, 'Die Ausländerfeindlichkeit in Deutschland ist gering', *Frankfurter Allgemeine Zeitung*, 18 August 1993.

282 *Notes*

54. Jürgen Krönig, 'Britannien schreckt auf', *Die Zeit*, 24 September 1993, p. 14.
55. Kenan Malik. 'Are they more racist than us?', *The Independent*, 29 November 1992.
56. *The Observer*, 13 August 1992, p. 10, appendix to John McGhle, 'Tide of race attack greets refugees to "promised land"'.
57. Robert Marmoz, 'La cour d'assises a condamné les quatre vigiles de Lyon pour crime contre la dignité humaine', *Le Monde*, 10 October 1992.
58. 'Jugendliche niedergeschossen', *Frankfurter Rundschau*, 8 April 1993, p. 2.
59. 'Skudangreb mod indvandrere', *Politiken*, 18 July 1994, p. 8.
60. Niels Levinsen, 'Fremmedhad præger valgkampen', *Morgenavisen/Jyllandsposten*, 16 March 1994, p. 2, section 2.
61. 'Dukke-bombe', *Morgenavisen-Jyllandsposten*, 15 March 1995.
62. Ernesto Sollberger, 'Polizisten werden des Serienmordes beschuldigt', *Frankfurter Rundschau*, 30 November 1994.
63. 'Angriff auf "Illegale"', *Frankfurter Allgemeine Zeitung*, 3 December 1992, p. 8.
64. Peter v. Heygendorff, 'Politisches Erdbeben für die Regierung Lubbers', *Das Parlament*, 18 March 1994.
65. Bundesministerium des Innern, 1994: 76–8.
66. Bundesministerium des Innern, 1994: 79.
67. *Der Spiegel*, 13/1995, p. 50.
68. In 1993 there were 326 000 asylum seekers, about 116 000 less then the year before. *Statisches Jahrbuch für die Bundesrepublik Deutschland 1994*, Wiesbaden, 1994, p. 73 (henceforth SJBRD, 1994). The figures fell in particular in the second half of 1993, after the new regulations became effective. Compared to the first half, the figures fell by about 50 per cent.
69. Schmalz-Jacobsen, 1993: 311.
70. Between 1973 and 1992 1 035 000 immigrants became German citizens; in 1992 alone the figure was 180 000. Schmalz-Jacobsen, 1993: 317 and SJBRD, 1994: 73.
71. *Der Spiegel*, 1995/12, p. 44,
72. Bade, 1994b: 88.
73. Schmalz-Jacobsen, 1993: 317; SJBRD, 1994: 73.
74. Faruk Şen and Andreas Goldberg, *Türken in Deutschland. Leben zwischen zwei Kulturen*, Munich, 1994, p. 41.
75. Sen and Goldberg, 1994: 92.
76. Sen and Goldberg, 1994: 118.

CHAPTER 17   SUMMARY: HOW A MELTING-POT WORKS

1. Richard D. Alba, 'Ethnicity', in Edgar F. Borgatta and Maire L. Borgatta (eds), *Encyclopedia of Sociology*, vol. 2, New York/Toronto/Oxford/Singapore/Sidney, 1992, pp. 575–84, esp. p. 577.

References

Abelshauser, Werner, *Wirtschaft in Westdeutschland 1945–1948. Rekonstruktion und Wachstumsbedingungen in der amerikanischen und britischen Zone*, Stuttgart, 1975.

Abelshauser, Werner, *Wirtschaftsgeschichte der Bundesrepublik Deutschland 1945–1980*, Frankfurt-am-Main, 1983.

Akten zur auswärtigen Politik 1918–1945. Aus den Archiven des Auswärtigen Amtes. Series A: 1918–1923, Vol. II, Göttingen, 1984.

Alba, Richard D., 'Ethnicity', in Borgatta and Borgatta, 1992: 575–84.

Andersen, Ellen et al., *Sønderjylland med Vadehavet og Rømø. Gyldendals Egnsbeskrivelser*, second edition, Copenhagen, 1977.

Angermund, Ralph, *Deutsche Richterschaft 1919–1945*, Frankfurt-am-Main, 1991.

von Aretin, Karl Otmar Freiherr, *Vom Deutschen Reich zum Deutschen Bund*, Göttingen, 1980.

Bade, Klaus J., 'Politik und Ökonomie der Auslanderbeschäftigung im preußischen Osten 1885–1914. Die *Internationalisierung des Arbeitsmarkts im "Rahmen der preußischen Abwehrpolitik"'*, in Puhle and Wehler, 1980: 273–99.

Bade, Klaus J. (ed.), *Deutsche im Ausland – Fremde in Deutschland. Migration in Geschichte und Gegenwart*, Munich, 1992.

Bade, Klaus J., *Homo Migrans – Wanderungen aus und nach Deutschland*, Essen, 1994a.

Bade, Klaus J., *Ausländer Aussiedler Asyl. Eine Bestandsaufnahme*, Munich, 1994b.

Barkai, Avraham, *Vom Boykott zur 'Entjudung'. Der wirtschaftliche Existenzkampf der Juden im Dritten Reich 1933–1943*, Frankfurt-am-Main, 1987.

Bauer, Franz J., 'Aufnahme und Eingliederung der Flüchtlinge und Vertriebenen. Das Beispiel Bayern 1945–1950', in Benz, 1985a: 158–72.

Bauer, Petra and Niedermayer, Oscar, 'Extrem rechtes Potential in den Ländern der Europäischen Gemeinschaft', *Aus Politik und Zeitgeschichte*, vol. 46–47, 1990, pp. 15–26.

Becker, Peter, Ostdeutsche und Westdeutsche auf dem Prüfstand psychologischer Tests, *Aus Politik und Zeitgeschichte*, vol. 24, 1992, pp. 27–36.

Benz, Wolfgang, *Die Gründung der Bundesrepublik. Von der Bizone zum souveränen Staat*, Munich, 1984.

Benz, Wolfgang (ed.), *Die Vertreibung der Deutschen aus dem Osten. Ursachen, Ereignisse, Folgen*, second edition, Frankfurt-am-Main, 1985a.

Benz, Wolfgang (ed.), *Die Bundesrepublik Deutschland. Geschichte in drei Bänden. Band 2: Gesellschaft*, Frankfurt-am-Main, 1985b.

Benz, Wolfgang, *Potsdam 1945. Besatzungsherrschaft und Neuaufbau im Vier-Zonen-Deutschlands*, Munich, 1986.

284   *References*

Benz, Wolfgang, 'Fremde in der Heimat: Flucht – Vertreibung – Integration', in Bade, 1992: 374–86.

Benz, Wolfgang (ed.), *Integration ist machbar. Ausländer in Deutschland*, Munich, 1993.

Berding, Helmut (ed.), *Wirtschaftliche und politische Integration in Europa im 19. und 20. Jahrhundert*, Göttingen, 1984.

Bergmann, Werner, 'Sind die Deutschen antisemitisch? Meinungsumfragen von 1946–1987 in der Bundesrepublik Deutschland', in Bergmann and Erb, 1990: 108–30.

Bergmann, Werner, 'Die Reaktion auf den Holocaust in Westdeutschland von 1945 bis 1989', *Geschichte in Wissenschaft und Unterricht*, vol. 6, 1992, pp. 327–50.

Bergmann, Werner and Erb, Rainer (eds), *Antisemitismus in der politischen kultur nach 1945*, Opladen, 1990.

Bernhardt, Hans-Michael, Heimpel, Heide and Schulzke, Leylâ, 'Minderheiten in der Mehrheit: Schulalltag in Kreuzberg', in Benz, 1993: 132–44.

Blaschke, Karlheinz, 'Alte Länder – Neue Länder. Zur territorialen Neugliederung der DDR', *Aus Politik und Zeitgeschichte*, vol. 27, 1990, pp. 39–54.

Boldt, Hans, *Deutsche Verfassungsgeschichte, Band 2. Von 1806 bis zur Gegenwart*, second edition, Munich, 1993.

Boog, Horst et al., *Der Angriff auf die Sowjetunion*, Frankfurt-am-Main, 1991.

Boos-Nünning, Ursula, 'Einwanderung ohne Einwanderungsentscheidung. Ausländische Familien in der Bundesrepublik Deutschland, *Aus Politik und Zeitgeschichte*, vol. 23–4, 1990, pp. 16–26.

Borchardt, Knut, 'The Industrial Revolution in Germany 1700–1914', in Cippola, 1973: vol. 4(1), pp. 76–100.

Borchardt, Knut, 'Trend, Zyklus, Strukturbrüche, Zufälle: Was bestimmt die deutsche Wirtschafsgeschichte des 20. Jahrhundert?', *Vierteljahrsschrift für Sozial- und Wirtschaftsgeschichte*, vol. 64, no. 2, 1977, pp. 145–78.

Borgatta, Edgar F. and Borgatta, Maire L. (eds), *Encyclopedia of Sociology*, vol. 2, New York/Toronto/Oxford/Singapore/Sidney, 1992.

Bosl, Karl, Staat, 'Gesellschaft, Wirtschaft im deutschen Mittelalter', in Grundmann, 1970: 694–835.

Botzenhart, Manfred, *Reform, Restauration, Krise. Deutschland 1789–1847*, Frankfurt-am-Main, 1985.

Brandt, Harm-Hinrich, 'The revolution of 1848 and the problem of Central European nationalities', in Schulze, 1987: 107–34.

Broszat, Martin, *Zweihundert Jahre deutsche Polenpolitik*, Frankfurt-am-Main, 1972.

Broszat, Martin, *Der Staat Hitlers*, eleventh edition, Munich, 1986.

Broszat, Martin, *Die Machtergreifung. Der Aufstieg der NSDAP und die Zerstörung der Weimarer Republik*, second edition, Munich, 1987.

Broszat, Martin and Weber, Hermann (eds), *SBZ-Handbuch. Staatliche Verwaltungen, Parteien, gesellschaftliche Organisationen und ihre Führungskräfte in der Sowjetischen Besatzungszone Deutschlands 1945–1949*, Munich, 1990.

Bundesministerium des Innern (eds), *Verfassungsschutzbericht 1992*, Bonn, 1993.

Bundesministerium des Innern (eds), *Verfassungsschutzbericht 1993*, Bonn, 1994.

Burg, Peter, *Der Wiener Kongreß. Der Deutsche Bund im europäischen Staatensystem*, Munich, 1984.

Carsten, Francis L., *Geschichte der preußischen Junker*, Frankfurt-am-Main, 1988.

Chamberlain, William Henry, *Die Russische Revolution 1917–1921*, vol. 1, Frankfurt-am-Main, 1958.

Christ, Peter and Neubauer, Ralf, *Kolonie im eigenen Land. Die Treuhand, Bonn und die Wirtschaftskatastrophe der fünf neuen Länder*, Reinbek, 1991.

Cipolla, Carlo M., *Literacy and Development in the West*, Harmondsworth, 1969.

Cipolla, Carlo (ed.), *The Fontana Economic History of Europe*, six vols, Glasgow, 1973.

Crew, David, *Bochum. Sozialgeschichte einer Industriestadt 1860–1914*, Frankfurt-am-Main/Berlin/Vienna, 1980.

Dahrendorf, Ralf, *Class and Class Conflict in Industrial Society*, London, 1972.

Deist, Wilhelm et al., *Ursachen und Voraussetzungen des Zweiten Weltkrieges*, Frankfurt-am-Main, 1989.

Delfs, Silke, 'Heimatvertriebene, Aussiedler, Spätaussiedler. Rechtliche und politische Aspekte der Aufnahme von Deutschstämmigen aus Osteuropa in der Bundesrepublik Deutschland', *Aus Politik und Zeitgeschichte*, vol. 48, 1993, pp. 3–11.

D'Elia, Costanza, 'Miracles and mirages in the West German economy: a survey of the literature of the 1980s, *Journal of European Economic History*, vol. 22, no. 2, 1993, pp. 381–401.

Deuerlein, Ernst, *Die Gründung des Deutschen Reiches in Augenzeugenberichten 1870/71*, Düsseldorf, 1977.

Dinkel, Reiner Hans and Lebok, Uwe, 'Demographische Aspekte der vergangenen und zukünftigen Zuwanderung nach Deutschland', *Aus Politik und Zeitgeschichte*, vol. 48, 1994, pp. 27–36.

Düding, Dieter, 'The ninenteenth-century German nationalist movement as a movement of societies', in Schulze, 1987: 19–50.

van Dülmen, Richard, *Entstehung des frühneuzeitlichen Europa 1550–1648*, Frankfurt-am-Main, 1982.

van Dülmen, Richard, *Reformation als Revolution. Soziale Bewegung und religiöser Radikalismus in der deutschen Reformation*, Frankfurt-am-Main, 1987.

Dumke, Rolf H., 'Der Deutsche Zollverein als Modell ökonomischer Integration', in Berding, 1984: 71–101.

Dumke, Rolf H., 'Reassessing the *Wirtschaftswunder*: reconstruction and postwar growth in West Germany in an international context', *Oxford Bulletin of Economics and Statistics*, vol. 52, no. 2, 1990, pp. 451–92.

Dyhr, Mogens, 'Hybridisiertes Südjütisch', *Germanistische Linguistik*, 101–103, 1990, pp. 25–47.

286   *References*

Eggers, Hans, *Deutsche Sprachgeschichte. Band 2. Das Frühneuhochdeutsche und das Neuhochdeutsche*, Reinbek, 1986.

Eggers, Hans, *Deutsche Sprachgeschichte. Band 1. Das Althochdeutsche und das Mitteldeutsche*, 2nd edn, Reinbek, 1991.

Ehlers, Joachim (ed.), *Ansätze und Diskontinuität deutscher Nationsbildung im Mittelalter*, Sigmaringen, 1989.

Ehlers, Joachim, 'Die deutsche Nation des Mittelalters als Gegenstand der Forschung', in Ehlers, 1989: 11–58.

Ehlers, Joachim, 'Mittelalterliche Voraussetzungen für nationale Identität in der Neuzeit', in Giesen, 1991: 77–99.

Endruweit, Günther and Trommsdorff, Gisela (eds), *Wörterbuch der Soziologie*, Stuttgart, 1989.

Engelberg, Ernst, *Bismarck. Urpreuße und Reichsgründer*, Munich, 1991.

Engelberg, Ernst, *Bismarck. Das Reich in der Mitte Europas*, Munich, 1993.

Engelsing, Rolf, *Analphabetentum und Lektüre*, Stuttgart, 1973.

Epstein, Klaus, *Matthias Erzberger und das Dilemma der deutschen Demokratie*, Frankfurt-am-Main/Berlin/Vienna, 1976.

Esser, Hartmut, 'Gastarbeiter', in Benz, 1985b: 127–56.

Falter, Jürgen W., *Hitlers Wähler*, Munich, 1991.

Fenske, Hans (ed.), *Im Bismarckschen Reich 1871–1890 (Quellen zum politischen Denken der Deutschen in 19. und 20. Jahrhundert. Freiherr vom Stein Gedächtnisausgabe, Band VI)*, Darmstadt, 1978.

Fest, Joachim, *Staatsstreich. Der lange Weg zum 20. Juli*, Berlin, 1994.

Fischer, Fritz, *Griff nach der Weltmacht. Die Kriegszielpolitik des kaiserlichen Deutschland 1914/1918*, Kronberg/Ts., 1977.

Fleckenstein, Josef, *Grundlagen und Beginn der deutschen Geschichte*, Göttingen, 1974.

Fohlen, Claude, 'The Industrial Revolution in France 1700–1914', in Cipolla, 1973: vol. 4 (1), pp. 7–75.

Foitzik, Jan, 'Domowina, Zwjazk luzikich Serbow' ['Heimat, Verband der Lausitzer Sorben'], in Broszat and Weber: 802–11.

Förster, Jürgen, 'Hitlers Entscheidung für den Krieg gegen die Sowjetunion', in Boog et al., 1991: 27–68.

Förster, Peter and Roski, Günther, *DDR zwischen Wende und Wahl. Meinungsforscher analysieren den Umbruch*, Berlin, 1990.

Frei, Norbert, *Der Führerstaat. Nationalsozialistische Herrschaft 1933 bis 1945*, Munich, 1987.

Friedländer, Saul, 'Vom Antisemitismus zur Judenvernichtung: Eine historiographische Studie zur nationalsozialistischen Judenpolitik und Versuch einer Interpretation', in Jäckel and Rohwer, 1987: 18–60.

Friedrich, Walter, 'Mentalitätswandlungen in der Jugend in der DDR', *Aus Politik und Zeitgeschichte*, vol. 16–17, 1990, pp. 25–37.

Geiss, Imanuel, *Juli 1914, Die europäische Krise und der Ausbruch des Ersten Weltkrieges*, third edition, Munich, 1986.

Geißler, Rainer, *Die Sozialstruktur Deutschlands. Ein Studienbuch zur Entwicklung im geteilten und vereinigten Deutschland*, Opladen, 1992a.

Geißler, Rainer, 'Die ostdeutsche Sozialstruktur unter Modernisierungsdruck', *Aus Politik und Zeitgeschichte*, vol. 29–30, 1992b, pp. 15–28.

Gellner, Ernest, *Nations and Nationalism*, Oxford, 1983.

Gerhardt, Dietrich, 'Das Elb- und Ostseeslavische', in Rehder, 1986: 103–10.

Giddens, Anthony, *Sociology. A Brief but Critical Introduction*, second edition, London, 1986.

Giesen, Bernd (ed.), *Nationale und kulturelle Identität. Studien zur Entwicklung des kollektiven Bewussteins in der Neuzeit*, Frankfurt-am-Main, 1991.

Giordano, Ralph, *Ostpreußen ade. Reise durch ein melancholisches Land*, Cologne, 1994.

Goldhagen, Daniel J., *Hitler's Willing Executioners. Ordinary Germans and the Holocaust*, New York, 1996.

Graml, Hermann, *Reichskristallnacht. Antisemitismus und Judenverfolgung im Dritten Reich*, Munich, 1988a.

Graml, Hermann, *Die Alliierten und die Teilung Deutschlands. Konflikte und Entscheidungen 1941–1948*, Frankfurt-am-Main, 1988b.

Graml, Hermann, *Antisemitism in the Third Reich*, Oxford, 1992 (English version of Graml, 1988a).

Greenfeld, Liah, *Nationalism. Five Roads to Modernity*, Cambridge, Mass., 1992.

Griewank, Karl, *Der Wiener Kongress und die europäische Restauration 1814/1815*, Leipzig, 1954.

Gritschneder, Otto, *Bewährungsfrist für den Terroristen Adolf H. Der Hitler-Putsch und die bayerische Justiz*, Munich, 1990.

Grundmann, Herbert (ed.), *Gebhardt. Handbuch der deutschen Geschichte*, vol. 1, ninth edition, Stuttgart, 1970.

Günther, Rigobert und Köpstein, Helga et al., *Die Römer an Rhein und Donau. Zur politischen, wirtschaftlichen und sozialen Entwicklung in den römischen Provinzen an Rhein, Mosel und oberer Donau im 3. und 4. Jahrhundert*, Vienna/Cologne/Graz, 1975.

Hachmann, Rolf, *Die Germanen*, Munich, 1971.

Hæstrup Jørgen, . . . *Til Landets Bedste – Hovedtræk af departementschefsstyrets virke 1943–45*, vol. 1, Copenhagen, 1966.

Hagen, William W., *Germans, Poles, and Jews. The Nationality Conflict in the Prussian East, 1772–1914*, Chicago/London, 1980.

Hardach, Gerd, *The First World War 1914–1918*, Harmondsworth, 1987.

Hartmann, Stefan, 'Zur nationalpolnischen Bewegung und zur preußischen Politik in Masuren vor dem Ersten Weltkrieg', *Zeitschrift für Ostforschung – Länder und Völker im östlichen Mitteleuropa*, vol. 42, no. 1, 1993a, pp. 40–83.

Hartmann, Stefan, 'Zu den Nationalitätenverhältnissen in Westpreußen vor dem Ausbruch des Ersten Weltkrieges', *Zeitschrift für Ostforschung – Länder und Völker im östlichen Mitteleuropa*, vol. 42, no. 3, 1993b, pp. 391–405.

Hauser, Oswald, 'Obrigkeitsstaat und demokratisches Prinzip im Nationalitätenkampf. Preußen in Nordschleswig', *Historische Zeitschrift*, vol. 192, 1961, pp. 318–61.

Heckel, Martin, *Deutschland im konfessionellen Zeitalter*, Göttingen, 1983.

Heiber, Helmut, *Die Republik von Weimar*, nineteenth edition, Munich, 1990.

Heidemeyer, Helge, *Flucht und Zuwanderung aus der SBZ/DDR 1945/1949–*

1961. Die Flüchtlingspolitik der Bundesrepublik Deutschland bis zum Bau der Berliner Mauer, Düsseldorf, 1994.

Heider, Paul et al., *Geschichte der Militärpolitik der KPD 1918–1945*, Berlin (East), 1987.

Heilbroner, Robert, *The Worldly Philosophers. The Lives, Times, and Ideas of the Great Economic Thinkers*, Harmondsworth, 1983.

Henderson, William Oscar, *The Zollverein*, third edition, London, 1984.

Herbert, Ulrich, *Die Geschichte der Ausländerbeschäftigung in Deutschland 1880–1980. Saisonarbeiter, Zwangsarbeiter, Gastarbeiter*, Berlin/Bonn, 1986.

Herder, Johann Gottfried, *Ideen zur Philosophie der Geschichte der Menschheit*, ed. Martin Bollacher, Frankfurt-am-Main, 1989.

Herrmann, Joachim (ed.), *Die Slawen in Deutschland. Geschichte und Kultur der slawischen Stämme westlich von Oder und Neisse vom 6. bis 12. Jahrhundert. Ein Handbuch – Neubearbeitung*, Berlin (East), 1985.

Higounet, Charles, *Die deutsche Ostsiedlung im Mittelalter*, Munich, 1990.

Hobsbawm, Eric J., *Industry and Empire*, Harmondsworth, 1979.

Hobsbawm, Eric J., *Nations and Nationalism since 1780: Programme, Myth, Reality*, second edition, Cambridge, 1992.

Hoffmann, Joachim, 'Die Kriegsführung aus der Sicht der Sowjetunion', in Boog et al., 1991: 848–964.

Hofstede, Geert, *Interkulturelle Zusammenarbeit. Kulturen – Organisationen – Management*, Wiesbaden, 1993.

Hradil, Stefan, 'Die "objektive" und die "subjektive" Modernisierung. Der Wandel der westdeutschen Sozialstruktur und die Wiedervereinigung', *Aus Politik und Zeitgeschichte*, vol. 29–30, 1992, pp. 3–14.

Hubatsch, Walter, *Deutschland zwischen dem Dreißigjährigem Krieg und der Französischen Revolution*, Frankfurt-am-Main/Berlin/Vienna, 1973.

Iggers, Georg, *Deutsche Geschichtswissenschaft. Eine Kritik der traditionellen Geschichtsauffassung von Herder bis zur Gegenwart*, Munich, 1971.

Inglehart, Ronald, *The Silent Revolution – Changing Values and Political Styles Among Western Publics*, Princeton, 1977.

Jäckel, Eberhard and Rohwer, Jürgen (eds), *Der Mord an den Juden im Zweiten Weltkrieg. Entschlußbildung und Verwirklichung*, Frankfurt-am-Main, 1987.

Jacobmeyer, Wolfgang, 'Ortlos am Ende des Grauens: Displaced Persons in der Nachkriegszeit', in Bade, 1992: 367–73.

James, Harold, *A German Identity 1770–1990*, London, 1989.

Jánossy, Franz (with contributions by Maria Holló), *Das Ende der Wirtschaftswunder. Erscheinung und Wesen der wirtschaftlichen Entwicklung*, Frankfurt-am-Main, 1966.

Janßen, Karl-Heinz und Tobias, Fritz, *Der Sturz der Generäle. Hitler und die Blomberg-Fritsch-Krise 1938*, Munich, 1994.

Jaworski, Rudolf, 'Die Sudetendeutschen als Minderheit in der Tschechoslowakei 1919–1938', Benz, 1985a: 29–38.

Jespersen, Otto, *Growth and Structure of the English Language*, Oxford, 1967.

Jordan, W. M., *Great Britain, France and the German Problem 1918–1939*, London, 1943, pp. 218–25, reproduced in Lederer, 1965: 73–7.

Jung, Matthias, 'Parteiensystem und Wahlen in der DDR. Eine Analyse der Volkskammerwahl vom 18. März 1990 und der Kommunalwahlen vom 6. Mai 1990', *Aus Politik und Zeitgeschichte*, vol. 27, 1990, pp. 3–15.

Jung, Matthias and Roth, Dieter, 'Kohls knappster Sieg. Eine Analyse der Bundestagswahl 1994', *Aus Politik und Zeitgeschichte*, vol. 51–2, 1994, pp. 3–15.

Kasper, Martin, *Geschichte der Sorben, Band 3. Von 1917 bis 1945*, Bautzen, 1976.

Kearney, Hugh, *The British Isles. A History of Four Nations*, Cambridge, 1989.

Kesselman, Mark et al. (eds), *European Politics in Transition*, Lexington, Mass./Toronto, 1992.

Keynes, John Maynard, 'The economic consequences of the peace', *Collected Writings*, vol. II, London, 1971.

Kiesewetter, Hubert, *Industrielle Revolution in Deutschland 1815–1914*, Frankfurt-am-Main, 1989.

Kitsikis, Dimitri, *L'Empire Ottoman*, second edition, Paris, 1991.

Kleßmann, Christoph, *Polnische Bergarbeiter im Ruhrgebiet 1870–1945. Soziale Integration und nationale Subkultur einer Minderheit in der deutschen Industriegesellschaft*, Göttingen, 1978.

Kleßmann, Eckart (ed.), *Die Befreiungskriege in Augenzeugenberichten*, Düsseldorf, 1966.

Kocka, Jürgen, *Klassengesellschaft im Krieg. Deutsche Sozialgesellschaft 1914–1918*, Frankfurt-am-Main, 1988.

Kocka, Jürgen, 'Ein deutscher Sonderweg. Überlegungen zur Sozialgeschichte der DDR', *Aus Politik und Zeitgeschichte*, vol. 40, 1994, pp. 34–45.

Kocka, Jürgen, '1945: Neubeginn oder Restauration?', in Stern and Winkler, 1994: 159–92.

Koller, Barbara, 'Aussiedler in Deutschland. Aspekte ihrer sozialen und beruflichen Eingliederung', *Aus Politik und Zeitgeschichte*, vol. 48, 1993, pp. 12–22.

Koselleck, Reinhart, *Preußen zwischen Reform und Revolution. Allgemeines Landrecht, Verwaltung und soziale Bewegung von 1791 bis 1848*, Munich, 1989.

Krausnick, Helmut, *Hitlers Einsatzgruppen. Die Truppen des Weltanschauungskrieges 1938–1942*, Frankfurt-am-Main, 1985.

Krekeler, Norbert, 'Die deutsche Minderheit in Polen und die deutsche Revisionspolitik des Deutschen Reiches 1919–1933', in Benz, 1985: 15–28.

Krüger, Bruno et al., *Die Germanen. Geschichte und Kultur der germanischen Stämme in Mitteleuropa. Ein Handbuch in zwei Bänden. Band II: Die Stämme und Stammensverbände in der Zeit vom 3. Jahrhundert bis zur Herausbildung der politischen Vorherrschaft der Franken*, Berlin (East), 1983.

Krüger, Peter, *Versailles. Deutsche Außenpolitik zwischen Revisionismus und Friedenssicherung*, Munich, 1986.

Kruse, Wolfgang, *Krieg und nationale Integration. Eine Neuinterpretation des sozialdemokratischen Burgfriedensschlusses 1914/15*, Essen, 1994.

Kühl, Jürgen, 'Arbeitslosigkeit in der vereinigten Bundesrepublik Deutschland', *Aus Politik und Zeitgeschichte*, vol. 35, 1993, pp. 3–15.

Leciejewski, Klaus, 'Zur wirtschaftlichen Eingliederung der Aussiedler', *Aus Politik und Zeitgeschichte*, vol. 3, 1990, pp. 52–62.

Lederer, Ivo (ed.), *The Versailles Settlement. Was It Foredoomed to Failure?*, Boston, 1965.

Lepsius, M. Rainer, 'Parteiensystem und Sozialstruktur: zum Problem der Demokratisierung der deutschen Gesellschaft', in Ritter, 1973: 56–80.

Leuschner, Joachim, *Deutschland im späten Mittelalter*, Göttingen, 1975.

Lindemann, Hans, 'Stichwort: Domowina', *Deutschland-Archiv*, no. 10, 1987, pp. 1025f.

Loock, Hans-Dietrich, '*Weserübung* – a step towards the Greater Germanic Reich', *Scandinavian Journal of History*, vol. 2, 1977, pp. 67–88.

Lüttinger, Paul, 'Der Mythos der schnellen Integration. Eine empirische Untersuchung zur Integration der Vertriebenen und Flüchtlinge in der Bundesrepublik Deutschland bis 1971', *Zeitschrift für Soziologie*, vol. 15, no. 1, 1986, pp. 20–36.

Mai, Gunther, *Das Ende des Kaiserreiches. Politik und Kriegsführung im Ersten Weltkrieg*, Munich, 1987.

Marschalck, Peter, *Bevölkerungsgeschichte Deutschlands im 19. und 20. Jahrhundert*, Frankfurt, 1984.

Marx, Karl and Engels, Friedrich, *Marx Engels Werke*, ed. Institut für Marxismus-Lenismus beim ZK der SED, Berlin (East).

Marz, Lutz, 'Dispositionskosten des Transformationsprozesses. Werden mentale Orientierungsnöte zum wirtschaftlichen Problem?', *Aus Politik und Zeitgeschichte*, vol. 24, 1992, pp. 3–14.

Messerschmidt, Manfred, 'Preußens Militär in seinem gesellschaftlichen Umfeld', in Puhle and Wehler, 1980: 43–88.

Michaelis, Herbert and Schraepler, Ernst (eds), *Ursachen und Folgen. Vom deutschen Zusammenbruch 1918 und 1945 bis zur staatlichen Neuordnung Deutschlands in der Gegenwart*, vol. 3, Berlin, 1960.

Michalk, Siegfried, 'Deutsch und Sorbisch in der Lausitz', *Germanistische Linguistik*, 101–103, 1990, pp. 427–44.

Michalka, Wolfgang, *Das Dritte Reich. Band 1: 'Volksgemeinschaft' und Großmachtpolitik 1933–1939*, Munich, 1985.

Michalka, Wolfgang, *Das Dritte Reich. Band 2: Weltmachtanspruch und nationaler Zusammenbruch 1939–1945*, Munich, 1985.

Michalka, Wolfgang (ed.), *Der Zweite Weltkrieg. Analysen, Grundzüge, Forschungsbilanz*. Munich/Zürich, 1989.

Mill, John Stuart, *Principles of Political Economy with some of their Applications to Social Philosophy*, ed. and intro. Sir William Ashley, London, 1904; reprinted Fairfield, NJ, 1987.

Mitchell, Brian R., *European Historical Statistics 1750–1975*, second revised edition, London/Basingstoke, 1981.

Moeller, Bernd, *Deutschland im Zeitalter der Reformation*, Göttingen, 1977.

Möller, Horst, 'Wie, aufgeklärt war Preußen?', in Puhle and Wehler, 1980: 176–201.

Möller, Kurt, 'Zusammenhänge der Modernisierung des Rechstextremismus mit der Modernisierung der Gesellschaft', *Aus Politik und Zeitgeschichte*, vol. 46–7, 1993, B46–47, pp. 3–9.

Mommsen, Wolfgang, *Imperialismustheorien*, third edition, Göttingen, 1987.

Mommsen, Wolfgang J., *Der autoritäre Nationalstaat. Verfassung, Gesellschaft und Kultur im deutschen Kaiserreich*, Frankfurt-am-Main, 1990.

Müller, Rolf-Dieter, 'Das Scheitern der wirtschaftlichen "Blitzkriegstrategie"', in Boog et al., 1991: 1116–226.

Neuberg, A. et al., *Der bewaffnete Aufstand. Versuch einer theoretischen Darstellung. Eingeleitet von Erich Wollenberg*, Frankfurt-am-Main, 1971.

Nipperdey, Thomas, *Deutsche Geschichte 1866–1918. Erster Band. Arbeitswelt und Bürgergeist*, third edition, Munich, 1993.

Nolte, Ernst, *Der Europäische Bürgerkrieg 1917–1945. Nationalsozialismus und Bolschewismus*, fourth edition, Frankfurt-am-Main, 1989.

Nolte, Ernst, *Der Faschismus in seiner Epoche. Action française – italienischer Faschismus – Nationalsozialismus*, eighth edition, Munich/Zürich, 1990.

Overesch, Manfred, *Deutschland 1945–1949. Vorgeschichte und Gründung der Bundesrepublik. Ein Leitfaden in Darstellung und Dokumenten*, Königsstein/Ts., 1979.

Overmans, Rüdiger, 'Die Toten des Zweiten Weltkrieges in Deutschland. Bilanz der Forschung unter besonderer Berücksichtigung der Wehrmacht- und Vertreibungsverluste', in Michalka, 1989: 858–73.

Pohl, Karl Heinrich, 'Die "Krisenkonferenz" vom 8. Dezember 1912', *Geschichte in Wissenschaft und Unterricht*, no. 2, 1994, pp. 91–104.

Priewe, Jan, 'Die Folgen der schnellen Privatisierung der Treuhandanstalt. Eine vorläufige Schlußbilanz', *Aus Politik und Zeitgeschichte*, vol. 43–4, 1994, pp. 21–30.

Priewe, Jan and Hickel, Rudolf, *Der Preis der Einheit. Bilanz und Perspektiven der deutschen Vereinigung*, Frankfurt-am-Main, 1991.

Puhle, Hans-Jürgen and Wehler, Hans-Ulrich (eds), *Preußen im Rückblick*, Göttingen, 1980.

Rautenberg, Hans-Werner, 'Deutsche und Deutschstämmige in Polen – eine nicht anerkannte Volksgruppe', *Aus Politik und Zeitgeschichte*, vol. 50, 1988, pp. 14–25.

Rehder, Peter (ed.), *Einführung in die slavischen Sprachen*, Darmstadt, 1986.

Rerup, Lorenz, *Slesvig og Holsten efter 1830*, Copenhagen, 1982.

Richter, Ludwig, 'Die Weimarer Reichsverfassung', *Aus Politik und Zeitgeschichte*, vol. 32–4, 1994, pp. 3–10.

Ritter, Gerhard A. (ed.), *Die deutschen Parteien vor 1918*, Cologne, 1973.

Ritter, Gerhard A. (ed.), *Das Deutsche Kaiserreich 1871–1914. Ein historisches Lesebuch*, fifth edition, Göttingen, 1992.

Ritter, Gerhard A. and Miller, Susanne (eds), *Die deutsche Revolution 1918–1919 – Dokumente*, Frankfurt-am-Main/Hamburg, 1968.

Rogall, Joachim, 'Die Tragödie einer Grenzlandbevölkerung – polnische Forschungen über die Masuren', *Zeitschrift für Ostforschung – Länder und Völker im östlichen Mitteleuropa*, vol. 41, no. 1, 1992, pp. 102–11.

Rogall, Joachim, 'Die deutschen Minderheiten in Polen heute', *Aus Politik und Zeitgeschichte*, vol. 48, 1993, pp. 31–43.

Rohe, Karl, *Wahlen und Wählertraditionen in Deutschland. Kulturelle Grundlagen deutscher Parteien und Parteiensysteme im 19. und 20. Jahrhundert*, Frankfurt-am-Main, 1992.

Rokkan, Stein, 'Nation building, cleavage formation and the structuring of mass politics', *Citizens, Elections, Parties. Approaches to the Comparative Study of the Processes of Development*, Oslo, 1970, pp. 73–144.

Ronge, Volker, 'Loyalty, voice or exit? Die Fluchtbewegung als Anstoß und Problem der Erneuerung der DDR', in Wewer, 1990: 29–46.

Schäuble, Wolfgang, *Der Vertrag. Wie ich über die deutsche Einheit verhandelte*, Munich, 1993.

Schieder, Theodor et al. (eds), *Dokumentation der Vertreibung der Deutschen aus Ost-Mitteleuropa*, Bonn, 1954; reprinted Munich, 1984.

Scheuch, Erwin K., *Wie deutsch sind die Deutschen? Eine Nation wandelt ihr Gesicht*, Bergisch-Gladbach, 1991.

Schiller, Klaus J. and Thiemann, Manfred, *Geschichte der Sorben, Band 4. Von 1945 bis zur Gegenwart*, Bautzen, 1979.

Schillinger, Reinhold, 'Der Lastenausgleich', in Benz, 1985a: 183–92.

Schirmann, Léon, *Justizmanipulationen. Der Altonaer Blutsonntag und die Altonaer bzw. Hamburger Justiz 1932–1994*, Berlin, 1995.

Schleunes, Karl A., 'Nationalsozialistische Entschlußbildung und die Aktion T 4', in Jäckel and Rohwer, 1987: 70–83.

Schmalz-Jacobsen, Cornelia et al., *Einwanderung – und dann? Perspektiven einer neuen Ausländerpolitik*, Munich, 1993.

Schmidt, Paul, *Statist auf diplomatischer Bühne 1923–1945. Erlebnisse des Chefdolmetschers im Auswärtigen Amt mit den Staatsmännern Europas*, Bonn, 1950.

Schnell, Rüdiger, 'Deutsche Literatur und deutsches Nationsbewusstsein im Spätmittelalter und Früher Neuzeit', in Ehlers, 1989: 247–320.

Schöllgen, Gregor (ed.), *Flucht in den Krieg? Die Außenpolitik des kaiserlichen Deutschland*, Darmstadt, 1991.

Schönhoven, Klaus, *Die deutschen Gewerkschaften*, Frankfurt-am-Main, 1987.

Schulte, Axel, 'Multikulturelle Gesellschaft: Chance, Ideologie oder Bedrohung', *Aus Politik und Zeitgeschichte*, vol. 23–4, 1990, pp. 3–14.

Schulze, Hagen, *Der Weg zum Nationalstaat. Die deutsche Nationalbewegung vom 18. Jahrhundert bis zur Reichsgründung*, second edition, Munich, 1986.

Schulze, Hagen (ed.), *Nation-Building in Central Europe*, Leamington Spa/ Hamburg/New York, 1987.

Seiring, Kerstin, 'Ostdeutsche Jugendliche fünf Jahre nach der Wiederver-einigung', *Aus Politik und Zeitgeschichte*, vol. 20, 1995, pp. 43–55.

Şen, Faruk and Goldberg, Andreas, *Türken in Deutschland. Leben zwischen zwei Kulturen*, Munich, 1994.

Siemann, Wolfram, *Gesellschaft im Aufbruch. Deutschland 1849–1871*, Frank-furt-am-Main, 1990.

Sinn, Gerda and Sinn, Hans-Werner, *Kaltstart. Volkswirtschaftliche Aspekte der deutschen Vereinigung*, second edition, Tübingen, 1992.

Skocpol, Theda, 'Emerging agendas and recurrent strategies in historical sociology', in Theda Skocpol (ed.), *Vision and Method in Historical Sociology*, Cambridge University Press, 1984, pp. 356–91.

Smith, Anthony D., *National Identity*, Reno/Las Vegas/London, 1991.

Statistik des Deutschen Reiches. Neue Folge, Band 427, Berlin, 1932; reprinted Osnabrück, 1978.

Statistisches Jahrbuch für die Bundesrepublik Deutschland 1979, Wiesbaden, 1979.

Statisches Jahrbuch für die Bundesrepublik Deutschland 1994, Wiesbaden, 1994.

References   293

Stauber, Reinhard, 'Nationalismus vor dem Nationalismus'? Eine Bestandsaufnahme zu "Nation" und "Nationalismus" in der Frühen Neuzeit', *Geschichte in Wissenschaft und Unterricht*, vol. 47, 1996, pp. 139–65.

Steensen, Thomas, *Die friesische Bewegung in Nordfriesland im 19. und 20. Jahrhundert (1879–1945)*, Neumünster, 1986.

Stern, Carola and Winkler, Heinrich-August (eds), *Wendepunkte deutscher Geschichte 1848–1990*, Frankfurt-am-Main, 1994.

Stern, Leo and Voigt, Erhard, *Deutschland in der Epoche des vollentfalteten Feudalismus von der Mitte des 13. bis zum ausgehenden 15. Jahrhundert*, Berlin (East), 1976.

Stone, Gerald, *The Smallest Slavonic Nation. The Sorbs of Lusatia*, London, 1972.

Stone, Lawrence, 'The educational revolution in England 1560–1640', *Past and Present*, vol. 28, 1964, pp. 41–80.

Stratemann, Ingrid, 'Psychologische Bedingungen des wirtschaftlichen Aufschwungs in den neuen Bundesländern', *Aus Politik und Zeitgeschichte*, vol. 24, 1992, pp. 15–26.

Streim, Albert, 'Zur Eröffnung des allgemeinen Judenvernichtungsbefehls gegenüber den Einsatzgruppen', in Jäckel and Rohwer, 1987: pp. 107–19.

Stürmer, Michael (ed.), *Das kaiserliche Deutschland. Politik und Gesellschaft 1870–1918*, Kronberg/Ts., 1979.

Stürmer, Michael, *Die Reichsgründung. Deutscher Nationalstaat und europäisches Gleichgewicht im Zeitalter Bismarcks*, Munich, 1990.

Taddey, Gerhard (ed.), *Lexikon der deutschen Geschichte. Personen, Ereignisse, Institutionen. Von der Zeitenwende bis zum Ausgang des 2. Weltkrieges*, Stuttgart, 1977.

Ternes, Charles-Marie, *Die Römer an Rhein und Mosel. Geschichte und Kultur*, Stuttgart, 1975.

von Thun-Hohenstein, Romedio Galeazzo Graf, *Der Verschwörer. General Oster und die Militäropposition*, Munich, 1984.

Tilly, Richard H., *Vom Zollverein zum Industriestaat. Die wirtschaftlich-soziale Entwicklung Deutschlands 1834 bis 1914*, Munich, 1990.

Tress, Madeleine, 'Germany's new Jewish question, or German Jewry's "Russian question"?', *New Political Science*, no. 24/5, 1993, pp. 75–86.

Trommer, Aage, 'Programm eller ej? Om udforskningen af Tyskland i den anden verdenskrig', *Historisk Tidsskrift*, vol. 87, no. 2, 1987, pp. 318–34.

Vester, Michael et al., *Soziale Milieus im gesellschaftlichen Strukturwandel. Zwischen Integration und Ausgrenzung*, Cologne, 1993.

Walker, Alastair, 'Nordfriesland als Sprachenkontaktraum', *Germanistische Linguistik*, 101–3, 1990, pp. 407–26.

Walter, Franz, 'Milieus und Parteien in der deutschen Gesellschaft. Zwischen Persistenz und Erosion', *Geschichte in Wissenschaft und Unterricht*, vol. 46, 1995, pp. 479–93.

Wassermann, Rudolf, 'Plädoyer für eine neue Asyl- und Ausländerpolitik', *Aus Politik und Zeitgeschichte*, vol. 9, 1992, pp. 13–20.

Waterman, John, *A History of the German Language*, Washington, 1966.

Weber, Hermann, *Geschichte der DDR*, second edition, Munich, 1989.

Weber, Max, *Wirtschaft und Gesellschaft*, Cologne/Berlin, 1964.

Wegner, Manfred, 'Produktionsstandort Ostdeutschland. Zum Stand der Modernisierung und der Erneuerung der Wirtschaft in den neuen Bundesländern', *Aus Politik und Zeitgeschichte*, vol. 17, 1994, pp. 14–23.

Wehler, Hans-Ulrich, *Bismarck und der Imperialismus*, fourth edition, Munich, 1976.

Wehler, Hans-Ulrich, *Krisenherde des Kaiserreiches 1871–1918. Studien zur deutschen Sozial- und Verfassungsgeschichte*, Göttingen, 1979.

Wehler, Hans-Ulrich, *Deutsche Gesellschaftsgeschichte. Erster Band. Vom Feudalismus des Alten Reiches bis zur Defensiven Modernisierung der Reformära 1700–1815*, second edition, Munich, 1989.

Wehler, Hans-Ulrich, *Deutsche Gesellschaftsgeschichte. Zweiter Band. Von der Reformära bis zur industriellen und politischen 'Deutschen Doppelrevolution' 1815–1845/49*, second edition, Munich, 1989.

Wehler, Hans-Ulrich, *Deutsche Gesellschaftsgeschichte. Dritter Band. Von der 'Deutschen Doppelrevolution' bis zum Beginn des Ersten Weltkrieges 1849–1914*, Munich, 1995.

Weiß, Hermann, 'Die Organisationen der Vetriebenen und ihre Presse', in Benz, 1985a: 193–208.

Wendt, Bernd-Jürgen, *Großdeutschland. Außenpolitik und Kriegsvorbereitung des Hitler-Regimes*, Munich, 1987.

Werth, Alexander, *Rußland im Krieg*, Munich/Zürich, 1965.

Wette, Wolfram, 'Ideologien, Propaganda und Innenpolitik als Voraussetzungen der Kriegspolitik des Dritten Reiches', in Deist et al., 1989: 25–208.

Wetzel, Juliane, 'Integration im Großbetrieb – Das Beispiel BMW', in Benz, 1993: 93–108.

Wewer, Göttrick (ed.), *DDR – Von der friedlichen Revolution zur deutschen Vereinigung*, Opladen, 1990.

Wiesemann, Falk, 'Flüchtlingspolitik in Nordrhein-Westfalen', in Benz, 1985a: 173–82.

Wiesinger, Peter, 'Regionale und überregionale Sprachausformung im Deutschen vom 12. bis zum 15. Jahrhundert unter dem Aspekt der Nationsbildung', in Ehlers, 1989: 321–43.

Winkler, Heinrich-August, *Von der Revolution zur Stabilisierung. Arbeiter und Arbeiterbewegung in der Weimarer Republik 1918 bis 1924*, second edition, Berlin/Bonn, 1985.

Winkler, Heinrich-August, *Der Weg in die Katastrophe. Arbeiter und Arbeiterbewegung in der Weimarer Republik 1930 bis 1933*, Berlin/Bonn, 1987.

Winkler, Heinrich-August, '1989/1990: Die unverhoffte Einheit', in Stern and Winkler, 1994: 193–226.

Wistrich, Robert, *Wer war wer im Dritten Reich? Ein biographisches Lexikon. Anhänger, Mitläufer, Gegner aus Politik, Wirtschaft und Militär, Kunst und Wissenschaft*, Frankfurt-am-Main, 1987.

Woydt, Johann, *Ausländische Arbeitskräfte in Deutschland. Vom Kaiserreich bis zur Bundesrepublik*, Heilbronn, 1987.

Wynot, Edward D., 'The Poles in Germany, 1919–1939', *East European Quarterly*, vol. 30, no. 2, 1996, pp. 171–86.

Zank, Wolfgang, 'Nur aus Ruinen auferstanden? – Das "Wirtschaftswunder DDR" im Licht einiger theoretischer Erklärungsansätze', *Deutsche Studien*, no. 92, 1985, pp. 327–47.

Zank, Wolfgang, *Wirtschaft und Arbeit in Ostdeutschland 1945–1949. Probleme des Wiederaufbaus in der Sowjetischen Besatzungszone Deutschlands*, Munich, 1987.

Zank, Wolfgang, 'Wirtschaftliche Zentralverwaltungen und Deutsche Wirtschaftskommission (DWK)', in Broszat and Weber, 1990: 253–96.

de Zayas, Alfred M., *Nemesis at Potsdam. The Anglo-Americans and the Expulsion of the Germans. Background, Execution, Consequences*, London/Henley/Boston, 1977.

de Zayas, Alfred M., *Die Anglo-Amerikaner und die Vertreibung der Deutschen. Vorgeschichte, Verlauf, Folgen*, Munich, 1980.

Zwahr, Hartmut, *Sorbische Volksbewegung. Dokumente zur antisorbischen Staatspolitik im preußischen Reich, zur Oberlausitzer Bauernbewegung und zur sorbischen nationalen Bewegung 1872–1918*, Bautzen, 1968.

Index

Words very frequently used (e.g. Prussia) are not listed. Personal names are listed when directly quoted or when having theoretical influence on this book, otherwise only when of exceptional importance.

298		*Index*